TEACHING MUSIC PERFORMANCE IN HIGHER EDUCATION

Teaching Music Performance in Higher Education

Exploring the Potential of Artistic Research

Edited by
*Helen Julia Minors, Stefan Östersjö, Gilvano Dalagna,
and Jorge Salgado Correia*

https://www.openbookpublishers.com

©2024 Helen Julia Minors, Stefan Östersjö, Gilvano Dalagna, and Jorge Salgado Correia (eds). Copyright of individual chapters remains with the chapters' authors.

This work is licensed under a Creative Commons Attribution-NonCommercial 4.0 International license (CC BY-NC 4.0). This license allows you to share, copy, distribute and transmit the work for non-commercial purposes, providing attribution is made to the author (but not in any way that suggests that he endorses you or your use of the work). Attribution should include the following information:

Helen Julia Minors, Stefan Östersjö, Gilvano Dalagna, and Jorge Salgado Correia (eds), *Teaching Music Performance in Higher Education: Exploring the Potential of Artistic Research*. Cambridge, UK: Open Book Publishers, 2024, https://doi.org/10.11647/OBP.0398

Further details about CC BY-NC licenses are available at https://creativecommons.org/licenses/by-nc/4.0/.

Copyright and permissions for the reuse of many of the images and other media included in this publication differ from the above. This information is provided in the captions and in the list of illustrations and media examples. Every effort has been made to identify and contact copyright holders and any omission or error will be corrected if notification is made to the publisher.

All external links were active at the time of publication unless otherwise stated and have been archived via the Internet Archive Wayback Machine at https://archive.org/web.

Any digital material and resources associated with this volume will be available at https://doi.org/10.11647/OBP.#resources.0398

ISBN Paperback: 978-1-80511-272-3
ISBN Hardback: 978-1-80511-273-0
ISBN Digital (PDF): 978-1-80511-274-7
ISBN Digital eBook (EPUB): 978-1-80511-275-4
ISBN HTML: 978-1-80511-277-8

DOI: 10.11647/OBP.0398

Cover image: Cover image: Wassily Kandinsky, *Gelb, Rot, Blau* (1925), https://commons.wikimedia.org/wiki/File:Kandinsky_-_Gelb-Rot-Blau,_1925.png

Cover design: Jeevanjot Kaur Nagpal

This book was produced as a deliverable for the Erasmus + project 2020-1-PT01-KA203-078541.

The European Commission's support for the production of this publication does not constitute an endorsement of the contents, which reflect the views only of the authors, and the Commission cannot be held responsible for any use which may be made of the information contained therein. https://react.web.ua.pt

Contents

Acknowledgements	vii
Introduction	1
Helen Julia Minors, Stefan Östersjö, Gilvano Dalagna, and Jorge Salgado Correia	
PART I: ARTISTIC RESEARCH IN HIGHER MUSIC EDUCATION	**9**
Introduction to Part I	9
Stefan Östersjö	
1. A Swedish Perspective on Artistic Research Practices in First and Second Cycle Education in Music	13
Stefan Östersjö and Carl Holmgren with Åsa Unander-Scharin	
2. Experimentation as a Learning Method: A Case Study Exploring Affordances of a Musical Instrument	47
Fausto Pizzol	
3. Finding Voice: Developing Student Autonomy from Imitation to Performer Agency	87
Mikael Bäckman	
4. Teaching Musical Performance from an Artistic Research-Based Approach: Reporting on a Pedagogical Intervention in Portugal	107
Gilvano Dalagna; Jorge S. Correia; Clarissa Foletto; Ioulia Papageorgi	
PART II: NOVEL APPROACHES TO TEACHING INTERPRETATION AND PERFORMANCE	**133**
Introduction to Part II	133
Gilvano Dalagna	
5. Artistic Practice as Embodied Learning: Reconnecting Pedagogy, Improvisation, and Composition	135
Robert Sholl	
6. Working Together Well: Amplifying Group Agency and Motivation in Higher Music Education	165
Jacob Thompson-Bell	

7. Score-Based Learning and Improvisation in Classical Music Performance   181
Mariam Kharatyan

8. Intercultural Musicking: Reflection in, on, and for Situated Klezmer Ensemble Performance   195
Richard Fay, Daniel J. Mawson, and Nahielly Palacios

PART III: CHALLENGES AND OPPORTUNITIES OF MUSIC PERFORMANCE EDUCATION IN SOCIETY   **221**

Introduction to Part III   221
Helen Julia Minors

9. The Musical Object in Deep Learning   225
Odd Torleiv Furnes

10. Rethinking Music Performance Education Through the Lens of Today's Society   251
Randi Margrethe Eidsaa and Mariam Kharatyan

11. Experience, Understanding and Intercultural Competence: The Ethno Programme   271
Sarah-Jane Gibson

12. Employability Skills within an Inclusive Undergraduate and Postgraduate Performance Curriculum in the UK   287
Helen Julia Minors

13. Conclusion: Probing, Positioning, (Re)Acting   307
Helen Julia Minors and Stefan Östersjö

About the Contributors   315

List of Figures   321

List of Tables   323

List of Audio and Video Musical Examples   325

Index   327

Acknowledgements

The editors would like to thank all of the authors for dedicated work on their chapters across the entire production process. Similarly, many thanks to the staff at Open Book Publishers, without whom this book would never have seen the light of day. Further, the editors are grateful to the Portuguese team at the University of Aveiro for their enthusiastic administration of the Erasmus+ REACT project and to the Swedish team for organising the REACT symposium, held in the Piteå School of Music on 21–23 September 2022, which provided the initial spark for the creation of the present book. Many thanks also to our respective home universities: York St John University, University of Aveiro, and the Luleå University of Technology. Last, but indeed not least, we would like to thank our student partners for their invaluable contributions.

Introduction

Helen Julia Minors, Stefan Östersjö, Gilvano Dalagna, and Jorge Salgado Correia

This book is the first publication to address the potential of artistic research in music to innovate the teaching and learning of music performance in Higher Music Education (HME) in Europe. Across the past twenty years, method development in artistic research has introduced experimental approaches[1,2,3] and artistic application of reflexive methods[4,5] in Higher Education Institutions (HEIs). While artistic research entered academia as something of a Trojan horse (as described by Marcel Cobussen in 2007),[6] our book traces how the practices of artistic research, and their practitioners, have become increasingly integrated in HME. At the same time, we also identify how important aspects of the potential of artistic research to provide critical and novel perspectives to HME are immediately related to how artistic researchers are also situated in Art worlds and its music industries.

As a response to the Bologna process (since 1999), HME has been in a state of transformation, which has often been referred to as an academization of formerly more practice-based teaching institutions. This publication seeks to bring out a different trajectory, through which processes of renewal in HME has led to developing student-centred approaches, employability skills, and greater student autonomy, with the further argument that artistic research practices have provided

---

1 Paulo de Assis, *Logic of Experimentation: Rethinking Music Performance through Artistic Research* (Leuven: Leuven University Press, 2018), p. 150, https://doi.org/10.11116/9789461662507
2 Ben Spatz, *Making A Laboratory. Dynamic Configurations with Transversal Video* (Santa Barbara, CA: Punctum Books, 2020), https://doi.org/10.2307/jj.2353794
3 Stefan Östersjö, 'Artistic knowledge, the laboratory and the hörspiel.' in *Gränser och oändligheter – Musikalisk och litterär komposition, en forskningsrapport /'Compositional' Becoming, Complexity, and Critique*, ed. by Anders Hultqvist and Gunnar. D. Hansson (Gothenburg: Art Monitor, 2020).
4 Darla Crispin, 'The Deterritorialization and Reterritorialization of Artistic Research', *Online Journal for Artistic Research*, 3 (2019), 45–59.
5 Darla Crispin, 'Looking back, Looking through, Looking beneath. The Promises and Pitfalls of Reflection as a Research Tool', in *Knowing in Performing: Artistic Research in Music and the Performing Arts*, ed. by Annegret Huber, Doris Ingrisch, Therese Kaufmann, Johannes Kretz, Gesine Schröder, and Tasos Zembylas (Bielefeld: Transcript Verlag, 2021), pp. 35–50.
6 Marcel Cobussen, 'The Trojan Horse. Epistemological Explorations Concerning Practice Based Research', *Dutch Journal of Music Theory*, 12/1 (February 2007), 18–33.

novel opportunities in this development. This has entailed a development of teaching models that would promote student self-determination, capacity to autonomously identify needs for further knowledge, and competencies, and also an emphasis on lifelong learning.

Some of the challenges that HME has been seeking to address are related to the questioning of the traditional conservatoire model. Practices associated with the teaching and learning of music performance have focused on values and expectations established in the nineteenth-century Western conservatory context and its master-apprentice practice.[7] This resulted in a predominantly mono-directional teaching and learning environment, emphasising the development of technical skills rather than critical and creative abilities.[8] Furthermore, such practices do not sufficiently prepare the student to meet the current professional demands and to envision alternatives beyond traditional institutional contexts for musical performance.[9] Current professional demands require the development of new, innovative pedagogical models as integrated alternatives to existing traditional practices.[10,11]

REACT – *Rethinking Music Performance in European Higher Education Institutions* is a Strategic Partnership funded by ERASMUS+ that seeks a response to these problems and to communicate best practices in this domain, with the aim of furthering a new teaching and learning paradigm in HME. REACT is developed by an international consortium[12] that mobilises an international cooperative network to develop new approaches to the teaching and learning of music performance in Higher Music Education. This strategic partnership collaboratively explores the potential of artistic research to propose new approaches to lifelong learning and student-centred pedagogical approaches.

Hence, the core pedagogical idea is that teachers share their experience of artistic research practices with their students. This entails an approach built on reflective practice and critical thinking. Rather than top-down transmission of knowledge, the aim is to create teaching and learning contexts that enable student and teacher to contextualise, explore, and share artistic research practices in music performance, from within the framework of Higher Music Education. At the same time, this also

---

7 Harold Jørgensen, 'Western Classical Music Studies in Universities and Conservatoires', in *Advanced Musical Performance: Investigations in Higher Education Learning*, ed. by Ioulia Papageorgi and Graham Welch (Ashgate: Surrey, 2014), pp. 3–20.
8 Randi Eidsaa, 'Dialogues between Teachers and Musicians in Creative Music-Making Collaborations', in *Musician-Teacher Collaborations: Altering the Chord*, ed. by Catharina Christophersen and Ailbhe Kenny (Abingdon: Routledge, 2018), pp. 133–45.
9 Guadalupe López-Íñiguez and Dawn Bennett, 'A Lifespan Perspective on Multi-Professional Musicians: Does Music Education Prepare Classical Musicians for their Careers?', *Music Education Research*, 22 (2020) 1, 1–14. https://doi.org/10.1080/14613808.2019.1703925
10 Jennifer Rowley, Dawn Bennett, and Patrick Schmidt, *Leadership of Pedagogy and Curriculum in Higher Music Education* (Abingdon: Routledge, 2019) p. 178.
11 Chris Dromey and Julia Haferkorn, *The Classical Music Industry* (Abingdon: Routledge, 2018), p. 30.
12 University of Aveiro (Portugal), University of Agder (Norway), University of Nicosia (Cyprus) Uniarts/Sibelius Academy (Finland), and Luleå University of Technology (Sweden).

entails situating the study of music performance in a wider context, in immediate interaction with the music art worlds and their music industries. Finally, and perhaps most importantly, by inviting students to an approach to learning music performance through artistic research, we put the individual capacities, interests, and inner motivation of the student at the centre.

In Figure I.1, the core perspectives of contextualising, exploring, and sharing are organised in three spheres, with the notion of artistic research based-learning at the centre, as a representation of how the student's individual wishes, intentions, possibilities, and challenges must be at the heart of the matter.

The left sphere embraces different perspectives of how a student may further contextualise their practice. Artistic research has brought to light the multiplicity of the knowledge production in musical practice. To fully embrace the embodied, artistic, and discursive knowledge forms also entails identifying possibilities for artistic development. At the same time, it also brings light to how some knowledge forms are deeply situated in practices developed in the art worlds of music and others situated in the science worlds of music research. For the purposes of this book, and considering the forms of knowledge activated in artistic research, it is essential to see this distinction as a way for each individual to navigate their practices within these wider fields of knowledge production. It is not a matter of choosing alliances but, rather, constitutes a means to situate one's practices and abilities in a wider context and identify the many different agencies with which a musician must interact in their studies as well as in their professional life. The ethos of critical thinking also demands that the process of contextualising practice involves the consideration of equitable and inclusive practices in order to inform and make meaningful change.

The right sphere includes explorative practices drawn from artistic research. We find essential how artistic research has come to be understood as built on the notion of experimentation in exploratory artistic lab settings. This may entail experimentation with artefacts like scores and instruments, and with musical traditions by challenging and blending performance practices. These explorations may also entail subjective perspectives such as finding a personal voice as well as the extension of such artistic experimentation in intersubjective negotiations of a shared, or discursive, voice through artistic collaboration.[13]

The bottom sphere reflects how the outcomes of artistic research may be effectively shared, both within academic contexts and in relation to art worlds as well as in wider societal perspectives. This may entail the development of further institutional collaboration beyond the academy, seeking to increase employability skills and societal relevance in our education.

---

13 David Gorton and Stefan Östersjö, 'Negotiating the Discursive Voice in Chamber Music', in *Performance, Subjectivity, and Experimentation*, ed. by Catherine Laws (Leuven: Leuven University Press, 2020).

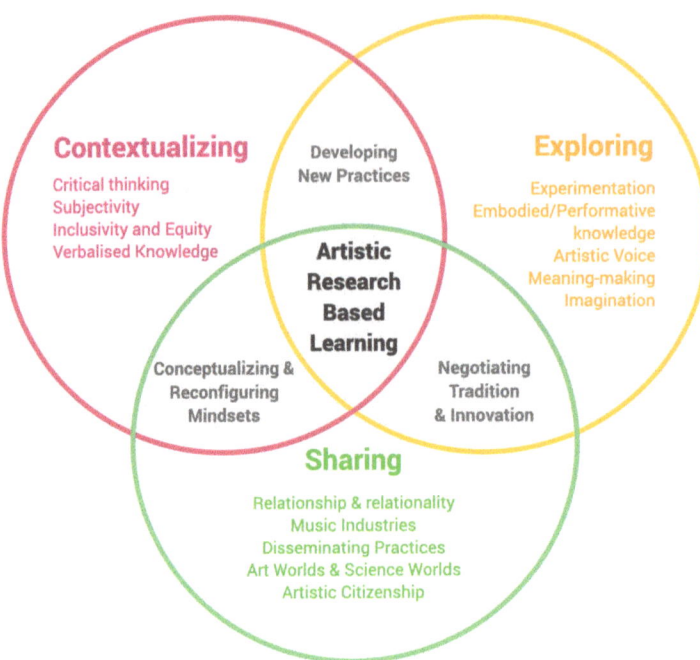

Fig. I.1 A student-centred perspective on the teaching and learning of music performance grounded in artistic research practices.

Introducing approaches to knowledge through critical thinking and a wide range of embodied, artistic and discursive knowledge forms, this book is complemented by a series of videos, as part of a MOOC[14] produced by teachers and researchers, which offer a first-person perspective of the artistic research in action, from teachers and researchers from within the consortium.

A student-centred approach was the basis for formulating the above figure. This was done in multiple ways: first REACT training schools engaged directly with students testing new ideas and involving both staff and students in partnership in the various experiences (articulated in Chapters 4 and 10). Moreover, the research presented within REACT and this book, all utilise student-centred approaches to considering the benefit and impact of the teaching and learning experience. In many of the examples, such as in Chapter 10, 11, and 12, students work as partners with colleagues to lead on making such artistic changes. The student voice is frequently cited throughout this book, enabling readers to engage directly with the feedback given in response to the creative interventions leading to the novel pedagogic ideas and findings shared here.

The present book is composed of chapters mainly drawn from peer reviewed contributions from the REACT symposium held at the Piteå School of Music, Luleå University of Technology in September 2022. The professional experience of the collected authors represents many decades of developing new approaches to their teaching through

---

14   The MOOC is available in the following website: https://react.web.ua.pt

artistic research. The discrepancy in how artistic research has been implemented in varying degrees in different European countries is at this point becoming a concern in the development of the teaching of music performance in HME.[15] It is a concern because there remains an over-reliance on traditional methods. The need for sharing practices across institutions is imperative to deepen understanding of the potential of artistic research in this context as well as sharing pedagogic tools and methods in advancing the centring of the student voice. Whilst the need for sharing these experiences and practices in teaching performance in HME is great, the differing institutional and structural conditions make such sharing less feasible. Hence in some countries, as exemplified in Chapter 1, artistic research has formed the basis for the development of the degree projects, and the structure of both first and second cycle education in music performance across the past decade and more, while in other countries, such as Germany, such processes are initiated at around the same time as the REACT project was created. In addition, the funding structures for HME vary greatly, which impacts not only the access to education, but the pedagogic models for delivering performance. For example, in the UK, there are fees paid via loan for every degree, currently £9,250 per year, which means there are limited resources for one-to-one tuition, and, as such, universities have fewer one-to- one performance-hour delivery per year than the specialist providers, including conservatoires, who gain more funding. By contrast, in many European countries, the education is fully funded by the state, which facilitates access and does not limit the resourcing of performance tuition.

While such differences have been observed also within the consortium of REACT, the project seeks to develop innovative means for sharing practices across institutions and, thereby, to develop impact which can substantially strengthen the development of more inclusive and dynamic teaching practices. The aim of the present book is to contribute to such a development by focussing more on the practices developed by an author, or a group of authors, rather than on theoretical perspectives. Further, all chapters address these practices in varying degrees from a student-centred perspective, sometimes by providing examples of a practical nature, or by reporting on research that draws on accounts and experiences of students, and by incorporating PhD artistic researchers in their own reflections on their own learning processes, as well as how such experience can be applied in teaching.

The book is structured in three parts: I) Artistic Research in HME; II) Novel Approaches to Teaching Interpretation and Performance; III) Challenges and Opportunities of Music Performance Education in Society. The four editors all have significant long-term experience of carrying out artistic research across European institutions, as well as of developing, leading, and managing music performance teaching in HEIs and have themselves developed novel teaching formats and curricula.

Part I, 'Artistic Research in HME', provides perspectives on how artistic research has developed in Higher Education Institutions in Europe since the beginning of the implementation of the Bologna process. Through a range of practice-based examples,

---

15 Robin Nelson, *Practice as Research in the Arts (and Beyond): Principles, Processes, Contexts, Achievements*, 2nd edn (London: Palgrave MacMillan, 2022).

drawing both on accounts from students and teachers, it is suggested that artistic research has increasingly contributed to reconfiguring music-performance teaching and learning also at undergraduate levels. From different perspectives, each chapter in this section provides examples of how artistic research practices have been central in the development of methods for teaching and learning of music performance across different European countries. A central factor appears to be a focus on artistic processes, and how these can be both scrutinised and deepened, through approaches to practice through research. Further, many examples point to how the artistic research practices of teachers may be shared with students, to the effect of enabling greater student autonomy and the development of lifelong learning.

Stefan Östersjö, Carl Holmgren, and Åsa Unander-Scharin's chapter, 'A Swedish Perspective on Artistic Research Practices in First and Second Cycle Education in Music', explores student-centred formats for HME. Fausto Pizzol, in 'Experimentation as a Learning Method: A Case Study exploring Affordances of a Musical Instrument', and Mikael Bäckman, in 'From Imitation to Creation', both seek to explore how the processes of developing a creative voice and personal performance voice may be effectively shared with students in the HME setting, through exploratory and innovative curriculum design. Gilvano Dalagna, Clarissa Foletto, Jorge Salgado Correia, and Ioulia Papageorgi's chapter, 'Teaching Musical Performance from an Artistic Research-Based Approach: Reporting on a Pedagogical Intervention', reports on a pedagogical intervention testing an artistic research-based approach to teaching and learning music performance, as a part of the REACT project.

Part II, 'Novel Approaches to Teaching Interpretation and Performance', presents a series of innovative educational approaches, ranging from the use of improvisation in the teaching of classical music performance, approaches bridging music theory and performance, as well as critical-response theory and reflexive methods. Each chapter is built on accounts of individual teaching practices rather than on general teaching models. All of which converge in promoting student autonomy and critical thinking, paving the way for novel creative approaches to music performance teaching and learning.

Mariam Kharatyan's chapter, 'Score-Based Learning and Improvisation in Classical Music Performance', is based on personal reflections on how a classical pianist may develop individual approaches to the interpretation and performance of classical music by contextualising the compositions and experimenting with their performance practice through the use of improvisation. Further, Kharatyan explores how sharing such practices with students has created new opportunities for students to develop their voices. Robert Sholl, on the other hand, employs improvisation as a tool in a performance-oriented approach to music theory. His chapter, entitled 'Reconnecting Theory: Pedagogy, Improvisation, and Composition' introduces students to the craft of improvised counterpoint through exercises based on Bach's Goldberg variations. Jacob Thompson-Bell, in his chapter 'Shared Learning Environments: Amplifying Group Agency and Motivation with Conservatoire Musicians', introduces the reader to a practice of applying a Critical Response Process feedback framework (CRP) to the teaching and learning of music performance. The chapter provides a theoretical framework through which CRP can be understood but also critically assessed and evaluated. Finally, Richard Fay, Daniel Mawson, and Nahielly Palacios, in their chapter 'Intercultural Musicking: Reflection in, on, and for Situated Klezmer Ensemble Performance', provide an outline of how reflective practices in music performance may form a basis for intercultural learning.

Part III, 'Challenges and Opportunities of Music Performance Education in Society', provides four perspectives on the challenges and possibilities for Higher Music Education. Perspectives address a range of issues including performance in intercultural contexts to several approaches to innovate in the design of educational programmes and curricula in response to changes in society. These changes include course developments which ensure that the higher music education curriculum is truly inclusive and diverse, with a global approach to pedagogy. Beyond the already existing skill-centred model of music performance education, the authors in this section propose a teaching/learning environment based on critical self-reflection and broader social reflexivity, meeting new artistic and societal challenges, such as linking artistic practice to the music industry (pedagogic approaches to embedding employability skills into the curriculum), community intervention (engaging with student and staff identities and creative voices to ensure an authentic education is crafted to develop individual needs), and inclusion (ensuring that students can see themselves represented in the curriculum).

Sarah-Jane Gibson's chapter, 'Experience, Understanding and Intercultural Competence: The Ethno Programme', explores how the Arts and Humanities Research Council-funded Ethno project, in the UK, develops participants' cross-cultural understanding, across genres and in improvisatory live spaces, in order to prepare HME students for professional employment. Odd Torleiv Furnes's chapter, 'The Musical Object in Deep Learning', defines, clarifies, and critiques how deep learning can be facilitated within a HME curriculum to ensure both an aesthetic and embodied experience of music performance during the learning process. Randi Margrethe Eidsaa and Mariam Kharatyan reflect on an initial stage of the REACT project in relation to their own teaching, learning and creative practice in Norway. In 'Rethinking Music Performance Education Through the Lens of Today's Society' they advocate for a student-centred interdisciplinary approach to facilitating students' understanding of the multiple possibilities of making music in contemporary society. Helen Julia Minors's chapter, 'Integrating Employability Skills within an Inclusive Undergraduate and Postgraduate Performance Curriculum', explores specific case study projects, which she led in the UK, which resulted in a revision of the HME curriculum to ensure it was both inclusive for all students and that the HME approach was relevant to contemporary employability skills. There is variability in these four chapters (two based in Norway and two in the UK), which intentionally shows different ways to develop a performance curriculum that is contemporary, placing students' creative voices and their individual developmental musical needs at the core of the educational design.

This book is developed also with the aim of addressing the increasing need for HME to reassess the relation to other professional music institutions. It brings together diverse voices working within HME—ranging from artistic researchers, who are also often professional performers, lecturers, postgraduate researchers, performance tutors, heads of department, and senior managers—to encourage the creation of closer collaborative bonds with music industries. Hereby, HME can develop teaching approaches that more efficiently further students' professional career opportunities. In combination with the videos in the MOOC, the final aim of this book is to fuel such developments and to instigate future actions in this field.

References

Cobussen, Marcel, 'The Trojan Horse. Epistemological Explorations Concerning Practice Based Research', *Dutch Journal of Music Theory*, 12/1 (February 2007), 18–33.

Crispin, Darla, 'The Deterritorialization and Reterritorialization of Artistic Research', *Online Journal for Artistic Research*, 3 (2019), 45–59

Crispin, Darla, 'Looking back, Looking through, Looking beneath. The Promises and Pitfalls of Reflection as a Research Tool', in *Knowing in Performing: Artistic Research in Music and the Performing Arts*, ed. by Annegret Huber, Doris Ingrisch, Therese Kaufmann, Johannes Kretz, Gesine Schröder, and Tasos Zembylas (Bielefeld: Transcript Verlag, 2021), pp. 35–50

Dalagna, Gilvano, Sara Carvalho and Graham Welch, *Desired Artistic Outcomes in Music Performance* (Abingdon: Routledge, 2021), https://doi.org/10.4324/9780429055300

De Assis, Paulo, *Logic of Experimentation: Rethinking Music Performance through Artistic Research* (Leuven: Leuven University Press, 2018)

Dromey, Chris and Julia Haferkorn, *The Classical Music Industry* (Abingdon: Routledge, 2018)

Eidsaa, Randi, 'Dialogues between Teachers and Musicians in Creative Music-Making Collaborations', in *Musician-Teacher Collaborations: Altering the Chord*, ed. by Catharina Christophersen, Ailbhe Kenny (Abingdon: Routledge, 2018), pp. 133–45

Jørgensen, Harold, 'Western Classical Music Studies in Universities and Conservatoires', in *Advanced Musical Performance: Investigations in Higher Education Learning*, ed. by Papageorgi, Ioulia and Welch, Graham (Ashgate: Surrey, 2014), pp. 3–20

López-Íñiguez, Guadalupe and Dawn Bennett, 'A Lifespan Perspective on Multi-Professional Musicians: Does Music Education Prepare Classical Musicians for their Careers?', *Music Education Research*, 22 (2020) 1, 1–14, https://doi.org/ 10.1080/14613808.2019.1703925

Nelson, Robin, *Practice as Research in the Arts (and Beyond): Principles, Processes, Contexts, Achievements*, 2nd edn (London: Palgrave MacMillan, 2022)

Östersjö, Stefan, 'Artistic knowledge, the laboratory and the hörspiel.' in Gränser och oändligheter –Musikalisk och litterär komposition, en forskningsrapport /'Compositional' Becoming, Complexity, and Critique, ed. by Anders Hultqvist and Gunnar. D. Hansson (Gothenburg: Art Monitor, 2020).

Rowley, Jennifer, Dawn Bennet, and Patrick Schmidt, *Leadership of Pedagogy and Curriculum in Higher Music Education* (Abingdon: Routledge, 2019) p. 178

Sloboda, John, *Musicians and Their Live Audiences: Dilemmas and Opportunities. Understanding Audiences* ([n. p.]: Scribd, 2013), https://pt.scribd.com/document/538118141/Sloboda-John-Musicians-and-their-live-audiences-dilemmas-and-opportunities

PART I

ARTISTIC RESEARCH IN HIGHER MUSIC EDUCATION

Introduction to Part I

Stefan Östersjö

Since its introduction in many European countries in the beginning of the twenty-first century, artistic research in music has proven its potential to enhance artistic development in individual practices as well as in collaborative projects. Artistic research in music has developed methods for the study of creative processes, often through introspective and reflexive approaches, and contributed new knowledge in cross-disciplinary music-research settings.[1] A characteristic feature of artistic research in Europe is how institutions have targeted artists with extensive professional experience to enter their artistic PhD programmes. This approach has ensured high artistic quality in the outcomes and that these have 'force and effect'[2] in an art world. At the same time, artistic research is characterised by the singularity of the knowledge produced, a typical factor in research built on challenges and possibilities in the practice of the individual artist. What might such research into specialised practices bring to the teaching practices in HME? And, indeed, what roles have artistic researchers developed in these institutions?

---

1 See, for instance, the role of artistic research in the CMPCP project, as reflected in a series of publications, including *Distributed Creativity: Collaboration and Improvisation in Contemporary Music*, ed. by Eric Clarke and Mark Doffman (Oxford: Oxford University Press, 2017) and in *Musicians in the Making: Pathways to Creative Performance*, ed. by John Rink, Helena Gaunt, and Aaron Williamon (New York: Oxford University Press, 2018).

2 Barbara Bolt, 'Artistic Research: A Performative Paradigm?' *Parse*, 3 (2016), 129–42, http://parsejournal.com/article/artistic-research-a-performative-paradigm/.

While initially, artistic research may have typically been experienced as a Trojan horse,[3] a foreign intruder—disturbing and threatening the established workings of the teaching and learning of music performance in HME, by providing space for the experimentation of individual artists in their premises—in Part I, we consider how artistic research has become instead an integrated feature, providing novel approaches. The notion of artistic research as a laboratory practice is useful,[4] since it allows for an understanding of experimentation as an approach which draws on the affordances of technologies, such as those of video recording,[5] and inter-subjective approaches to knowledge production, enabled through audio and video technologies.[6] By considering artistic research from the perspective of the laboratory, the exploratory practices that are developed in the lab come to the fore. What artistic research offers to HME is, therefore, explorative and experimental practices, and tools that enable and enhance these. However, it is also essential to stress the nomadic nature of artistic research, through which the researcher continuously provides an outsider perspective, bringing a critical gaze at the practices and traditions of these teaching institutions.

In Part I of this book, experimental approaches to individual practice are central perspectives in two chapters, building on ongoing artistic PhD projects: Fausto Pizzol's chapter 'Experimentation as a Learning Method: A Case Study Exploring Affordances of a Musical Instrument' offers a detailed account of a cycle of experimentation designed to explore the harmonic potential of the electric bass. The author proposes that the artistic research approach tested in the project may be relevant in artistic research on instruments other than the electric bass, but furthermore, that his methods, grounded in ecological psychology, offers new possibilities for the teaching and learning of playing the electric bass. Mikael Bäckman, in his chapter, 'From Imitation to Creation', employs a similar theoretical framework, grounded in embodied music cognition, in a project which explores how experimentation with transcription and imitation may lay the grounds for a transformation of individual voice. In the final analysis, Bäckman assesses how the learning outcomes of his individual artistic research process may be applied in teaching the harmonica to students in HME. This is also the central theme of the entire of Part I, addressed in a somewhat wider perspective in the first and final chapters. First, Stefan Östersjö, Carl Holmgren, and Åsa Unander-Scharin's chapter, 'A Swedish Perspective on Artistic Research Practices in First and Second Cycle Education in Music', provides an analysis of method development in the Piteå School of Music, at Luleå University of Technology, taking the independent degree project, and the courses

---

3 Marcel Cobussen, 'The Trojan Horse. Epistemological Explorations Concerning Practice Based Research', *Dutch Journal of Music Theory*, 12/1 (February 2007), 18–33.
4 Stefan Östersjö, 'Artistic Knowledge, the Laboratory and the Hörspiel', in *Gränser och oändligheter–Musikalisk och litterär komposition, en forskningsrapport /'Compositional' Becoming, Complexity, and Critique*, ed. by Anders Hultqvist and Gunnar. D. Hansson (Gothenburg: Art Monitor, 2020).
5 Ben Spatz, *Making A Laboratory. Dynamic Configurations with Transversal Video* (Santa Barbara, CA: Punctum Books, 2020).
6 Stefan Östersjö, Nguyễn Thanh Thủy, David Hebert, and Henrik Frisk, *Shared Listenings: Methods for Transcultural Musicianship and Research* (Cambridge: Cambridge University Press, 2023).

preparing students for these, as the point of departure. This is relevant, since the impact of artistic research in HME has been found to be substantial in the development of methods and forms of representation in student theses.[1] In such method development, artistic research practices have also been important when the centre of the independent project becomes an opportunity for the student to identify their individual interests, challenges, difficulties or opportunities, that they wish to develop in their studies, and bring with them into the next stages of education or professional work. The fourth chapter in this Part develops an analysis of the second Training School which formed part of the REACT project, and which was hosted by the University of Aveiro in May 2022. Building on their experience as participating teachers, Gilvano Dalagna, Clarissa Foletto, Jorge Salgado Correia, and Ioulia Papageorgi's chapter, 'Teaching Musical Performance from an Artistic Research-Based Approach: Reporting on a Pedagogical Intervention', reports on a pedagogical intervention seeking to develop and test an artistic research-based approach to teaching and learning music performance. The chapter builds largely on a focus-group interview with participating students but also relates these to a literature review looking at current curriculum development in HME, and an assessment of the relation between HEIs and the music industry.

A significant feature of Part I of the book is how it is built on qualitative interviews, seeking to assess how individual students in first and second cycle education have experienced the application of artistic research approaches in their studies. Three out of four chapters draw on small-scale interview studies, which also bring out student voices, with the aim of focusing on individual experience rather than curriculum design and overarching pedagogical strategies. While this approach has obvious beneficial qualities, this section of the book also illustrates the need for more comprehensive studies of the impact of artistic research in HME. It suggests that such further study should employ multiple perspectives—starting with findings by artist researchers in their individual research projects—to further trace how these findings may be applied in teaching. Through combinations of qualitative and quantitative approaches, we should be able to document how such findings have been systematically employed in curriculum development across European countries, and, finally, to assess the outcomes through analysis of student publications and through interviews with students and alumni.

---

1   Karin Johansson and Eva Georgii-Hemming, 'Processes of Academisation in Higher Music Education: the case of Sweden', *British Journal of Music Education*, 38 (2) (2021).

References

Bolt, Barbara, 'Artistic research: A performative paradigm?' *Parse*, 3 (2016), 129–42. Retrieved from: http://parsejournal.com/article/artistic- research-a-performative-paradigm/.

Clarke, Eric and Mark Doffman (eds), *Distributed Creativity: Collaboration and Improvisation in Contemporary Music* (Oxford: Oxford University Press, 2017)

Cobussen, Marcel, 'The Trojan Horse. Epistemological Explorations Concerning Practice Based Research', *Dutch Journal of Music Theory*, 12/1 (February 2007), 18–33.

Craenen, Paul, 'Artistic research as an integrative force. A critical look at the role of master's research at Dutch conservatoires', *FORUM+*, 27.1 (2020), 45–55, https://doi.org/10.5117/FORUM2020.1.CRAE

Crispin, Darla, 'The Deterritorialization and Reterritorialization of Artistic Research', *Online Journal for Artistic Research*, 3(2019), 45–59.

Johansson, Karin, and Eva Georgii-Hemming, 'Processes of Academisation in Higher Music Education: the case of Sweden', *British Journal of Music Education*, 38 (2) (2021).

Östersjö, Stefan, 'Artistic knowledge, the laboratory and the hörspiel.' in *Gränser och oändligheter –Musikalisk och litterär komposition, en forskningsrapport /'Compositional' Becoming, Complexity, and Critique*, ed. by Anders Hultqvist and Gunnar. D. Hansson (Gothenburg: Art Monitor, 2020).

Östersjö, Stefan, Nguyễn Thanh Thủy, David Hebert, and Henrik Frisk. *Shared Listenings: Methods for Transcultural Musicianship and Research* (Cambridge: Cambridge University Press, 2023).

Rink, John, Helena Gaunt, and Aaron Williamon (eds), *Musicians in the Making: Pathways to Creative Performance* (New York: Oxford University Press, 2018).

Spatz, Ben, *Making A Laboratory. Dynamic Configurations with Transversal Video* (Santa Barbara, CA: Punctum Books, 2020).

1. A Swedish Perspective on Artistic Research Practices in First and Second Cycle Education in Music

Stefan Östersjö and Carl Holmgren with Åsa Unander-Scharin

Introduction

This chapter seeks an understanding of the ways in which practices of artistic research are contributing to the development of the teaching and learning of music performance in Higher Music Education (HME). It is built on the authors' long-term experience of teaching artistic research methods and supervising theses in first and second cycle programmes in Sweden. First, we provide a brief historical overview of how artistic research in music was implemented in Sweden, with particular attention to knowledge claims and method development.[1] Second, we consider the impact of the Bologna process on HME in Sweden, a process in which the authors have been personally involved. It has, among other things, demanded a shift from teacher-driven provision toward 'student-centred higher education'.[2] The third section is the most substantial, and first outlines the role of the thesis project in the bachelor's and master's

---

[1] Darla Crispin, 'Looking back, Looking through, Looking beneath: The Promises and Pitfalls of Reflection as a Research Tool', in *Knowing in Performing: Artistic Research in Music and the Performing Arts*, ed. by Annegret Huber, Doris Ingrisch, Therese Kaufmann, Johannes Kretz, Gesine Schröder, and Tasos Zembylas (Bielefeld: Transcript Verlag, 2021), pp. 35–50; Stefan Östersjö, 'Thinking-through-Music: On Knowledge Production, Materiality, Subjectivity and Embodiment in Artistic Research' in *Artistic Research in Music: Discipline and Resistance*, ed. by Jonathan Impett (Leuven: Leuven University Press, 2017), pp. 88–107; Stefan Östersjö, 'Art Worlds, Voice and Knowledge: Thoughts on Quality assessment of artistic research outcomes', *ÍMPAR Online Journal for Artistic Research*, 3(2) (2019), 60–69; Robin Nelson, *Practice as Research in the Arts (and Beyond): Principles, Processes, Contexts, Achievements,* 2nd edn (London: Palgrave MacMillan, 2022).

[2] European Ministers Responsible for Higher Education, 'London Communiqué: Towards the European Higher Education Area: Responding to Changes in a Globalised World' (2007), http://www.ehea.info/Upload/document/ministerial_declarations/2007_London_Communique_English_588697.pdf, p. 2.

programmes in the Piteå School of Music, at Luleå University of Technology (LTU), and the courses that prepare students to undertake thesis projects. We present an overarching qualitative and quantitative analysis of completed theses from 2020–2022 with regard to aims, research questions, and methods. For each of the six identified categories, one thesis was selected for a more detailed qualitative analysis. Finally, each of these six students was interviewed. Hereby, the central material of the chapter is constituted of student voices, the experience manifested in their thesis projects as well as their retrospective reflections on the role of the projects in their individual artistic development, as expressed in individual interviews carried out by the authors.

Artistic Research in Sweden

Artistic research was implemented in the early 2000s in Sweden, with the first PhD students employed in 2002.[3] A fundamental characteristic of artistic research in the country has been a consistent focus on artistic excellence, as expressed by Gertrud Sandqvist, 'artistic-research education should be given to artists who have a well-developed practice of their own'.[4] This approach generated a set of highly independent PhD projects with a firm grounding in their respective art worlds,[5] carried out by artists who sought means for challenging their individual practices and creating a wider understanding of their role. As further argued by Sandqvist, the rationale for this approach was that only when they have fully 'mastered their own artistic projects can artists decide which methods they need in order to develop the specific parts of their artistic projects that are oriented towards the production of new knowledge'.[6] Hence, while the point of departure was the qualities of the individual artistic practice of the PhD student, the further aim would always be to 'produce a new kind of information that is not introspective but combinative, outward-looking and seeking new connections'.[7] The first Swedish PhD theses in artistic research in music were defended in 2008, and the past ten years have given clear indications of an increasing maturity in the field, with stronger research environments, and also, as argued by Lundström, with projects 'increasingly conducted by research groups or research teams that often involve more than one university and more than one discipline'.[8]

Although a comprehensive analysis of the methods and practices developed in the field of artistic research in Europe across the past twenty years is still lacking, it

---

3   Håkan Lundström, 'Svensk forskning i musik: De senaste 100 åren' [Swedish Research in Music: The Last 100 Years], *Swedish Journal of Music Research*, 101 (2019), 1–47.
4   Gertrud Sandqvist, 'New Knowledge from the Artist's Perspective: On artistic research', in *Artistic Research in Music: Discipline and Resistance*, ed. by Jonathan Impett (Leuven: Leuven University Press, 2017), p. 184.
5   Howard S. Becker, *Art Worlds*, 25. anniversary ed., updated and expanded (Berkeley: University of California Press, 1982/2008).
6   Sandqvist, p. 184.
7   Mika Hannula, Juha Suoranta and Tere Vadén, *Artistic Research: Theories, Methods and Practices*, trans. by Gareth Griffiths and Kristina Kölhi (Helsinki: Academy of Fine Arts, 2005), p. 22.
8   Lundström, p. 46.

is clear that one important feature is the application of reflexive methods in artistic projects.[9] For instance, Darla Crispin, observes how, in artistic research, 'attention has increasingly turned to ways in which auto-ethnography and self-reflexivity can continue to be developed as viable approaches to conducting musical research'.[10] From the perspective of other research domains, in which autoethnography has become an important vehicle, Bartleet observes how

> autoethnography and artistic research have enjoyed a dynamic relationship—the former enabling the latter, and the latter fuelling the former, and both have found themselves privileging the subjectivity of the artist-researcher, the materiality of the researcher's body, and the intersubjectivities that emerge through the researcher's artistic encounters with the world.[11]

Crispin further notes how the method development in artistic research 'has become concomitant with innovations around musical language and notions concerning its "truth content"'.[12] At the same time, Crispin observes how the outcomes of artistic research also have 'been a driving force behind various innovations in art-making'.[13] Hence, professional artists, carrying out artistic research using reflexive methods have demonstrated substantial impact on the development of their individual research projects. Another factor, common to these projects, is the role of artistic experimentation, as a means for challenging the individual practice of the researcher.[14] Of particular interest for the purposes of the present chapter is however whether the methods and practices of artistic research have indeed also affected the teaching and learning in HME.

In a recent article, Karin Johansson and Eva Georgii-Hemming argue that '[i]n Sweden, the artistic PhD degree has established artistic research as the main way of enquiry for developing new knowledge in the field of music';[15] and they make the further claim that this has laid the grounds for creating formats for a research-based education, a perspective which will be further examined in the next section. They also find that reflection has constituted a basis for the introduction of research-based methods, and

---

9   In general, the studies carried out so far typically approach a single context in smaller scale studies, as is the case in the present chapter and others across this book. Another very useful example of the same nature is Paul Craenen's paper 'Creative and Social Intentions of Research Proposals of Music Performance Students. A reality check of curriculum discourse in higher music education' (2024, in press), which presents a thematic analysis of almost 300 project proposals by master's students at the Royal Conservatoire The Hague, submitted between 2021 and 2023.
10 Crispin, p. 71.
11 Bartleet Brydie-Leigh, 'Artistic Autoethnography: Exploring the Interface Between Autoethnography and Artistic Research', in *Handbook of Autoethnography*, ed. by Tony E. Adams, Stacy Holman Jones and Carolyn Ellis (New York: Routledge, 2021), p. 133.
12 Crispin, p. 73.
13 Ibid.
14 For examples of how experimentation may drive artistic PhD projects, see the two following chapters in this book, by Fausto Pizzol and Mikael Bäckman respectively. For further theoretical framing, see Paulo de Assis, *Logic of Experimentation: Rethinking Music Performance through Artistic Research* (Leuven: Leuven University Press, 2018).
15 Karin Johansson and Eva Georgii-Hemming, 'Processes of Academisation in Higher Music Education: the case of Sweden', *British Journal of Music Education*, 38(2) (2021), p. 181.

Georgii-Hemming, Johansson, and Nadia Moberg note how 'teachers and leaders [in HME] view reflection as a method for students' self-improvement as the students develop written and oral skills by which they can document and consider their performances and artistic development'.[16] In the following section, we will further examine the results of their large-scale comprehensive study, as a part of outlining the curriculum development in HME in Sweden, largely built on the process launched by the Bologna agreement.[17]

The Bologna Process and HME in Sweden

As indicated in a recent literature review, instrumental teaching and learning in HME have been reported as largely based on the master–apprentice model.[18] However, the way in which this model is implemented has been found to be in direct conflict with three of the changes that the Bologna process entailed, since such education should be research-based, use student-centred teaching models aiming to activate students in their learning, and aim for students' lifelong learning (i.e., emphasise the need for generalisation and transfer of learning, and meta-cognitive aspects such as learning of learning). Although no specific requirements for music are given in Swedish legislation,[19] students shall, for a degree of bachelor of fine arts, demonstrate abilities including autonomously identifying, formulating, and solving artistic and creative problems; making assessments informed by relevant artistic, social, and ethical issues; and identifying their need for further knowledge and taking responsibility for their learning.[20] Second-cycle education shall, in addition, further develop students' ability to integrate and make use of their knowledge and students' potential for professional activities or research that demand considerable autonomy.[21] Thus, based on these formulations, artistic education in music post-Bologna shall be research-based, student-centred, and develop students' capacity for lifelong learning.

The research project 'Discourses of Academization and the Music Profession in Higher Music Education' (DAPHME, 2016–2018), sought a comprehensive understanding of the impact of the Bologna process on artistic education in music in Europe. Hence, the outcomes of the Swedish study within the DAPHME project constitute a central reference regarding the implementation of the Bologna process in HME in Sweden. A major portion

---

16   Eva Georgii-Hemming, Karin Johansson, and Nadia Moberg, 'Reflection in Higher Music Education: what, why, wherefore?', *Music Education Research*, 22.3 (2020), p. 251.
17   See also Chapter 8 of this book, in which Fay et al. discuss the use of reflexive methods in a module for intercultural music teaching and learning in HME from the perspective of a UK University.
18   Carl Holmgren, 'Dialogue Lost? Teaching Musical Interpretation of Western Classical Music in Higher Education' (PhD thesis, Luleå University of Technology, 2022), http://urn.kb.se/resolve?urn =urn:nbn:se:ltu:diva-88258, pp. 54–73.
19   Swedish Council for Higher Education, 'The Higher Education Ordinance. Annex 2. System of Qualifications' (SFS 1993:100), https://www.uhr.se/en/start/laws-and-regulations/ Laws-and-regulations/The-Higher-Education-Ordinance/Annex-2/
20   The Higher Education Ordinance. Annex 2. System of Qualifications (SFS 1993:100).
21   Ibid.

of papers from the Swedish study within the DAPHME project are based on interviews with teachers and leaders in HME. For instance, Johansson and Georgii-Hemming cite extensively from their informants, who generally describe the establishment of artistic research as a decisive factor for the renewal of the degree project in music performance in HME.[22] It is argued that practices from artistic research have demonstrated how 'to integrate reflective and artistic activities, and how to document and present research in multimodal formats'.[23] Furthermore, informants observe how the degree projects are not typically designed to conform with 'ready-made forms and stereotypes' but 'are both conventional and experimental, they cross borders and investigate new things'.[24]

To summarize the outcomes of the Swedish part of the DAPHME project, the leaders and teachers in HME were found to use four types of justifications for including reflection in artistic programmes in music. First, reflection was described as having the ability to enable students to take individual responsibility for their artistic development.[25] Second, reflection was viewed as a tool for personal branding and expanding musicians' capacity to verbally communicate about their performances.[26] Third, it was described as a tool that enables musicians to situate themselves, and that may produce musicians 'who have a voice'.[27] And, finally, reflections were found to show 'potential to develop the common professional field of knowledge'.[28]

While Johansson and Georgii-Hemming emphasise that the degree project was 'initially much debated',[29] their study confirms our impression that, in Swedish HME, the degree project, built on artistic research practices and methods, has become an integrated building block in the curricula in all teaching institutions. Furthermore, their study also proposes that the use of reflexive methods is a typical feature of these practices, as discussed and problematized by Crispin.[30]

In a recent article, Moberg[31] makes contrasting observations drawn from a qualitative content analysis, followed by a discourse analysis, of finished master's thesis projects. She puts forth a more critical view on the implementation of reflexive methods in second-cycle degree projects, claiming that 'sought-after practices within HME such as critical thinking, reflection, reflexivity and metacognitive engagement [...] are conspicuous by their absence'.[32] Moberg further claims that 'theses reproduce music as an object independent of social and political concerns along with practitioner

---

22 Johansson and Georgii-Hemming, 2021.
23 Ibid., p. 182.
24 Ibid., p. 183.
25 Georgii-Hemming et al., 2020, pp. 250–51.
26 Ibid., p. 251.
27 Ibid., p. 253.
28 Ibid.
29 Johansson and Georgii-Hemming, 2021, p. 182.
30 Crispin, 2021.
31 Nadia Moberg, 'The Place of Master Theses in Music Performance Education in Sweden: subjects, purposes, justifications', *Music Education Research*, 25.1 (2023), 24–35.
32 Ibid, p. 9.

preoccupation with the self in search of individual advancement', arguing that such a point of departure in individual artistic practice entails that 'arguments beyond the self are rendered redundant'.[33] However, in the method description, Moberg describes how her analysis 'focused on purpose formulations and/or research questions (or sections serving a similar function) and justifications for the theses'.[34] Thus, it is unclear how claims can be made regarding the students' abilities to contextualise their practice, since the study is explicitly limited to the purpose formulations, research questions, or 'sections serving a similar function'.[35] Throughout this chapter, we will seek a deeper understanding of the role of reflexive methods and how the degree project may, indeed, promote critical thinking and the ability to situate artistic practice in wider socio-cultural contexts. We note how the study of artistic learning processes is challenging when it comes to the collection and analysis of data.

Description of Programmes in the Piteå School of Music

The three-year bachelor programme in music, as well as the two-year master's, have been given at the Piteå School of Music since 2007. The programmes have, since the beginning, been constructed with a clear progression with the student's degree project in mind. The overarching aim has been to identify each student's individually experienced artistic possibilities, challenges, and motivations, in order to involve both student and teachers in the design of the studies. Hereby, the degree project should be an integrated and central component in the artistic development of the student. The design also aims to develop student autonomy and reflexivity, an objective which is addressed in the introductory courses, in which students are taught critical thinking and reflexive methods, based on practices of artistic research.[36]

Bachelor	Master
The Research Process (7.5 credits)	Artistic research processes: theory and method (15 credits)
Degree project (15 credits)	Degree Project (30 credits)

Table 1.1. The basic design of introductory courses and degree projects in the bachelor's and master's programmes in Music Performance at Piteå School of Music, Luleå University of Technology (LTU).[37]

---

33   Ibid.
34   Ibid., p. 4.
35   Ibid.
36   Consider, however, the chapter by Jacob Thompson-Bell in this book, where he proposes, emphasising collective perspectives on learner agency, that in the development of student-centred learning environments. Rather than promoting autonomy, a more holistic perspective on criticality and learning informs the alternative paradigm of 'ontonomy'.
37   Syllabi for the courses are found on the university website, according to the links in the reference list.

In Table 1.1, the upper row refers to the introductory courses in both programmes, each of which leads to the formulation of a project plan for the thesis project to follow (as listed in the second row). The introductory course in the bachelor's programme is carried out in the spring of the second year, with the course stretching across the entire term. Similarly, the 15-credit thesis project stretches across the entire third year. A seminar at a 70% milestone is held in March and a final seminar in May, followed by an examination wherein both the artistic outcomes and the written submission are discussed and assessed as a whole.

In the master's programme, the introductory course stretches across the entire first year. The degree project is carried out in the second year, although many students start their thesis project with a pilot study, which concludes the first term of the first year. Thereby, the thesis work can extend across three terms, occupying more or less the entire duration of the studies. In the master's thesis course, there are part-time seminars at 40% and 70% milestones, followed by a final seminar in May. As in the bachelor course, the final examination of the thesis takes place after the final seminar.

Design of the Study

This chapter builds on a study of the role of the thesis project in the Piteå School of Music, in which the authors have been directly involved as teachers, supervisors, and examiners. The greater part of the study is concerned with the documented outcomes of the students' independent degree projects. Since the courses for both artistic research methods and theories, as well as the thesis project itself, have been in constant development, we decided to focus this study on the theses produced in 2020–2022.

The study consisted of five main parts: first, a preliminary qualitative content analysis of the bachelor's (n = 56) and master's theses (n = 11); second, a quantitative analysis of selected key words in the theses; third, a qualitative analysis of aims and research questions serving to validate the analysis in the two previous stages; fourth, for each of the categories identified in the first qualitative analysis, one student thesis was selected subjected to a closer study; and fifth, we interviewed the students whose theses we had analysed, asking them to provide feedback on our analysis of their project and asked additional questions regarding how they had experienced their artistic education and how they had experienced the role of the degree project in their studies. In sum, the design of the study has sought to provide insights regarding the implementation of artistic research practices in the students' theses project and to foreground students' own accounts, both through their written publications and through interviews.

Preliminary Qualitative Content Analysis

We first approached the data through a qualitative content analysis[38] based on a summative reading of all the theses from 2020 to 2022, aiming to identify overarching topics and methods used. This initial step in the research design is similar to the study by Moberg mentioned above, in which a qualitative content analysis of 266 master's theses with 'a classical music orientation' from three institutions for higher music education in Sweden 2013–2020 was carried out.[39] Our analysis led to a preliminary set of six categories in which the student projects could be structured:

- 'Collaborative Practices and Ensemble Interaction'
- 'Interpretation, Expression, and Voice'
- 'Performer-Instrument Interactions'
- 'Rehearsal and Efficient Practising'
- 'Musical Gesture in Performance and Conducting'
- 'Performance Anxiety'

It should be noted that several of these categories are closely linked. 'Performer-Instrument Interactions', 'Rehearsal and Efficient Practising', and 'Musical Gesture in Performance and Conducting' all build on the embodied interactions between performers and instruments. Moberg's findings have many similarities, wherein more than half of the theses were concerned with the following seven topics: technique and expression (12.8%); musical works and composers (10.2%); interpretation (9%); auditions and competitions (8.6%); mental health and preparation (6.8%); arranging, composing, and improvisation (4.5%); and practice (4.5).[40] Our impression was that the outcomes of the content analysis were less precise than we had wished for, a concern which appears to be relevant also for the similar type of categorisations found in Moberg's paper.

Quantitative Analysis of Student Theses

After the preliminary qualitative thematic analysis, we sought a wider understanding of the findings by conducting a quantitative content analysis[41] using automated bash scripts. Hereby, we examined the frequency of 40 selected keywords, relating to the methods used in all bachelor's (n = 56) and master's (n = 11) theses (in total, n = 67). In the search, we set the threshold for inclusion at three occurrences of the respective search term, striving

---

38 James W. Drisko and Tina Maschi, *Content Analysis* (New York: Oxford University Press, 2016).
39 Moberg, 2023, p. 3.
40 Ibid., pp. 4–5.
41 Drisko and Maschi, 2016.

to filter out theses making only passing mention of the terms. The theses were written in either Swedish or English; therefore, parallel searches were made in both languages.

The raw output from the searches of the selected keywords was then inserted into a spreadsheet, where the data was further analysed. Two general observations were made: first, the term 'process' is mentioned in almost all bachelor's and all master's theses, typically always with reference to a description or discussion of the individual artistic process, hence indicating that this aspect of artistic research practice has had a prominent role in the inquiry. Second, the term 'reflection' (and the Swedish 'reflektion'), although occurring in some of the bachelor's theses, is substantively more common in master's theses, thus possibly indicating the advanced students' higher level of metacognitive awareness, or at least suggesting a greater ability to conceptualise their learning process.

The analysis of methods confirmed some expected patterns, wherein projects addressing aspects of performance typically employed both audio and/or video for the documentation of artistic process, while projects related to composition and related practices would focus more on other modes of documentation. An increase in the use of video documentation was noted among master's projects. The use of logbooks was found more frequently in bachelor's than in master's theses. Interviews were also used by students in both programmes, however more frequently in the master's theses. Furthermore, in some master's theses, stimulated-recall analysis was used, indicating an increased interest in achieving intersubjective understanding. Moreover, a tendency was found that the combination of 'interview' and 'teacher' was more frequent in master's theses, possibly indicating that the students' regular teachers had had a more substantial involvement in these projects, an observation that we will return to below.

Qualitative Analysis of Aims and Research Questions

In order to obtain a deeper understanding of the data, a further qualitative analysis of all the studied theses' aims and research questions was carried out, which entailed identifying central categories, beyond those found in the first analysis. The findings were triangulated against these six categories, and the number of occurrences was quantified, allowing more than one category for each thesis.

This analytical process indicated clearly that the initially identified category of 'Performance Anxiety' was not relevant, since the phrase occurred only twice in bachelor's theses (see Fig. 1.1). At the same time, an additional category, labelled as 'Structural Analysis Aimed at Arranging or Composition', was found to be quite central as it occurred in 49% of the bachelor's theses and in 74% of the master's theses. Furthermore, we found that this category could be subdivided into projects that either sought to develop skills in arranging or in composition. It should be noted that 'arranging' here refers to a wide range of skills, often related to either individual performance or to studio production.[42] Additionally, some projects also referred to 'structural analysis' but as an aspect of musical 'interpretation', and are hence found in that category (see, further, Fig. 1.1).

The excluded category of 'Performance Anxiety' is a topic that has tended to recur across institutions in Sweden, in particular among students in classical music performance, as evidenced in Moberg who reports that 6.8% of the analysed master's theses falls within this category.[43] It is beyond the scope of the present chapter to discuss this phenomenon,[44] but it does suggest that there are issues with psychological well-being among classical music students. Notably, in the present study, very few occurrences of Music Performance Anxiety-related topics were found, instead leaving space for projects exploring musical performance as creative practice.

The final six categories found in the analysis of aims and research questions were:

1. 'Structural Analysis Aimed at Arranging or Composition' (49% bachelor, 74% master).

2. 'Collaborative Practices and Ensemble Interaction' (13% bachelor, 27% master) where the focus is on the interaction between performers, as well as between performer and composer (more prominent within master's theses).

3. 'Interpretation, Expression, and Voice', denotes projects which sought to develop students' personal musicianship, striving to form their own musical identity as performers (16% bachelor, 64% master).

4. 'Performer-Instrument Interactions' focused on the performers' relation to their instrument and how this could be developed to meet their artistic goals (54% bachelor, 36% master).

5. 'Rehearsal and Efficient Practising' denotes theses that sought to develop more efficient ways of practising (mostly bachelor) and rehearsing (32% bachelor, 18% master)

6. 'Musical Gesture in Performance and Conducting', are projects studying and exploring gestures in performance and conducting (2% bachelor, 27% master)

---

42 There is an interesting parallel between degree projects in this category (using structural analysis as a tool in the artistic process) and the performative approach to teaching theory advocated and outlined in the chapter by Robert Sholl in this book.

43 Moberg, 2023, p. 5.

44 For a recent literature review of Music Performance Anxiety in HME, see Erik Blair and Hendrik van der Sluis, 'Music Performance Anxiety and Higher Education Teaching: A systematic literature review', *Journal of University Teaching & Learning Practice*, 19.3 (2022), 5–15.

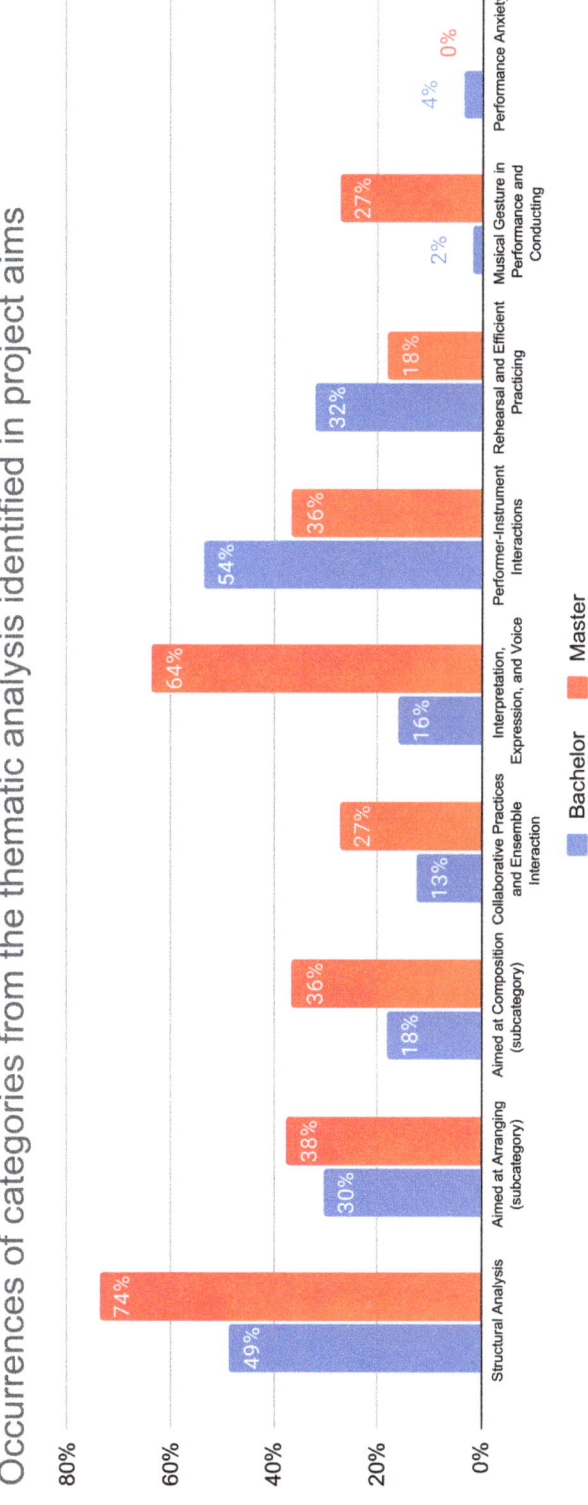

Fig. 1.1: A proportional representation of occurrences of the most prevalent categories in the qualitative content analysis.

Qualitative Analysis of Method and Design — a Closer Study of One Student Thesis per Category

For each of the six categories identified above (see Fig. 1.1), one student thesis was selected and subjected to a closer study. Our ambition has been to give voice to each student and, thereby, prioritise direct quotations.[45] Furthermore, we also interviewed the students whose theses we had analysed, asking them to provide feedback on our analysis of their thesis also posing additional questions regarding how they had experienced their artistic education as well as the role of the degree project in their studies. The authors translated all Swedish quotes, and the originals are presented in the footnotes.

Structural Analysis Aimed at Arranging or Composition

The use of structural analysis to explore and develop practices of musical composition is a category which is commonly found both in bachelor- and master-level theses. We will, in the following, look at the master's thesis by Robin Lilja, which explores a particular method for algorithmic composition, using what he calls 'constraint-based patterns'.[46] This method sought to develop conditions for creating a convincing balance between contrast and coherence across musical parameters in a musical composition, an objective previously explored through a similar composition method within the frames of Lilja's bachelor's thesis project.[47] According to the aims of the project, the 'achieved contrasts should be apparent in multiple parameters, but the overall musical structure should still maintain some form of coherence', and the project was built on the hypothesis that 'the sequential nature of the contrasts within the constraint-based patterns should contribute to the desired level of coherence'.[48]

In the literature study, the writings of Gerhard Nierhaus were a central reference, and, in order to further substantiate the project's relation to research on algorithmic composition, Lilja followed two courses at Kunst Universität Graz (KUG), Nierhaus's home university.[49] The fundamental method of the project is described as artistic experimentation, and, to capture the outcome of this practice, two main methods were used to document the author's individual process: a structured logbook and

---

45   A side effect of this approach was that, despite the greater number and generally high quality of bachelor's theses, we decided to prioritise theses written in English rather than Swedish, which led to the selection of four master theses and only two on the bachelor level.

46   Robin Lilja, 'Constraint-based Patterns—An examination of an algorithmic composition method' (master's thesis, Luleå University of Technology, 2021), http://urn.kb.se/resolve?urn=urn:nbn:se:ltu:diva-85001

47   Robin Lilja, 'Musikaliska kontraster genom förbud: Undersökning av min kompositionsmetod antikomposition' [*Musical Contrasts through Prohibition: Investigation of my composition method anticomposition*] (bachelor's thesis, Luleå University of Technology, 2019), https://urn.kb.se/resolve?urn=urn:nbn:se:ltu:diva-74099

48   Ibid., p. 13.

49   Ibid., p. iv and p. 62.

the use of verbal annotations in the finished score, both contributing to capturing moments of decision-making. The analytical approach, however, was not merely an assessment of the artistic outcomes of the composition method, as experienced from a first-person perspective. A further perspective was provided through the collection of different forms of feedback from listeners. Such third-person perspectives on the artistic outcomes were drawn from differently designed focus-group interviews (which always included a full screening of a particular piece, typically a concert recording from the premiere). In these sessions, informants were selected according to the criteria that they have no knowledge with regard to the method used for the composition of the music. A different category of feedback was drawn from teachers and fellow composition students, whose feedback built on both listening and reading the score (most typically, drafts derived in the process of artistic experimentation). In the final discussion, Lilja concludes that both types of responses were useful, but the feedback from the more informed listeners provided valuable input in the creative process, identifying artistic challenges, issues, and potential. At the same time, it is interesting to note how it became difficult for Lilja to tell whether a perceived increase of coherence in the music was due to revisions in the score or if it was related to a particular listener becoming accustomed to the style of the music.[50] In an interview carried out in December 2022, Lilja further reflects on the role of feedback in relation to lifelong learning and notes how:

> While it might go without saying, I want to state the importance of the teachers, supervisors, and peers in the process of 'becoming your own teacher'. Their comments during feedback will echo in my head as I grow, and I will ask myself 'what would my teacher/supervisor/peer have said?'[51]

In the discussion, much emphasis is given to the relation between complexity in input and output. For example, in the section addressing the creation of the orchestral piece, Lilja explains that he eventually decided to use 'a simpler algorithm for a more complex result'.[52] Similar observations constitute the general response to the aim of the project: to explore how the use of the constraint-based patterns may shape the relation between coherence and contrast. In the final discussion, Lilja observes how:

> The greater the amount of composition parameters which are controlled through constraint-based patterns, the simpler each individual composition parameter has to be in order to reach contrasting results that I find satisfying. In other words: when the interference patterns of the multiple composition parameters become more complex, the less complex each individual parameter needs to be for the result to be interesting. What is truly delightful, is that this means that you can have high coherence in each individual parameter [...] while the resulting interference pattern provides high contrast.[53]

---

50   See Lilja, 2021, p. 52.
51   Lilja, Robin, personal communication, 31 December 2022.
52   Lilja, 2021, p. 60.
53   Lilja, 2021, p. 51.

Another recurring topic is the role of intuition in the compositional process and its relation to the compositional constraints. In his conclusion, Lilja reflects on how there is always more to be learnt with regard to the potential of the system he created, observing how 'satisfaction is never reached, and therein lies the beauty'.[54] In reflecting on the thesis project as a whole, Lilja notes how, '[i]n artistic endeavours we make a lot of choices, and artistic research is where we explain why we made these choices—to the extent that someone else can understand and learn from them'.[55] In the final analysis, therefore, Lilja's degree project appears to have provided tools for lifelong learning and an awareness of how such learning is dependent on interaction with others.

Collaborative Practices and Ensemble Interaction

The category of 'Collaborative Practices and Ensemble Interaction' was more prominent in master's theses compared to in the bachelor's in our study. One example is the project of jazz-pianist Ester Mellberg entitled 'A partner at the piano: Expanding musical and performative expressions in a duo with a vocalist'.[56] This thesis project was carried out through the study of an already existing duo: Mellberg and the vocalist Sofie Andersson. Andersson was a student in the same programme and, interestingly, her degree project was also a study of their collaboration, but more from her perspective as a vocalist.[57] Hence, artistic collaboration not only constituted the object of study, but it was also the artistic method through which two independent theses were eventually produced. Mellberg situates her project in a research context with reference to the work of Vera John-Steiner[58] but also through specific studies in artistic research in music, looking at how a shared voice can be developed through artistic collaboration.[59] In an interview with Mellberg, she claims that the combined collaborative perspectives facilitated different learning processes. She describes how, at times, the members of the duo were 'becoming each other's supervisors, and thus also our own'.[60]

For Mellberg, the personal motivation for the project lay in her relation to her instrument, the piano. She experienced how 'the link between expressing something

---

54 Ibid., p. 62.
55 Lilja, 2022.
56 Ester Mellberg, 'A Partner at the Piano: Expanding musical and performative expressions in a duo with a vocalist' (master's thesis, Luleå University of Technology, 2022), http://urn.kb.se/resolve?urn=urn:nbn:se:ltu:diva-91443
57 Sofie Andersson, 'Expressive Voice: Enhancing a vocalists performative tools in duo collaboration with a pianist' (Master's thesis, Luleå University of Technology, 2022), https://urn.kb.se/resolve?urn=urn:nbn:se:ltu:diva-91445
58 Vera John-Steiner, *Creative Collaboration* (Oxford University Press, 2000).
59 Mellberg, 2022, pp. 7–8.
60 Ester Mellberg, personal communication, 6 January 2023. Swedish original: 'Vi blev varandras handledare och därmed våra egna'.

and the practice of piano performance are separated in the teaching, at least in my genre'.[61] She describes how she had learnt 'a lot of crafts such as music theory, chords and scales and how to use them for improvisation'. However, the issue that she wished to address was the experience of having 'rarely practised the use of the crafts or improvisation in an expressive way. One practises techniques to play fast, loud or to understand complex harmonies but forget the part where to use the crafts to express something'.[62] Hence, Mellberg's research aim was to deepen her 'understanding of what it means to be an expressive and interactive pianist and expand those skills in duo performance with a vocalist'.[63] The project emerged in collaboration with Andersson as they created arrangements of three songs, recorded them, and analysed their interactions and the emergence of joint expression.

To efficiently address the artistic processes that emerged through the collaboration, video and audio documentation was employed. This data was analysed through the use of stimulated recall,[64] motivated by the pianist's wish to create a joint understanding of the developing practice, together with the singer. A flowchart drawn from Mellberg's thesis describes how this method formed part of the artistic process (see Fig. 1.2). In discussing the choice of methods, Mellberg observes how '[s]timulated recall has been used both as we have created our arrangements and also to analyse the outcome of our recordings. While creating arrangements we have used stimulated recall to get a 3rd person perspective of our musical interpretation'.[65] Thereby,

> we can give ourselves constructive criticism and make the changes we need to reach the intended expression. [...] Using stimulated recall interspersed with open coding has been a great way of reaching a deeper understanding of the knowledge we have gained through this project, and also the knowledge we already possessed.[66]

In the final analysis, they used a model of performer's voice, based on embodied music cognition, with particular interest in how a shared voice can emerge through the blending of individual voices.

---

61 Mellberg, 2022, p. 3.
62 Ibid.
63 Ibid., p. 4.
64 For an introduction to the history of this method and its usage in music research, see Stefan Östersjö, Nguyễn Thanh Thủy, David Hebert, and Henrik Frisk, *Shared Listenings: Methods for Transcultural Musicianship and Research* (Cambridge: Cambridge University Press, 2023), pp. 1–81.
65 Mellberg, 2022, p. 52.
66 Ibid.

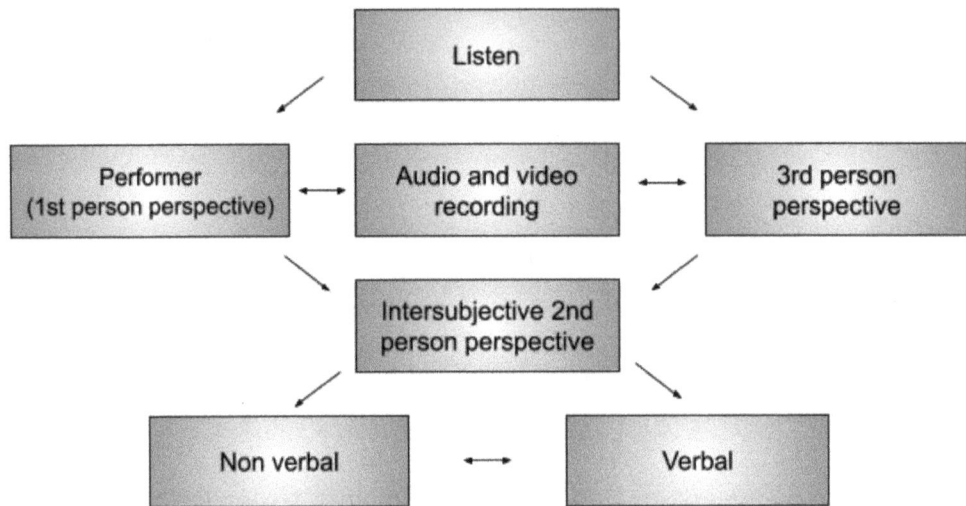

Fig. 1.2: A flowchart of the interaction between Mellberg and Andersson through the use of stimulated recall analysis.[67]

When reflecting on the role of the thesis project within their studies, Mellberg observes how it

> was by far the most important for us. [...] It created a clear direction, a clear focus and a goal to aim for. Both Sofie [Andersson] and I were completely invested in the work, and we became better at reflecting, deepening our understanding and thinking in several steps.[68]

The full project can perhaps only be understood by a reading of the two theses, but in our interview with Mellberg, she concludes that, for her, the project had most of all contributed to developing greater 'autonomy and self-confidence'.[69]

Interpretation, Expression, and Voice

The category of 'Interpretation, Expression, and Voice' was the second most prominent among master's thesis projects but was much less common in the bachelor's theses. In Simon Perčič's master's thesis 'Temporal Shaping: A conductor's exploration of tempo and its modifications in Weber's *Der Freischütz Overture*',[70] the aim was to explore the historical 'conception of "tempo modification" and its overall relevance in the temporal shaping of

---

67 Ibid., p. 14.
68 Swedish original: 'Examensarbetet var det absolut viktigaste för oss under utbildningen (...) [det] skapar en tydlig riktning, ett tydligt fokus och ett mål att sikta mot. Både jag och Sofie blev helt uppslukade av arbetet och vi blev bättre på att reflektera, fördjupa oss och tänka i flera steg.'
69 Mellberg, 2023. Swedish original: 'att självständigheten och självsäkerheten är mer påtaglig'.
70 Simon Perčič, 'Temporal Shaping: A conductor's exploration of tempo and its modifications in Weber's *Der Freischütz Overture*' (master's thesis, Luleå University of Technology, 2020), http://urn.kb.se/resolve?urn=urn:nbn:se:ltu:diva-80528

music in orchestral conducting'.[71] While this entailed a study of historical performance practice, further aims were to relate tempo modification to present-day conventions and to explore tempo modification through Perčič's own practice as an orchestral conductor, thus providing important insights into the development of a musical interpretation.

Tempo modification as a historical practice was researched through a multi-method design consisting of a literature study, an in-depth interview with the composer Marko Mihevc, and, finally, through analysis of recordings by Toscanini, Walter, and Kleiber. The study focused on the overture to Carl Maria von Weber's *Der Freischütz*, first through a detailed study of historical recordings of the piece and, second, through a similar study of recordings of two different performances conducted by Perčič. The historical analysis suggested that tempo modification has become less of a common practice, as indicated in Table 1.2 below in the decreasing number of occurrences of unstable bar groups in the performances by Walter (6), Toscanini (4), and Kleiber (3), represented here in chronological order. Another artistic method was to develop approaches to score reduction, and an entire chapter is dedicated to a description of this process, which encompassed the two years of the degree project. In this, Perčič sought to 'extract the balance and structural development, which constitute a firm ground for tempo nuancing'.[72]

Group nr.	Relative bar nr.	Bar nr. /reh. letter	Bar group	Walter	Toscanini	Kleiber	Dynamics
1	1	37	5	U	U	U	pp <>
2	6	42	4	U	U	S	<>
3	10	46	4	S	S	S	f
4	14	50	3	U	U	U	<
5	17	53	4	U	S	U	<
6	21	57	4	S	S	S	<
7	25	A	4	S	S	S	ff
8	29	65	4	U	S	S	
9	33	69	4	U	S	S	
10	37	73	4	S	S	S	
11	41	77	4	S	S	S	
12	45	B	6	S	S	S	<
13	50	87	4	S	U	S	

Table 1.2. *Der Freischütz*; stable (S) and unstable (U) bar groups, drawn from Perčič, 2020, p. 26.

---

71 Ibid., p. 5.
72 Ibid., p. 53.

Although the study of historical practices of tempo modification lays the ground for the entire thesis, the core results are drawn from the analysis of Perčič's practice as a conductor. The first performance of Weber's *Der Freischütz Overture* was carried out with the Norrlandsoperan Symphony Orchestra. The second performance, scheduled with The Gävle Symphony Orchestra, was cancelled due to the COVID-19 pandemic and substituted by a rehearsal and recording of the piece in a version for two pianists. This makeshift solution provided both limitations and a potential for further experimentation. The comparative audio analysis identified no 'unstable' bar-groupings in Perčič's first recording (as compared to the findings represented in Table 1.2) but four in the second version. Importantly, Perčič also highlights the deepened interaction between conductor and performers in the later version, a feature which appears to have strongly contributed to their exploration of the phenomenon of tempo modification.

In an interview carried out in January 2023, Perčič reflects on the thesis project and notes how 'it addresses an issue that cannot be solved immediately, but needs to be explored from within—we could find an analogy in organic development—an approach that goes from the inside out'.[73] The embodiment and subjectivity of the student are therefore integrated in the learning process in ways that are central to artistic research practices.

In the concluding discussion, the combination of methods in the project are considered in relation to conventional forms of teaching in HME. Perčič suggests that research-based approaches have the potential to enable 'a more detailed understanding of the potential in conducting'[74] and, further, proposes that different pedagogies could be developed by defining

> what skills are best taught in a master-apprentice way, and what skills could be further developed through the use of scientific approaches and novel forms of teaching, that encourage independence and personal judgement. Learning conducting is more often than not connected with master-apprentice way of knowledge passing, therefore, I would argue, building new knowledge, using technologies, research papers and especially experimental testing is from my point of view the way forward.[75]

Building on these ideas, in the interview, Perčič describes the thesis project as providing 'a basic tool for thinking about your own daily learning – a kind of resilience generator'.[76] Hence, this thesis not only provides an account of individual artistic development and how a historical study of performance practice can contribute to developing individual approaches to musical interpretation, but, also, it reflects on how this learning process may inform the development of pedagogical approaches to the teaching and learning of music performance.

---

73   Simon Perčič, personal communication, January 2 2023.
74   Perčič, 2020, p. 58.
75   Perčič, 2020.
76   Perčič, 2023.

Performer–Instrument Interactions

The fourth category addresses 'Performer-Instrument Interactions'. As an example of this category, we will look at the bachelor's thesis of jazz drummer Jakob Sundell entitled 'The Drum Also Sings: A study exploring playing tonal melody on the jazz drum set'.[77] When he introduces what sparked his ideas for this project, he writes 'I would like the melodical [sic] expression of the drum set to be a natural part of my musicianship. The aim has been for me as a musician to be able to use rhythm, phrasing, melody and harmony just like any other instrumentalist'.[78] Thus, Sundell's thesis is an example of how explorative approaches to the relation between performer and instrument can give rise to expanded possibilities and novel modes of expression.

Literature studies were a considered part of the project design, providing a historical outline of the development of melodic drumming in jazz. This also entailed an interest in how the modern drum kit evolved, identifying a direct connection between the modified setup and the emergence of melodic drumming in the 1960s in the playing of Max Roach and Art Blakey. Another fundamental reference is the work of the drummer Ari Hoenig, whose approach to tuning the drumkit, and techniques for modifying pitch, are adopted by Sundell.

The project was structured as an iterative cycle consisting of four steps. Practicing was the first step, which entailed testing different tunings for a number of jazz standards and devising techniques for modifying the pitch of individual drums while playing. The second step was to make studio recordings with a full group. Thirdly, feedback sessions on these recordings were held with peers, teachers, and other established musicians. Fourth and finally, Sundell undertook an analysis of the recordings, which was to a great extent focused on the playing techniques and tuning systems devised for the drum kit. Comparing this cycle with how Paulo de Assis[79] conceives of experimentation in artistic research—as integrated in cyclical processes intertwined with other forms of knowledge construction—we find interesting how the first step in Sundell's cycle could be better described as artistic experimentation. Furthermore, the component of feedback from teachers and peers differentiates his model from that of Assis, providing a stronger focus on the learning processes. This step in the explorative cycle seems very fruitful in a bachelor's thesis project and also establishes a more dynamic relation between student and teacher.

The discussion is largely focused on technical aspects of the experimentation carried out in the first step, such as how to tune the drums and manage the melodic intonation. It also covers the setup itself, including drumheads but also the choice

---

77 Jakob Sundell, 'The Drum Also Sings: A study exploring playing tonal melody on the jazz drum set' (bachelor's thesis, Luleå University of Technology, 2022), http://urn.kb.se/resolve?urn=urn:nbn:se:l tu:diva-91898
78 Ibid., p. 2.
79 Paulo de Assis, *Logic of Experimentation: Reshaping Music Performance in and through Artistic Research* (Leuven: Leuven University Press, 2018).

of striking implements. Taken together, the approach developed in the project entails a redefinition of the drum kit, demanding a new practice and also affording a series of musical challenges.[80] Sundell notes that there are, indeed, parts of melodic improvisation on other instruments that are transferable to the drum set,

> such as phrasing, tension and release, call and response and melodic contour. But the melodic content in tonal improvisation is not. The drum set can be able to play improvisational lines based on scales. For this to happen the intonation and melodic intention has to be of high precision.[81]

Reflecting back on the thesis project, Sundell notices that: 'I became fully aware of my musical ability and weaknesses and what I needed to do to come closer to my goal'.[82] Sundell further observes how this was 'the point at which the studies went from being instructive to constructive' and that the students were invited to 'generate their own knowledge through the process of the thesis course'.[83] To conclude, Sundell expresses how his exploration of the 'melodic possibilities of the drum set' has given rise to a novel awareness of a 'target sound', which is a characteristic of a personal 'musical voice', and also provided new and more goal-directed methods for artistic development.[84]

Rehearsal and Efficient Practising

Many students decide to focus their degree project on developing or testing techniques for efficient rehearsal and practising. Such projects demand a thorough design for assessing the outcomes of such experimentation with the embodied practice of performance. Sara Hernandez, in her bachelor's thesis 'Fiolen i kvinter: En ny metod att hitta en handställning som förbättrar intonationen' ('The Violin in Fifths: A novel method for finding a hand position that improves intonation'), provides a convincing example of how such work can be carried out and assessed.[85] Her thesis starts out by acknowledging the complexity of obtaining good intonation on the violin, which, apart from developing one's listening, involves a practice deeply embodied in the performers' left-hand technique. Hernandez points to how the many aspects of left-hand technique have been previously explored by Schradieck, Flesch, and Sevcik. However, her project

---

80 In this regard, Sundell's project may serve as an example of how perceptual learning based in artistic experimentation can be a foundational structure for a degree project, as proposed by Fausto Pizzol in the next chapter.
81 Sundell, 2022, p. 21.
82 Jakob Sundell, personal communication, January 9 2023.
83 Sundell, 2023.
84 Ibid.
85 Sara Hernandez, 'Fiolen i kvinter: En ny metod att hitta en handställning som förbättrar intonationen' [The Violin in Fifths: A novel method for finding a hand position that improves intonation] (bachelor's thesis, Luleå University of Technology, 2022), http://urn.kb.se/resolve?urn=urn:nbn:se:ltu:diva-91435

is built on the novel approach proposed by the violinist Rodney Friend, which seeks to develop a better left-hand position with a grounding in the performance of fifths, and how this enables the development of a better left-hand technique with the further aim of improving intonation. Her project follows the meticulous process of testing these exercises and applying them in the study of two pieces: the fugue from Bach's first violin sonata in G minor, BWV 1001, and the first movement of Samuel Barber's violin concerto, Op. 14. To assess potential progress in the development of technical skills, a sufficient time span is necessary. The first documentation was, therefore, carried out in March 2021, with audio recordings of selected exercises from Friend's method[86]. After using this practice method for a year, the same exercises were recorded again in April 2022. Sections in Bach's fugue and Barber's concerto that were found to be particularly challenging in terms of intonation were selected and recorded within the same time span as designed for the selected exercises. In the thesis, Hernandez provides detailed examples of how these sections were prepared in several steps, by applying technical exercises built on fifths, according to Friend's method. Effectively, these examples also provide an analytical parsing of the challenges to the left-hand technique in each sequence.

An interesting feature of Hernandez's project design is the use of a reference group of two fellow students and one teacher, who were invited to listen to recordings of both technical exercises and rehearsal performances of the two works, grading the quality of the intonation on a scale from 1 to 5. Hernandez also carried out the same grading process as the reference group. The outcome of the project is clearly expressed in the assessment of the recordings, wherein the judgement is quite unanimous in all cases, generally shifting from 2 to 4 in the comparison between March 2021 and April 2022. The development and application of methods for practising and rehearsal in the study of music performance are a major contribution of this thesis. Hereby, the project indicates that basic skills can be efficiently developed through an individual degree project, if the project design is efficient and purposeful.

In an interview, Hernandez observed how her writing had 'encouraged reflection, since I've had to analyse and observe my playing from an outside perspective, in ways that were new to me. Writing about it has helped me articulate and understand myself better as a musician'.[87] Hence, the tasks of documenting and analysing her practising not only contributed to the learning process but also had been directly intertwined with and enhanced through the writing process. In a further reflection on the impact of the thesis project in her studies as a whole, Hernandez concludes that

---

86   Rodney Friend, *The Violin in 5ths: Developing Intonation and Sound* (London: Beares publishing, 2019).
87   Sara Hernandez, personal communication, 2 January 2023. Swedish original: 'Skrivandet har uppmuntrat till reflektion då jag har behövt analysera och observera mitt spel utifrån på ett nytt sätt. Att skriva om det har hjälpt mig formulera och förstå mig själv bättre som musiker.'

the project has been an exercise in looking at oneself from outside with new eyes – the eyes of a teacher. To make recordings and evaluate before and after practising gives an incredible amount of insight and information into one's own playing'.[88]

To conclude, an important contribution of this thesis project may ultimately lie in how the combination of methods have contributed to further developing the student's capacity for autonomous learning.

Musical Gesture in Performance and Conducting

The final thematic category is 'Musical Gesture in Performance and Conducting', exemplified here by the master's thesis 'Meaningless Movement or Essential Expression: A study about gestures' by the clarinettist Stina Bohlin.[89] She describes how the idea of studying musical gestures first came to her when her clarinet teacher told her

> that I was wasting my air by moving a lot when playing long phrases. Hearing this made me feel confused, since I thought I stood relatively still while playing. This led me to reflect upon the fact that there seemed to be a discrepancy between how I thought I was moving versus how others perceived my body language.[90]

We find this description, of how her initial interest in a study of gesture was sparked, to be revealing in relation to our thematic analysis. Bohlin expresses an experience which is grounded in the relation between performer and instrument, but, at the same time, the experience she describes is closely related to the type of issues addressed by many students in the category of 'Rehearsal and Efficient Practicing'. However, this initial observation led Bohlin to further reflection on the relation between body movement and expressiveness in music performance (effectively relating her project also to the category of 'Interpretation, Expression, and Voice'). The aim of her thesis was, therefore, formulated as seeking 'a more expressive performance by increasing awareness of the gestures I make while playing'.[91]

Bohlin further notes how 'It is hardly possible to conduct a study about gestures in music without coming across the concept of embodiment'.[92] Here, she turns to Randall Harlow, who claims that 'it is argued that musicians and their musical instruments exist in an ecological relationship at the level of embodied gesture'.[93] Inspired by

---

[88] Hernandez, 2023. Swedish original: 'Jag tycker arbetet har varit en övning i att se på sig själv utifrån med nya ögon– en lärares ögon. Att göra inspelningar och sedan utvärdera före och efter är något som ger otroligt mycket inblick och information i ens eget spel.'

[89] Stina Bohlin, 'Meaningless Movement or Essential Expression: A study about gestures' (master's thesis, Luleå University of Technology, 2021), http://urn.kb.se/resolve?urn=urn:nbn:se:ltu:diva-85247

[90] Bohlin, 2021, p. 1.

[91] Ibid., p. 2.

[92] Ibid., p. 4.

[93] Randall Harlow, 'Ecologies of Practice in Musical Performance'. *MUSICultures*, 45.1–2 (2018), 215–37 (p. 215).

previous research in systematic musicology—but also, more immediately, by the artistic research of her clarinet teacher, Robert Ek—her project had a mixed-methods approach, combining quantitative and qualitative data collection and analysis. Hence, it should be noted how, in Bohlin's project, a closer collaboration between teacher and student was possible because her teacher was already carrying out an artistic PhD project on a related topic.

Bohlin collected video data of her own performance, as well as of a fellow student and of her teacher, all performing the first movement of Brahms's second clarinet sonata in E-flat major, Op. 120 No. 2. Qualitative and quantitative coding of these videos were carried out, involving both the teacher and the fellow student in stimulated recall sessions. Further interviews with both informants added to the qualitative data. The outcomes of the project led Bohlin to conclude that 'for experienced performers, expressiveness is vital when playing music and musicians use a variety of tools for enhancing musical intentions when performing, gestures being one of them'.[94] She eventually concluded that '[h]ow these insights will influence my future performances remains to be seen but by turning attention towards my own gestural language I have not only been studying gestures, but also myself, as a performer'.[95] We observe how this thesis, even more than in the case of Sundell's bachelor project, shows evidence of instigating a different relationship between teacher and student. The research design has been instrumental in replacing the traditional master-apprentice model with a more dynamic interrelation. The reasons for this appear to be manifold, since her clarinet teacher is himself involved in similar research on gesture: their interactions in the collection and analysis of data became a vehicle for collaboration and, perhaps even, mutual learning. In addition to this collaborative design, the study itself brought insight into the student-teacher interaction, and the widened understanding of these relations appear to have further sparked more autonomous modes of working. In an interview in January 2023, Bohlin made the observation that her work on the thesis has provided several tools for lifelong learning. She mentions getting 'inspiration from what others have done previously, to be introduced to different ways of analysing and reflecting on one's music making and to get tools for concretizing things one already "knows" but which are difficult to verbalise'.[96] Again, these reflections emphasise how the task of situating one's artistic practice—as a part of designing and then writing a thesis, as well as of acquiring methods for critical reflection—may contribute to laying the groundwork for student autonomy and student-driven learning.

---

94 Bohlin, 2021, p. 46.
95 Ibid.
96 Stina Bohlin, personal communication, 8 January 2023. Swedish original: 'att få inspiration av vad andra har gjort innan, att presenteras för olika sätt att analysera och reflektera över sitt eget musicerande och att få verktyg för att konkretisera sådant man kanske "vet" men har svårt att sätta ord på.'

Discussion

The discussion is structured according to the three main perspectives promoted in the Bologna Declaration. Hence, we will consider whether and how the degree projects analysed in the study embrace forms of learning that are research-based, student-centred, and contribute to developing students' capacity for lifelong learning. Outside of these three perspectives, our study has also indicated that experimentation has proven to be an important factor in a majority of the analysed projects, just as can be observed in the development of artistic PhD programmes in music,[97] and we address this perspective and its implications for HME in a final section.

Research-Based Approaches

Just as concluded by Georgii-Hemming et al.,[98] a central trace of the impact of artistic research in HME is the predominant use of reflexive methods in the design of degree projects. In our study, we have found many different approaches to how qualitative and reflexive methods can be integrated to enhance artistic development.

In all of the theses discussed, reflexive methods are interwoven with artistic development, which we understand as a result of the implementation of methods and practices from artistic research. Moreover, we find the use of such methods to have created learning situations that contributed to the students' development of self-understanding, situatedness, and an interest in lifelong learning.

It appears that the degree project has typically played a central role in the students' education. For example, Mellberg described how, for the artistic development of their duo, the thesis project was 'by far the most important', creating a 'clear focus and a goal to aim for'.[99] As examples of artistic outcomes, Sundell points to an increased awareness of a personal 'musical voice' and of how to develop it,[100] while Bohlin observes the emergence of 'a more expressive performance' and claims that the origin of this development is found in an 'increasing awareness of the gestures' she makes in performance.[101]

Regarding methods used, we see, as noted in the preliminary qualitative content analysis, that logbooks and various forms of audio-visual documentation are used. Several master's theses employ stimulated recall methods, which allows students to combine second- and third-person perspectives with the first-person accounts otherwise typical of many reflexive methods. For instance, in Mellberg, intersubjective approaches were employed both in the artistic work as well as in the analysis of the creative collaboration in their duo, using 'stimulated recall to get a 3rd person

---

97 Östersjö, 2017; de Assis, 2018.
98 Georgii-Hemming et al., 2020.
99 Mellberg, 2023.
100 Sundell, 2023.
101 Bohlin, 2021, p. 2.

perspective of [their] musical interpretation'.¹⁰² Furthermore, Mellberg claims that stimulated recall analysis has enabled 'constructive criticism' and increased awareness of how 'to reach the intended expression' and, ultimately, contributed a 'deeper understanding of the knowledge we have gained through this project, and also the knowledge we already possessed'.¹⁰³

In reflecting back on the design of his thesis project, Lilja observes how 'there is a difficulty in observing oneself', and his project sought to methodologically address this challenge by introducing feedback from different groups of listeners, in combination with his own reflections as captured in logbooks and score annotations.¹⁰⁴ With these, Lilja sought to capture how artistic research can allow for the creation of new knowledge 'that someone else can understand and learn from'.¹⁰⁵

Lilja's thesis points to the usefulness of obtaining more developed methodological awareness when it comes to the negotiation of subjective and intersubjective perspectives in artistic research. It further exemplifies how students may benefit from developing self-reflexive skills. On the same note, Hernandez observed how the degree project prompted her to 'analyse and observe my playing from an outside perspective, in ways that were new to me'.¹⁰⁶ But, the development of such skills is also particularly useful as tools for lifelong learning, a perspective which we address further below.

However, a recent paper by Moberg instead notes how students' formulations of the purpose-statements in their master's theses 'typically include "I", "me", "mine" or "my"' and connecting this tendency with a 'focus on individual competences rather than collective knowledge'.¹⁰⁷ In Moberg's discourse analysis, it is claimed that such introspective perspectives were rendered hegemonic in these theses as justifications were premised on individualistic wants, needs, or interests: 'Here, the "I" is centred not only as the object of study, but also as an authority and source of knowledge, as a problem and as a means'.¹⁰⁸ Hence, Moberg suggests that these degree projects are 'primarily expected to be self-serving, occasionally serve colleagues, and, in exceptional cases, an audience'.¹⁰⁹

While we sympathise with Moberg's wish to emphasise the need for degree projects to situate the student in a wider context and address issues that are of relevance for a wider audience, we believe that reflexive methods have a wider usefulness in the teaching and learning of music performance in HME. As stated by Lilja, '[i]n artistic endeavours we make a lot of choices, and artistic research is where we explain why we made these choices – to the extent that someone else can understand and learn from

---

102 Mellberg, 2022, p. 52.
103 Ibid.
104 Lilja, 2022.
105 Ibid.
106 Hernandez, 2023.
107 Moberg, 2023, p. 5.
108 Ibid., p. 9.
109 Ibid.

them'.[110] Thus, as also clarified through Lilja's reflection regarding the difficulties of self-observation, with reference to the methodological design of his thesis project, it seems clear that the use of reflexive methods should not immediately be equated to what Moberg describes as focussing 'on individual competences rather than collective knowledge'.[111]

Georgii-Hemming et al. describe how teachers and institutional leaders conceptualise reflection as demanding the ability to situate 'yourself in relation to society as well as to how certain *musical ideas* and *ideals* have developed historically'.[112] Johansson and Georgii-Hemming further note how '[t]he research-oriented degree project in the first and second cycles of HME has gradually emerged as a discipline-specific instrument for individual as well as institutional development'.[113] At the same time, in Moberg's study, it is claimed that, in degree projects, 'justifications are not anchored in previous research or situated within a field of research'.[114] However, our observation in regard to the students' awareness of research contexts is rather the opposite to Moberg's.[115] We find that the theses discussed here explicitly refer to previous research and were understood to build directly on music-research practices. Bohlin expressed this when noting how her 'goal was to use methods and practices from artistic research, to the greatest extent possible, [...] perhaps most of all in the coding and analysis of my recordings'.[116] It may be worth mentioning that, while qualitative analysis of video and audio recordings are not in themselves particular to artistic research, such methods have tended to be a typical feature of the design of artistic research projects. With the use of audio and video technologies, the student projects discussed above, have been designed through cycles of experimentation, documentation, and analysis, leading to the development of new practices. Furthermore, a historical perspective on the research questions has both situated the studies as well as informed the design, as can be seen in the projects of Sundell and Perčič.[117] Lilja, on the other hand, situates both the artistic practice and a research approach in the domain of algorithmic composition. The literature reviews in all of these six theses are substantial and situate the projects in various ways in relation to art worlds and science worlds.[118] Taken together, we find all of these qualities to suggest that the theses analysed in this chapter are all built on artistic research methods and practices.

---

110 Lilja, 2022.
111 Moberg, 2023, p. 5.
112 Georgii-Hemming et al., 2020, p. 252, emphasis in original.
113 Johansson and Georgii-Hemming, 2021, p. 182.
114 Moberg, 2023, p. 9.
115 Moberg, 2023.
116 Bohlin, 2023.
117 Perčič, 2020.
118 See Östersjö, 2019.

Student-Centred Teaching and Learning

As put forth above, the overarching aim of the course design of the bachelor's and master's programmes at the Piteå School of Music has been to identify each student's individually defined and experienced artistic possibilities and challenges. A further aim was to develop a project for which the student's individual motivation is strong and the potential for individual artistic development is central. As phrased by Perčič, in his reflection, a well-designed thesis project may address 'an issue that cannot be solved immediately, but needs to be explored from within' and may find 'an approach that goes from the inside out'.[119] Here, Perčič aligns with Hannula et al., who argue that, 'instead of a top-down model or intervention, there has to be enough room, courage and appreciation for organic, content driven development and growth'.[120] Furthermore, this student-centred approach has also entailed that students' understanding of their own needs for development became more clearly articulated, thus improving their capacity for autonomous learning. An example of this is when Lilja notes that learning is a matter of 'understanding what there is to understand'.[121] Sundell, in reflecting on the role of the thesis project, goes further to observe how the project went 'from being instructive to constructive'.[122] The student was no longer required to acquire knowledge from the teacher but to 'generate their own knowledge'.[123] In reflecting on the degree project, Sundell notes how he has found that 'most teachers at the university work on a principle of teaching the student to learn by themselves' and, further, observes how 'this approach was also a big part of the thesis course. The student is given the tools to learn and develop skills on their own'.[124]

On a different note, and bringing forth a set of critical reflections, Mellberg finds a lack of connections in the teaching 'between expressing something and the practice of piano performance'.[125] She further describes how one 'practises techniques to play fast, loud or to understand complex harmonies but forget the part where to use the crafts to express something'.[126] Similarly, but in a different genre, Hernandez, as a classical violinist, observes that what she 'can sometimes find missing in teaching is finding the source of the problem, not just identifying it',[127] and her thesis project sought ways to address such shortcomings. This observation is in line with previous research suggesting that, to avoid limiting the potential for students' development of

---

119 Perčič, 2023.
120 Mika Hannula, Juha Suoranta, and Tere Vadén, *Artistic Research: Theories, Methods and Practices*, trans. by Gareth Griffiths and Kristina Kölhi (Helsinki: Academy of Fine Arts, 2005), p. 13.
121 Lilja, 2022.
122 Sundell, 2023.
123 Ibid.
124 Ibid.
125 Melberg, 2022, p. 3.
126 Ibid.
127 Hernandez, 2023.

metacognitive skills, teachers should involve students in discussions regarding their problems, the sources of these, as well as how they could be solved.[128]

Perčič, in turn, takes such institutional critique even further, asking 'what skills are best taught in a master-apprentice way, and what skills could be further developed through the use of scientific approaches and novel forms of teaching'.[129] He argues that conducting is seldom a practice that is best taught by copying a master. Rather, he advocates the development of independence, personal judgement, but also 'building new knowledge, using technologies, research papers and especially experimental testing', which, he suggests, is 'the way forward'[130] for the teaching and learning of music performance. An outcome of such student-centred approaches, which is highlighted in several interviews, are, as expressed by Mellberg, the emergence of a stronger sense of 'autonomy and self-confidence'.[131] Lilja, in turn, notes how '[i]ndependence may be one of the most important qualities if you want to become a freelance composer'.[132] This suggests that a student-centred approach may indeed be a means for properly preparing students for professional life and for lifelong learning.

Approaches to Lifelong Learning

Lilja makes useful observations regarding how abilities for lifelong learning may be drawn out of interactions with teachers and supervisors, noting how '[t]heir comments during feedback will echo in my head as I grow, and I will ask myself 'what would my teacher/supervisor/peer have said?'.[133] Furthermore, by developing a deeper understanding for how artistic collaboration may serve as a tool for lifelong learning and artistic growth, Mellberg expresses how the combined collaborative perspectives made the duo partners become at times, 'each other's supervisors, and thus also our own'.[134] Mellberg further notes how

> becoming one's own teacher, I believe is a matter of perspective. To manage to make observations of your own music making from several perspectives, than those from inside the experience of performing. It is great to be able to record oneself and show and discuss what is heard and seen with others, and thereby get perspectives to utilise in an analytical moment.[135]

A similar observation is made by Lilja, who relates an increased ability in the development of autonomy as an artist, which he connects to the different forms of feedback that formed a central aspect of the project design in his master's thesis:

---

128 Holmgren, 2022.
129 Perčič, 2020, p. 58.
130 Perčič, 2020, p. 58.
131 Mellberg, 2023.
132 Lilja, 2022.
133 Lilja, 2022.
134 Mellberg, 2023. Swedish original: 'Vi blev varandras handledare och därmed våra egna'.
135 Ibid.

> Feedback is crucial in becoming your own teacher, because if you comment on someone else's creative decisions, you will look at your own work and ask yourself 'what would I have said if this was someone else's work?'. I would argue that continuously giving and receiving feedback to and from my peers is one of the main reasons why I reached the point I am at today, and due to the importance of synergy between classes I find this point to be of relevance to this question.[136]

To summarise, the student theses appear to have provided different methodological tools and encouraged personal abilities that may promote lifelong learning. Perhaps such meta-cognitive processes[137] can be summarised through Perčič's observation of how the thesis project may function as 'a basic tool for thinking about your own daily learning – a kind of resilience generator'.[138]

Experimentation

Experimentation is not only a long-standing component of research in the hard sciences but also a decisive factor in the development of music and other arts since the early twentieth century. In fact, it played an important role much before then, although sometimes under a different label. As argued by Stefan Östersjö, 'the core of an artistic research project is where the subjectivity of an artist encounters an experimental approach, a challenge to one's practice, and perhaps often to one's habits'.[139] Along similar lines, Hannula et al. claim that the artistic researcher 'must be able – even by bending the rules – to find or create courage for experimentation, for taking risks and, above all, for enjoying the uncertainty, detours and failures of research'.[140] In this final section of the discussion, we will consider to what extent artistic experimentation has characterised the degree projects in the study.

In the theses of four students—Lilja, Mellberg, Perčič, and Sundell—experimentation is present (to varying degrees) as a way of conceptualising different aspects of their music making and learning but also as a method for artistic development. Thus, Lilja describes artistic experimentation as a 'main research method',[141] while Sundell's thesis exemplifies how explorative approaches to the relation between performer and instrument can give rise to expanded possibilities and novel modes of expression through the design of iterative cycles that involve experimentation. In Mellberg, the experimental dimension of the project is a stylistic measure, while Perčič refers to his 'experiments with reductive analysis' as a central artistic method.[142] While the

---

136 Lilja, 2022.
137 Susan Hallam, 'The Development of Metacognition in Musicians: Implications for Education', *British Journal of Music Education*, 18.1 (2001), 27–39.
138 Perčič, 2023.
139 Östersjö, 2017, p. 104.
140 Hannula, Suoranta, and Vadén, 2005, p. 168.
141 Lilja, 2021, p. 15.
142 Perčič, 2020, p. 30.

prominence of reflexive methods has been rightly observed to be a central trace of the impact of artistic research methods and practices in HME, we believe that a further development of methods based on artistic experimentation has the potential to deepen the students' understanding of artistic research and its potential for the teaching and learning of music performance.

Final Thoughts

The present study has obvious limitations. First of all, it scrutinises in depth a relatively limited number of theses and, secondly, it focuses on theses produced in one single school of music. Furthermore, the initial stages of the qualitative and quantitative analysis were tentative, though built on our pre-understanding of the material (since two of the authors had either been examining or supervising the theses studied). As discussed above with reference to Moberg's study, also in this chapter, it has been difficult to produce a transparent argument through content analysis of student theses. However, despite the limitations in the method and design, the initial analysis provided the necessary structural understanding, which allowed us to select theses for the following, more detailed, qualitative analysis.

Hence, there is a need for a deeper understanding of both the development of methods and practices in the artistic PhD education in HME, and its impact on first and second cycle education in these institutions. Moreover, as Moberg notes,[143] the relationship between the written text and the artistic artefacts should be explored more in-depth in future studies.

In a publication created by the Swedish partners of the REACT project, based on interviews with students, alumni, staff, and stakeholders outside of HME, it is argued that, in Sweden, 'artistic research is not fully implemented in the current curricula, and especially in the first and second cycle. As a result, students do not gain enough experience of and skills in critical thinking and academic writing'.[144] However, through our study of the theses discussed above, we observe that research methodologies and practices drawn from artistic research are successfully employed in degree projects. Or, to put it differently, while a wider group of informants in Correia et al.[145] argues that there is a need to strengthen the role of artistic research in HME, our analysis of student theses at the Piteå School of Music suggests that a process of implementation of artistic research methods and practices is already well underway. The resulting learning processes for the students can be observed to be fruitful, both in terms of project results as well as expressed in their retrospective self-assessment. Many

---

143 Moberg, 2023.
144 Jorge Correia and others, REACT–Rethinking Music Performance in European Higher Education Institutions, *Artistic Career in Music: Stakeholders Requirement Report* (Aveiro: UA Editora, 2021), p. 19, https://doi.org/10.48528/wfq9-4560
145 Ibid.

means for developing students' capacity for lifelong learning and for increasing their understanding of music, musical performance, and themselves as artists are brought forth, both in the written theses as well as in interviews cited above. We also wish to underline the importance of having faculty that have pursued PhD studies, as such involvement, as evidenced in Bohlin's project, opens up for different forms of student-teacher collaboration, in the exploration of more student-centred and research-based approaches to the teaching and learning of music performance.[146] Again, we believe that herein lies the potential for what Perčič advocates as 'the way forward'.[147]

To conclude, we find that the study proposes three main implications for HME. First, that artistic research has shown potential to enable more student-centred forms of teaching and learning, based to a great extent on its use of reflexive methods. Second, that employing artistic research practices and methods shows great potential to enhance lifelong learning. Third, that the role of artistic experimentation, as expressed in the student theses, suggests that the notion of the artistic research laboratory[148] is a potential model for how the teaching and learning in HME may be reconsidered.

At the same time, we would be the first to acknowledge that there is still so much to learn; and the path ahead is, indeed, not clearly mapped out. The final argument of this chapter is, therefore, that results such as presented in this small-scale study should be cross-referenced with similar data from other countries, a research approach which in turn could lay the ground for a more substantial re-imagining of curricula in HME, grounded in artistic research practices.

References

Andersson, Sofie, 'Expressive Voice: Enhancing a vocalists performative tools in duo collaboration with a pianist' (master's thesis, Luleå University of Technology, 2022), https://urn.kb.se/resolve?urn=urn:nbn:se:ltu:diva-91445

de Assis, Paulo, *Logic of Experimentation: Reshaping Music Performance in and through Artistic Research* (Leuven: Leuven University Press, 2018), https://doi.org/10.11116/9789461662507

Bartleet, Brydie-Leigh, 'Artistic Autoethnography: Exploring the Interface Between Autoethnography and Artistic Research', in *Handbook of Autoethnography*, ed. by Tony E. Adams, Stacy Holman Jones, and Carolyn Ellis (New York: Routledge, 2021), pp. 133–45, https://doi.org/10.4324/9780429431760-14

Becker, Howard S., *Art Worlds*, 25th anniversary edn., updated and expanded (Berkeley: University of California Press, 1982/2008)

Blair, Erik and Hendrik van der Sluis, 'Music Performance Anxiety and Higher Education Teaching: A Systematic Literature Review', *Journal of University Teaching & Learning Practice*, 19.3 (2022), 5–15, https://doi.org/10.53761/1.19.3.05

---

146 See further the REACT model, presented in the introduction to this book.
147 Perčič, 2020, p. 58.
148 Ben Spatz, *Making A Laboratory. Dynamic Configurations with Transversal Video* (Santa Barbara, CA: Punctum Books, 2020).

Bohlin, Stina, personal communication, 8 January 2023

——, 'Meaningless Movement or Essential Expression: A study about gestures' (master's thesis, Luleå University of Technology, 2021), http://urn.kb.se/resolve?urn=urn:nbn:se:ltu:diva-85247

Correia, Jorge and others, REACT–Rethinking Music Performance in European Higher Education Institutions, *Artistic Career in Music: Stakeholders Requirement Report* (Aviero: UA Editora, 2021), https://doi.org/10.48528/wfq9-4560

Crispin, Darla, 'Looking Back, Looking Through, Looking Beneath. The Promises and Pitfalls of Reflection as a Research Tool', in *Knowing in Performing: Artistic Research in Music and the Performing Arts*, ed. by Annegret Huber, Doris Ingrisch, Therese Kaufmann, Johannes Kretz, Gesine Schröder, and Tasos Zembylas (Bielefeld: Transcript Verlag, 2021), pp. 35–50, https://doi.org/10.1515/9783839452875-006

Drisko, James W. and Maschi, Tina, *Content Analysis* (New York: Oxford University Press, 2016), https://doi.org/10.1093/acprof:oso/9780190215491.001.0001

European Ministers Responsible for Higher Education, 'London Communiqué: Towards the European Higher Education Area: Responding to Changes in a Globalised World', 18 May 2007, http://www.ehea.info/Upload/document/ministerial_declarations/2007_London_Communique_English_588697.pdf

Friend, Rodney, *The Violin in 5ths: Developing Intonation and Sound* (London: Beares Publishing, 2019)

Georgii-Hemming, Eva, Karin Johansson, and Nadia Moberg, 'Reflection in Higher Music Education: what, why, wherefore?', *Music Education Research*, 22.3 (2020), 245–56, https://doi.org/10.1080/14613808.2020.1766006

Hallam, Susan, 'The Development of Metacognition in Musicians: Implications for Education', *British Journal of Music Education*, 18.1 (2001), 27–39, https://doi.org/10.1017/s0265051701000122

Hannula, Mika, Juha Suoranta, and Tere Vadén, *Artistic Research: Theories, Methods and Practices*, trans. by Gareth Griffiths and Kristina Kölhi (Helsinki: Academy of Fine Arts, 2005)

Harlow, Randall, 'Ecologies of Practice in Musical Performance'. *MUSICultures*, 45.1–2 (2018), 215–37

Hernandez, Sara, personal communication, 2 January 2023

——, 'Fiolen i kvinter: En ny metod att hitta en handställning som förbättrar intonationen' [*The Violin in Fifths: A novel method for finding a hand position that improves intonation*] (bachelor's thesis, Luleå University of Technology, 2022), http://urn.kb.se/resolve?urn=urn:nbn:se:ltu:diva-91435

Holmgren, Carl, 'Dialogue Lost? Teaching Musical Interpretation of Western Classical Music in Higher Education' (PhD thesis, Luleå University of Technology, 2022), http://urn.kb.se/resolve?urn=urn:nbn:se:ltu:diva-88258

Johansson, Karin and Eva Georgii-Hemming, 'Processes of Academisation in Higher Music Education: the case of Sweden', *British Journal of Music Education*, 38.2 (2021), 173–86, https://doi.org/10.1017/S0265051720000339

John-Steiner, Vera, *Creative Collaboration* (Oxford University Press, 2000)

Lilja, Robin, personal communication, December 31 2022

——, 'Constraint-based Patterns – An Examination of an Algorithmic Composition Method' (Master's thesis, Luleå University of Technology, 2021), http://urn.kb.se/resolve?urn=urn:nbn:se:ltu:diva-85001

——, 'Musikaliska kontraster genom förbud: Undersökning av min kompositionsmetod antikomposition' [*Musical Contrasts through Prohibition: Investigation of my Composition Method Anticomposition*] (bachelor's thesis, Luleå University of Technology, 2019), https://urn.kb.se/resolve?urn=urn:nbn:se:ltu:diva-74099

Luleå University of Technology, C7010G, *Artistic Research Processes: Theory and Method, 15 Credits* [course syllabus] (Luleå: Luleå University of Technology, 2022a), https://webapp.ltu.se/epok/dynpdf/public/kursplan/downloadPublicKursplan.pdf?kursKod=C7010G&lasPeriod=208&locale=en&locale=en

——, *X0005G, Research Process C, 7.5 Credits* [course syllabus] (Luleå University of Technology, 2022b), https://webapp.ltu.se/epok/dynpdf/public/kursplan/downloadPublicKursplan.pdf?kursKod=X0005G&lasPeriod=214&locale=en&locale=en

——, *F0316G, Thesis, Bachelor Programme in Music – Classical Musician, 15 Credits* [course syllabus] (Luleå University of Technology, 2022c), https://webapp.ltu.se/epok/dynpdf/public/kursplan/downloadPublicKursplan.pdf?kursKod=F0316G&lasPeriod=212&locale=en&locale=en

Lundström, Håkan, 'Svensk forskning i musik: De senaste 100 åren' [Swedish Research in Music: The Last 100 Years], *Swedish Journal of Music Research*, 101 (2019), 1–47

Mellberg, Ester, personal communication, 6 January 2023

——, 'A Partner at the Piano: Expanding Musical and Performative Expressions in a Duo with a Vocalist' (Master's thesis, Luleå University of Technology, 2022), http://urn.kb.se/resolve?urn=urn:nbn:se:ltu:diva-91443

Moberg, Nadia, 'The Place of Master Theses in Music Performance Education in Sweden: Subjects, Purposes, Justifications', *Music Education Research*, 25.1 (2023), 24–35, http://doi.org/10.1080/14613808.2023.2167966

Nelson, Robin, *Practice as Research in the Arts (and Beyond). Principles, Processes, Contexts, Achievements*, 2nd edn (London: Palgrave MacMillan, 2022), https://doi.org/10.1007/978-3-030-90542-2

Östersjö, Stefan, Nguyễn Thanh Thủy, David Hebert, and Henrik Frisk, *Shared Listenings: Methods for Transcultural Musicianship and Research* (Cambridge: Cambridge University Press, 2023), https://doi.org/10.1017/9781009272575

Östersjö, Stefan, 'Thinking-through-Music: On Knowledge Production, Materiality, Subjectivity and Embodiment in Artistic Research' in *Artistic Research in Music: Discipline and Resistance*, ed. by Jonathan Impett (Leuven: Leuven University Press, 2017), pp. 88–107, https://doi.org/10.2307/j.ctt21c4s2g.6

——, 'Art Worlds, Voice and Knowledge: Thoughts on Quality Assessment of Artistic Research Outcomes', *ÍMPAR Online Journal for Artistic Research*, 3.2 (2019), 60–69, https://doi.org/10.34624/impar.v3i2.14152

——, 'Nordic Contexts', in *Practice as Research in the Arts (and Beyond). Principles, Processes, Contexts, Achievements*, 2nd edn, ed. by Robin Nelson (London: Palgrave MacMillan, 2022), pp. 147–54, https://doi.org/10.1007/978-3-030-90542-2_9

Perčič, Simon, personal communication, January 2 2023

——, 'Temporal Shaping: A Conductor's Exploration of Tempo and its Modifications in Weber's Der Freischütz Overture' (Master's thesis, Luleå University of Techology, 2020), http://urn.kb.se/resolve?urn=urn:nbn:se:ltu:diva-80528

Sandqvist, Gertrud, 'New Knowledge from the Artist's Perspective: On artistic research', in *Artistic Research in Music: Discipline and Resistance*, ed. by Jonathan Impett (Leuven: Leuven University Press, 2017), pp. 181–86, https://doi.org/10.2307/j.ctt21c4s2g.12

Spatz, Ben, *Making A Laboratory: Dynamic Configurations with Transversal Video* (Santa Barbara, CA: Punctum Books, 2020), https://doi.org/10.2307/jj.2353794

Sundell, Jakob, personal communication, 9 January 2023.

——, 'The Drum Also Sings: A Study Exploring Playing Tonal Melody on the Jazz Drum Set' (Bachelor's thesis, Luleå University of Technology, 2022), http://urn.kb.se/resolve?urn=urn:nbn:se:ltu:diva-91898

The Higher Education Ordinance. Annex 2. System of Qualifications (SFS 1993:100), https://www.uhr.se/en/start/laws-and-regulations/Laws-and-regulations/The-Higher-Education-Ordinance/Annex-2/

2. Experimentation as a Learning Method:
A Case Study Exploring Affordances of a Musical Instrument

Fausto Pizzol

Introduction

Artistic research typically starts out from a creative challenge. For a bass player, the conventional understanding of the instrument could in itself be a limitation, given its monophonic characteristic, typically with an accompanying role. The possibility of exploring a different understanding of the instrument's potential for polyphonic and harmonic playing became the impetus for my entry into artistic research in music, and an exploration characterised by artistic method development. Looking for a method to learn, develop, and systematise the study of this potential, I adopted the concept of affordances[1] and a theory derived from it, called perceptual learning and development.[2] Artistic research is a way for me to develop systematic approaches to initiate artistic development and design the path to new creative insights.

From immersion in the perspectives of affordance theory and perceptual learning, I created a research design meant to conduct experiments on the possibilities of playing vertical harmonies on the electric bass. These experiments were expanded to include simultaneous execution of harmony and melody, a technique known as the chord-melody style of playing. In this sense, this chapter exposes the research that I made to learn, develop, and systematise this unconventional use of the instrument, as well as a discussion about affordances and perceptual learning and its use in music research. Along with these main goals, I suggest that the method I create should be tested by

---

1   James Jerome Gibson, *The Ecological Approach to Visual Perception* (Boston: Houghton Mifflin, 1979).
2   Eleanor Jack Gibson and Anne D. Pick, *Perceptual Learning and Development: An Ecological Approach* (New York: Oxford University Press, 2000).

other musicians who want to explore unconventional ways to play their instruments. Implementing these tests should be the next step in this work in progress.

Alongside the method based on the concept of affordances and perceptual learning and development theory, this research has its theoretical musical contents based on the LCCTO—Lydian Chromatic Concept of Tonal Organization.[3] The choice of the LCCTO concept as a musical foundation has to do with its emphasis on the relationship between chords and scales, which places it in line with this work. Applying its premises through the proposed research design led to the creation of a harmonic vocabulary for the electric bass, containing a chord dictionary, a thesaurus of patterns articulating chords and scales, and compositions organised as studies, called creative applications.

Affordances

The term 'affordances' was coined in the 1960s by James Jerome Gibson (1904–1979) within the scope of Ecological Psychology, a field in which the psychologist and his wife Eleanor Jack Gibson (1910–2002), another relevant name for this study, were pioneers. A concise definition of ecological psychology is given by Lorena Lobo, Manuel Heras-Escribano, and David Travieso:

> [...] is an embodied, situated, and non-representational approach pioneered by J. J. Gibson and E. J. Gibson. This theory aims to offer a third way beyond cognitivism and behaviorism for understanding cognition. The theory started with the rejection of the premise of the poverty of the stimulus, the physicalist conception of the stimulus, and the passive character of the perceiver of mainstream theories of perception. On the contrary, the main principles of ecological psychology are the continuity of perception and action, the organism-environment system as a unit of analysis, and the study of affordances as the objects of perception, combined with an emphasis on perceptual learning and development.[4]

J. Gibson aimed to present an innovative perspective for understanding perception and perceptual learning that would overcome the dichotomies of perception/action, organism/environment, subjective/objective, and mind/body characteristics of predecessor theories.[5] In this context, he developed the concept of affordances, defending the idea of mutualism in the relationship between the organism and the environment in the perception of possibilities of action. The author defines affordances in this way:

---

3   George Russell, *Lydian Chromatic Concept of Tonal Organization: Volume 1: The Art and Science of Tonal Gravity*, Fourth Edition (Brookline: Concept Publishing, 2001).
4   Lorena Lobo, Manuel Heras-Escribano, and David Travieso, 'The History and Philosophy of Ecological Psychology', *Frontiers in Psychology*, 9.2228 (2018), 1—15 (p. 1), https://doi.org/103389/fpsyg.2018.02228.
5   Ibid., p. 1.

> The affordances of the environment are what it offers the animal, and what it provides or furnishes, either for good or ill. The verb to afford is found in the dictionary, but the noun affordance is not. I have made it up. I mean by it something that refers to both the environment and the animal in a way that no existing term does. It implies the complementarity of the animal and the environment.[6]

Deepening his concept, J. Gibson states that the behaviours of individuals, in the sense of action, depend on the knowledge they obtain through the perception of the affordances of the environment.[7] Such perception is the result of a direct process, which begins with the detection of specific information from the environment, such as patterns and regularities, which are named invariants.[8] Rejecting the idea of perception as a passive process, Pablo Covarrubias, paraphrasing J. Gibson, points out that the animal actively seeks information through exploratory movements.[9] The authors Luke Windsor and Christophe de Bézenac exemplify: '(...) a pen might afford writing (...). A pen will be a shape that fits the hand, exudes a coloured liquid, which can mark a surface: to discover these properties would require exploration, a key element of ecological psychology.' Interpreting J. Gibson, the same authors use their own words to define the concept of affordances, and, in my opinion, create a simple and clarifying version: 'An affordance is a property of an event or object, relative to an organism, which represents its potential for action.'[10] Another equally interesting statement about the concept of affordances is put forward by Agnes Szokolszky:

> This mutualist concept [affordances] captures the codeterminate character of functional meaning in the O-E [organism-environment] system. A given environment offers directly perceivable possibilities for action, and agents take advantage of these possibilities, which have intrinsic relational value, and therefore are directly meaningful, in a situated way.[11]

Although the definition of affordances proposed by J. Gibson is considered very broad by some researchers, giving rise to several interpretations,[12] he describes the detailed study undertaken over almost two decades that gave rise to it and offers a wealth of examples of what it synthesises. Considering that his main interest is related to the

---

6 J. Gibson, p. 127.
7 See Mina Khatibi and Razieh Sheikholeslami, 'Gibson's Ecological Theory of Development and Affordances: A Brief Review', *The International Journal of Indian Psychology*, 2.4 (2015), 140–44 (p. 143).
8 See Agnes Szokolszky, 'Perceiving Metaphors: An Approach from Developmental Ecological Psychology', *Metaphor and Symbol*, 34.1 (2019), 17–32 (p. 21),, https://doi.org/10.1080/10926488.2019.1591724>
9 Pablo Covarrubias, et al., 'The Senses Considered as Perceptual Systems: The Revolutionary Ideas of Gibson's 1966 Book, 50 Years Later—part 1', *Ecological Psychology*, 29.2 (2017), 69–71 (p. 70),, https://doi.org/10.1080/10407413.2017.1297680>
10 Luke W. Windsor and Christophe de Bézenac, 'Music and affordances', *Musicae Scientiae*, 16.1 (2012), 102–20 (p. 3),, https://doi.org/10.1177/1029864911435734>
11 Szokolszky, p. 20.
12 See Lorenzo Jamone and others, 'Affordances in Psychology, Neuroscience, and Robotics: A Survey', *IEEE Transactions on Cognitive and Developmental Systems*, 10.1 (2018), 4–25 (p. 5),, https://doi.org/10.1109/TCDS.2016.2594134>

perception of the environment by human beings, J. Gibson argues the following four things:

> The theory of affordances is a radical departure from existing theories of value and meaning. It begins with a new definition of what value and meaning are. The perceiving of an affordance is not a process of perceiving a value—free physical object to which meaning is somehow added in a way that no one has been able to agree upon; it is a process of perceiving a value—rich ecological object. Any substance, any surface, any layout has some affordance for benefit or injury to someone. Physics may be value—free, but ecology is not [...]. The medium, substances, surfaces, objects, places, and other animals have affordances for a given animal. They offer benefits or injury, life or death. This is why they need to be perceived. The possibilities of the environment and the way of life of the animal go together inseparably. The environment constrains what the animal can do [...]. Within limits, the human animal can alter the affordances of the environment but is still the creature of his or her situation.
>
> An affordance cuts across the dichotomy of subjective-objective and helps us to understand its inadequacy. It is equally a fact of the environment and a fact of behaviour. It is both physical and psychical, yet neither. An affordance points both ways, to the environment and to the observer.
>
> [W]hat we perceive when we look at objects are their affordances, not their qualities. We can discriminate the dimensions of difference if required to do so in an experiment, but what the object affords us is what we normally pay attention to.
>
> The affordance of something does not change as the need of the observer changes. The observer may or may not perceive or attend to the affordance, according to his needs, but the affordance, being invariant, is always there to be perceived. An affordance is not bestowed upon an object by a need of an observer and his act of perceiving it. The object offers what it does because it is what it is.[13]

Regarding the relationship between music studies and the concept of affordances and perceptual learning and development, I highlight three texts that dialogue with this work: (1) Adnan Marquez-Borbon (2009) 'Perceptual Learning and the Emergence of Performer-Instrument Interactions with Digital Music Systems';[14] (2) Simon Waters (2007): 'Performance Ecosystems: Ecological approaches to musical interaction';[15] (3) Luke Windsor and Christophe de Bézenac (2012): 'Music and Affordances'.[16]

Waters discusses the notion of a performance ecosystem, focusing on the performer-instrument-environment interrelationship within the scope of electroacoustic music. Important for the present work and in line with E. Gibson's theory that will be

---

13 J. Gibson, The Ecological Approach to Visual Perception, pp. 140—43.
14 Adnan Marquez-Borbon, 'Perceptual Learning and the Emergence of Performer-Instrument Interactions with Digital Music Systems', *A Body of Knowledge* (2018), 2–23, https://escholarship.org/uc/item/5p45g68p>
15 Simon Waters, 'Performance Ecosystems: Ecological approaches to musical interaction', *Electroacoustic Music Studies Network* (2007), http://www.ems—network.org/spip.php?article278
16 Windsor and de Bézenac.

discussed later, he points out the mutation in this interrelationship as potentiated by engagement in exploratory activities of a perceptual nature. Another point of dialogue between Waters's and the present work is his framing of musical instruments as tools, from an ecological perspective:

> It enables us to deal with the instrument as a tool, instrument as prosthesis (mimetic, relating to a perceived 'lack', and integral to a specific body), instrument as sensor (and thus integral to our intersensoriality), and instrument as a measure of engagement [...]. It allows us to acknowledge that precise acoustic conditions and aggregates of bodies have been critical for much musicking [...].[17]

Marquez-Borbon investigates the interaction between performers and digital musical instruments from the perspective of perceptual learning and development. He points out:

> [...] as the performer learns to play the instrument, they attune their perception to the multiple capacities of the system and are capable, in some instances, to perceive new possibilities that may yield possible paths towards the development of new musical or sonic practices. Interactions, more than operating a device, are represented by a rich history of engagement in which the performer develops a deep understanding of the system and what it may artistically afford. It is suggested that achieving this aim can be prompted by the introduction of alternative learning or pedagogical strategies that go beyond traditional music conservatory pedagogy. These multiple approaches invest in the development of other creative musical skills, such as improvisation, listening, and collaboration, which are often ignored by the dominant Western music tradition.[18]

Marquez-Borbon uses key terms for the theory of perceptual learning and development of new affordances: attune, perception, interactions, engagement. These terms will take part in this work when exposing the method adopted for carrying out the proposed experiments.

The text by Windsor and de Bézenac points out a way to understand the relationships between musicians and their musical instruments in the creation of new affordances: '[...] instruments can have different affordances when in the hands of individuals with different or deliberately changed effectivities.'[19] The authors add:

> In fact, many musical traditions incorporate actions that deliberately go against the characteristics of the instruments that are used. Musicians often go to great lengths to overcome bodily and instrumental constraints in order to achieve particular aesthetic or functional goals (e.g., learning lines that are characteristic of another instrument or instrumentalist). In this process, musicians change their effectivities through the development of new perceptual sensitivities and levels of motor complexity.[20]

---

17 Waters, p. 5.
18 Marquez-Borbon, p. 19.
19 Windsor and de Bézenac, p. 9.
20 Ibid., p. 8.

In line with the above statement, the contemporary practice of the electric bass, in the aspect explored here, incorporates actions that deliberately go against the characteristics of its conventional practice. The new affordances of this aspect involve the development and systematisation of techniques and mechanisms to create a harmonic vocabulary for the instrument. Then, this vocabulary is used in the creation of artistic interventions, materialised in the form of musical compositions that approach the electric bass as a harmonic instrument.

Continuing the discussion about the use of the concept of affordances in this work, I begin by framing the electric bass in one of the categories of ecological objects listed by J. Gibson (that is, medium, substances, surfaces, objects, places, and other animals), namely, objects. Within this category, there is also a subdivision: attached objects and detached objects. The electric bass falls into the latter.

> The affordances of what we loosely call objects are extremely various. It will be recalled that my use of the terms is restricted and that I distinguish between attached objects and detached objects [...]. Detached objects must be comparable in size to the animal under consideration if they are to afford behavior. But those that are comparable afford an astonishing variety of behaviors, especially to animals with hands. Objects can be manufactured and manipulated. Some are portable in that they afford lifting and carrying, while others are not [...].[21]

The definition of the characteristics of the electric bass through the perception of the affordances of the instrument, as this is being done, does not aim to reclassify or give it a new name. Rather, the objective is to declassify it from established practice, pointing out broader characteristics that may contribute to the perception of new affordances. In this logic, the electric bass, being a musical instrument, can still be characterised within one of the categories of detached objects, a tool. This last characterization has already been mentioned before when quoting Waters and portrays a personal perception that, in part, motivated the beginning of this investigation. I believe that the electric bass (as well as other musical instruments) can be approached beyond the established paradigm for its practice, starting from the conception that it is only a tool for musical expression, that is, a musical object at its disposal of creativity.

Using ecological psychology terms, this proposal of exploring the affordances of the electric bass beyond conventional practice (melodic/monophonic), and approaching the instrument as harmonic/polyphonic, reflects my perception that this musical tool enables ('affords') the individual, in this case, myself, specific and potentially prolific actions in this regard.[22] This proposal is supported by J. Gibson's statement about the perception of the affordances of a detached object:

---

21 J. Gibson, p. 133.
22 I think it is appropriate to point out that this is a proposal considerably at odds with the canon of electric bass performance, when it comes to evaluating its current reference literature. In this sense, and in view of the results that will be presented later, I believe that this text has the potential to contribute

To Perceive an Affordance is not to Classify an Object

The fact that a stone is a missile does not imply that it cannot be other things as well. It can be a paperweight, a bookend, a hammer, or a pendulum bob. It can be piled on another rock to make a cairn or a stone wall. These affordances are all consistent with one another. The differences between them are not clear-cut, and the arbitrary names by which they are called do not count for perception. If you know what can be done with a graspable detached object, what it can be used for, you can call it whatever you please. The theory of affordances rescues us from the philosophical muddle of assuming fixed classes of objects, each defined by its common features and then given a name. As Ludwig Wittgenstein knew, you cannot specify the necessary and sufficient features of the class of things to which a name is given. They have only a 'family resemblance'. But this does not mean you cannot learn how to use things and perceive their uses. You do not have to classify and label things in order to perceive what they afford.[23]

Once this initial framework is made, the development of the harmonic affordances of this detached object-tool, the electric bass, is based on a complementary theory, or extension,[24] of James Gibson's concept, the notion of perceptual learning and development, developed in parallel by Eleanor Gibson.[25] Her theory seeks to explain the process of learning and developing new affordances according to the ecological psychology paradigm. Therefore, based on the concept of affordances, the work proposed here seeks, in conjunction with the theoretical/musical content of the LCCTO, to develop the harmonic potential of the electric bass through the application of J. Gibson and E. Gibson's theory and its ramifications, as detailed next.

Perceptual Learning and Development

In the context of ecological psychology, 'perceptual learning refers to the basic epistemic process of how the perceptual system becomes sophisticated in the detection of novel and relevant aspects of the environment and thereby becomes able to guide action in ever changing contexts'.[26] According to E. Gibson, learning and development take place through processes of adjustment of the individual's behaviour in accordance with the information available in the environment. She calls these processes 'attunement' and 'calibration'.[27] The authors Lobo, Heras-Escribano, and Travieso clarify:

---

significantly to the advancement of knowledge about the possibilities of musical application of the electric bass.

23 J. Gibson, p. 134.
24 Szokolszky, 'Perceiving Metaphors', p. 18.
25 E. Gibson and Pick, *Perceptual Learning and Development: An Ecological Approach*.
26 Agnes Szokolszky and others, 'Ecological approaches to perceptual learning: learning to perceive and perceiving as learning', *Adaptive Behavior*, 27.6 (2019), 363–88 (p. 373).
27 E. Gibson and Pick, p. 141; p. 179.

The ecological approach to perceptual learning aims to explain how perceivers take advantage of the specific and redundant information available in the ambient energy arrays (E. J. Gibson, 1969; E. J. Gibson and Pick, 2000). This is, perceptual learning has to do with the processes of attunement and calibration. First, organisms must engage into an attunement process (to learn how to detect specific information for affordances); second, they need to adjust their behavior to an informational variable (a calibration process).[28]

Exploration is placed as an essential procedure for this process of learning and development of new possibilities of action and, according to E. Gibson, such procedure involves engaging in activities of perception of different natures, such as visual, oral, or haptic (tactile system). The author also points out the influence of mental processes and social context in detecting information for affordances.

Still on the importance of the exploratory procedure according to the bias of ecological psychology, Marquez-Borbon observes the construction of new knowledge and, consequently, new affordances:

> Consistent with E. J. Gibson's description of information pickup, performers engaged in exploratory actions to reveal information about the system. Additionally, performatory actions where participants engaged in a process of expectation and confirmation contributed to yielding new knowledge and further spurred exploration [...]. E. J. Gibson observes that as action capabilities change (i.e, sensorimotor skills), new affordances can be learned. In effect, in developing skills one also develops or attunes their perception to the environment.[29]

In this logic, E. Gibson, considering that the perceptual development that leads to the learning of new affordances is driven by a complex interaction between the environment and human motivation, describes the behavioural aspects that contribute to such development. These can be summarised as follows:

> Agency: Self-control, intentionality in behaviour. Agency is learning to control both one's own activity and external events.
>
> Prospectively: Intentional, anticipatory, playful, future-oriented behaviours [...] Tendency to see order, regularity, and pattern to make sense of the world.
>
> Flexibility: Perception can adjust to new situations and bodily conditions (such as growth, improved motor skills, ...).[30]

A more recent development of E. Gibson's proposal involves a theory called 'direct learning'. This approach seeks to reveal the regularities in the learning path, which

---

28 Lobo et al., p. 12.
29 Marquez-Borbon, p. 12.
30 See Khatibi and Sheikholeslami, p. 142. These three behavioural aspects, to some extent, resemble the deep learning guidelines discussed by Odd Torleiv Furnes in Chapter 10 of this book. However, the notion of deep learning, widespread in the field of (New) Learning Sciences, also focuses on building long-term understanding and on interdisciplinarity of contents, subjects that are not central to E. Gibson's perceptual learning and development theory.

is characterised as an information-driven process. The theory relies on the possibility that learning is a direct event, rather than one based solely in cognitive processes.[31] Inspired by the concept of affordances and perceptual learning and development, it details a set of behavioural processes that imply a change in perception (learning) and actions guided by perception. They are:

Education of Intention: '[...] one of the functions of intention is to set up perceptual or perceptual-motor systems to detect a particular informational variable.'[32] This variable is called the 'specifying variable', and, as the name suggests, it is a variable that specifies the property that an observer intends to perceive. David Jacobs and Claire Michaels state that certain perceptions and actions, among many possible ones, are more beneficial than others and, with experience, the individual can improve the choice of which of these he or she intends to update.[33] Regarding the importance of intentions in the exploratory learning process, Jacobs and Michaels point out:

> Ecological studies therefore often proceed by choosing situations in which a particular intention can be assumed. In catching experiments, for instance, it is generally assumed that perceivers intend to catch balls and not to hit or to avoid balls. Such assumptions are necessary because intentions define task situations, for instance—and this is important for the remainder of the article—assuming a particular intention is required to define and identify specifying and non specifying variables.[34]

Education of Attention: J. Gibson addressed the importance of educating attention for the detection of relevant variables. In his opinion, this is an active process wherein the individual seeks to concentrate on the most useful informational variables.[35] Attention, which guides perception, is understood as the driving force in the detection of information.[36] It can be understood that, perception, continuously guided by attention to an intentionally selected variable (education of intention), can be redirected by new events or information towards new and more useful variables.[37] 'Education of attention is an action-based process, involving research and active exploration.'[38]

Calibration: Although Jacobs and Michaels have created a quantitative approach to the calibration process, something that the present work does not intend to adopt, this process also points to behaviours that can be approached qualitatively. I refer to the perception-action loop: (1) 'perceptual systems orient the perceptual organs and make adjustments in the exploration to resonate when ecological information is

---

31   David Jacobs and Claire Michaels, 'Direct Learning', *Ecological Psychology*, 19.4 (2007), 321–49 (p. 330), https://doi.org/10.1080/10407410701432337
32   Ibid., p. 327.
33   Ibid., p. 326.
34   Ibid.
35   J. Gibson, pp. 235–43.
36   Szokolszky and others, 'Ecological approaches', p. 367.
37   Jacobs, 'Direct Learning', p. 327.
38   Szokolszky and others, 'Ecological approaches', p. 370.

picked up';[39] (2) the circularity in the interaction between new motor skills and new possibilities of action: 'New motor skills bring new action possibilities;[40] and (3) the refinement of the education of intention and education of attention processes, which can feed back into each other. Jacobs and Michaels state: '[...] the sophistication of expert performance derives from the improved fits of experts to their environments [...].'[41]

Based on these ecological psychology principles discussed so far, I propose a method to guide artistic experiments aimed at developing new affordances (harmonic in nature) for the electric bass and creating a harmonic vocabulary, as summarised in the research design[42] below.

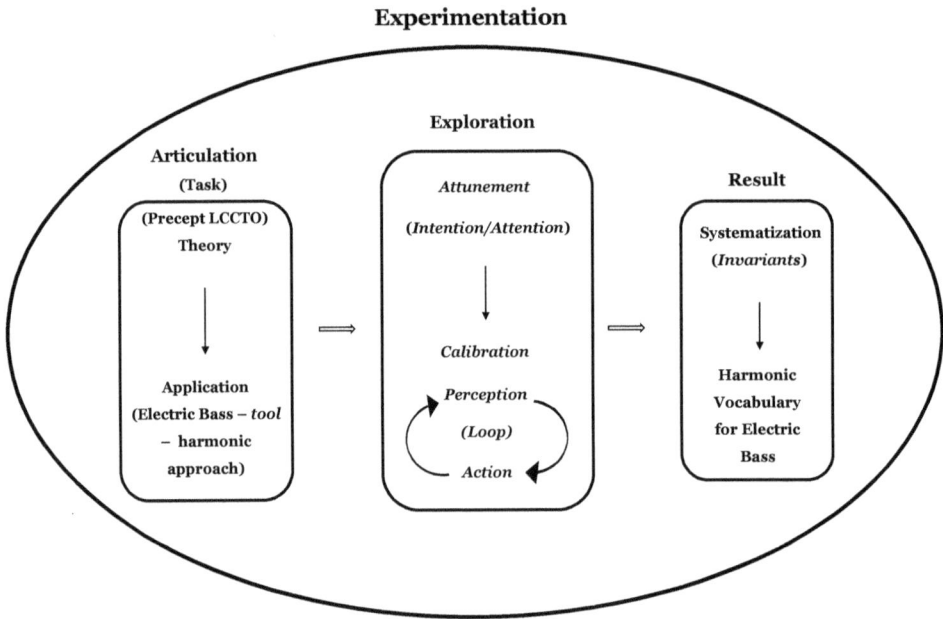

Fig. 2.1: Research design summarising the method adopted for the empirical experiments

---

39   Michael Richardson and others, 'Ecological Psychology: Six Principles for an Embodied-Embedded Approach to Behavior', in *Handbook of Cognitive Science: An Embodied Approach*, ed. by Paco Calvo and Tony Gomila (Amsterdam: Elsevier, 2008), pp. 159–87 (p. 174), https://doi.org/10.1016/B978-0-08-046616-3.00009-8

40   Lorenzo Jamone and others, 'Affordances in Psychology, Neuroscience, and Robotics: A Survey', *IEEE Transactions on Cognitive and Developmental Systems*, 10.1 (2018), 4–25 (p. 4), https://doi.org/10.1109/TCDS.2016.2594134

41   Jacobs, 'Direct Learning', p. 322.

42   This is the research design that is mentioned in the chapter introduction. Fed with theoretical data from the LCCTO (precepts), it works as a mechanism aimed at exploration and consequent generation of results related to the possibilities of harmonic execution of the electric bass.

Conducting the Experiments

The artistic experiments are divided into three groups. Each of these groups was conceived with the aim of structuring a harmonic vocabulary for the electric bass. The three groups are:

- First Group—Detection of possibilities to play the chords proposed in the LCCTO, on the electric bass. (Generating chapter 1 of the harmonic vocabulary: chord dictionary)
- Second Group—Detection of possibilities for harmonising the LCCTO's principal scales on the electric bass. (Generating Chapter 2: thesaurus of patterns articulating chords and scales)
- Third Group—Harmonic relationships between the chords from the harmonic fields of the principal scales of the LCCTO. (Generating Chapter 3: harmonic relationships between chords)

The exposition of the method of conducting the experiments will be done through commentary on examples. There will be three examples, one for each group of experiments.

1st Group—Detection of Possibilities to Play the Chords Proposed in the LCCTO, on the Electric Bass

The first group of artistic experiments focuses on the exploration of ways of performing, on the electric bass, the chords from the harmonic fields suggested in the LCCTO. To register such execution forms, diagrams representing the scale of the instrument will be used (Fig. 2.2).

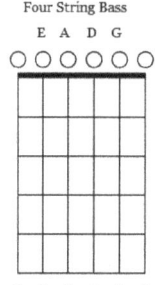 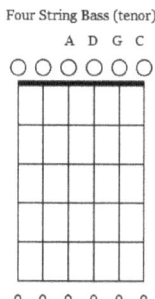 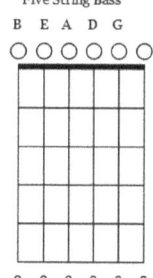 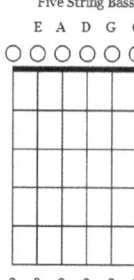

Fig. 2.2: Diagrams for four and five-string electric bass.

Attunement

Between pages 23 and 28 of George Russell's reference book on the LCCTO is presented the score notation of the principal chords (chord mode) and sub-principal chords constructed from each of the degrees of the Lydian Scale. Each group of chords proposed for a certain degree is treated as a premise, and different possibilities of playing these chords on the electric bass are explored. As an example, for the #IV degree of the harmonic field of the Lydian Scale, the following harmonic structures are placed:

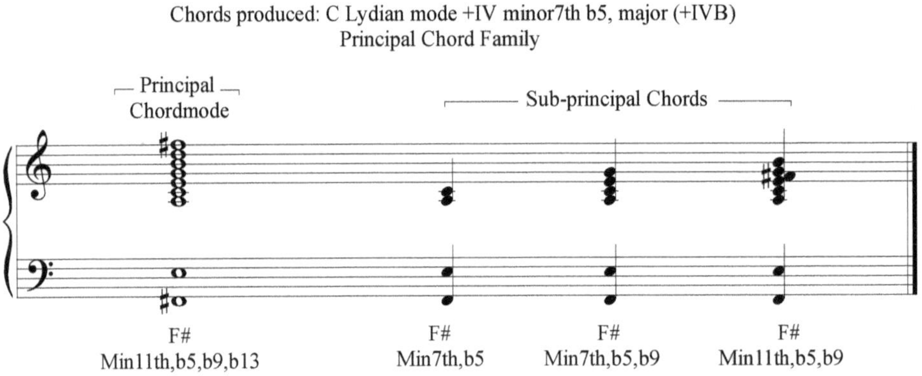

Fig. 2.3: Lydian Mode +IV Minor Seventh b5/Major(+IVb) – Principal Chord Family. From Russell, p. 27.

The first suggested sub-principal chord is F#min7(b5), composed by the notes F Sharp (T), A (b3rd), C (b5th), E (b7th). The score notation is the starting point of the experiment, and represents, in relation to the proposed research design, the theory component to be applied to the practice of electric bass (task). Then begins the attunement process, wherein the intention (education of intention) is to play the chord exactly as specified in the author's score on the electric bass, that is, at the same pitch and with the same interval order. Therefore, the education of attention is focused on locating, visually and tactilely, the ergonomic possibilities of executing said harmonic structure. As a result of this perceptual exploration, the following forms of execution were detected for the F#Min(b5) chord, as represented in the diagrams, Fig. 2.4a–p, below:

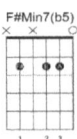

Fig. 2.4a. Possibility of performing the same harmonic structure proposed by the LCCTO.

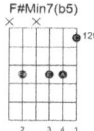

Fig. 2.4b. Possibility of performing the same harmonic structure/execution form an octave higher.

Calibration

Starting the second process, calibration, it is possible to detect other ways of executing the F#min7(b5) chord by adjusting the perception for new informational variables. The chord in question is formed by the notes F#, A, C, E, which are repeated in different locations of the electric bass scale.

Keeping F sharp as the lowest sound of a harmonic structure composed of four notes, it is possible to create different voicings by varying the order of notes A, C, E, as well as the height (frequency) and position, in the scale, of all the four notes. By calibrating attention to these variables, the perception-action loop is fed, revealing new execution possibilities, ergonomically and sonically viable.[43] As a result of this exploratory process, the following forms of execution were detected:

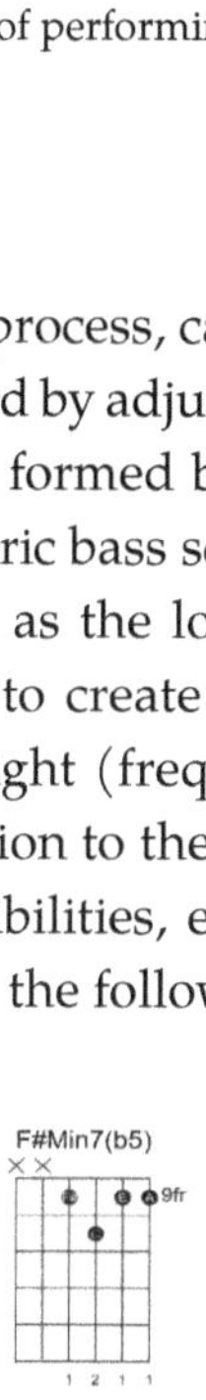

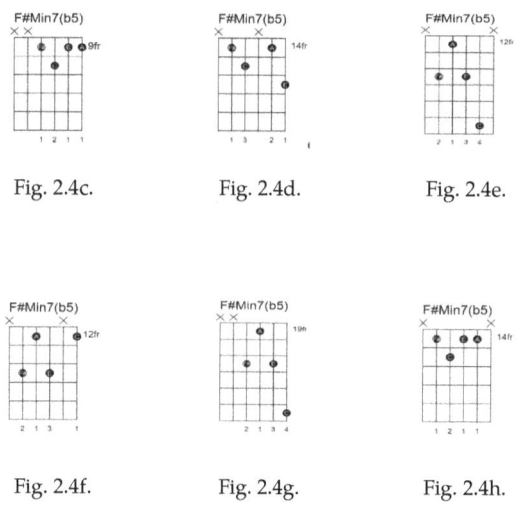

Fig. 2.4c. 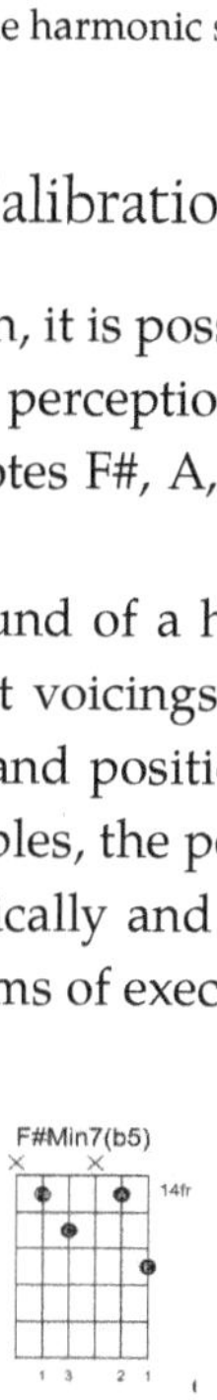 Fig. 2.4d. 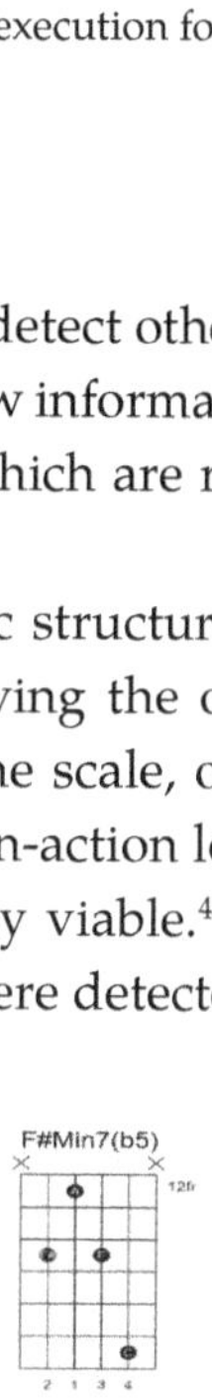 Fig. 2.4e.

Fig. 2.4f. Fig. 2.4g. Fig. 2.4h.

The execution forms registered so far were gradually perceived in visual, tactile, and aural ways, through the exploration of the instrument's scale and from each new piece

---

43   This calibration process, applied as a method for exploration, based on the perception-action loop, bears some degree of similarity with the procedure for 'creating variations' as described by Mikael Bäckman in Chapter 3 of this book, in relation to what he calls a 'creative process of generating licks' for the harmonica.

of information detected. Each form of execution produced information for the progress of the experiment, resulting, in a cyclical way, in the perception of new forms. The next process, as dictated by the research design, is the systematisation of the results.

The implemented systematisation proposal aims to facilitate the learning and internalisation of the results of the experiments practically and logically. For this purpose, systematisation is divided into two stages: (1) initial, aimed at organising the results associated with each experiment, and (2) final, encompassing the set of results of all experiments, originating the harmonic vocabulary for the electric bass. The systematisation stage that will be exposed below fits as initial, that is, it represents the organisation of the results of the experimentation of the possibilities of execution in the electric bass of the F#min7(b5) chord. The systematisation of the results of this one, as well as of the other experiments of detection of possibilities of execution of the chords proposed in the LCCTO, takes place through the grouping of the diagrams of each chord explored according to its highest note (leading tone). This higher note constitutes the invariant[44] of systematisation chosen by me. Following this logic, the F#min7(b5) chord diagrams are organised as follows:

Systematization

F#Min7th b5 chord with minor 3rd (A) as Leading Tone:

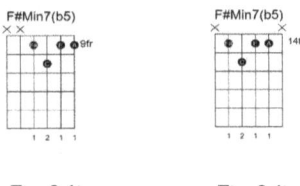

Fig. 2.4i.   Fig. 2.4j.

F#Min 7th b5 chord with diminished 5th (C) as Leading Tone:

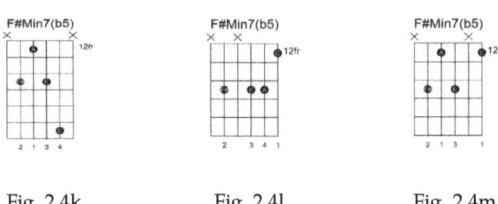

Fig. 2.4k.   Fig. 2.4l.   Fig. 2.4m.

---

44   See J. Gibson; E. Gibson and Pick.

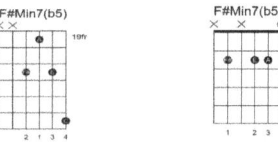

Fig. 2.4n. Fig. 2.4o.

F#Min 7th b5 chord with minor 7th (E) as Leading Tone:

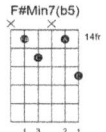

Fig. 2.4p.

Fig. 2.4 (a–p): Diagrams representing execution forms for the F#Min(b5) chord.

The choice of systematisation based on the invariant highest note (leading tone) reflects prospective behavioural conduct.[45] Anticipating a future behaviour, this initial systematisation proposal will help the following artistic work, which deals with the articulation of scales and, subsequently, melodies, with the chords that are now being studied. In this reasoning, the chord forms detected and systematised are added to the harmonic vocabulary and made available for harmonising scales and melodies. For each degree of a given scale, there is a set of diagrams available, where the highest note of the voicing represents the note of the melody to be harmonised.

For clarification purposes, I present a brief video example (Video 2.1) of this articulation which is covered in detail in specific experiments. In this example, a Lydian melody is harmonised with the chord from the first-degree in root position and inversions.

Video 2.1. Video of author presenting CMaj triad and inversions, uploaded by Fausto Lessa, 14 February 2022. https://hdl.handle.net/20.500.12434/c7435c81

---

45 For prospective behaviour, see E. Gibson and Pick, pp. 168–76.

Second Group—Detection of Possibilities for Harmonising the LCCTO's Principal Scales on the Electric Bass. (Articulations between Chords and Scales)

The exploration to be carried out in this second group of experiments aims to produce theoretical knowledge and develop technical skills related to the simultaneous execution of melodic lines and harmonic accompaniment on the electric bass. Qualitatively, possibilities of harmonising on the electric bass will be experimented with involving articulations between the principal scales of the LCCTO and chords from their respective harmonic fields. The five chord categories listed by Russell were experimented with, namely: Major, Minor, Dominant, Augmented, and Diminished.[46]

Referring to the proposed research design, the theory/practice articulation of this entire group of experiments takes place through the application of the chord/scale relational content, as presented in the LCCTO, to the harmonic approach of the electric bass. In the case of this particular experiment, the theory concerns the harmonisation of the C Lydian diminished Scale using the C diminished triad.

Attunement

In the attunement process, where exploration begins, the aim is to detect a viable possibility of executing already registered forms (diagrams) of the diminished triad suggested by Russell (closed position), simultaneously with the execution of the Lydian Diminished Scale. Inversions are also contemplated.

In my view (intention/attention), the first perceptibly viable possibility is the execution of the Lydian Diminished Scale in ascending and descending forms, with block harmonisation of the notes that belong to the diminished triad of C.[47] The result of this initial exploration is listed below (Video 2.2 and Fig. 2.5). [48]

Video 2.2. Video of author presenting the harmonisation of Lydian Diminished Scale notes belonging to the first degree triad—closed position, uploaded by Fausto Lessa, 5 February 2022. https://hdl.handle.net/20.500.12434/df0f8785

---

46 Russell, p. 17.
47 I believe it is important to emphasise the personal character of this initial perception and, although it is not the object of study in this work, it seems reasonable to me to say that other musicians can suggest different approaches.
48 All results of the second group of experiments are recorded, in addition to the score, with the support of diagrams and respective audios and videos.

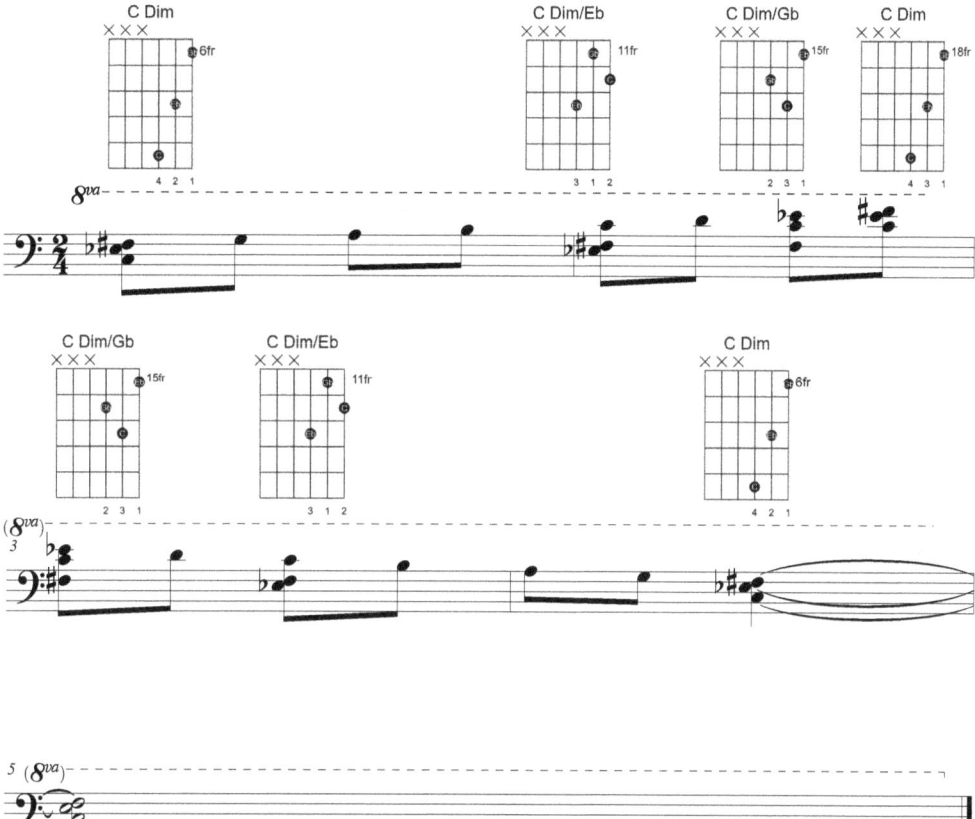

Fig. 2.5: Harmonising the notes of the Lydian Diminished Scale that belong to the first—degree triad—closed position.

Calibration

In the calibration process, possibilities of harmonising the scale are explored using different voicings of the diminished triad. In addition to harmonising the notes of the triad, I also sought to detect viable ways of harmonising the other notes of the scale. This harmonisation results in the construction of chords with sixth, seventh, or triads with an added note (add).

Video 2.3. Video of author demonstrating the harmonisation of all notes of the Lydian Diminished Scale with the first-degree triad—closed position, uploaded by Fausto Lessa, 5 February 2022. https://hdl.handle.net/20.500.12434/e6c0b76e

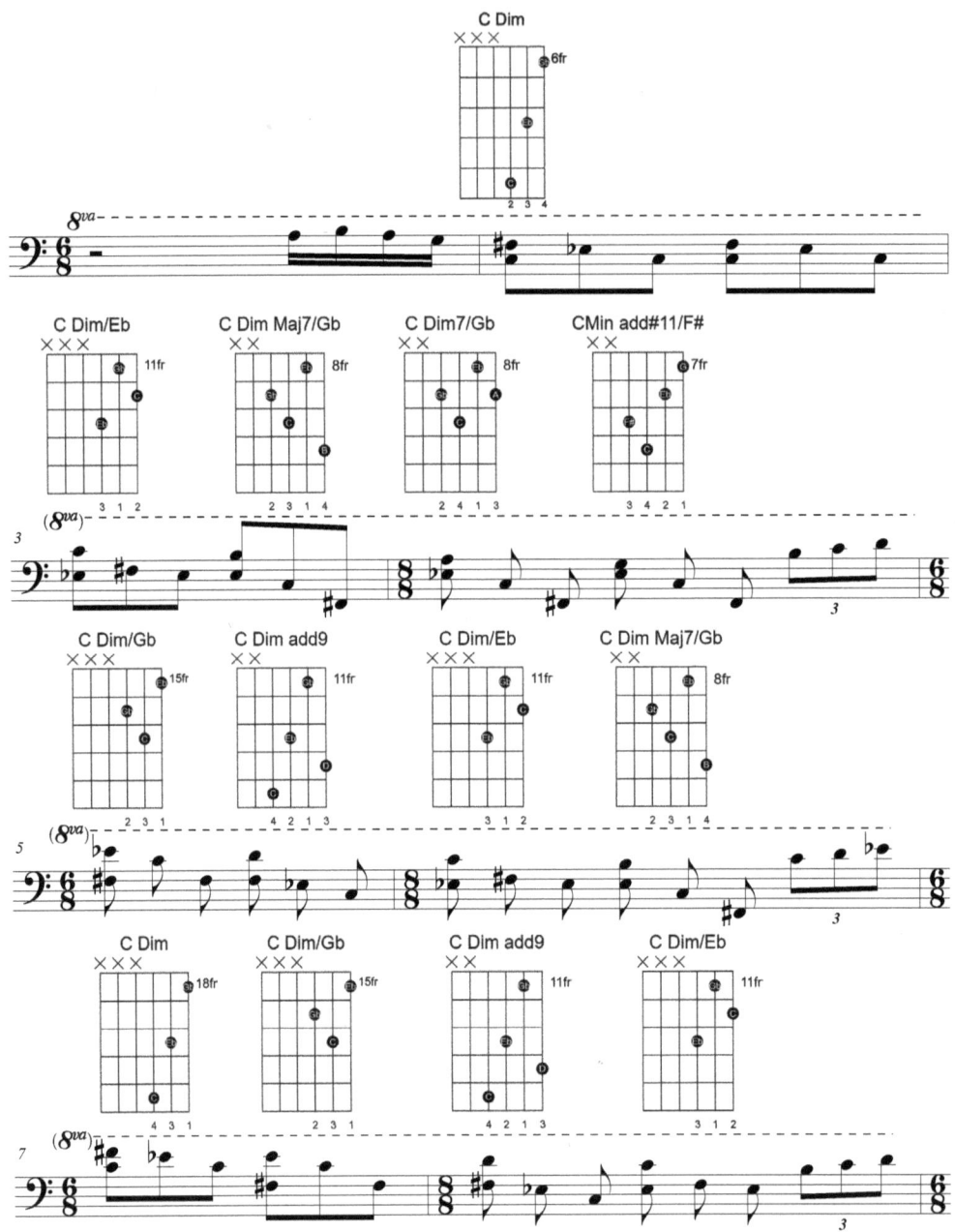

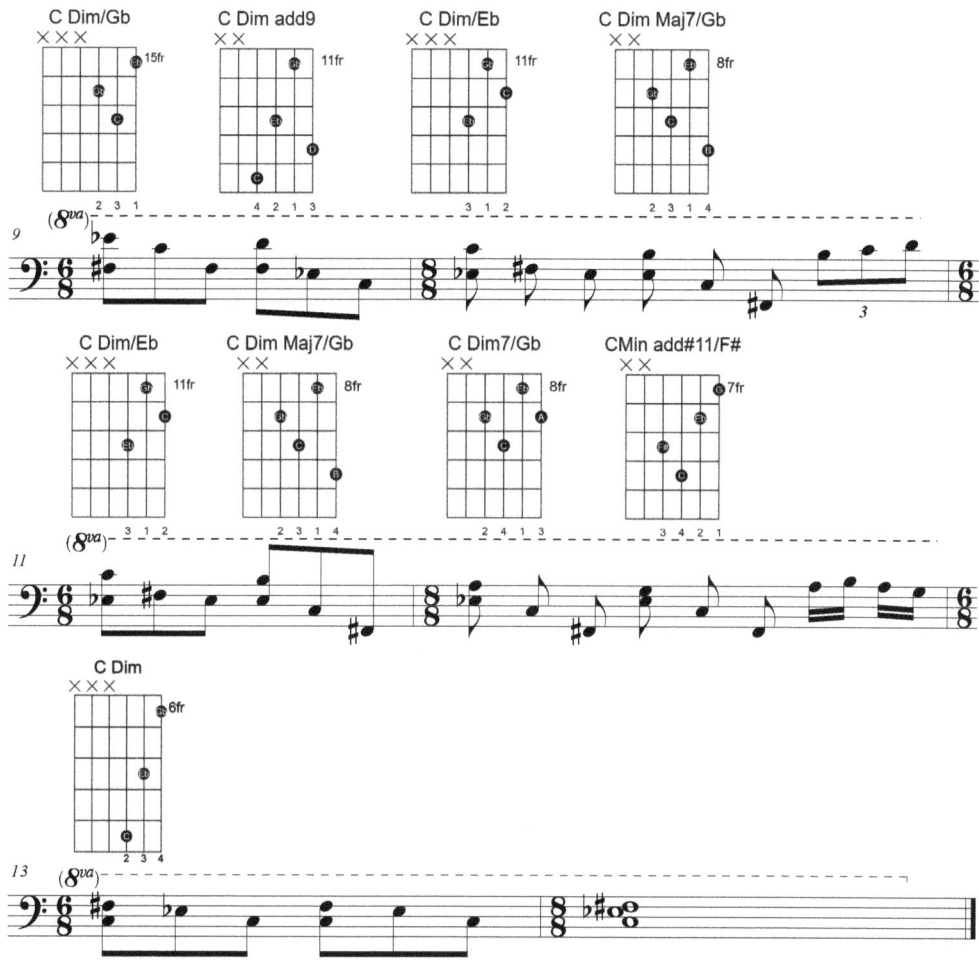

Fig. 2.6: Harmonizing all notes of the Lydian Diminished Scale with the first-degree triad – closed position.

Harmonisation of all Notes of the Lydian Diminished Scale with the First-Degree Triad—Drop 2 Position

The execution of the chords listed below proved to be unfeasible in the drop 2 position. As an alternative to continuing the exploration, these same chords were executed in closed position:

- Cdim/Gb with A as the highest note of the voicing
- Cdim Maj7/Gb with B as the highest note of the voicing
- Cdim add9 with D as the highest note of the voicing
- CMin add#11/F# with G as the highest note of the voicing

Video 2.4. Video of author demonstrating the harmonisation of all notes of the Lydian Diminished Scale with the first degree triad—drop 2 position, uploaded by Fausto Lessa, 5 February 2022. https://hdl.handle.net/20.500.12434/0cb2636e

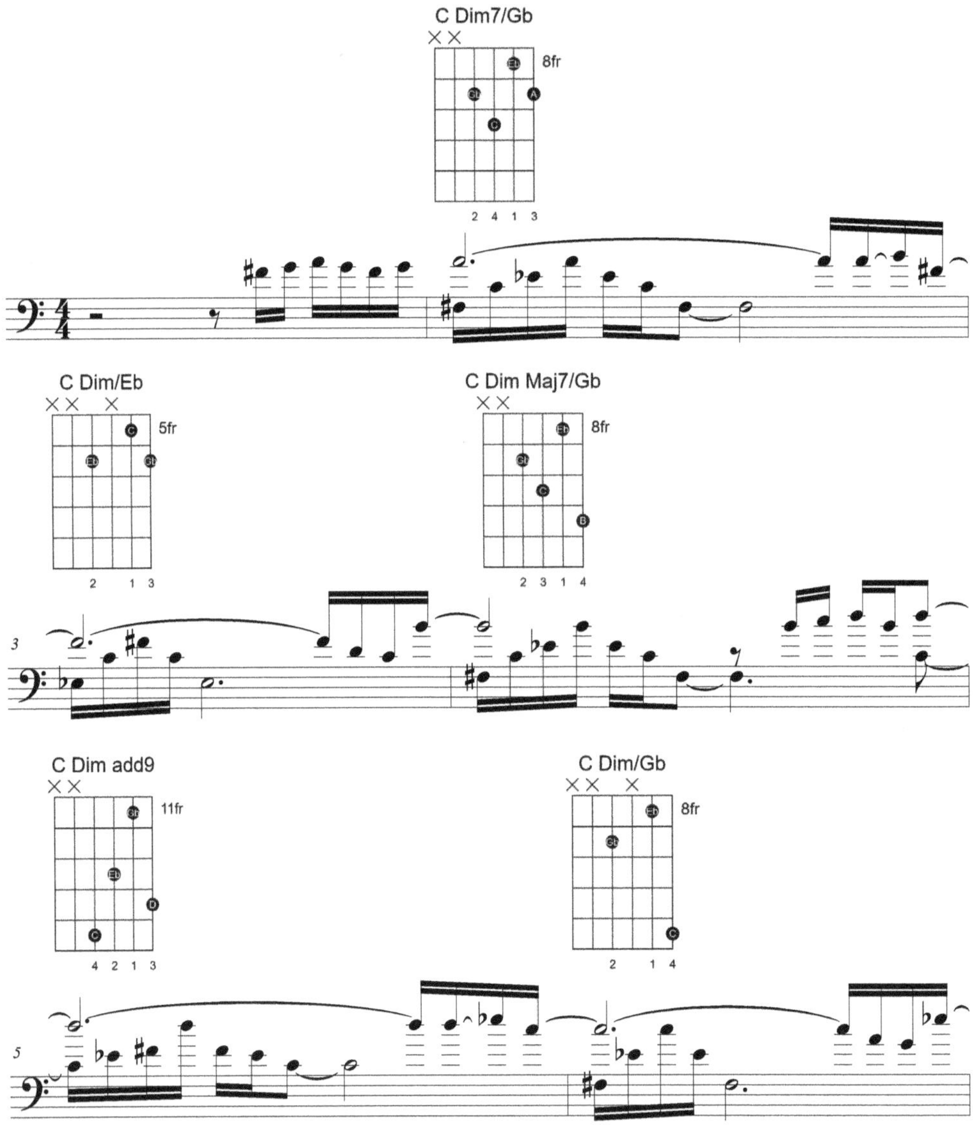

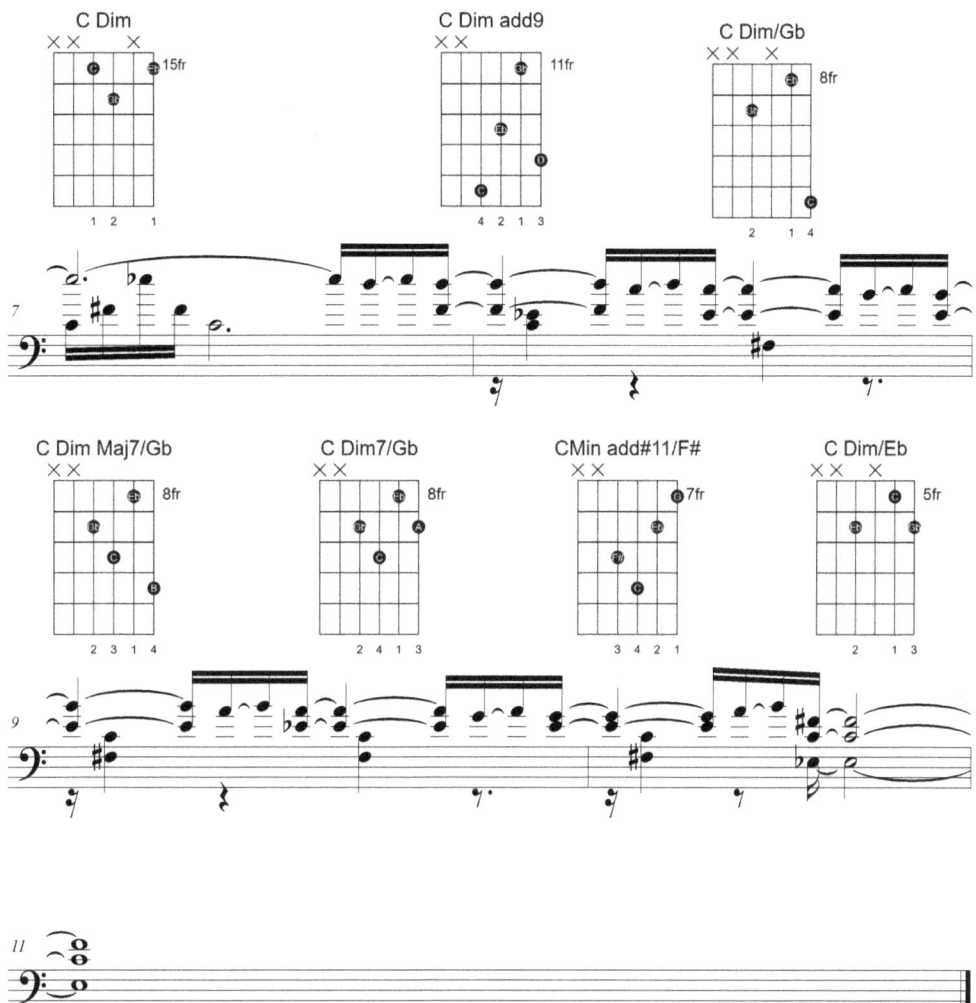

Fig. 2.7: Harmonising all the notes of the Lydian Diminished Scale with the first—degree triad—drop 2 position.

Execution of the Lydian Diminished Scale, on More than one String, Accompanied by Harmonisation with the First-Degree Triad—Open Position

Another possibility explored was the execution of the scale accompanied by the chord. After having harmonised the notes individually in the previous explorations, the perception/action loop led my practice toward the search for possibilities of executing phrases or melodic motifs accompanied by their harmonisations. One way I found to make the study of this new affordance viable and systematic was to use the scale, with beginning and end in different degrees in each measure, contemplating all seven degrees. With the mastery of this affordance, that is, possessing the technical ability to execute this discovered potential, it becomes possible to freely manipulate the scale to create different melodies and harmonise them.

Video 2.5. Video of author executing the Lydian Diminished Scale, on more than one string, accompanied by harmonisation with the first degree triad—open position, uploaded by Fausto Lessa, 5 February 2022. https://hdl.handle.net/20.500.12434/0874b874

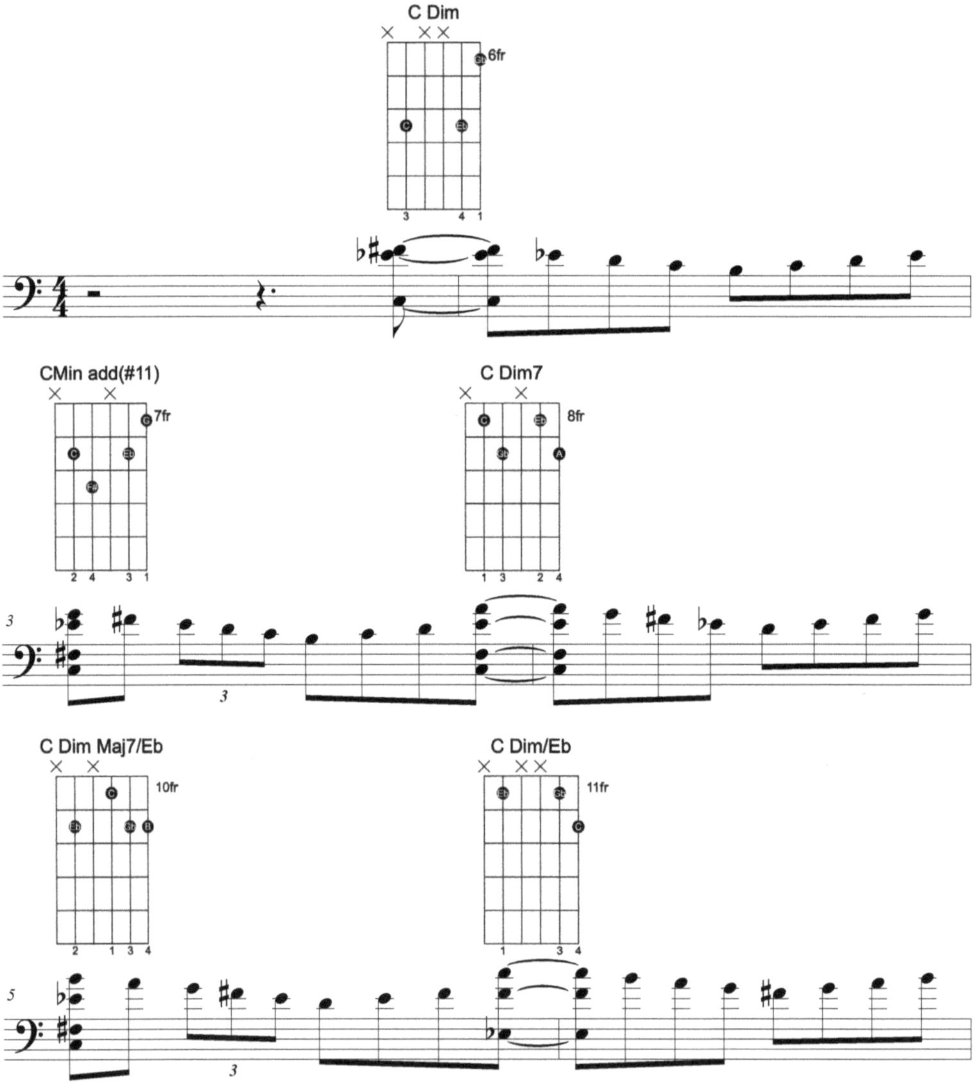

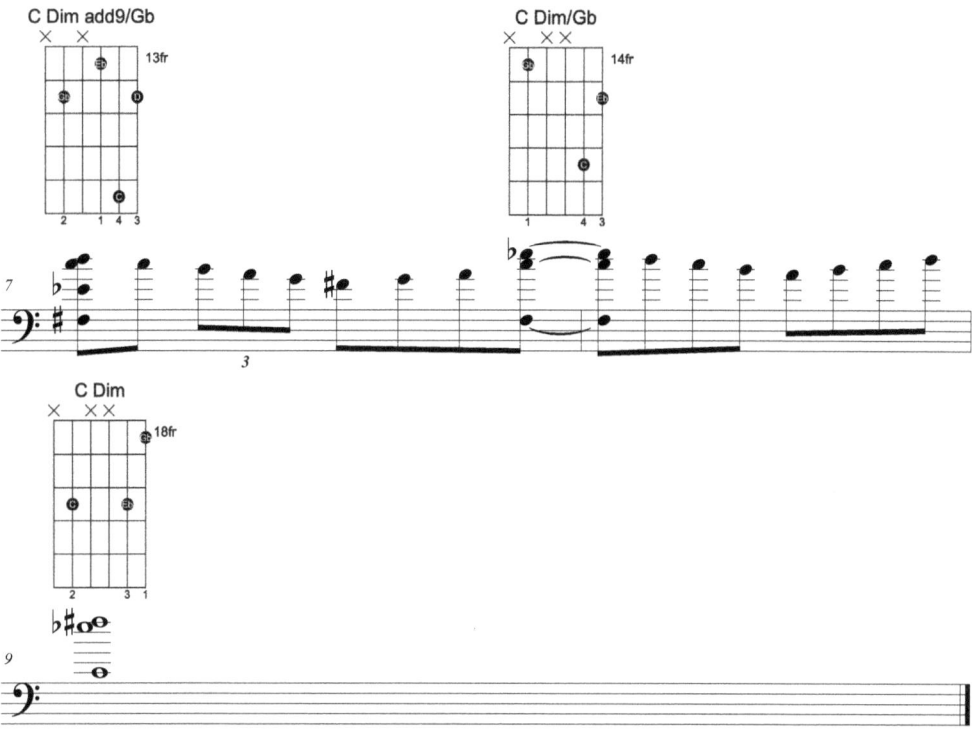

Fig. 2.8: Execution of the Lydian Diminished Scale, on more than one string, accompanied by harmonisation with the first-degree triad – open position.

After exposing the exploration of the possibilities of harmonising the Lydian Diminished Scale, two observations can already be made. The first concerns the dimension that the work could take if the possibilities were explored to the point of exhaustion. Opportunely, these experiments have a qualitative bias, to detect relevant aspects to produce the necessary knowledge to build a consistent vocabulary for the harmonic performance of the electric bass. In this sense, based on the experiments, the three positions explored—closed, drop 2, and open—prove to provide the content required for this purpose.

The second observation refers to the research design, more specifically to the calibration process and the subsequent systematisation of results based on invariants. By feeding the perception-action loop with the result of the first exploration, the search for new affordances was directed towards moving the notes away from the voicings gradually and in an organised way. As a consequence of this procedure, invariant elements were naturally imposed that can be taken as a reference for systematisation. I am referring, again, to the positions of the triad, that is: closed, drop 2, open. Therefore, based on the two observations, I defined that the experiments of the second group would have as one of the delimitation and systematisation criteria these previously defined positions, which proved to be viable and adequate when applied to the harmonic approach of the electric bass.

I believe it is reasonable to state that the results obtained so far with this Lydian Diminished Scale harmonisation experiment constitute a qualitatively satisfactory collection of viable execution possibilities to be added to the proposed harmonic vocabulary. Therefore, once this experimentation is over, I find that in addition to the previously selected invariants, associated with the chord position (closed, drop 2, open), a second set of invariants has imposed itself, contributing to the efficient complementation of the delimitation and systematisation of the results. I refer to the sequence of explorations generated by the perception-action loop. In this sequence, the following order of procedures was outlined, which was then adopted in the other experiments of this group: (1) harmonising only the notes of the scale that belong to the chord being explored; (2) harmonising all notes of the scale with the chord being explored; (3) execution of the scale, fragment, motif or rhythmic/melodic pattern thereof, in more than one electric bass string, accompanied by harmonisation with the chord being explored. In this logic, the delimitation and process of systematisation of the results of each experiment in this second group can be illustrated from two complementary sets of invariants, as outlined below.

Delimitation

Invariants – group 1	Invariants – group 2
A- Chord in closed position	1-Harmonization only of the scale notes that belong to the explored chord.
B- Chord in drop 2 position	2-Harmonization of all scale notes with the explored chord.
C- Chord in open position	3- Execution of the scale, fragment, motif or rhythmic/melodic pattern of this, in more than one electric bass string, accompanied by harmonization with the explored chord.

Fig. 2.9: Delimitation scheme of the experiments of the second group.

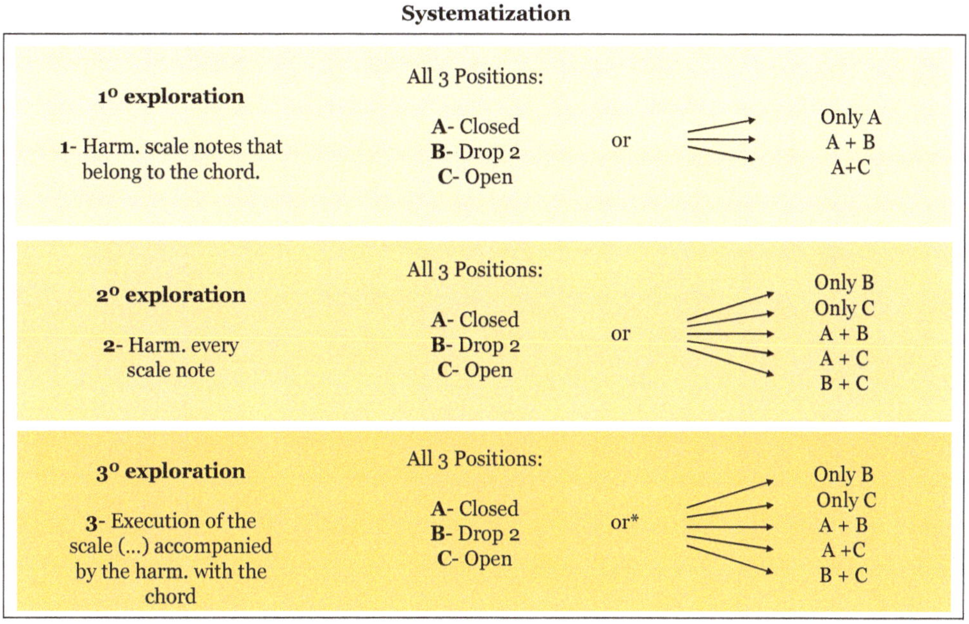

Systematization

	All 3 Positions:			
1º exploration 1- Harm. scale notes that belong to the chord.	A- Closed B- Drop 2 C- Open	or	→	Only A A + B A+C
2º exploration 2- Harm. every scale note	A- Closed B- Drop 2 C- Open	or	→	Only B Only C A + B A + C B + C
3º exploration 3- Execution of the scale (...) accompanied by the harm. with the chord	A- Closed B- Drop 2 C- Open	or*	→	Only B Only C A + B A +C B + C

*If ≠ 2nd exploration.

Fig. 2.10: Scheme of systematisation of the experiments of the second group.

Thus, regarding systematisation, if all explorations of a given experiment are ergonomically viable, the set of results obtained will contemplate the exploration of all positions and forms of articulation defined by the two sets of invariants that make up the delimitation.

Creative Application

The proposed creative application intends to use the contents resulting from the experiments in the form of composition. As an example, the creative application of the results of experiments with dominant chords articulated with the Lydian Dominant Scale will be exposed below.

This creative study has the C Lydian Flat Seventh Scale as its central tonality and is based on the articulation between melodies elaborated from this scale and the dominant tetrad formed by the harmonisation of its first-degree. However, chords of the dominant type (flat seventh) from different degrees and/or belonging to other tones and harmonic fields are used. This intentional use of different contents and assumptions of the LCCTO in the same composition is in line with what was previously defined in my research, in the sense of favouring and gradually intensifying the transversality of the addressed subjects. In this logic, the composition has dominant chords such as G7sus4 (measure 14) and G7(#5) (measures 14 and 15), coming respectively from the harmonic fields of the Lydian scale (second-degree) and Lydian Flat Augmented (fifth degree augmented). It also has chromatic passages in the melody and a Lydian major seventh chord in C#maj7/9(#11).

The musical instrument used to record the composition was a five-string electro-acoustic bass. In contrast to the solid body of the conventional electric bass, the instrument has a resonance box that adds a peculiar tone to the instrument, even with the traditional electric pickup and electronic circuit. Another differential of the electroacoustic bass is its strings, composed of a metallic alloy formed mainly by bronze. The tuning used, starting from the highest string, follows the order: C, G, D, A, E.

Video 2.6. Video of author demonstrating the creative application: articulation between the Lydian Flat Seventh Scale and the dominant chord of the first degree, uploaded by Fausto Lessa, 5 February 2022. https://hdl.handle.net/20.500.12434/56e02acf

2. Experimentation as a Learning Method

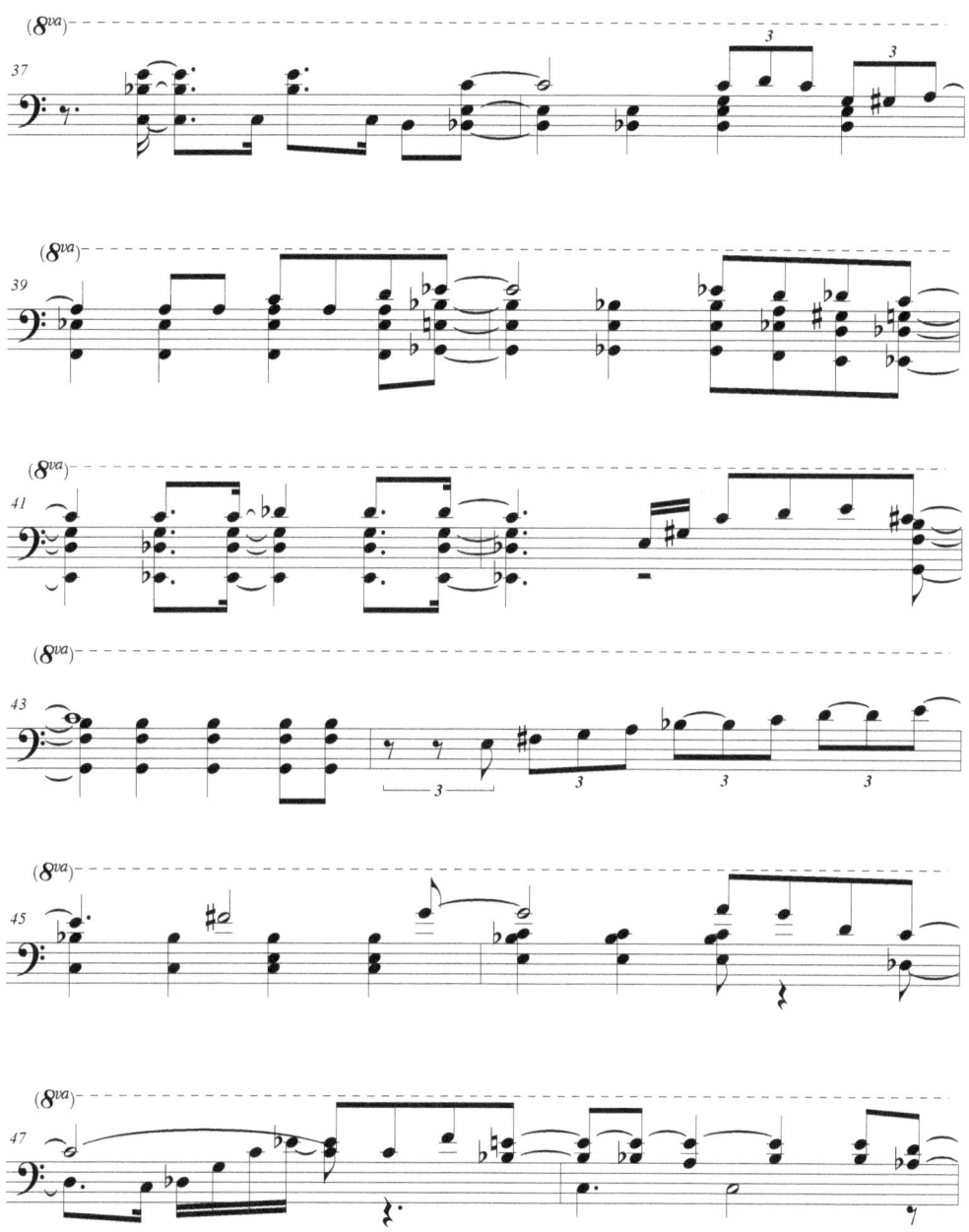

Fig. 2.11: Creative application: results from the articulation between the Lydian Flat Seventh Scale and the dominant chord of the first degree.

Third Group—Harmonic Relationships between the Chords from the Harmonic Fields of the Principal Scales of the LCCTO

The harmonic relationships were explored in two fashions. The first was between chords from the same primary modal tonic degree of the different principal scales of the LCCTO. The second was between chords from different degrees and scales, exploring the alternate and conceptual modal tonic degrees, according to LCCTO. The example shown next deals with the chords from primary modal tonic I.

Referring to the research design, the first procedure is to choose the premise to be articulated with the harmonic approach of the electric bass. In this exemplification, it will be the harmonic relationship between the primary modal tonic chords. From the statement of this task begins the attunement process. The intention was to play, in a sequence established by the tonal-gravity principle (from close to distant), each chord and principal scale of the first degree, aiming to display and internalise their sonority.

Attunement

Video 2.7. Video of author demonstrating the articulation between LCCTO's principal scales and chords from the first degree—closed position, uploaded by Fausto Lessa, 16 May 2022. https://hdl.handle.net/20.500.12434/3636d83c

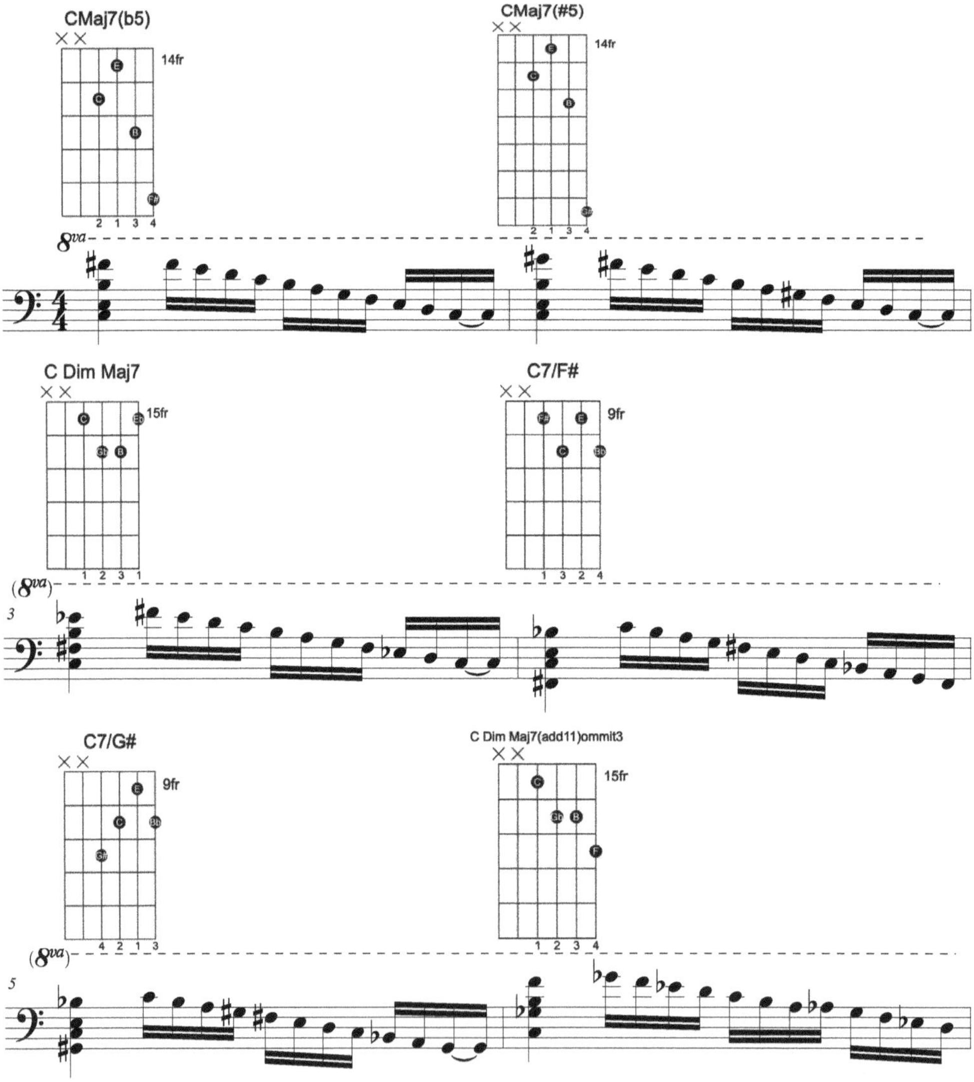

Fig. 2.12: Articulation between LCCTO's principal scales and chords from the first—degree—closed position.

Having the result of this first exploration, the experiment goes to the next process, the calibration. In this process, the chords from other degrees were explored using different voicings and scale patterns. Since the chords from the first degree were explored exclusively in the closed position, the other chords will use a different voicing type or a combination of voicings. The example below (Video 2.8 and Fig. 2.13) explores the chords from the second degree in a mix of drop 2 and open position.

Video 2.8. Video of author demonstrating the articulation between LCCTO's principal scales and chords from the second degree, uploaded by Fausto Lessa, 28 November 2022. https://hdl.handle.net/20.500.12434/35b6eccf

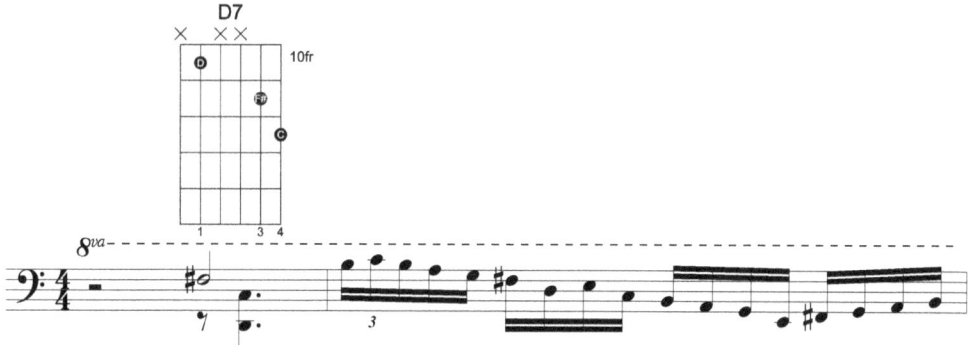

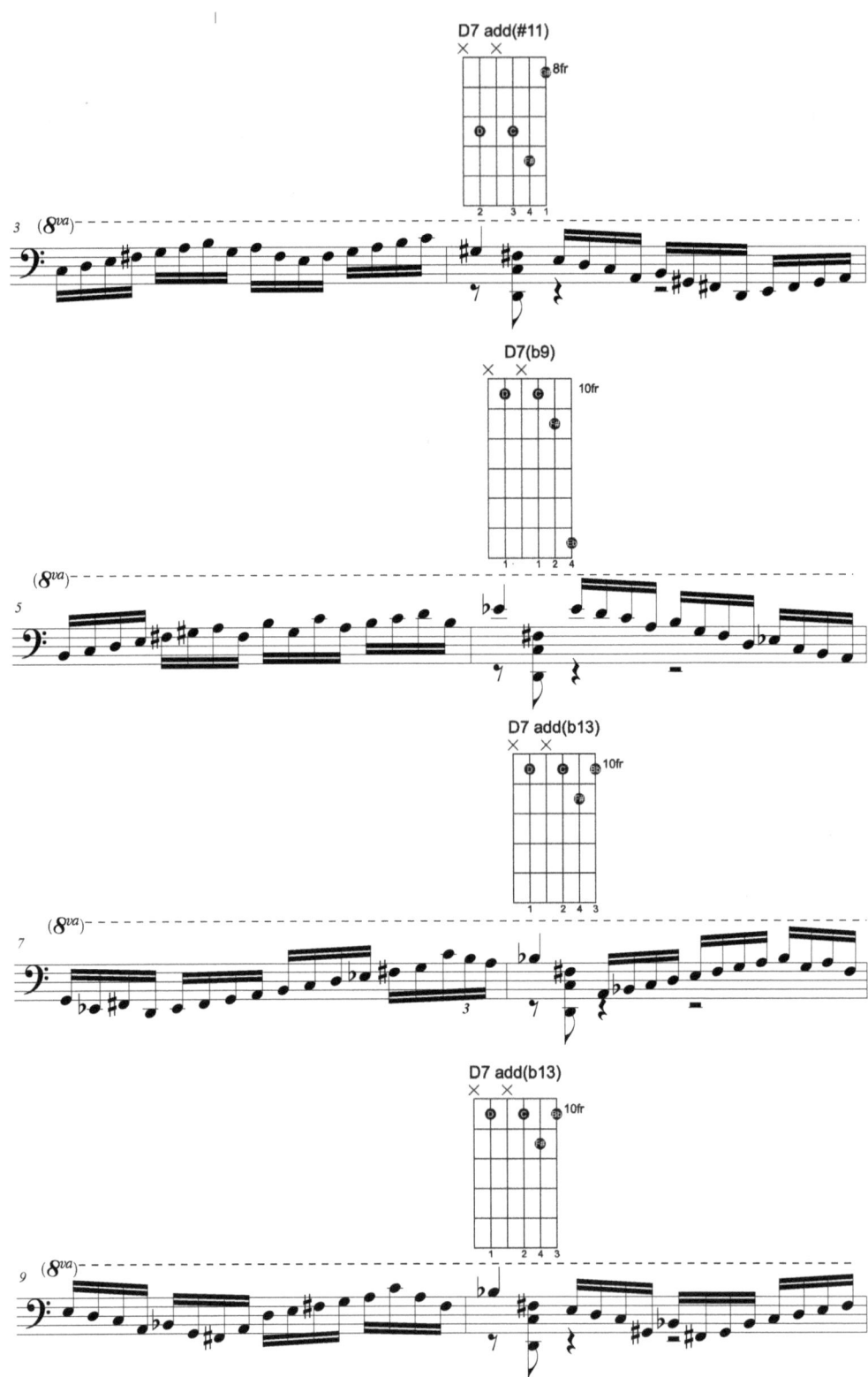

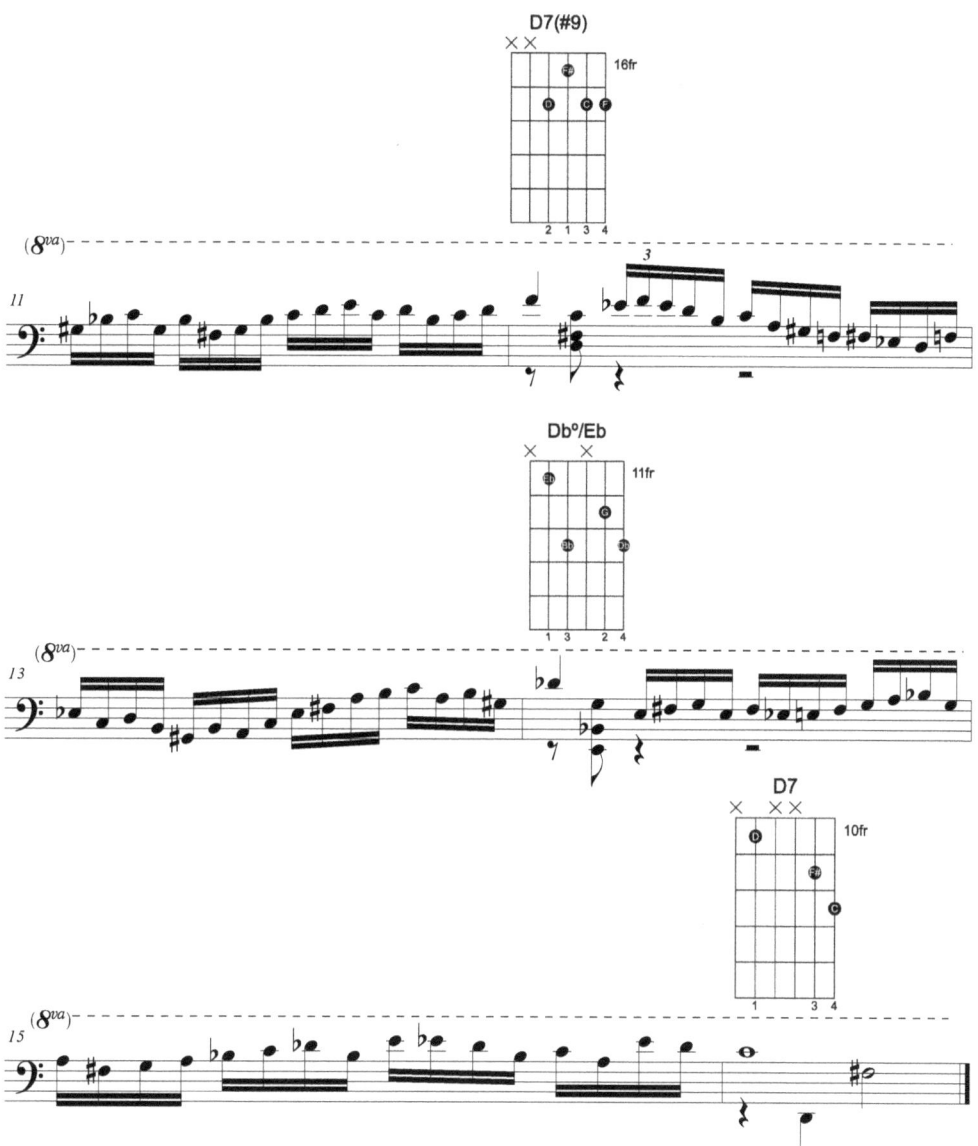

Fig. 2.13: Articulation between LCCTO's principal scales and chords from the second—degree.

Each degree explored has its own creative application. The invariant for the systematisation for this group of experiments was, obviously, the scale degree. The score below portrays the result of this application for the first degree.

Video 2.9. Video of author demonstrating the creative application: results from the articulation between LCCTO's principal scales and chords from the first degree, uploaded by Fausto Lessa, 28 November 2022. https://hdl.handle.net/20.500.12434/0dd3a1d7

2. Experimentation as a Learning Method

Fig. 2.14: Creative Application: results from the articulation between LCCTO's principal scales and chords from the first—degree.

Considerations and Conclusions

Applying the concept of affordances to musical practice with a focus on technical development and creation proves to be convenient and productive. The proposed research design, also based on the perceptual learning and development theory, is an instrument with potential yet to be explored and discussed.

The results of these artistic experiments, even considering the qualitative character of the explorations, were numerous. The set of results from the first group of experiments add up to more than a thousand diagrams representing ways of playing chords on the electric bass. The second and third groups of artistic experiments also bring together a considerable amount of articulation patterns between chords and scales, as well as harmonic relationships. The perception/action loop appears to be limited only by creativity, intention, and attention, thus constituting a versatile and individualised tool for musical learning and development.

The creative applications also have a didactic purpose. Initially conceived to assess the musical applicability of the results obtained in the experiments, these syntheses of the results can be seen as musical studies. From this perspective, the teaching-learning activity related to the harmonic approach of the electric bass can benefit, diverting the route from mechanical learning of repetition of exercises with scales to the path of assimilation of contents associated with musical practice, creation, and interpretation.

Finally, I believe that this material that I am producing from the artistic experiments, namely the harmonic vocabulary content for the electric bass, could have several uses: as teaching material, for those bass players who wish to learn or develop this instrument's potential; to consolidate the position of the electric bass as a harmonic instrument; and for composers, as a reference book, if they wish to compose musical works in which the electric bass has a harmonic approach. I also think that the research design I created can contribute to investigations that propose the development of unconventional techniques (extended techniques) for playing instruments other than the electric bass.

References

Carello, Claudia and Michael T. Turvey, 'Physics and Psychology of the Muscle Sense', *Current Directions in Psychological Science*, 13.1 (2004), 25–28, https://doi.org/10.1111/j.0963-7214.2004.01301007.x

Covarrubias, Pablo, Ángel A. Jiménez, Felipe Cabrera, and Alan Costall, 'The Senses Considered as Perceptual Systems: The Revolutionary Ideas of Gibson's 1966 Book, 50 Years Later – part 1', *Ecological Psychology*, 29.2 (2017), 69–71, https://doi.org/10.1080/10407413.2017.1297680

Fajen, Brett R., Michael A. Riley and Michael T. Turvey, 'Information, Affordances, and the Control of Action in Sport', *International Journal of Sport Psychology*, 40 (2009), 79–107

Gibson, Eleanor Jack and Anne D. Pick, *Perceptual Learning and Development: An Ecological Approach* (New York: Oxford University Press, 2000)

Gibson, James Jerome, *The Ecological Approach to Visual Perception* (Boston: Houghton Mifflin, 1979)

Jacobs, David and Claire Michaels, 'Direct Learning', *Ecological Psychology*, 19.4 (2007), 321–49, https://doi.org/10.1080/10407410701432337

Jamone, Lorenzo, Emre Ugur, Angelo Cangelosi, Luciano Fadiga, Alexandre Bernardino, Justus Piater, and José Santos-Victor, 'Affordances in Psychology, Neuroscience, and Robotics: A Survey', *IEEE Transactions on Cognitive and Developmental Systems*, 10.1 (2018), 4–25, https://doi.org/10.1109/TCDS.2016.2594134

Khatibi, Mina and Razieh Sheikholeslami, 'Gibson's Ecological Theory of Development and Affordances: A Brief Review', *The International Journal of Indian Psychology*, 2.4 (2015), 140–44

Lee, David N., 'General Tau theory: evolution to date', *Perception*, 38.6 (2009), 837–50, https://doi.org/10.1068/pmklee

Lobo, Lorena, Manuel Heras-Escribano, and David Travieso, 'The History and Philosophy of Ecological Psychology', *Frontiers in Psychology*, 9.2228 (2018), 1–15, https://doi.org/10.3389/fpsyg.2018.02228

Marquez-Borbon, Adnan, 'Perceptual Learning and the Emergence of Performer-Instrument Interactions with Digital Music Systems', *A Body of Knowledge* (2018), 2—23, https://escholarship.org/uc/item/5p45g68p

Norman, Donald Arthur, *The Design of Everyday Things* (New York: Basic Books, 1988)

Richardson, Michael, J., Kevin Shockley, Brett R. Fajen, Michael A. Ryley, and Michael T. Turvey, 'Ecological Psychology: Six Principles for an Embodied-Embedded Approach to Behavior', in *Handbook of Cognitive Science: An Embodied Approach*, ed. by Paco Calvo and Tony Gomila (Amsterdam: Elsevier, 2008), 159–87, https://doi.org/10.1016/B978-0-08-046616-3.00009-8

Russell, George, *Lydian Chromatic Concept of Tonal Organization: Volume 1: The Art and Science of Tonal Gravity, Fourth Edition* (Brookline: Concept Publishing, 2001)

Szokolszky, Agnes, Catherine Read, Zsolt Palatinus, Kinga Palatinus, 'Ecological Approaches to Perceptual Learning: Learning to Perceive and Perceiving as Learning', *Adaptive Behavior*, 27.6 (2019), 363–88

Szokolszky, Agnes, 'Perceiving Metaphors: An Approach from Developmental Ecological Psychology', *Metaphor and Symbol*, 34.1 (2019), 17–32, https://doi.org/10.1080/10926488.2019.1591724

Travieso, David and others, 'Dynamic Touch as Common Ground for Enactivism and Ecological Psychology', *Frontiers in Psychology*, 11.1257 (2020), 1–10, https://doi.org/10.3389/fpsyg.2020.01257

Turvey, Michael T. and Robert E. Shaw, 'Ecological Foundations of Cognition: I. Symmetry and Specificity of Animal–Environment Systems', *Journal of Consciousness Studies*, 6 (1999), 95–110

Waters, Simon, 'Performance Ecosystems: Ecological Approaches to Musical Interaction', *Electroacoustic Music Studies Network* (2007), 1–20, http://www.ems-network.org/spip.php?article278

Windsor, W. Luke and Christophe de Bézenac, 'Music and Affordances', *Musicae Scientiae*, 16.1 (2012), 102–20, https://doi.org/10.1177/1029864911435734

Withagen, Rob and Margot Van Wermeskerken, 'Individual Differences in Learning to Perceive Length by Dynamic Touch: Evidence for Variation in Perceptual Learning Capacities', *Attention Perception & Psychophysics*, 71.1 (2009), 64–75, https://doi.org/10.3758/APP.71.1.64

3. Finding Voice: Developing Student Autonomy from Imitation to Performer Agency

Mikael Bäckman

Introduction

Across the past twenty years, artistic research has offered new approaches to the study of artistic process. This development can be divided in two types: those that study individual process and those who study collaborative process.[1,2] In Blom et al, such study of individual artistic process is also found to have implications for education, since '[t]he process of engaging in, reflecting and analyzing, writing, and feeding back into one's own arts practice and teaching is, itself, an 'artistic action research' model that contributes to the discipline area as well as the development of the individual artist-academic'.[3] This chapter unfolds such a process of applying artistic research findings in teaching in Higher Music Education.

Since the implementation of the Bologna process, there is an expectation that teachers in higher music education (henceforth HME) should promote student autonomy and lifelong learning.[4] Previous research suggests that informal learning

---

1 Concerning study of individual process, see for example Sten Sandell, 'På Insidan Av Tystnaden: En Undersökning' (PhD thesis, Göteborgs Universitet, Art Monitor, 2013). See also Paul Craenen, *Composing Under the Skin: The Music-Making Body at the Composer's Desk* (Leuven: Leuven University Press, 2014).

2 Concerning study of collaborative process, see Henrik Frisk and Stefan Östersjö, *(re)Thinking Improvisation: Artistic Explorations and Conceptual Writing* (Lund University, Elanders Sverige AB, 2013). Paul Roe, 'A Phenomenology of Collaboration in Contemporary Composition and Performance' (unpublished doctoral thesis, University of York, 2007). Stefan Östersjö, 'Shut Up 'N' Play: Negotiating the Musical Work' (PhD thesis, Lund University, Media-Tryck, 2008).

3 Diana Blom, Dawn Bennett and David Wright, 'How Artists Working in Academia View Artistic Practice as Research: Implications for Tertiary Music Education', *International Journal of Music Education*, 29(4), (2011), 359–73 (p. 369), https://doi.org/10.1177/0255761411421088

4 European Ministers Responsible for Higher Education, 'London Communiqué: Towards the European Higher Education Area: Responding to Changes in a Globalised World' (2007), http://www.ehea.

practices are effective tools in order to enable student autonomy.[5] An important aspect of informal learning is that, unlike traditional learning, there are no definable goals, the ends are not defined in advance.[6] This has the implication that the student can be involved in planning the content of the learning experience, to take charge of their own learning, thus leading to meta-cognitive skills such as learning about learning (as discussed above in Chapter One), and finding lifelong learning strategies.[7] In such a learning situation, the teacher's role is 'mainly to assist students to become aware of their strengths and weaknesses in relation to future challenges'.[8] In order to help the student to obtain lifelong learning strategies, the teacher must meet the student where s/he is, and adapt the content to each individual.[9]

In what follows, I will attempt to explore how results from my artistic research project may be applied in my own teaching.[10] Through my practice as a harmonica player, I have investigated how a personal expression, or voice, may emerge from a process initiated by transcription and imitation. The aim of the project was to explore the transformation of a performer's voice through a process of transcribing and practicing solos by the iconic harmonica player Charlie McCoy. When applying my findings from this artistic research project in my teaching in HME, the challenge was to initiate a similar process with my students, with the aim of promoting student autonomy and lifelong learning. So how does the idea of copying someone's playing relate to student autonomy? The answer may lie in informal learning practices, since they 'may allow students to develop a degree of musical autonomy as well as experimenting with and formulating their own unique musical voice'.[11] Up until the inclusion of jazz studies in HME, the only way to learn how to play was through informal learning.[12] The same goes for Blues and Country music. Today, 'it could be said that the jazz tradition underwent

---

info/Upload/document/ministerial_declarations/2007_London_Communique_English_588697.pdf, p. 2.

5 See, for example, Cecilia K. Hultberg, 'Artistic Processes in Music Performance. A Research Area Calling for Inter-Disciplinary Collaboration', *Swedish Journal of Music Research/Svensk Tidskrift för Musikforskning*, 95 (2013), 79-94. See also Phil Jenkins, 'Project Muse: Formal and Informal Music Educational Practices', *Philosophy of Music Education Review*, 19:2 (2011), 179-97.

6 Phil Jenkins, 'Project Muse: Formal and Informal Music Educational Practices', *Philosophy of Music Education Review*, 19.2 (2011), p. 179-97.

7 Susan Hallam, 'The Development of Metacognition in Musicians: Implications for Education', *British Journal of Music Education*, 18.1 (2001), p. 27–39.

8 Nadia Moberg and Eva Georgii-Hemming, 'Musicianship—discursive constructions of autonomy and independence within music performance programmes'. Proceedings of the Conference 'Becoming Musicians. Student Involvement and Teacher Collaboration in Higher Music Education', Oslo, October 2018, ed. by Stefan Gies and Jon Helge Sætre ([n.p.]: NMH publications, 2019) pp. 67–88.

9 Rineke Smilde, 'Change and the Challenges of Lifelong Learning', in *Life in the Real World: How to Make Music Graduates Employable*, ed. by Dawn Bennett (Champaign, IL: Common Ground Publishing, 2012), p. 99–123.

10 This artistic research project was developed and carried out for my PhD thesis in Musical Performance.

11 Juliet Hess, 'Finding the "both/and": Balancing informal and formal music learning', *International Journal of Music Education*, 38:3 (2020), 441–55 (p. 451).

12 See, for example, Paul F. Berliner, *Thinking in Jazz. The Infinite Art of Improvisation* (Chicago: University of Chicago Press, 1994).

a change for the worse when it became a subject formally studied in schools'.[13] This formalization of how you learn how to play jazz, at the expense of the traditional informal way of learning, has been critiqued.[14] There is a paucity of studies concerning this shift from informal to formal regarding Country music and Blues within HME, most likely since they entered the world of HME at a much later stage. However, as a musician mostly active within the field of Country music and Blues, I would argue that those genres run the risk of being institutionalized, in the same way as one may argue that Jazz has been.

This chapter builds on an analytical perspective, informed by embodied music cognition, and engages with concepts of voice and affordance to try to clarify these processes. According to the research paradigm 'embodied music cognition' (EMC), the involvement of our body is central to understanding our interaction with music.[15] EMC builds on embodied-cognition theories and applies them to music. I view *voice* as the sum of all the choices a musician makes—choices that become patterns, which, in turn, make a musician unique.[16] For a further discussion of voice, see Mikael Bäckman.[17] In order to fully understand a musician's voice, one needs to engage with the concept of affordances. This concept originates from James Gibson and his work in ecological psychology, where he argues that we perceive objects based on how we can use them, i.e., what they afford us.[18] This is a relational concept, since objects do not afford the same thing to different animals or, indeed, different humans. This is easily applicable to musical instruments, as a harmonica in the hands of a professional affords many things that is unavailable for a beginner (see also Chapter 2 of this book).

In what follows, I show how the transformation of voice took place within my own artistic practice, with a particular attention to challenges I came across. Furthermore, I will show how I have applied my method in my teaching in HME, focusing on students' challenges.[19] I will also briefly touch upon the impact of the affordance of the diatonic harmonica in this specific voice transformation process. In the first section, I will describe the overall method of my artistic research project. Then I will present the preliminary artistic results, giving extra attention to two examples where my method encountered challenges. In the next section, I will describe and present some tentative results from my educational study. Once again, I will put the spotlight on what proved to be difficult, this time focusing on the challenges that my students experienced. In

---

13 Jenkins, p. 195.
14 See, for example, Eitan Wilf, *School for Cool: The Academic Jazz Programme and the Paradox of Institutionalized Creativity* (Chicago: University of Chicago Press, 2014).
15 Marc Leman, Luc Nijs, Pieter-Jan Maes and Edith Van Dyck, 'What is Embodied Music Cognition?', *Springer Handbook of systematic Musicology*, ed. Rolf Bader (Berlin: Springer, 2017), 747–60.
16 Naomi Cumming, *The Sonic Self: Musical Subjectivity and Signification* (Bloomington: Indiana University Press, 2000).
17 Mikael Bäckman, 'In Search of My Voice', *Music & Practice*, 10 (2023), unpaginated.
18 James J. Gibson, *The Ecological Approach to Visual Perception* (New York: Psychology Press, 1979).
19 I have worked as a lecturer at The School of Music in Piteå at the Luleå University of Technology, Sweden, since 2005, teaching harmonica, music history, ensemble, and music theory.

the final section, I will discuss the challenges that my students and I encountered and reflect on how the similarities and differences of these challenges relate to our various experiences as musicians.

A Performative Study of Idiolect

This chapter is based on the results of my artistic research project, as well as a qualitative study of my teaching in HME. The first stage of my project was to immerse myself in the playing style of country harmonica legend Charlie McCoy. McCoy has been active as a session musician, as well as a recording and performing artist, since the early 1960s. He has recorded more than 14,000 sessions during his still-ongoing career.[20] I transcribed McCoy's first thirteen albums as a featured artist, representing his recorded output during the 1960s up until 1978.[21] These transcriptions were notated, more specifically, written down in a tablature notation. The transcriptions were also aural, i.e., I learned to play the transcriptions along with the original recordings. This was a very important part of the process, since this is how I attempted to embody the idiolect of McCoy. Based on these transcriptions, McCoy's playing style, particularly the charting of his musical idiolect, was analysed. From this analysis, a number of frequently occurring licks and strategies were identified. I argue that these licks are important features of McCoy's idiolect. In addition to the transcriptions, in-depth interviews were conducted—with McCoy as well as two other prominent country harmonica players: Buddy Greene and Mike Caldwell. The aim of these interviews was to test the accuracy of my analysis. With McCoy's licks as a point of departure, I have created my own variations of these. This lick-creation process was documented with video/audio recordings.[22] This journey, from analysis to creation, is the focus of my artistic research project. In the next section, I will present my artistic results, thus far. I will also present a few challenges I encountered.

Results

The first part of my artistic research project was to transcribe and imitate the harmonica playing of Charlie McCoy. The analysis of those transcriptions, combined with the results from the interview with McCoy, as well as the interviews with Caldwell and Greene, informed me in two ways. Firstly, I became quite knowledgeable concerning McCoy's idiolect, not only in an analytical way, but also in a very practical way since I learned to play my transcriptions. One might say that I became proficient at McCoy's

---

20   Margie Goldsmith, *Masters of Harmonica* (Alpharetta, GA: Mountain Arbor Press, 2019), p. 165.
21   Not including his work as a session player during this time period.
22   Examples of this documentation are stored in the online 'Research Catalogue', an international and non-commercial database for artistic research. See https://www.researchcatalogue.net/profile/show-exposition?exposition=1964122

idiolect, both intellectually and in musical practice. Second, since McCoy's playing has been, and still is, so influential, mapping his idiolect also functions as an audit of country harmonica playing in general. The mapping is thus not only of an idiolect, but also a significant mapping of country harmonica playing from the 1960s and onwards. This mapping was important for the next phase of my project; when I created new licks, I had an embodied knowledge of what was innovative and what was derivative.

The results thus far are twofold. First, I came up with results that are musicological, i.e., the transcriptions and my analysis of McCoy's idiolect based on said transcriptions and complementary interviews. Second, based on the knowledge I gained through interviews and transcriptions, I have sought to transform my own artistic voice as a country harmonica player, thus producing artistic results. In what follows, I will describe how the musicological results have inspired and informed my artistic results.

As described above, my artistic research project has provided me with a thorough mapping of McCoy's idiolect. This has resulted in two publications, one of those focuses specifically on how McCoy found his own style, by relating to his influences. These influences were mainly other musicians—guitarists, fiddle players, and pedal steel guitarists—that McCoy worked with in the recording studios of Nashville. Therefore, the role of instruments other than the harmonica in this process is discussed in the paper.[23] The other publication presents McCoy's idiolect in a more artistic way; it is an audio paper, which also deals with how I have used my McCoy idiolect study to transform my own voice.[24]

Another result was my creative process of lick generation. I chose 10 McCoy licks, using these as starting points to create original material. I devoted a practice session to each of these McCoy licks, which I documented with video and audio recordings. In each session, I played a McCoy lick verbatim, over and over, until my inner hearing presented, or rather suggested, a variation of this lick. I played that variation and, if it was to my liking, I continued to play this new lick over and over until I came up with a variation of that lick. This process produced more than 200 new licks based on McCoy's original licks (see Figure 3.1). The goal of each session was to let the original McCoy lick inspire me to create variations, thus creating licks which are no longer McCoy's but, instead, my own original material. Important to note here is that each of these ten licks have many variants in McCoy's output. In other words, my variations on McCoy's licks can also be seen as a logical continuation of what he himself has been doing throughout his career. McCoy has recorded licks he liked, and, at later recordings, these licks have recured, usually slightly changed. I, in my turn, have identified McCoy licks which I like, then I have consciously changed them. However, that is only the beginning. As I now implement these licks in my playing with my

---

23 Mikael Bäckman, 'The Real McCoy. Tracking the Development of Charlie McCoy's Playing Style', *International Country Music Journal* (2022), 184–231.
24 Mikael Bäckman, 'In Search of My Voice', *Music and Practice*, 10 (2023), unpaginated, DOI: 10.32063/1012

band 'John Henry', my licks are sometimes being altered as I improvise my solos.[25] Sometimes I start out playing a lick and, as I am playing it, I hear a new way to resolve the phrase. This might be inspired by what someone else in the band is playing, or the chord changes of the song, or the groove we are playing, or someone's previous solo in the song. In the moment of playing the lick, I am usually unaware of what inspires me to make a change, it is a very intuitive process which draws upon all my embodied knowledge as a musician. The number of licks produced is significant since, in the next phase of my project, I commenced to practice my own licks, embodying them in my bag of licks. Therefore, I would consider a session successful if it produced many variations on the original McCoy lick. As can be seen in Figure 3.1 below, some licks were more productive than others.

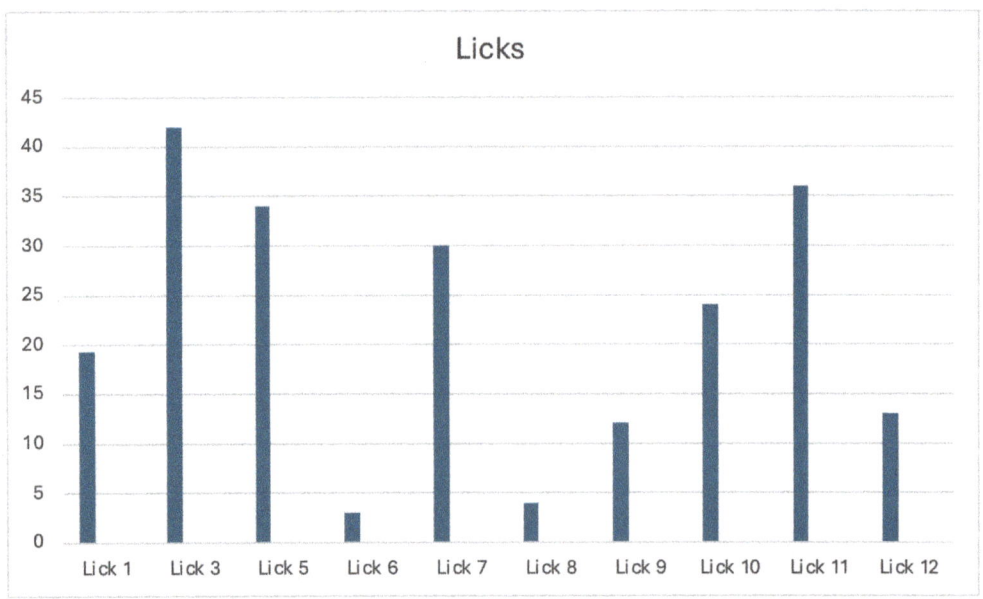

Fig. 3.1: Overview of the 10 McCoy licks I chose with the intent of creating original licks inspired by the original recordings. Lick 2 and 4 are omitted since I chose not to engage with those.

When I transcribed McCoy's playing, I realized that certain licks were reminiscent of pedal steel guitar playing. This suspicion of mine was confirmed during the interview with McCoy, where he pointed out that his style is based on adapting licks by other

---

25 For examples of documentation of my playing during my artistic research project, see the following YouTube videos: 'Turn the Cards Slowly', uploaded by BD Pop, 11 March 2021, https://www.youtube.com/watch?v=5VChN5y_dKI; 'Roly Poly', 11 March 2021, uploaded by BD Pop, https://www.youtube.com/watch?v=fAf8VJibMMw; 'Turn the Cards Slowly', uploaded by John Henry, 12 November 2021, https://www.youtube.com/watch?v=zfTqqOYsn-Q; 'Flip That Rock', uploaded by John Henry, 12 November 2021, https://www.youtube.com/watch?v=w4QW9AcAWB4. Also, for the main artistic output of my PhD thesis, see John Henry, 'Lucky Luck', *Spotify* album, uploaded by John Henry, https://open.spotify.com/artist/2V9BG3gxbAY6QZEQ76c7tm?si=4yMsHA_0RL2P9Zv5t-ryGA

typical country instruments, the pedal steel guitar being one of them, to the harmonica. As I realized that I was very fond of playing these pedal steel-like licks I found in my transcriptions, I decided to do what McCoy had done, i.e., transcribe pedal steel solos and licks. This proved to be quite fruitful; it produced very interesting licks when I adapted the original solos and licks to work with the affordances of the diatonic harmonica. Rather than taking the detour of transcribing a harmonica player's version of pedal steel licks, I cut out the middleman and went straight to the source, i.e., the pedal steel. Niklas Lundblad and Fredrik Stjernberg write about the distinction between emulation and imitation.[26] When emulating, X does what Y did to achieve a specific goal. Emulating means that X focuses on what specifically led Y to achieve that goal. When imitating, by contrast, X does what Y did, duplicating not only the behaviour that specifically led to the achievement of the desired goal but also other behaviours.[27] In my project, I would consider learning to play McCoy's solos an act of imitation. However, transcribing pedal steel solos—since the interviews revealed to me that this was McCoy's method—is an act of emulation. I am, at the same time, imitating pedal steel playing and emulating Charlie McCoy.

Another type of lick which McCoy has recorded on a few occasions, is his harmonica adaptation of a vocal yodel.[28] McCoy's yodels occur in songs originally performed by Jimmie Rodgers and Hank Williams. When I practise these yodel-licks, I use a technique known as corner switching, taught to me by Robert Bonfiglio, which makes them more accessible on the harmonica.[29] During the interview, McCoy confirmed that he does not use the same technique as me, which might explain why he has not explored the concept of yodelling on the harmonica in more depth than he has. It made me realise that this is a perfect area for me to delve deeper into. So, once again, I stopped taking the detour of transcribing a harmonica player's imitation of the original source, i.e., the yodels, and started transcribing the vocal yodels themselves. In other words, I chose the path of emulation rather than imitation. Some yodels work quite well on the harmonica without the need to adapt them. However, most of them need to be altered to make them work well with the affordances of the harmonica. I found that the most interesting sound is when I can use chromaticism, playing with portamento through bending notes. This transformation, adapting the vocal source to fit the affordances of the harmonica, has been a very rewarding negotiation that has taught me much about my instrument, what it offers, and what it resists.

One of McCoy's most significant contributions to the field of country harmonica playing is his use of the so-called 'country-tuned' harmonica. McCoy did not invent

---

26 Niklas Berild Lundblad and Fredrik Stjernberg, *Frågvisare. Människans viktigaste verktyg* (Stockholm: Volante, 2021), p. 44.
27 Ibid.
28 'Yodeling is a series of rapid changes (breaks) between Overdrive in fuller density and Neutral in falsetto. These singers often use note leaps of sixths or sevenths.' Catherine Sadolin, *Complete Vocal Technique* (Copenhagen: CVI Publications, 2021), p. 306.
29 Robert Bonfiglio, b. 1950, is the world's premier classical harmonica player.

this tuning, but he is the first to record with it; hence, he is responsible for disseminating this tuning throughout the harmonica world. McCoy uses this tuning to make the affordances of the harmonica better fit his musical needs. The country tuning turned out to be especially applicable on the dominant chord. In my own playing, I found the major supertonic chord to be a challenge, where the harmonica resisted more than it offered.[30] Since this chord is quite common in Western Swing, I realised there might be a need to change the affordances of my instrument. Therefore, I started exploring a tuning I had devised in 2019, which I call Western Swing tuning. This tuning alters the affordances of the harmonica and offers the same advantages on the supertonic chord that the country-tuned harmonica does on the dominant chord.

Difficulties

Having described the results of my artistic research project in the previous section, I will now move on to present some challenges experienced by myself and by the students. Whereas some of the practice sessions I did based on McCoy licks generated more than forty new original licks, two of the sessions produced less than five new versions (see Fig. 3.1). In this section, I will direct my focus to these two, less fruitful, lick-generating sessions.

Lick Eight

Video 3.1. Video of author documenting lick-generation session eight, https://hdl.handle.net/20.500.12434/f09a5320

When I start lick-generation session eight, as in all my sessions, I verbally define the lick which I am about to start working on. In this particular session, I start out by stating that lick eight '…is not as clearly defined as some of the other licks…' (0.19). After some hesitation, I define lick eight as 'a descending motion followed by an ascending interval jump [leap]' (0.35). Most sessions last for approximately twenty minutes, and some licks were explored in two or more such sessions. Lick eight's session, however, only lasted for fourteen minutes, then I gave up. At one point in the session, after several fruitless attempts at creating an interesting new lick, I simply state that 'hmmm, that just sounds like Charlie' (03.41). In most of these sessions, an interesting variation of McCoy's original lick arrives within the first minute or two.

---

30   For example, an A major chord in the key of G major.

With lick eight, it took more than nine minutes to produce the first variation that I found to be worthy of preservation. Watching the video recording of the session, it is clear that I am quite ambivalent about that new lick, stating that 'Not sure if I like it or not, but yeah, maybe' (10.49).

At 14.34, the camera's battery ran out and interrupted the session. While replacing the battery, I realise that this lick is a dead-end and decide not to resume the session. When listening back to these four licks at the time of writing this chapter, approximately two years after the session, I find these less than impressive. Even after practising and performing my corpus of new licks for nearly two years' time, I still found a vast majority of these licks to be to my liking. The licks derived from lick eight however, are not quite up to scratch. One reason this lick failed to produce more material might be the somewhat unclear definition of the McCoy lick itself. In most cases during these sessions, I had a clear lick, or strategy, to work with. The licks had a solid construction, yet they were easy to turn into malleable material. However, when the original lick seemed to lack such clarity, it paradoxically lacked the ability to become malleable. It was almost as if the licks that produced many variations were made from clay with a perfect texture. The clay was not too hard, which would have made it difficult to shape it into new forms. On the other hand, it was hard enough not only to have an original shape, but also to maintain the shape I altered them into.

Lick Six

Video 3.2. Video of author documenting lick-generation session six, https://hdl.handle.net/20.500.12434/8ef03205

Lick six is played over a II-V-I progression, and it was the least productive of all my lick-creation sessions. The first lick took approximately three minutes to come up with, but then it took almost ten minutes to produce the next one. Even though this session lasted for twenty minutes, it only produced three new licks. However, unlike lick eight, the licks produced during this session were to my liking, and I have found versions of them popping up in my playing ever since they were first discovered. However, when the session was over, I had a feeling that I had not been creating, but rather that I was playing, or perhaps constructing, an exercise.[31] In other words, I was struggling to find

---

31 Not unlike what you can find in a how-to-play-jazz instruction book. See, for example, Jamie Aebersold, *How to Play Jazz and Improvise* (New Albany, NY: Jamey Aebersold Jazz Inc, 1992).

creative material. What I came up with sounded correct over the chord changes, but most of what I played did not excite me.

One possible reason for the meagre output of lick-session six might be that I am playing over a predefined chord progression, which may have limited my imagination. In other sessions, I would hear a chord or chord progression in my mind, but I would allow myself to be free to make changes to that progression as a new lick developed. However, during this session, I was locked into a set chord progression. Another possible reason for the relative failure of the session is related to the affordances of the harmonica. As stated in the section concerning my Western Swing-tuned harmonica, the major supertonic is, when playing in second position on a diatonic harmonica, quite challenging.[32] Both the tonic and the third of the chord are bent notes, i.e., notes which are not available on the harmonica simply by exhaling or inhaling, hence, an extended technique is required. This very limitation is why I designed the Western Swing-tuned harmonica, but unfortunately, I did not use that tuning in this particular session. In other words, playing the major supertonic with a regular country-tuned harmonica has its limitations, and this I believe to be one reason why I was having trouble coming up with creative material in this session. I am not saying that it cannot be done, Charlie McCoy has played very well over a major supertonic chord countless times, however, in this session, it was an obstacle for me.

Having examined the difficulties that I encountered in my creative process, I will now direct my focus to my harmonica students and consider the challenges they experienced.

My Harmonica Students

In this section I will describe my HME study with harmonica students. This study resonates well with the goal of the REACT training school, which aimed to encourage artistic creation rather than uncritical imitation (as discussed in Chapter 4 in this book). My goal was not only that students would learn from and be inspired by the transcription of harmonica recordings but that they would not stop there. The aim was to create original material, based on the transcription and imitation. This was, however, not easy for the students, so in this section I will focus on the challenges they encountered. They are, as we shall see, quite different from the challenges I experienced. The above-described method of deliberate transformation of individual voice has constituted my central artistic method. Since this method was found to be productive and useful to me, I have sought to further explore its possibilities for my teaching in HME. However, since my project took place over the timespan of several years, and the students would be working with this concept in a 7.5 credit course, I had to

---

32 Positions are the term used by harmonica players when referring to playing diatonic harmonica in different keys. This is most often done by playing in the various modes which the major scale affords. The most commonly used positions are 2nd (mixolydian), 1st (ionian), and 3rd (dorian).

delimit their endeavour. In my artistic research project, I aimed to transform my artistic voice, which would have been a bit ambitious to achieve in a single course. Hence, I chose to focus on the process of using transcription and imitation as a springboard for artistic creation. In order to explore this further, I created this single-subject course for harmonica students with the aim of exploring how the process of transcription may lead to the formation of original licks. I have conducted one study with five students and a second study with four students.

The course was set up so that the students would do what I have done in my artistic research project, although on a much smaller scale. They were to choose at least one harmonica solo to transcribe. Allowing them to choose solos, as opposed to me selecting the solos for them, was important to ensure that student autonomy played a major role in the course. They chose solos which they are particularly fond of, thus increasing their motivation to devote the many hours which are necessary to transcribe the music played. In the first study, two of the students chose one solo, two chose two solos, and one chose three solos. In the second study, all students chose one solo each. During the transcription process, they were guided by me; they sent me their transcriptions, and I provided them with feedback. Then they had another go at the transcription based on my feedback. After that, we agreed on a final version, which they now had the task of learning to play, along with the original recording, as well as they could. At this point in the course, they are strictly working with imitation. The goal of this process is twofold, 1) they improve their playing technique while striving to play as close to the original as possible. This process allows the students a chance to find the areas where they need to improve. 2) The imitation stage gives them the opportunity to, at least partly, embody the original solo. I provided them with feedback during this process as well. This feedback was mostly concerned with technical advice, e.g., how to perform certain phrases on the harmonica, which techniques to use, and so on. When they played the transcription to the best of their ability, we moved on to the next stage of the course where they chose at least three favourite licks from their transcriptions. Once again, it was important for student autonomy that they choose the licks they wanted to work with. The students were then given the task of creating variations on these licks, i.e., new licks based on the originals from their transcriptions. We initially discussed various possible strategies to create variations, both based on available literature as well as my own experiences of this process.[33]

Preliminary results indicate that this is a fruitful method, however, there are challenges which need to be addressed. It is at this point important to point out that the students who have participated in this study are not enrolled in our regular bachelor's or master's programmes, simply because we have no harmonica students in those programmes at present. This entails a few implications: 1) Students who

---

33 See, for example, Paul F. Berliner, *Thinking in Jazz. The Infinite Art of Improvisation* (Chicago: University of Chicago Press, 1994) and Matt Pivec, 'Maximizing the Benefits of Solo Transcription', *JazzEd*, January (2008), 23–26.

are in the midst of a university education are quite used to reflecting on their own learning process, since this is a natural part of many courses. The harmonica students in my study are not currently active as full-time university students, therefore they tend to be unaccustomed to reflecting on their own learning process. This is a skill which needs practice, and it is difficult to achieve proficiency at this during the rather short time span of a 7.5 credit course.[34] This possible lack of reflective skill may have affected the feedback I received from them in my interviews. 2) The level of playing skills was quite varied amongst these students, and the first study indicated that this type of voice development benefits from a rather high level of instrumental skill. 3) Since eight of these nine students lack a formal music education, they are comfortable with an informal learning situation. A student in our regular bachelor's programmes might feel that a course like this is more informal that what they are used to, since the outcome is not clearly defined in advance.[35] However, several of these students spoke of the value of the high level of structure they imposed on their practising during the course.

Another important aspect is the students desire to actually come up with original material. This is not the goal of every student; some are quite content with learning to play a solo as closely to the original recording as they are capable of. After learning to play that solo, some students had no desire to further explore the possibilities of creating original licks inspired by the transcriptions. They only did so because it was required in the course.

There were a lot of challenges for the students during the course, the hardest and most interesting being the creation of new licks. Three main challenges were brought forth by the students:

Challenge A: Trying to Improve a Lick which is Already Great

All students expressed, in different ways, that it was almost overwhelming to try to create something new from a material which was, in their view, already perfect. They had chosen a favourite solo to transcribe, then selected their very favourite phrases, or licks, from that solo. They felt almost intimidated by the perfection of the original lick, just the thought of changing it ever so slightly was almost considered blasphemy. Student A said 'How can I change this? This is fantastic. Anything I will do [to change the lick] feels like it would just trash this song'.[36] This implies a fear of destroying

---

34   A student is expected to put in 200 hours of work for a 7.5 credit course. Approximately 12 hours consisted of workshops and individual lessons, the remaining time is devoted to individual practice.
35   See Phil Jenkins, 'Project Muse: Formal and Informal Music Educational Practices', *Philosophy of Music Education Review*, 19:2 (2011), 179–97.
36   Group interview, my translation. Original quotation in Swedish: 'Hur ska man kunna göra om det här, det här är ju fantastiskt. Allt jag kommer göra känns ju som att det...bara krascha den här låten.'

something beautiful and replacing it with something of perceived lesser beauty. As student D put it: 'It's good the way it is'.[37]

Challenge B: All the Great Ideas have Already been Played and Recorded

Student D said that 'It's hard to come up with something which hasn't already been done, because the stuff that has been done earlier, you know they sound good…'.[38] It is clear to me, from the interviews and lessons I had with student D, that s/he has studied the genre, in this case blues, well. S/he would quite often refer to various influential blues harmonica players and what they typically play on recordings. This is a knowledge which can be both a blessing and a curse. It is a blessing since it means that you, through extensive listening, know what is appropriate to play in a traditional blues, and the licks you come up with are going to sound true to the genre. It is, perhaps, simultaneously a curse, since this knowledge might make you compare everything you play with that produced by masters of the genre. Or it might lead you to be guided by your inner hearing and play someone else's lick when trying to create something original. As Karin Johansson writes, 'The relationship between artistic independence and the preservation of traditions can be a difficult topic to handle on a personal level.'[39]

Challenge C: Falling into Old Habits

When trying to change the original lick, there is a risk of falling into old habits and playing what you usually do, hence nothing new is brought to the table. Student B refers to this challenge, stating that it is hard to come up with something original from a great lick, since '…In a way you have your own vocabulary, your style […] Then [when you try to come up with an original version of the lick] it just becomes that stuff you usually play […] You have your little toolbox'.[40]

Discussion

Both my students and I found the method of transcription and imitation to be a prosperous springboard to create original material. This could be used to initiate a process which ultimately strives towards finding one's own voice. The informal

---

37 Individual interview, my translation. Original quotation in Swedish: 'Den är ju så bra som den är.'
38 Group interview, my translation. Original quotation in Swedish: 'Det är svårt att hitta på något som inte är gjort tidigare. För de grejorna som är gjorda tidigare dom vet man ju att de låter bra många gånger.'
39 Karin Johansson, 'Undergraduate students' ownership of musical learning: obstacles and options in one-to-tone teaching', *British Journal of Music Education*, 30.2 (2013), 277–95 (p. 279).
40 Group interview, my translation. Original quotation in Swedish: 'Man har ju på något sätt sitt vokabulär och sin stil […] Då blev det ju det där vanliga töntet som man brukar hålla på med […] Man har ju sin lilla verktygslåda.'

learning, which was an important part of the process, granted the students autonomy since they, in many ways, were masters of their own learning. They were allowed to choose the songs they transcribed, and they chose their favourite licks to use as models in the lick-creation process. As Phil Jenkins states, 'Informal learning implies a self-motivated effort to reach competence in some task or skill'.[41] In her studies on how popular music is learned, Lucy Green points to the increase in motivation when the students are allowed to work with music of their choice.[42] I feel that it is especially important to include a high degree of informal learning when you work with genres such as Blues and Country music, which are ones all the students in my study did. These genres, just like early Jazz, have a history of informal learning which we should respect, even when we include them in HME. In the interviews, student C commented on the freedom to choose the material to transcribe, thinking it an excellent way to start this process. However, the students were not always realistic in their choices, what they wanted to learn was sometimes far above their own playing level. That is when my role as a teacher becomes important, I could advise them to choose a recording which was at a more appropriate level for them.

I have used a fair amount of informal learning in these harmonica courses, but it is important to note that the traditional formal teaching and learning methods have merit, too. All of the students needed help with the transcriptions, and I spent time with each student working on and discussing different playing techniques used by the harmonica players in the original recordings. During the process of transcription and imitation, the students developed their metacognitive skills in that they identified their own weaknesses when being unable to play, or indeed hear, parts of the solos. This often resulted in me giving them exercises to work on in order to improve their technique. Formal learning with a well-defined goal indeed. Research points to the importance of finding a balance between formal and informal learning, or 'transfer learning and transformational learning', as Gemma Carey and Catherine Grant refer to this type of learning.[43] Also interesting thing to note is that I, who have worked as a university lecturer for the better part of the past twenty years, consider this course to contain a high amount of informal learning. However, that view was not shared by all students. Those who were completely self-taught found that one benefit of this course was that it inspired them to become more structured in their practising routine, i.e., to impose a higher amount of what could be considered formal learning with explicit goals.

---

41 Jenkins, p. 181.
42 Lucy Green, *How Popular Musicians Learn: A Way Ahead for Music Education* (Aldershot: Ashgate, 2002).
43 Gemma Carey and Catherine Grant, 'Teachers of instruments, or teachers as instruments? From transfer to transformative approaches to one-to-one pedagogy', in *Becoming and Being a Musician: The Role of Creativity in Students' Learning and Identity Formation*, Proceeding of the 20th International Seminar of the ISME Commission on the Education of the Professional Musician, July 2013, https://doi.org/10.13140/2.1.2916.3204; see also Hess.

Though the students greatly appreciated the autonomy they were allowed, I was surprised by one aspect in the interviews. The part of the course, which in my mind was the most autonomous, i.e., the lick-generation process, was not viewed as such by all students. They experienced ownership of their learning when they worked with the transcriptions of their own choice, but when it came time to create licks of their own, some of the students paradoxically felt constrained. The perceived lack of autonomy was that they *had to* create licks of their own. Though they were free to create *what* they wanted, if they wanted to pass the course, they were not free to refrain from creating new licks. As Smilde writes, 'Perhaps the most important aspect [of lifelong learning strategies] is that this is never a matter of simply giving out ready-made recipes: it starts with considering the mindset and identity of each individual.'[44]

If I would have had more time with the students, I could have implemented the lick-generation process at different (later) stages in their education, some earlier than others. This perceived lack of autonomy relates to their (lack of) desire to create new, original materiel. As discussed earlier, most of the students would have been perfectly happy if the course had only contained transcription of solos and getting guidance from me concerning how to play the solos. This likely has to do with where they are in their musical journey. Jenkins states that 'like any other creative activity, the quality of what one creates greatly depends on the quality of one's experiences, and here, perhaps more than in other informal techniques, skill obtained from formal instruction will affect quality as well'.[45] Once again, this points to the need of a balance of formal and informal learning. Susan Hallam writes that 'students need to acquire this "musical" knowledge base prior to or concurrently with knowledge about specific learning and support strategies'.[46] So, my ambition to provide these students with lifelong-learning strategies and autonomy, was, in a way, a little premature. Most of these students would need to work more with formal learning concerning transcription and technical skill on the harmonica. This formal learning can, of course, go hand in hand with informal learning and autonomy, allowing the students to choose what they want to learn. It is my job to guide them and inspire them to search for their own voice, not to be content to be a copycat. Carl Holmgren writes, regarding the development of a personal artistic voice, that:

> given that a personal artistic voice is a complex amalgamation that demands an intricate interplay between philosophical and aesthetic judgments and stances, as well as an adequate technical command on the instrument, it is not possible to develop merely through imitation.[47]

---

44   Smilde, p. 115.
45   Jenkins, p. 195.
46   Susan Hallam, 'The Development of Metacognition in Musicians: Implications for Education', *British Journal of Music Education*, 18.1 (2001), 27–39 (p. 21).
47   Carl Holmgren, 'Dialogue Lost? Teaching Musical Interpretation of Western Classical Music in Higher Education', PhD thesis, Luleå University of Technology, 2022, p. 50.

So, during the formal studies of transcription and imitation, it might be fruitful to carefully add the lick-generation process, bit by bit, aiming towards the creation of a unique voice.

Granted, we all had our difficulties along the way. My challenges deal exclusively with lack of inspiration due to the original lick being either too rigid or too loose in its structure. The less-productive licks were either not clearly enough defined to provide me with a solid foundation to experiment with, or too constrained, thus inhibiting creativity. On the other hand, the students' challenges mainly concerned what might be considered a misconception, i.e., that you are supposed to create something of higher aesthetic value than the original recording. I will return to that thought later, but first I would like to point out two important differences between me and the students, one difference concerning our sources of inspiration. They based their lick-creation sessions strictly on discrete licks from the solo(s) they had chosen. My variations were based on what I call 'lick-families', i.e., licks that had many recorded variations. One way of viewing this is that the licks I based my variations on had, in most cases, already been altered. McCoy had, in fact, made plenty of his own variations, which inspired my own investigations. However, since we were limited by the time span of a short course during one semester, there was obviously not enough time for the students to find such a pool of lick variants to work with. Another difference between the students and myself is where we are as harmonica players and musicians. I am playing at a professional level, and they are not quite there (yet). Hallam's research indicates that professional musicians have developed considerable metacognitive skills, such as learning of learning, simply because they must in the competitive world in which they work.[48] These types of skills were present among advanced students, too, in Hallam's study, but not as well developed.

Challenges A and B refer to the students' experience of not being able to better the originals. This I would argue is a misconception, since the goal is not to try to improve on the licks you love, the object is to let them guide you in your search for your own voice. This requires that you lose your ego and stop comparing yourself with the original, or as student D put it: 'That you don't care so much, that you just go.'[49] Let the masters of past and present inspire you, allow their voices to be heard in your own playing. To me, copying what someone else has done with the aim of finding your own voice is the utmost sign of respect. Regardless of how you alter the lick, you are not going to damage it. The original recording will remain the same. It is my role as a teacher to help the students to get into this mindset: they should not see their task as trying to improve on something beautiful, rather, to see themselves reflected in that beauty. This is an important part of the process, where I, as the teacher, am much needed as a mediator between the original recordings and the students.

---

48 Hallam.
49 Individual interview, my translation. Original quotation in Swedish: 'Att man inte bryr sig så mycket, att man bara kö.'

Although the comparison with the solos on the recordings clearly is an obstacle for the students, there is something beautiful about Challenges A and B. They feel intimidated because they love and respect the tradition in which they are working. I feel the same way about McCoy's playing, it does not need improvement. However, if I am to play licks I have learned from McCoy, they will benefit from the addition of my own voice. After all, McCoy plays McCoy better than anyone else. Mike Caldwell stated in our interview that he wanted to add his own personality to the licks, careful not to claim his ideas to be better than McCoy's: 'It's ok to play it a little different than Charlie, because it's me.'[50]

Challenge C, on the other hand, deals with the risk of falling into old habits, thus preventing yourself from letting the source of your inspiration guide you to new solutions. There is certainly a tension here, when you want to bring yourself into the lick, to put your own stamp on it, you are running the risk of moving too far from your source of inspiration, i.e., the original lick. By 'too far', I mean that you end up playing one of your own clichés without a trace of the original, which was meant to inspire you to come up with something of your own. One might say that the point is to meet halfway or, rather, to bring yourself into the lick and then go beyond. However, you need to be careful not to leave it behind completely. In your new lick, you should be able to, in some way, trace your way back to the original lick. In other words, you should be able to explain to yourself why you made the choices you made. On the other hand, there is certainly nothing wrong with coming up with a lick that in no way resembles the original, as long as it is new to yourself, and not one of the licks you already had in your little toolbox, as student B put it.

When helping students to strive towards the goal of creating their own voice, one powerful tool is reflection.[51] During the interviews, both individual and in group form, the students were given plenty of opportunity to reflect on their own learning. These reflections not only increased their autonomy and strengthened their lifelong-learning strategies but also helped them in their voice development. Moberg and Georgii-Hemming write that 'students must reflexively become aware of who they *are*, what musical preferences they *have*, and where they *are* located in the musical field' in order to develop artistic freedom.[52] This resonates well with my study, since the students reflected on their own abilities to copy other harmonica players in their field. Their musical preferences were front and centre in the course, since they chose the material we worked with. They also reflected on these preferences when I interviewed them regarding why they chose certain licks. I would argue that one important step towards finding your own voice is the very *choice* of solos and licks. There are reasons why the students chose what they did; student A said that certain licks 'lay well in my mouth'

---

50   Mike Caldwell interview.
51   See, for example, Moberg and Georgii-Hemming.
52   Moberg and Georgii-Hemming, p. 81, emphasis in original.

when explaining why s/he chose to work with those licks.[53] There is something in these solos and licks which resonates within the students, something which points to who they are. This very resonance is what they need to pay attention to, to develop, to nurture, and adapt into their own playing. Through their choices of solos, they have begun the journey of identifying what they really love, and this, I believe, is the way to find out not only who you are but also who you want to be as a musician.

As far as the challenges we all experienced, it is interesting to note that my challenges and the students' challenges are entirely different. I never felt intimidated by the original recording, only inspired. One possible explanation for this might be that I was able to play the transcriptions along with the recordings, sounding close to the original, without the need of slowing the speed of the recording down. However, the students were all, more or less, struggling to play their chosen solos and licks. They all had to slow the recordings down and were still, in many aspects, not sounding like the original. There is nothing remarkable about that: I have spent thousands of hours honing my skills at aural transcriptions; they have not. Not yet anyway.

In sum, the preliminary results of my educational study encourage me to continue working in this manner. That is, to apply the knowledge I gain through my artistic research and my artistic practice in my teaching in HME. There is nothing particularly novel about that ambition, my colleagues at my university do, to greater or lesser extent, precisely that. However, when you formalize this process as you do in a research project, the potential gain increases. Granted, there will always be a need to adapt the methods used in your artistic research when applying them within the framework of HME. For example, to adjust to the timeframe of a single course, a semester or even the three-year span of a bachelor's programme. Also, it will be necessary to adapt my methods to meet the students where they are, and to meet the needs of the students. Regarding the various challenges I have outlined, I do not necessarily see a need to eliminate these challenges. On the contrary, working *with* these challenges is what gives the students opportunity to grow, become autonomous, and to work towards fostering an individual voice. Trying to work around or to eliminate the challenges might mean less opportunity for learning.

In short, I am confident that all students, teachers, and researchers will benefit from HME being informed by up-to-date artistic research. It is my hope that presenting what I am doing will inspire teachers in HME to do artistic research, as well as artistic researchers to apply their findings in HME.

---

53   Group interview, my translation. Original quotation in Swedish: '...att det låg bra i munnen.'

References

Aebersold, Jamie, *How to Play Jazz and Improvise* (New Albany, NY: Jamey Aebersold Jazz Inc, 1992)

Bäckman, Mikael, 'The Real McCoy. Tracking the Development of Charlie McCoy's Playing Style', *International Country Music Journal* (2022), 184–231

Bäckman, Mikael, 'In Search of My Voice', *Music & Practice*, 10 (2023), unpaginated, DOI: 10.32063/1012

Berild Lundblad, Niklas, and Fredrik Stjernberg, *Frågvisare. Människans Viktigaste Verktyg* (Stockholm: Volante, 2021)

Berliner, Paul F, *Thinking in Jazz. The Infinite Art of Improvisation* (Chicago: University of Chicago Press, 1994)

Blom, Diana, Dawn Bennett, and David Wright, 'How Artists Working in Academia View Artistic Practice as Research: Implications for Tertiary Music Education', *International Journal of Music Education*, 29(4), (2011), 359–73, https://doi.org/10.1177/0255761411421088

Caldwell, Mike, interview, conducted 3 September 2020

Carey, Gemma and Grant, Catherine, 'Teachers of Instruments, or Teachers as Instruments? From Transfer to Transformative Approaches to One-To-One Pedagogy' in *Becoming and Being a Musician: The Role of Creativity in Students' Learning and Identity Formation*, Proceeding of the 20th International Seminar of the ISME Commission on the Education of the Professional Musician, July 2013, https://doi.org/10.13140/2.1.2916.3204

Craenen, Paul, *Composing Under the Skin: The Music-Making Body at the Composer's Desk* (Leuven: Leuven University Press, 2014)

Frisk, Henrik and Östersjö, Stefan, *(re)Thinking Improvisation: Artistic Explorations and Conceptual Writing* (Lund University, Elanders Sverige AB, 2013)

Gibson, James J., *The Ecological Approach to Visual Perception* (New York: Psychology Press, 1979)

Goldsmith, Margie, *Masters of Harmonica* (Alpharetta, GA: Mountain Arbor Press, 2019)

Green, Lucy, *How Popular Musicians Learn: A Way Ahead for Music Education* (Aldershot: Ashgate, 2002)

Hallam, Susan, 'The Development of Metacognition in Musicians: Implications for Education', *British Journal of Music Education*, 18.1 (2001), 27–39, https://doi.org/10.1017/S0265051701000122

Hess, Juliet, 'Finding the "both/and": Balancing Informal and Formal Music Learning', *International Journal of Music Education*, 38:3 (2020), 441–55, https://doi.org/10.1177/0255761420917226

Holmgren, Carl, 'Dialogue Lost? Teaching Musical Interpretation of Western Classical Music in Higher Education', PhD thesis, Luleå University of Technology, 2022.

Hultberg, Cecilia K., 'Artistic Processes in Music Performance. A Research Area Calling for Inter-Disciplinary Collaboration', *Swedish Journal of Music Research/Svensk Tidskrift för Musikforskning*, 95 (2013), 79–94

Jenkins, Phil, 'Project Muse: Formal and Informal Music Educational Practices', *Philosophy of Music Education Review*, 19:2 (2011), 179–97, https://doi.org/10.2979/philmusieducrevi.19.2.179

Johansson, Karin, 'Undergraduate Students' Ownership of Musical Learning: Obstacles and Options in One-To-One Teaching', *British Journal of Music Education*, 30:2 (2013), 277–95, https://doi.org/10.1017/s0265051713000120

Leman, Marc; Luc Nijs, Pieter-Jan Maes, and Edith Van Dyck, 'What is Embodied Music Cognition?', in *Springer Handbook of systematic Musicology*, ed. by Rolf Bader (Berlin: Springer, 2017), pp. 747–60

Moberg, Nadia and Eva Georgii-Hemming, 'Musicianship – Discursive Constructions of Autonomy and Independence within Music Performance Programmes', Proceedings of the Conference 'Becoming Musicians. Student Involvement and Teacher Collaboration in Higher Music Education', Oslo, October 2018, ed. by Stefan Gies and Jon Helge Sætre, NMH publications, 2019, p. 67–88

Pivec, Matt, 'Maximizing the Benefits of Solo Transcription', *JazzEd*, January (2008), 23–26

Roe, Paul, 'A Phenomenology of Collaboration in Contemporary Composition and Performance' (unpublished doctoral thesis, University of York, 2007)

Sadolin, Catherine, *Complete Vocal Technique* (Copenhagen: CVI publications, 2021)

Sandell, Sten, 'På Insidan Av Tystnaden: En Undersökning' (PhD thesis, Göteborgs Universitet, Art Monitor, 2013)

Smilde, Rineke, 'Change and the Challenges of Lifelong Learning', in *Life in the Real World: How to Make Music Graduates Employable*, ed. by Dawn Bennett (Champaign, IL: Common Ground Publishing, 2012), pp. 99–123

Wilf, Eitan, *School for Cool: The Academic Jazz Programme and the Paradox of Institutionalized Creativity* (Chicago, University of Chicago Press, 2014)

Östersjö, Stefan, 'Shut Up 'N' Play: Negotiating the Musical Work' (PhD thesis, Lund University, Media-Tryck, 2008)

4. Teaching Musical Performance from an Artistic Research-Based Approach:
Reporting on a Pedagogical Intervention in Portugal

Gilvano Dalagna; Jorge S. Correia; Clarissa Foletto; Ioulia Papageorgi

Introduction

This book chapter reports on the outcomes of the second REACT training school, a pedagogical intervention to test an artistic research-based approach to teaching and learning music performance. This extracurricular course was created at the University of Aveiro, leading institution in the strategic REACT project. The intervention was tested as extracurricular to pilot interventions, solutions, and feedback prior to formalising such changes within the validated curriculum. The chapter is structured in four parts. The first part discusses existing practices of music performance teaching and learning in European higher education institutions. This part explores the historical development of music performance education and the influence of the values and expectations established in the context of the nineteenth-century Western Music Conservatoire and its traditional master-apprentice one-to-one pedagogical model. The consequences of this model, referred to here as 'the conservatoire model', are outlined, along with a summary of the career requirements of music performance professionals, in 'Artistic Careers in Music: Stakeholders Requirements Report', the first output published by the consortium of the REACT project.[1] Connections are drawn between the conservatoire model and artistic research in order to inform innovative practices and launch an alternative pedagogical intervention. In the second part, the implementation of the pedagogical intervention

---

[1] Jorge Correia and others, REACT–Rethinking Music Performance in European Higher Education Institutions, *Artistic Career in Music: Stakeholders Requirement Report* (Aveiro: UA Editora, 2021), p. 20, https://doi.org/10.48528/wfq9-4560

at a Portuguese university is described. Details about types of activities and contents included in the programme, selection of participants, data collection (from focus groups interviews), and data analysis are presented. The results are presented in the third part of the chapter. They are based on students' collected feedback on their experiences regarding their participation in the intervention. We utilise the student voice in order to assess the effectiveness of the training school itself. An account of the thematic analysis and its results are presented through the sharing of student voices from the focus-group interviews. In the final section, the theoretical and pedagogical implications of the intervention are evaluated, with reference to the student feedback and the process of the implementation undertaken. We also address the methodological limitations of the study and, finally, propose suggested directions for future research.

Background

Since the nineteenth century, two different ways of conceptualising the teaching and learning of music performance in higher education have been established in mainland Europe. Higher education institutions are considered to have two approaches: that of universities, which is described as academic, and that of conservatoires, which is described as performance based.[2,3] In practice, many university courses do include performance, but they are structured differently, and likewise, conservatoires do include academic programmes, but for a smaller modular proportion. Moreover, university-degree courses, for the most part, are three years, while conservatoire courses are usually four years in length (referring to full-time registration). The Bologna model (see further below), however, posits the structure of three years of undergraduate study, plus two years of postgraduate taught master's study. Despite the apparent differences, these two educational environments—university departments and conservatoires—have similarities. Both aim to create a student-centred approach, but they vary in the hours each dedicates to performance, particularly to one-to-one teaching, referred to here as the master-apprentice model. Conservatoires usually dedicate a smaller percentage of their students' time to theoretical courses. [4,5,6] Universities, on the other hand, usually

---

2   Harold Jørgensen, 'Western Classical Music Studies in Universities and Conservatoires', in *Advanced Musical Performance: Investigations in Higher Education Learning*, ed. by Ioulia Papageorgi and Graham Welch (Ashgate: Surrey, 2014), pp. 3–20 (p. 15).
3   Ioulia Papageorgi; Andrea Creech; Elizabeth Haddon; Frances Morton; Christophe De Bezenac; Evangelos Himonides; John Potter; Celia Duffy; Tony Whyton, and Graham Welch, 'Perceptions and Predictions of Expertise in Advanced Musical Learners', *Psychology of Music*, 38 (2010) 1, 31–66, https://doi.org/10.1177/0305735609336044
4   Gemma Carey and Don Lebler, 'Reforming a Bachelor of Music Programme: A Case Study', *International Journal of Music Education*, 30 (2012), 4, 312–27.
5   *Advanced Musical Performance: Investigations in Higher Education Learning*, ed. by Ioulia Papageorgi and Graham Welch (Surrey: Ashgate, 2014), p. 15.
6   Michael Stepniak and Peter Sirotin, *Beyond the Conservatoire Model: Reimagining Classical Music Performance Training in Higher Education* (Abingdon: Routledge, 2020), p. 72.

tend to reduce the time students dedicate to performance practice.[7] While university music programmes usually offer a variety of modules such as musicology, performance studies, music technology, composition, and music education, conservatoires also offer these, but their focus is on what these subjects can help improve performance.

Several institutions continue to train young musicians primarily using a curriculum built on principles institutionalised in the Paris Conservatoire in the nineteenth century.[8] These principles are deduced from a view of performance as essentially a question of interpreting a composer's score. This understanding aligns with the paradigmatic influence of *werktreue*, which led to the development of the following practices: (i) specialism in a single instrument or vocal type; (ii) a pursuit of virtuosic technique; (iii) focus on accurately performing what is written in the score; (iv) a standardisation of exams and prizes as a means by which to monitor the quality of music performance; (v) teacher-directed as opposed to student-centred teaching; and (vi) dominance of Western art music.[9] This teaching paradigm encourages performance students to interpret pre-existing scores in line with traditional and hegemonic performance practices.[10] The excessive focus on imitation moves away from encouraging student-centred learning, where the voice of the students' own creativity and critical thinking is made the focal point.

The conservatoire model has also influenced how students envision their future careers in music industries, largely as performers in dominant classical music institutions.[11] Historical evidence from the last decade suggests that students have had some difficulty finding ways to relate their practice with their creativity,[12],[13] due to the excessive focus on developing competences. Other authors, more radically, have suggested that the conservatoire model neither prepares students for their likely freelance futures nor helps them to achieve their artistic aspirations, since the professional music field is changing

---

[7] Ioulia Papageorgi, Andrea Creech, Elizabeth Haddon, Frances Morton, Christophe De Bezenac, Evangelos Himonides, John Potter, Celia Duffy, Tony Whyton, and Graham Welch, 'Institutional Culture and Learning I: Perceptions of the Learning Environment and Musicians' Attitudes to Learning', *Music Education Research*, 12 (2010) 2, 151–78.

[8] See Gilvano Dalagna, Sara Carvalho, and Graham Welch, *Desired Artistic Outcomes in Music Performance* (Abingdon: Routledge, 2021), p. 108; John Sloboda, *Musicians and Their Live Audiences: Dilemmas and Opportunities. Understanding Audiences* ([n. p.]: Scribd, 2013), https://pt.scribd.com/document/538118141/Sloboda-John-Musicians-and-their-live-audiences-dilemmas-and-opportunities

[9] Biranda Ford and John Sloboda, 'Learning from Artistic and Pedagogical Differences Between Musicians' and Actors' Traditions Through Collaborative Processes, in *Collaborative Learning in Higher Music Education*, ed. by Helena Gaunt and Heidi Westerlund (Aldershot: Ashgate, 2013), pp. 27–36. See also Sloboda.

[10] Roland S. Persson, 'The Subjective World of the Performer', in *Handbook of Music and Emotion: Theory Research and Applications*, ed. by Patrick N. Juslin and John Sloboda (New York: Oxford University Press, 2001), pp. 275–89.

[11] Dalagna, Carvalho, and Welch, p. 150.

[12] Helena Gaunt, Andrea Creech, Marion Long, and Susan Hallam, 'Supporting Conservatoire Students Towards Professional Integration: One-to-One tuition and the Potential of Mentoring', *Music Education Research*, 14 (2012) 1, 25–43.

[13] Angela Beeching, 'Musicians Made in USA: Training Opportunities and Industry Change', in *Life in the Real World: How to Make Music Graduates Employable*, ed. by Dawn Bennett (Champaign, IL: Common Ground, 2012), pp. 27–43.

faster than training programmes. This may create a tension between the skills prioritised and what is needed to sustain a career in music.[14] The perceived tension highlights the importance of continuing to design approaches that effectively equip musicians for sustainable careers and integrate the student-voice in such design processes.[15]

This gap between the conservatoire model and career demands motivated the development of a strategic partnership of REACT (as discussed in the introduction to this book). The consortium of institutions in the aforementioned countries conducted a cross-European study with the aim of identifying current artistic career demands in the music-performance industry. This interview-based study involved a large number of stakeholders, and the proportions are different for each case study, but all comprise professional performers, students, teachers, artistic directors, career coaches, heads of music departments, composers, and music producers. The analysis revealed common challenges and demands for an artistic career, but also some differences across the countries represented. The final report summarised the data collected in the qualitative study and a literature review. The authors propose a list of professional requirements and a number of suggestions which would enable HME to respond to referred requirements (see Table 4.1).

Professional Requirements	Suggestions for HME
• Entrepreneurship, versatility, flexibility, and networking; • Psychological endurance, resilience, and wellness; • Practicalities of working life, financial constraints of the profession in which competition is fierce; • The capacity to rethink music artistically in a rapidly changing society and the role of the artist in such a society; • Improvisation; • Agile musicianship, e.g., adjustability to the "sound-bite" culture and "liquid" society; • Competencies in working in community settings and communal institutions;	• Increasing tuition in music pedagogy; • Connecting music performance modules in HME curricula with other music-related courses, and with the music performance industry as a whole; • Establishing an international dialogue, collaboration, and exchange of ideas with other universities' students and faculty; • Proposing courses on technological literacy and competences; • Offering artistic mentoring support as well as career management; • Development of critical thinking and self-reflection skills • Importance of understanding authenticity in performance

Table 4.1. Professional competencies identified in the synthetic analysis.[16]

---

14 Rineke Smilde and Sigurdur Halldórsson, 'New Audiences and Innovative Practice: An International Master's Programme with Critical Reflection and Mentoring at the Heart of an Artistic Laboratory', in *Collaborative Learning in Higher Music Education*, ed. by Helena Gaunt and Heidi Westerlund (Surrey: Ashgate, 2013), pp. 225–30 (p. 220).

15 Dawn Bennet, Angela Beeching, Rosie Perkins, Glen Carruthers and Janis Weler, 'Music, Musicians and Careers', in *Life in the Real World: How to Make Music Graduates Employable*, ed. by Dawn Bennett (Champaign, IL: Common Ground, 2012), pp. 9-10.

16 Correia and others, p. 20.

In the following table, a triangulation involving the results of the cross-European study and a synthesis of the existing literature review on career development is presented. Table 4.2 shows a more detailed list of demands that integrates other competencies beyond technical and interpretative skills.

Cross-European study	Synthesis of the Literature Review
- Competition - Financial literacy - Psychological endurance - Entrepreneurship - Versatility - Musicianship - Musicianship skills (e.g., sight reading, staging, improvisation) - Marketing - Management - Critical thinking - Self-promotion - Networking - Identifying funding opportunities	- Strategic self-renewal of skills and knowledge[17] - Developing a learner identity[18] - Build and run a 'small business'; finding their niche; integrate a complex web of motivation, Time, educational systems, vocational concerns, and long-held perceptions of success; retaining and refining technical skills even when undertaking other work[19] - Philosophical underpinning; music-technical skills; interpersonal skills [20] - Leadership; transcultural understanding; creativity and awareness of the context within which Music work takes place[21,22]

---

17 Rosalind Gill, 'Cool, Creative and Egalitarian? Exploring Gender in Project-Based New Media Work in Europe', *Information, Communication and Society*, 5 (2002), 70–89, https://doi.org/10.1080/13691180110117668

18 Guadalupe López-Íñiguez and Dawn Bennett, 'A Lifespan Perspective on Multi-Professional Musicians: Does Music Education Prepare Classical Musicians for their Careers?', *Music Education Research*, 22 (2020) 1, 1–14, https://doi.org/10.1080/14613808.2019.1703925

19 Dawn Bennett and Ruth Bridgstock, 'The Urgent Need for Career Preview: Student Expectations and Graduate Realities in Music and Dance', *International Journal of Music Education*, 33 (2015) 3, 263–77, https://doi.org/10.1177/0255761414558653

20 Colin Durrant, 'Shaping Identity Through Choral Activity: Singers' and Conductors' Perceptions', *Research Studies in Music Education*, 24 (2005) 1, 88–98, https://doi.org/10.1177/1321103X050240010701

21 Katja Thompson, 'Fostering Transformative Professionalism Through Curriculum Changes within a Bachelor of Music', in *Expanding Professionalism in Music and Higher Music Education: A Changing Game*, ed. by Heidi. Westerlund and Helena Gaunt (Routledge: London, 2021), pp. 42–58 (pp. 44–50).

22 Martin Berger, 'Educing Leadership and Evoking Sound: Choral Conductors as Agents of Change', in *Leadership and Musician Development in Higher Music Education*, ed. by Dawn Bennett, Jennifer Rowley, and Patrick Schmidt (Routledge: New York, 2019), pp. 115–29 (pp. 115–20).

• Writing proposals • Branding • Public relations • Recording • Staging • Technological literacy • Understanding the role of music in society • Understanding how music industry works	• Critical thinking[23] • Exploring multiple genres[24] • Improvisational and compositional practice[25] • Disciplinary agility; social networking; enterprise and effective career self-management [26]

Table 4.2. Artistic career demands in music performance.

One can argue that the list of demands is vast and complicated to address through a single strategy. However, Pamela Burnard,[27] Mary Lennon, and Geoffrey Reed[28] have suggested that creativity and critical thinking should be highlighted in order to develop individual creative voices. Further, our report[29] identifies two fundamental approaches to supporting the transition from the role of student to professional musician: institutions must create a student-centred curriculum which enables their voices to speak (see Chapters 11 and 12 in this book) and project-based learning informed by artistic research practices (see Chapters 1 and 3 in this book). The currency of the aspects listed in the table has been evident throughout the process

---

23 Gareth Dylan Smith, 'Masculine Domination in Private Sector Popular Music Performance Education in England' in *Bourdieu and the Sociology of Music Education*, ed. by Pamela Burnard, Ylva Hofvander Trulsson, and Johan Söderman (Ashgate: Surrey, 2015), pp. 61–78.
24 Pamela Burnard, *Developing Creativities in Higher Music Education: International Perspectives and Practices* (Routledge: London, 2013). P.100.
25 Irene Deliège and Geraint Wiggins, *Musical Creativity: Multidisciplinary Research in Theory and Practice* (Psychology Press: East Sussex, 2006), p. 1.
26 Brydie-Leigh Bartleet, Dawn Bennett, Ruth Bridgstock, Paul Draper, Scott Harrison, and Huib Schippers, 'Preparing for Portfolio Careers in Australian Music: Setting a Research Agenda', *Australian Society for Music Education Corporation*, 1 (2012), 32–41, https://files.eric.ed.gov/fulltext/EJ1000243.pdf
27 Burnard, p. 100.
28 Mary Lennon and Geoffrey Reed, 'Instrumental and Vocal Teacher Education: Competences, Roles and Curricula', *Music Education Research*, 14 (2012) 3, 285–308.
29 Correia and others, p. 20.

of adapting pedagogy in HME in accordance with the Bologna Declaration.[30,31] As discussed above, HME, have historically been built on the conservatoire model and, therefore, have focused on one-to-one teaching.[32] Ford and Sloboda observe that HME have faced several managerial challenges to justify the financial viability of this one-to-one teaching model, notably from a social and political perspective, when resources are limited and costs increasing, and where inclusive practices and widening participation are central aims for regulators.[33]

Driven by an aim to create a unified European Higher Education sector, the Bologna Declaration encouraged many conservatoires and universities to rethink their pedagogical structure and, consequently, their relationship with the music industries, as well as to adhere to the principle that each educational area should be supported by research.[34,35,36] The agreement instigated a process of developing research cultures across all HME institutions. In this process, artistic research has emerged as an important factor in the creation of such research environments that meaningfully include research in music performance.[37,38]

The challenge of the Bologna Declaration, of grounding all education on research-led teaching, was to articulate how research findings were possible in practice. This turmoil was grounded in how artists felt the need to justify their artistic practice as research and could be valued as a contribution to knowledge.[39]

Artistic research has emerged as a solution to this state of affairs, since it has the potential to ground arts education in a student-centred, experiential way of learning, with a basis in research practice. As such, it has facilitated novel ways of teaching and assessing (see Chapter 12). The term 'generative'[40] describes artistic research

---

30 The Bologna Declaration refers to an agreement between 29 European countries to establish a European Higher Education area which supported the free movement of students, the acceptance of equivalent entry qualifications, and a standard approach to undergraduate and postgraduate degrees. See https://ehea.info/Upload/document/ministerial_declarations/1999_Bologna_Declaration_English_553028.pdf

31 Darla Crispin, 'Artistic Research and Music Scholarship: Musings and Models from a Continental European Perspective', in *Artistic Practice as Research in Music: Theory, Criticism, Practice*, ed. by Mine Doğantan-Dack (Surrey: Ashgate Publishing, 2015), pp. 53–72 (p. 68).

32 Crispin, p. 55.

33 Ford and Sloboda, p. 30.

34 Jorge Salgado Correia, Gilvano Dalagna, Alfonso Benetti, and Francisco Monteiro, *Cahiers of Artistic Research 1: When Is Research Artistic Research?* (Aveiro: Editora da Universidade de Aveiro, 2018), p. 40.

35 Dalagna, Carvalho, and Welch, p. 108.

36 Crispin, p. 55.

37 Jorge Salgado Correia and Gilvano Dalagna, *Cahiers of Artistic Research 3: A explanatory model for Artistic Research* (Aveiro: Editora da Universidade de Aveiro, 2018), p. 40.

38 Stefan Östersjö, 'Thinking-Through-Music: On Knowledge Production, Materiality, and Embodiment in Artistic Research', in *Artistic Research in Music: Discipline and Resistance*, ed. by Jonathan Impett (Leuven: Leuven University, Press, 2018), pp. 88–107 (p. 100).

39 Jorge Salgado Correia and Gilvano Dalagna, 'A Verdade Inconveniente sobre os Estudos em Performance', in *Performance Musical sob uma Perspectiva Pluralista*, ed. by Sonia R. Albano de Lima (Musa Editora: São Paulo, 2021), pp. 11–26 (p. 20).

40 Estelle Barrett, *Aesthetic Experience and Innovation in Practice–Led Research* (2010), conference paper, Deakin Research Online, https://hdl.handle.net/10536/DRO/DU:30032166

as an alternative to the existing qualitative and quantitative paradigm: 'artwork embodies research findings which are symbolically expressed, though not expressed through numbers and words'.[41] The inadequacy of scientific research[42] to ground arts education in practice could finally be overcome by an epistemological approach through artistic research as it enables a somatic experience within the context of the art world, often described as 'Practice Research'.[43] Artistic research offers a possibility to overcome the subject/object dichotomy of scientific research, since it allows the sharing of the artist's subjectivity and experience in the development of a new practice (which crosses all the arts, not only music). The development of this new practice is fundamental to a student-centred approach, which engages with contextualisation, exploration, and dissemination, as shown in the REACT model (see Introduction). In addition to the potential in observing, analysing, and describing musical practices from a multidisciplinary perspective, artistic researchers critically reflect on their subjective and inter-subjective experience of artistic practice, identifying and proposing new possibilities that are conveyed through their practice in their art world.[44]

Artistic research is not fully integrated in all HME bodies in Europe. Only a few institutions have explored the potential of artistic research as a new paradigm in music performance teaching in its full capacity.[45] It is not yet possible to grasp the impact of artistic research in the education of students in HME across the sector, though work is being done within individual institutions (see for instance Chapters 1, 3, and 11). Likewise, the impact of artistic research-informed teaching in students' transition to professional is clear, as, in the UK, the graduate outcomes demonstrate a benefit (see Chapter 12).

REACT Training School

In the REACT project, two training schools formed a basis for experimenting with educational models based on artistic research (the first, in Norway, discussed in Chapter 10), and the second in Portugal (discussed here). Both interactions tested project-based learning pedagogical strategies and student-centred approaches through practices of artistic research in music.

---

41 Brad Haseman, 'A Manifesto for Performative Research', *Media International Australia*, 118 (2006) 1, 98–106.
42 Sanjay Seth, Beyond the Reason: Postcolonial Theory and the Social Sciences (Oxford: Oxford University Press, 2021), p. 200.
43 James Bulley and Özden Şahin, *Practice Research - Report 1: What is practice research? and Report 2: How can practice research be shared?* (London: PRAG-UK, 2021), p. 80, https://doi.org/10.23636/1347
44 Stefan Östersjö, 'Art Worlds, Voice and Knowledge: Thoughts on Quality Assessment of Artistic Research Outcomes', *ÍMPAR Online journal for artistic research*, 3(2) (2019), 60–69.
45 Dalagna, Carvalho, and Welch, p. 180.

This change of perspective was the main objective of these interventions. Critical thinking and creativity were core elements in the pedagogical praxis, as can be seen further on in the 'Results' section, where we analyse the impact of the second training school via the interviews with participants. The first core element (critical thinking) refers to a reflexive process focused on the subjectivity of each individual, while the second (creativity) refers to a process of communicating this subjectivity in academic and professional contexts.

Students were invited to conceive, develop, and publicly present an artistic project based on challenges they experience during their practice. The activities proposed by the training school aimed to assist students in this process. Thus, music performance was conceived as a creative practice and a space for problematization. Students defined the focus of their projects, and pedagogical support was provided through mentoring by consortium members.

Structure and Implementation of the 2nd REACT Training School

Building on the evaluation of the first training school (see Chapter 10), as well as the outcomes of the Stakeholders Requirement Report,[46] the consortium members defined the following structure for the second training school, which encompassed four main modules:

(i) *philosophical stance* - aims to critically identify challenges in musical practice;

(ii) *exploration* - aims to develop a critical creative reaction to the challenges identified in module 1;

(iii) *self-disclosure* - facilitates students in making sense of their own experience to find ways to connect them with their own music making;

(iv) *social intervention* - aims to explore the impact of artistic research and its potential for change in art worlds and industry.

The course was held in May 2022, at the Department of Communication and Art at the University of Aveiro in Portugal. During a full teaching week (40 hours), 17 master's and bachelor's students (see Fig. 4.1) were involved in a total of 25 activities distributed throughout the week. Nine instrumental teachers from the department were invited to select potential student participants based on the following criteria: (i) interest in an artistic career and in developing a project of their own; (ii) some experience in research methods and developing their own career planning; (iii) sufficient performance experience to deal with this intervention; (iv) having completed 1 year of a bachelor's programme. The three figures below show the number of students at

---

[46] Jorge Correia and others, p. 20.

each level (Fig. 4.1), the instruments they play (Fig. 4.2), and the correlation between the students and their instruments (Fig. 4.3).

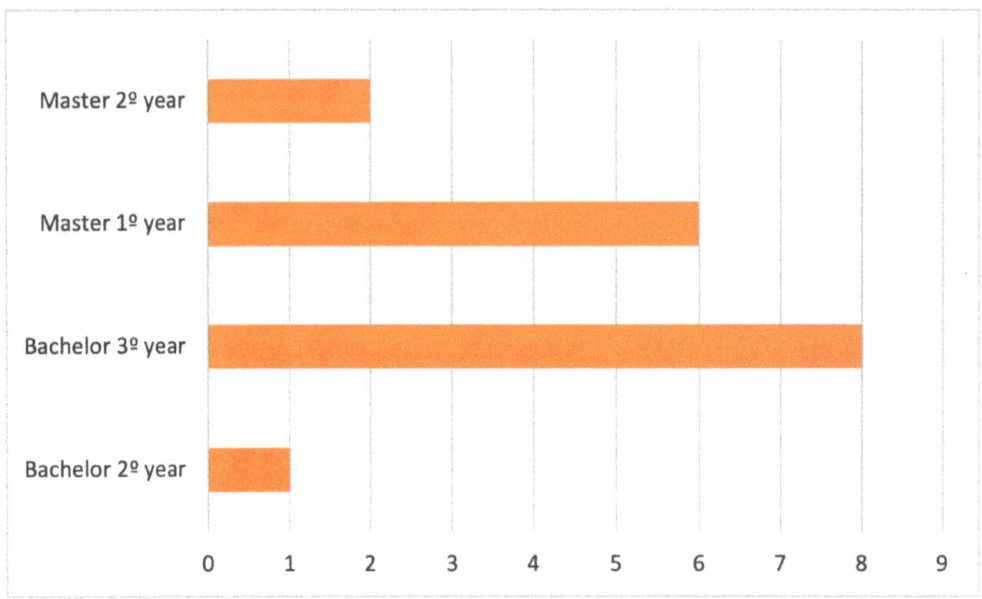

Fig. 4.1: Number of students by course and year of study.

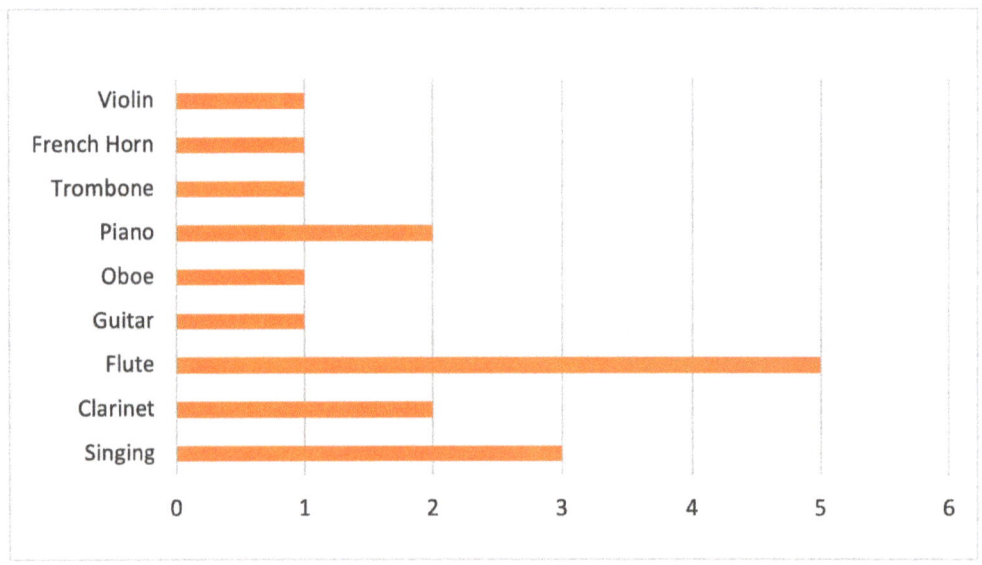

Fig. 4.2: Students by instrument.

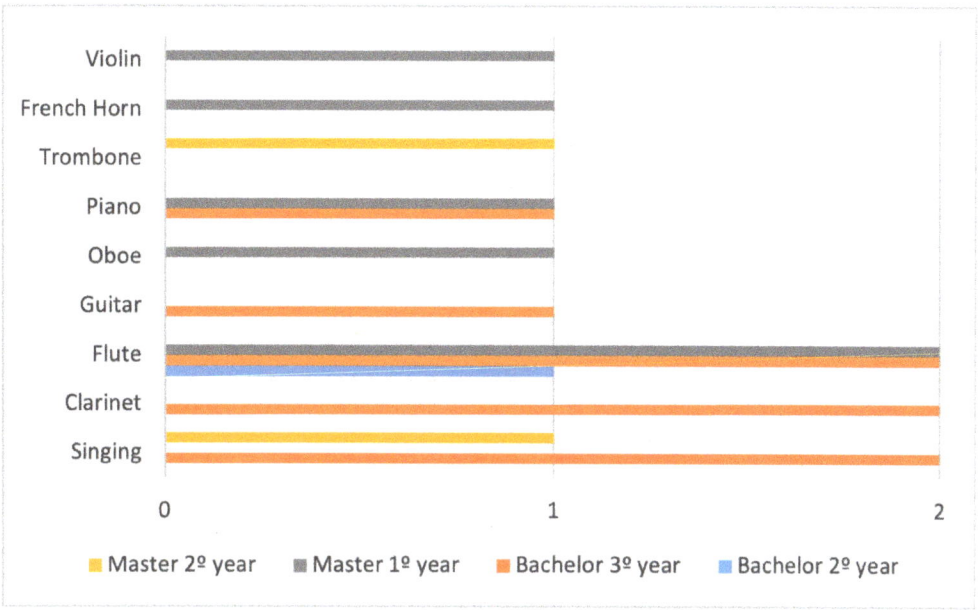

Fig. 4.3: Correlation between instruments and students.

The activities were based on the four modules previously described above. In each module, the consortium members proposed two units (that is, target topics addressed in each module) and invited feedback from others to indicate which units could be addressed in the school. In these modules, four main competencies were addressed: meaning making (A), finding one's own artistic voice (B), developing and managing projects (C), and seeking empathy (D).

Sixteen lectures, workshops, and demonstrations of projects were proposed by eleven REACT members. All of the activities distributed across the units can be seen in Table 4.3. Between the lectures, group mentoring sessions were offered on each day.

Modules (What are the areas covered by the REACT training school?)	Learning objectives (What should students be able to achieve?)	Associated competences (What competences of the AR-BL model are associated with each module?)	Units (what are the target topics addressed in each module?)	Content (what are the questions that should be answered in each unity?)	Lectures/workshops (what activities will you include in your lecture or workshop?)
1. Philosophical stance	Identifying and critically thinking on challenges in students' musical practice	A	1.1 The emancipated performer	What characterizes an emancipated performer?	Performance as artistic creation Towards an emancipated and artistic persona
			1.2 Challenging performance	How do normatives have challenged music performance practices and how to critically react to them?	Musical interpretation: What it is, could be, and might be Developing artistic projects: Interdisciplinary perspectives and arts integration in higher music performance education Through and Beyond the Notes: New Interpretational Possibilities in Music Performance
2. Self-disclosure	Formulating a critical and artistic stance	A, B, C	2.1 Subjective and intersubjective	What is subjectivity and how can it be explored in music performance practices?	From personal relevance to social pertinence
			2.2 Bridging practices and theory	How can research assist performers to react to challenges in music practices?	Well-being and professional education of musicians in time of crises
3. Exploration	Reacting creatively to these challenges taking the artistic stance into account	A, B, C	3.1 Choice and responsibility in remix culture	How to negotiate individual pertinence and social relevance in performance practices?	Performance and syncretic experiences Challenging Performance Rethinking the score Bridging musical and artistic knowledge in performance practice
			3.2 REACT Laboratory: experimentation and creation	How can artistic creation be documented? What is the relevance of monitoring musical practices?	Documenting artistic research in music performance
4. Social intervention	Planning a communication strategy to disseminate an artistic project to a wider community (in the academia and beyond)	A, B, C, D	4.1 Performance and career	What are the challenges and opportunities for higher education students to develop an artistic career?	Career development for performers: Identity and employability - Health, well-being and performance anxiety
			4.2 Performance in society: audience, relevance and outreach	What are the existing strategies to engage with audiences? How can I communicate the innovative aspect in an artistic project? How to identify a suitable channel of dissemination for my artistic project?	Artistic responses to Crisis. Reflections and examples Musical Performance in society: Art worlds, research and outreach

Table 4.3. React training school structure

Data Collection and Analysis

A focus-group interview was conducted one week after the end of the training school with the aim of assessing its impact on the students' learning and professional path.[47] All students were invited to take part in the interview. It was scheduled at a time when the majority of the participants could attend. However, nine of the seventeen students declined to participate in the interview because of other commitments. We adopted a semi-structured technique to guide the group interview[48] and solicit observations about the training school. The discussion centred around four questions:

(i) What do you think was most pertinent, for you in particular, during the week of the training school?

(ii) How has this experience impacted on your activity as a performing musician?

(iii) What improvements do you think are needed at the school?

(iv) Imagining the school's curriculum as a basis for the development of other courses, what impact could this kind of activity have on the teaching of music performance in the future?

Eight students participated in the discussion during the focus-group interview and the total length of the interview recording was one hour. We had four students in the third year of the bachelor's degree, three in the first year of the master's degree, and one in the second year of the master's programme. They encompassed six instruments. The original data was recorded in Portuguese and then transcribed verbatim using the F5 software. A thematic analysis, with the aid of the software NVivo 12, was conducted through a process of coding the data, then organising them into themes and sub-themes.[49] Themes and sub-themes were coded according to the four aforementioned questions that guided the interviews.[50]

---

47   The REACT project received approval for conducting this study by the Ethics and Deontology Committee of University of Aveiro (Approval no. 18-CED/2021) and by the Data Protection Officer of University of Aveiro. In addition, all participants signed an informed-consent document agreeing to participation, and they were assured that all data collected were confidential and anonymous. For the purpose of this chapter, participants are referred to as P1, P2, P3, P4, P5, P6, P7, and P8.
48   Colin Robson, *Real World Research* (West Sussex: Wiley, 2011), p. 400.
49   Paul Cooper and Donald McIntyre, *Effective Teaching and Learning: Teachers' and Students' Perspectives* (Berkshire: McGraw-Hill Education, 1998), p. 35.
50   Only selected parts of the interviews that exemplify each theme were translated into English when writing up the results.

Results

Four themes emerged in the analysis of the interview data.

(i) **Benefits**: the students' perspectives on their knowledge development during the training school and how this impacted their way of conceiving musical practice;

(ii) **Positive aspects**: students' positive feedback on the structure, delivery, engagement, and management of the training school;

(iii) **Improvements**: students' feedback on possible changes in the structure, content, and/or pedagogical approach adopted in the training school;

(iv) **Future implications**: students' feedback on a possible impact of the training school in HEIs.

Fig. 4.4 displays the four emergent themes and their correspondent set of sub-themes. Both, themes and sub-themes, listed in the figure will be explained further throughout the description that comes next.

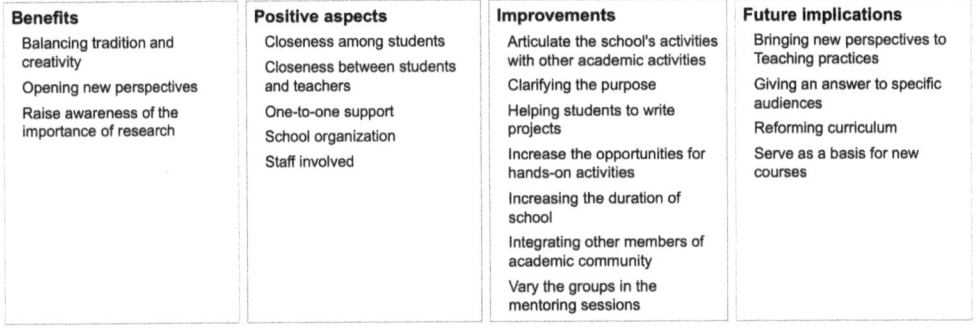

Fig. 4.4: Themes and their respective sub-themes identified in the data analysis of the interviews.

Benefits

Regarding the benefits, the participants talked about how the school could affect their artistic and professional path. One of the benefits mentioned during the focus-group discussion was the possibility of gradually adapting the approach proposed in the training school to the current conservatoire model. We coded this sub-theme as 'balancing tradition and creativity' as listed in Fig. 4.4. It appears that the school stimulated some of the students to explore creativity and take a critical standpoint towards their musical practice, exploring new interpretive possibilities in the repertoire.

> P3: But I think the REACT school was a kick-start for us to start exploring creativity, something I'd never done before, and it helped me open up my horizons a lot. It doesn't mean that now I'm going to do everything in an extremely creative way. We also (need to) follow a tradition in order to then deconstruct it, I think…

This quote summarises what all the participants ended up sharing in the interviews and is in line with the objective set by the REACT consortium for the training school. These objectives were not intended to teach artistic research methods but, rather, to provide students with experiences that would pave the way for them to become open to actively engage with other professional opportunities.

Another theme that emerged in the data analysis was coded as 'opening new perspectives', listed as the second sub-theme in Fig. 4.4. For the participants, the new perspectives were related to projects that they could develop in their future careers, other paths than those exclusively centred on playing in an orchestra or on teaching. The following two quotations refer to this sub-theme. The first concerns the opportunity to think differently about the scores and the concert itself, while the second is about the process of developing a project:

> P4: Everything we did in the workshops really helped to create new ideas for the projects and to give me a new way of thinking about scores and our concerts that I hadn't had before.

> P2: I really enjoyed the week. It was something I've never done before. Throughout the week, I had a lot of ideas about my project, and I don't think I could have done it on my own.

One of the main aims of the REACT training school was to encourage students to explore their own expectations and challenges through project-based learning, rather than proposing ready-made models of good practice. This was mainly achieved in the mentoring sessions, the focus of which was to help students integrate the topics discussed at the training school with their individual contexts.

The last sub-theme coded in Benefits was 'raising awareness of critical and creative thinking'. It describes student feedback on the role of critically exploring the decision-making process that is integral to project development.

> P5: The school gave us the freedom and 'wings' to consciously think in terms of research about what we really wanted to do and not explore aimlessly. We had this idea at the beginning that we were going to experiment without control, but I ended up realising that, more than control, experimentation within the framework of research leads to conscious freedom within the scope of our creative project. I was able to realise this better by attending the workshops…

The training school revealed that any meaningful change in the teaching and learning traditional model through artistic research requires much more than teaching artistic research methods to undergraduate students. If students are surrounded by a teaching culture where research is not a core value, it will be hard for them to understand this paradigm shift. This was highlighted in the above quotation, when the student explained that the school taught them to 'think in terms of research'. All of the students taking part in the training school had previous experience of learning research methods, but P5 suggests that the link between these research methods and their practice was not obvious.

Positive Aspects

The participants identified five positive aspects in the training school, coded as: closeness and partnership between students, closeness and partnership between teachers and students, individual support, school organisation, and staff involved in the school. Each of these aspects were coded as sub-themes. The first one (closeness and partnership between students) concerns the relationships established between participants in the training school. P9 and P2 referred to such relationships as more meaningful than others established in their usual courses. They appreciated the friendly environment that encouraged interaction between students and between students and teachers.

> P9: [There was] a deeper relationship with the participants in this training school than probably with many of the colleagues I've known in the music department since the beginning of the year
>
> P2: We spend more time with these people [the REACT training school colleagues] than with other colleagues on our course […] it's social, and social is extremely important and this Training School is centred on that too

Since the training school was developed on the basis of values such as collaboration and sharing, these quotes lead us to reflect further on why such a connection between the participants was so evident. These students were all enrolled at the same institution, but it seems that the training opened up an opportunity for them to discuss their challenges and expectations in a non-judgemental environment, where all participants had the chance to discuss and contribute individually to each other's projects.

The second sub-theme listed as a positive aspect was 'closeness and partnership between students and teachers'. P2 observed that the training school allowed students to share more about their feelings and ideas:

> P2: I think it was very good that there was no distance between teachers and students, I'm talking about the coffee break, I think this connection helped a lot and it's a form of sharing, because music is also what we do, we share a taste that we all have, however different it may be, it's always a way of getting together, of creating new connections, of creating small roots within the same area, so to speak.

This quotation refers to the general perceptions of the students: the training school followed a dialogical and horizontal approach that facilitated the relationship between students and teachers, despite age or cultural differences in the group. The students felt an openness from the teachers, which encouraged them to share their thoughts and ideas. This was particularly important in one-to-one interactions, such as in the mentoring sessions.

One of the main aspects highlighted by the students was the 'individual support' given to them during the mentoring sessions—the third sub-theme coded within the positive aspects. The tutorial sessions opened a space for students to share their personal ideas on a more personal level and receive feedback from teachers.

> P1: I think that, in my case, what was perhaps most important were the mentoring sessions. We talked about everything [...] but the mentoring was a bit more individual and specific to each case. In my case it helped more than probably for others, because on the last day we had mentoring with the teacher who gave the lecture on performance anxiety, and I think the lecture was super interesting, she was able to help me more directly. At least for me, for my problems, that moment gave me more space to talk about more private things. I think those sessions were the most important parts for me...

This observation suggests that a culture of mentoring should be fostered in HME. Although these students have individual lessons on a regular basis, the comment also suggests that creating opportunities to discuss wider topics with other experts could be very useful. P1's quotation also leads us to recognise that topics such as artistic enquiry and performance anxiety are closely linked and that this relationship could be explored further in future interventions.

Another two sub-themes coded as positive aspects were the 'school organisation' and the 'staff involved'. Participants found the programme to be balanced, with very good connections between lectures. P4 and P5 highlighted the fact that the programme was well balanced and that there was non-hierarchical relationship between student and staff.

> P4: I think the organisation of the school was quite good. It wasn't overwhelming, it wasn't too heavy. It was intense, but it was of an appropriate intensity. It wasn't too heavy for what I was expecting. Because when I saw the weekly timetable, I was frightened by how many different things we were going to have, but I think there was a good connection between them, and that got people motivated and wanting to know more.

> P5: I totally agree that the organisation was exemplary, these things are usually chaotic, with many teachers who never keep to the timetable and we're also Portuguese and consequently arrive late... this issue of there not being so much hierarchy between teachers and students is also something I've always valued a lot, I didn't know almost anyone in the group that took part, but out of the blue it seemed like everyone was my friend!

These last two comments constitute significant feedback for the organisation of the training school. Seemingly, these students were expecting topics to be presented in a one-directional, expository manner. Adopting project-based learning combined with a student-centred approach allowed the REACT staff to cover a wide variety of topics in an interactive and therefore light-hearted way.

Improvements

The participants in the focus group talked about a number of possible improvements for future interventions as well as for the proposed shift to the new paradigm, which were very relevant for this initiative. These improvements were coded as the following sub-themes: 'articulating the school's programme with other academic activities', 'integrating more teachers and students', 'helping students to write projects', 'increasing the opportunities for hands-on activities', 'increasing the duration of the school', and 'varying the groups' formation in mentoring sessions'. The first sub-theme, 'articulating the school's programme with other academic activities', concerns the importance of integrating the school activities with the existing curriculum. For example, some students were not allowed to participate all week because some teachers did not excuse them from their other regular activities, as indicated by P6.

> P6: But even so, for the experience I had, which was very limited, I think it was very enriching and I'm very sorry I couldn't stay the whole week and that's also something I can add to the things that could be better. We had a whole week to try and sort out our creativity (so to speak), but, for example, I had to leave in the middle of this very special and unusual project to take part in an orchestra activity that I've been doing since the beginning of my degree [...] just because no one was released from the orchestra.

This problem arose due to the difficulty of articulating intensive extracurricular courses with the institution's regular activities without overriding them. However, many students felt that their instrumental teacher should have been involved. This suggestion of improvement was coded as 'integrating other teachers and students'. The next two quotation exemplify the importance of involving teachers:

> P2: I think it's important that teachers have this way of understanding our idea and what we've done this week, because it can affect assessment; we can become demotivated when we're assessed. You can spend a whole week acquiring new knowledge that you then fail to apply. If the teachers are in tune with our ideas, or at least if they understand what this 'training school' stands for, then perhaps this is a way for us to make a significant change through the REACT project, rather than confronting two opposing forces.

> P3: To open up this thinking to the whole community, especially the instrument teachers, because as they said, the curriculum is very interesting, but the way it's put into practice sometimes doesn't match the objective. Often, teachers do with the modules what they want and not what is proposed by the module itself, and that makes everything very difficult [...] I'm talking specifically about the orchestra. For

example, I could have been exempted from doing [it for] the rest of the project, but that didn't happen. But there are a lot of problems, you have to deconstruct a lot of problems to be able to implement this kind of thing, but I think we've had some very interesting days.

Continuing in this line of thought, P3 highlighted the importance of involving more students in the training school. This participant emphasised the importance of informing others about the initiative:

P3: I wanted to address this point because I think it's really important that all students know that this school exists and that all teachers should be the main disseminators of this information among their students.

These previous three comments suggest that students are aware that the impact of this training school could be amplified if the instrument teachers were in tune with the main ideas of the training school. This corroborates the idea that the development of new pedagogical approaches to performance must integrate all parties involved.

In addition, some students felt that the training school would benefit from giving students opportunities to plan and organise a concrete project, 'helping students to write their own projects', the fourth sub-theme coded as improvement.

P7: Before the week started I had the idea that we were going to… like… with the mentoring sessions, draw up our projects and put them on paper, you know. And I missed that a bit, because sometimes it's important [...] sometimes it's important to learn how to structure a project, even to prepare it for a public call.

This feedback led us to reflect on the importance of the space opened up by the programme to understand the particularities of each individual case. Although mentoring sessions should naturally cover this aspect, there was still room to delve deeper into each student's particular project.

In terms of the structure of the school, it was suggested that 'increasing the opportunities for hands-on activities', the fifth sub-theme coded as improvement. should be considered:

P9: Have a practical component, even if it's on the day itself. Along with a kind of theoretical lecture, there should also be space in the mentoring session to help students with the practical aspects of realising the project.

In fact, several comments in the interviews emphasised the importance of practical activities for the school (especially those dedicated to developing the project), although the students recognised a good balance between the activities on offer. Some participants suggested that 'increasing the duration of the school' would improve it. This was specially highlighted by P1 and P2. In the second quotation, below, increasing the practical component is linked to the wish for increased opportunities for hands-on activities.

> P1: I would say that there are things that could have more time to discuss. There were moments when we organised ourselves in groups and we had to prepare presentations... but it would be much more effective and interesting if we had had more time. [...] Especially at the beginning of the week we had several practical things and I think this should be the path to continue; it is the one that is the most stimulating and that ends up making the biggest difference [...] I would say that some lectures are immensely theoretical and are interesting too... but, whatever is more practical I like it better. In short, I suggest extending the time with these teachers through more mentoring sessions and workshop sessions.

> P2: So, I think the school week is very well structured, I also think that the issue of specifying some subjects, or some workshops, or even broadening the mentoring sessions would be something that could benefit everyone [...] time could be more extended, it doesn't need to be a week, but also to give time so that we could focus at the theoretical level and have a practical component [...] and even make room for more mentoring sessions so that students have specific help more suited to their specific project.

Increasing the duration of the school, as suggested by these participants, is a challenge for the REACT consortium. In fact, organising interventions like this requires a deep negotiation that involves several parties in each of the five participating institutions.

During the school, the mentoring sessions always comprised the same group of students; only the facilitators changed. P7 and P4 suggested that the groups could also be varied, integrating the students even more, in terms of including the student voice in co-creating sessions. This concerns the seventh code within the improvement category: 'varying the groups' formation in mentoring sessions':

> P7: Really, a week is a short time, it would have to be a longer period, but I also think it's very nice the idea that after each group debate in the mentoring sessions, if we could get to know the ideas of the other groups, of the other projects, because that can help, one can get other ideas and suggestions too.

These suggestions for improvement are important for the planning of future interventions. They highlight the importance of balancing different types of activities and negotiating the pedagogical proposal with the idiosyncrasies of each institution. Although REACT teachers made themselves available to continue supporting the development of projects after the training school finished, the demobilisation caused by the end of face-to-face activities ended up resulting in, if not abandonment, a considerable slowdown in the implementation of individual projects. Only a few students got back in touch with the participating teachers to get further help.

Future Implications

The last theme described in this chapter encompasses two sub-themes, namely: 'giving an answer to specific audiences' and 'serving as a basis for new courses'. According to the students, future implementations of this training school could 'give answers to specific audiences'—the first sub-theme coded as future implications—who are interested in developing more performance and artistic skills to improve in their profession.

> P4: It is always personal, so I think, in the long run, it would help specific students who really want to integrate this new field of vision and lead to a new way of thinking as artists. Not everybody wants to be. There are a lot of people who want to be researchers, want to be artists, there are a lot of different specificities but I think this approach is something that is missing at the moment.

Finally, the students felt that this training school could have a huge impact on curriculum reconfiguration and could 'serve as a basis for new courses'.

> P4: we would really need to experience the REACT school as a master degree or at least as a branch of a course... This would be an effective way to offer this new perspective and knowledge.

P4 also suggested that the structure of the training school could be included as a module in the current plan of the master's degree.

> P4: I think it would be a good idea, not to change the system completely, not to do it in a brutal way, but to implement it little by little. For example, we have many subjects that are not taught at the moment, in the master's degree and bachelor's degree, but they do exist in the curricular plan. I think that, with the REACT training school, we should be able to replace those subjects that are frozen. And it would already be a path of slowly implementing a new way of restructuring the curriculum, and it would already help students in the future, close to those who are finishing the conservatory, to be able to have new subjects that can be very important for the curriculum and for the way of preparing themselves for the labour market.

The comments here suggest that the participating students recognised the potential of an artistic research-based learning for their artistic development and did clearly understand why it should be further explored. Despite feeding back on the potential for improvement, participants recognized that an intervention like the REACT training school should be integrated in the curriculum, not an isolated activity.

Discussion

This book chapter has reported on the second REACT training school, which was a pedagogical intervention testing an artistic research-based approach to teaching and learning music performance, offered as an extracurricular course. The rationale for this implementation is based on the limitations and shortcomings of the 'conservatoire model', which has restricted students' possibilities for developing critical and creative thinking in HEIs. Inspired by the practices and methods of artistic research, the second REACT training school was an initiative designed to foster creativity and critical thinking[51],[52] via a student-centred curriculum and project-based learning.[53] This approach addresses aspects that were mentioned as key issues by the literature referred to in section two. The purpose of the school was to provoke change in the students' perspective and attitude towards making music, by providing perspectives drawn from artistic research practice.

Overall, participants reported benefits related to the school and to their perspectives that seem to match the artistic career demands in music industries. These benefits included balancing tradition and creativity,[54] opening up new perspectives,[55] and raising awareness of critical[56] and creative thinking.[57] The outcomes of the study reported in this chapter reinforce the need to open space for new pedagogical and artistic perspectives that stimulate critical thinking in HME. Overall, the students reported a significant change in their attitude towards music practice and goals. They reported a shift in their creative focus from one of skill competency toward a personal reflective practice focused on project-based learning within their art world. We argue that this shift constitutes an important first step in students' development of their future professional career.

The second REACT training school was designed for the purpose of testing novel approaches in the teaching and learning of music performance. Here, we do not proposed a concrete solution but, instead, present a range of possibilities. Although this intervention offered a clear hint that the proposed approach could lead to a very promising change in mindsets, there is still a need to clarify how artistic research can interact with the conservatoire model, as well as how instrumental teachers, who are not familiar with artistic research, might come to participate. Further, the qualitative study which forms the basis of the chapter had its own limitations: the limited number of interviewees (just 8 from a total of 17 participants); the short duration of the intervention, which did not allow tutorial support until the public presentation

---

51 Burnard, p. 120.
52 Lennon and Reed, p. 258.
53 Correia and others, p. 80.
54 Dalagna, Carvalho, and Welch, p. 180.
55 López-Íñiguez and Bennett, p. 134.
56 Correia and others, p. 20.
57 Thompson, p. 44.

of the developed projects; the data analysis was based on students' reports of their experiences and did not include other sources such as the data related to their final projects' presentations. Nevertheless, the findings marginally suggest several benefits and positive aspects of integrating artistic research practice in the pedagogical structure of HEIs, as further supported by findings presented in other chapters of this book. Students seemed very aware of the importance of their learning development and pointed to the importance of new teaching approaches in HME.

The results here suggest that students highly valued the closeness and the open environment promoted by the training school, in terms of their interactions with staff. Future studies could explore the ways in which institutions encourage students in the deeper investigation of their feelings, activities, questions, and personal challenges. In this way, they would engage students in experiential terms in all the dimensions of the REACT model. The training school was limited, as noted, but it gave us insight into the potential of approaches to teaching and learning performance through artistic research. And, through the qualitative study, we have been encouraged to think of this as an opportunity to increase student autonomy and personal engagement in the design of their studies.

References

Barrett, Estelle, *Aesthetic Experience and Innovation in Practice–Led Research* (2010), conference paper, Deakin Research Online, https://hdl.handle.net/10536/DRO/DU:30032166

Bartleet, Brydie-Leigh, Dawn Bennett, Ruth Bridgstock, Paul Draper, Scott Harrison, and Huib Schippers, 'Preparing for Portfolio Careers in Australian Music: Setting a research agenda' *Australian Society for Music Education Corporation*, 1 (2012), 32–41, https://files.eric.ed.gov/fulltext/EJ1000243.pdf

Beeching, Angela, 'Musicians Made in USA: Training Opportunities and Industry Change', in *Life in the Real World: How to Make Music Graduates Employable*, ed. by Dawn Bennett (Champaign, IL: Common Ground, 2012), pp. 27–43

Bennett, Dawn and Ruth Bridgstock, 'The Urgent Need for Career Preview: Student Expectations and Graduate Realities in Music and Dance', *International Journal of Music Education*, 33 (2015) 3, 263–77, https://doi.org/10.1177/0255761414558653

Bennet, Dawn, Angela Beeching, Rosie Perkins, Glen Carruthers, and Janis Weler, 'Music, Musicians and Careers', in *Life in the Real World: How to Make Music Graduates Employable*, ed. by Dawn Bennett (Champaign, IL: Common Ground, 2012), pp 9-10.

Berger, Martin 'Educing Leadership and Evoking Sound: Choral Conductors as Agents of Change', in *Leadership and Musician Development in Higher Music Education*, ed. by Dawn Bennett, Jennifer Rowley, and Patrick Schmidt (Routledge: New York, 2019), pp. 115–29 (pp. 115–20)

Bulley, James and Özden Şahin, *Practice Research - Report 1: What is practice research? and Report 2: How can practice research be shared?* (London: PRAG-UK, 2021), p. 80, https://doi.org/10.23636/1347

Burnard, Pamela, *Developing Creativities in Higher Music Education: International Perspectives and Practices* (Routledge: London, 2013), p. 100

Carey, Gemma and Don Lebler, 'Reforming a Bachelor of Music Programme: A Case Study', *International Journal of Music Education*, 30 (2012) 4, 312–27

Cooper, Paul and Donald McIntyre, *Effective Teaching and Learning: Teachers' and Students' Perspectives* (Berkshire: McGraw-Hill Education, 1998)

Correia, Jorge and Gilvano Dalagna, 'A Verdade Inconveniente sobre os Estudos em Performance', in *Performance Musical sob uma Perspectiva Pluralista*, ed. by Sonia R. Albano de Lima (São Paulo: Musa Editora, 2021), pp. 11–26

Correia, Jorge and Gilvano Dalagna, *Cahiers of Artistic Research 3: An explanatory model for Artistic Research* (Aveiro: Editora da Universidade de Aveiro, 2018)

Correia, Jorge, Gilvano Dalagna, Alfonso Benetti, and Francisco Monteiro, *Cahiers of Artistic Research 1: When Is Research Artistic Research?* (Aveiro: Editora da Universidade de Aveiro, 2018)

Correia, Jorge and others, REACT–Rethinking Music Performance in European Higher Education Institutions, *Artistic Career in Music: Stakeholders Requirement Report* (Aviero: UA Editora, 2021), https://doi.org/10.48528/wfq9-4560

Crispin, Darla, 'Artistic Research and Music Scholarship: Musings and Models from a Continental European Perspective', in *Artistic Practice as Research in Music: Theory, Criticism, Practice*, ed. by Mine Doğantan-Dack (Surrey: Ashgate Publishing, 2015), pp. 53–72

Dalagna, Gilvano, Sara Carvalho, and Graham Welch, *Desired Artistic Outcomes in Music Performance* (Abingdon: Routledge, 2021)

De Assis, Paulo, *Logic of Experimentation: Rethinking Music Performance through Artistic Research* (Leuven: Leuven University Press, 2018)

Deliège, Irene, and Geraint Wiggins, *Musical Creativity: Multidisciplinary Research in Theory and Practice* (Psychology Press: East Sussex, 2006)

Durrant, Colin, 'Shaping Identity Through Choral Activity: Singers' and Conductors' Perceptions', *Research Studies in Music Education* 24 (2005) 1, 88–98, https://doi.org/10.1177/1321103X050240010701

Dylan Smith, Gareth, 'Masculine Domination in Private Sector Popular Music Performance Education in England', in *Bourdieu and the Sociology of Music Education*, ed. by Pamela Burnard, Ylva Trulsson Hofvander, and Johan Söderman (Ashgate: Surrey, 2015), pp. 61–78

Ford, Biranda and John Sloboda, 'Learning from Artistic and Pedagogical Differences Between Musicians' and Actors' Traditions Through Collaborative Processes', in *Collaborative Learning in Higher Music Education*, ed. by Helena Gaunt and Heidi Westerlund (Surrey: Ashgate, 2013), pp. 27–36

Gill, Rosalind, 'Cool, Creative and Egalitarian? Exploring Gender in Project-Based New Media Work in Europe', *Information, Communication and Society*, 5 (2002), 70–89, https://doi.org/10.1080/13691180110117668

Gaunt, Helena, Andrea Creech, Marion Long, and Susan Hallam, 'Supporting Conservatoire Students Towards Professional Integration: One-to-One Tuition and the Potential of Mentoring', *Music Education Research*, 14 (2012) 1, 25–43

Haseman, Brad, 'A Manifesto for Performative Research', *Media International Australia*, 118 (2006) 1, 98–106

Jørgensen, Harold, 'Western Classical Music Studies in Universities and Conservatoires', in *Advanced Musical Performance: Investigations in Higher Education Learning*, ed. by Ioulia Papageorgi and Graham Welch (Ashgate: Surrey, 2014), pp. 3–20

Jørgensen, Harold *Research into Higher Music Education* (Oslo: Novos Press, 2009)

Lennon, Mary and Geoffrey Reed, 'Instrumental and Vocal Teacher Education: Competences, Roles and Curricula', *Music Education Research*, 14 (2012) 3, 285–308

López-Íñiguez, Guadalupe and Dawn Bennett, 'A Lifespan Perspective on Multi-Professional Musicians: Does Music Education Prepare Classical Musicians for their Careers?', *Music Education Research*, 22 (2020) 1, 1–14, https://doi.org/ 10.1080/14613808.2019.1703925

López-Íñiguez, Guadalupe and Dawn Bennett, 'Broadening Student Musicians' Career Horizons: The Importance of Being and Becoming a Learner in Higher Education', *International Journal of Music Education*, 39 (2021) 2, 134–50, https://doi.org/10.1177/0255761421989111

López-Íñiguez, Guadalupe and Pamela Burnard, 'Towards a Nuanced Understanding of Musicians' Professional Learning Pathways: What Does Critical Reflection Contribute?', *Research Studies in Music Education*, 0 (2021) 0, 1–31, https://doi.org/10.1177/1321103X211025850

López-Íñiguez, Guadalupe and Dawn Bennett, 'A Lifespan Perspective on Multi-Professional Musicians: Does Music Education Prepare Classical Musicians for their Careers?', *Music Education Research*, 22 (2020) 1, 1–14, https://doi.org/10.1080/14613808.2019.1703925

Östersjö, Stefan, 'Art Worlds, Voice and Knowledge: Thoughts on Quality Assessment of Artistic Research Outcomes', *ÍMPAR Online journal for artistic research*, 3(2) (2019), 60–69

Östersjö, Stefan, 'Thinking-Through-Music: On Knowledge Production, Materiality, and Embodiment in Artistic Research', in *Artistic Research in Music: Discipline and Resistance*, ed. by Jonathan Impett (Leuven: Leuven University, Press, 2018), pp. 88–107

Papageorgi, Ioulia and Graham Welch, (eds), *Advanced Musical Performance: Investigations in Higher Education Learning* (Surrey: Ashgate, 2014)

Papageorgi, Ioulia, Andrea Creech, Elizabeth Haddon, Frances Morton, Christophe De Bezenac, Evangelos Himonides, John Potter, Celia Duffy, Tony Whyton, and Graham Welch, 'Perceptions and Predictions of Expertise in Advanced Musical Learners', *Psychology of Music*, 38 (2010a) 1, 31–66

Papageorgi, Ioulia, Andrea Creech, Elizabeth Haddon, Frances Morton, Christophe De Bezenac, Evangelos Himonides, John Potter, Celia Duffy, Tony Whyton, and Graham Welch, 'Institutional Culture and Learning I: Perceptions of the Learning Environment and Musicians' Attitudes to Learning'. *Music Education Research*, 12 (2010b) 2, 151–178.

Persson, Roland S., 'The Subjective World of the Performer', in *Handbook of Music and Emotion: Theory Research and Applications*, ed. by Patrick N. Juslin and John Sloboda (New York: Oxford University Press, 2001), pp. 275–89

Perkins, Rosie, 'Learning Cultures and the Conservatoire: An Ethnographically-informed Case Study', *Music Education Research*, 15 (2013) 2, 196–213

Robson, Colin, *Real World Research* (West Sussex: Wiley, 2011)

Seth, Sanjay, *Beyond the Reason: Postcolonial Theory and the Social Sciences* (Oxford: Oxford University Press, 2021)

Silverman, Marissa 'A Performer's Creative Processes: Implications for Teaching and Learning Musical Interpretation', *Music Education Research*, 10 (2008) 2, 249–69

Smilde, Rineke and Sigurdur Halldórsson, 'New Audiences and Innovative Practice: An International Master's Programme with Critical Reflection and Mentoring at the Heart of an Artistic Laboratory', in *Collaborative Learning in Higher Music Education*, ed. by Helena Gaunt and Heidi Westerlund (Surrey: Ashgate, 2013), pp. 225–30

Sloboda, John, *Musicians and Their Live Audiences: Dilemmas and Opportunities. Understanding Audiences*, ([n. p.]: Scribd, 2013), https://pt.scribd.com/document/538118141/Sloboda-John-Musicians-and-their-live-audiences-dilemmas-and-opportunities

Stepniak, Michael and Peter Sirotin, *Beyond the Conservatoire Model: Reimagining Classical Music Performance Training in Higher Education* (Abingdon: Routledge, 2020), p. 72

Thompson, Katja 'Fostering Transformative Professionalism Through Curriculum Changes Within a Bachelor of Music', in *Expanding Professionalism in Music and Higher Music Education: A Changing Game*, ed. by Heidi Westerlund and Helena Gaunt (Routledge: London, 2021), pp. 42–58

PART II

NOVEL APPROACHES TO TEACHING INTERPRETATION AND PERFORMANCE

Introduction to Part II

Gilvano Dalagna

How can musical interpretation be taught in a way that develops the lifelong skill of critical thinking and a reflective methodology built on artistic research? Musical interpretation is a core element of performance teaching in European HEIs, and it is a crucial outcome of learning programmes. It has, moreover, been central to artists whose research is developed and disseminated within the art world and, so, whose practice requires regular and insider reflection. Recent studies have suggested that musical interpretation is not negotiated and that students are responsible for developing their own artistic voice. However, the case studies in Part III of this book show how much the curriculum can support the development of the student voice when this is central to the design of the curriculum. The position of the student as apprentice is a consequence of a traditional pedagogical approach that developed in the nineteenth century and still informs teaching and learning practices. In this master-apprentice model, the role of the instructor is like that of the guru who passes on his or her own crafts and skills without any sense of co-creation or negotiation.

Part II of this volume shares four case studies that explore an alternative pedagogical perspective on music performance and musical interpretation, discussing and reconfiguring the master-apprentice approach. These four chapters informed the development of the REACT model, presented in the Introduction of this book. They provide insights and examples of how the topics and the spheres can be implemented. Inevitably, the chapters here presented are essentially focused on the spheres of contextualizing and exploring 'in' the model. The four case studies exemplify how students can be taught to address their subjectivity (*contextualizing*) and how to investigate it through sources and materials to develop their artistic voice (*exploring*). This is crucial for negotiating tradition and innovation when developing new practices that will reconfigure conceptual models. These chapters also show how teaching and learning can go beyond the master-apprentice approach and embrace improvisation, collaboration, and composition.

The case studies reported here were developed in two different countries, Norway and the UK, by expert performers and educators with extensive teaching experience in higher music education. Starting with the Norwegian context, Mariam Kharatyan draws on her experience of artistic research as a classically trained pianist, in Chapter 7, to explore pedagogical strategies based on (re)introducing improvisation in the teaching and learning of classical music performance. Turning to the UK context, Robert Sholl's Chapter 5 describes a hands-on approach to the teaching and learning of counterpoint, through improvisation and composition. Hereby, his chapter provides an example of Paul Craenen's claim, with reference to the design of master's studies in music performance, that

> artistic research suggests a potential to transcend the practice-theory dichotomy which we may still encounter in the way courses such as music history, music theory, aesthetics, and all kinds of optional courses are offered separately from the main subject of study.[1]

As both improvisation and composition are critical to the notion of collaboration and collaborative learning, Part II includes two further chapters that address these issues through case studies conducted in the UK. In Chapter 6, Jacob-Thompson Bell explores Critical Response Process (CRP) to expand models of individual student-centred learning to benefit from the 'distributive' agency in a classroom, with specific focus on performing arts in a conservatoire setting. Richard Fay, Daniel Mawson, and Nahielly Palacios focus in Chapter 8 on the reflective performer practices embedded in the Klezmer Ensemble Performance (KEP) module at The University of Manchester, UK. These authors introduce a reflective-performer framework into their klezmer ensemble and examine the resulting texts generated to accompany their assessed performance, that is, the reflective texts through which they situate their informed performance intentions. These two chapters explore further the notions of critical thinking, inclusivity, and equity, which are central to the sphere *contextualizing* in the artistic research-based approach proposed by the REACT consortium, representing practical examples of how to integrate these in HEIs.

We hope the readers find inspiration in these four chapters for how artistic research-based learning can be adapted and explored in different pedagogical settings—those in which the teacher is looking beyond the master-apprentice approach. The practices discussed here may play an important role in promoting a respectful pedagogical experience, which is a fundamental pillar in students' search for their artistic voice.

---

[1] Paul Craenen, 'Artistic research as an integrative force. A critical look at the role of master's research at Dutch conservatoires', *FORUM+*, 27.1 (2020), 45–55, https://doi.org/https://doi.org/10.5117/FORUM2020.1.CRAE

5. Artistic Practice as Embodied Learning: Reconnecting Pedagogy, Improvisation, and Composition

Robert Sholl

Introduction

'When you know what you're doing, you can do what you want'.[1]

More than forty years ago, Joseph Kerman proposed the notion of 'getting out of' musical analysis—a strategy, through criticism, to contextualise formalist analytical thought.[2] Kerman's argument was flawed in many respects as Kofi Agawu pointed out; analysis was necessary, in the latter's view, to teach 'undergraduate music theory' and 'basic musical literacy', something Kerman, doubtless, would not have denied.[3]

Yet these somewhat circuitous debates missed something more fundamental, especially as ideological and academic territories seemed to require protection.[4] Over at least the last forty years the rise of university theory courses, particularly in America, has

---

[1] A saying often used by the somatic educationalist Moshe Feldenkrais, including in a training session delivered on 9 June 1980 at Amherst. My thanks to Simon Rigby (University of West London) and Nicholas Walker (The Royal Academy of Music) for their thoughtful comments on this chapter. My thanks, too, to Daniel K. L. Chua who inspired this idea for this chapter. I taught 'Techniques of Composition' with Daniel at King's College London in the mid-1990s, and Daniel used the theme of the *Goldberg Variations* for teaching species counterpoint.

[2] See Joseph Kerman, 'How We Got into Analysis, and How to Get out', *Critical Inquiry*, 7.2 (Winter 1980), 311–31.

[3] Kofi Agawu, 'How We Got out of Analysis, and How to Get Back in Again', *Music Analysis*, 23:2/3 (July–October 2004), pp. 267–86 (p. 269).

[4] See Julian Horton, 'On the Musicological Necessity of Musical Analysis', *Musical Quarterly*, 103, 1–2 (2022), 62-104; and 'Valuing the Surplus: Perspectives on Julian Horton's Article "On the Musicological Necessity of Music Analysis"', with contributions by Kofi Agawu, Gurminder K. Bhogal, Esther Cavett, Jonathan Dunsby, Julian Horton, Alexandra Monchick, Ian Pace, Henry Stobart and Simon Zagorski-Thomas; compiled and edited by Esther Cavett, in *Music Analysis*, 32:3, 412–71, https://doi.org/10.1111/musa.12221

led to a schism between theory as a discipline and theory as a necessary precursor and as complementary to practice—for learning repertoire, improvisation, and for composition.

Analysts interested in performance, and attempting to inform performance, are not a new phenomenon.[5] Some recent attempts to bridge disciplinary boundaries are surveyed by Mine Doğantan-Dack, who has proposed a form of practice-based approach to music theory through artistic research.[6] Her work attempts to assimilate phenomenological insights and the 'highly situated embodied, affective, multimodal factors that shape a performer's (listening) experience' of music to create new interpretative knowledge through practice. She critiques the way scholars such as Gabriela Imreh (with psychologists, Roger Chaffin and Mary Crawford), Jeffrey Swinkin, Daphne Leong, and Janet Schmalfeldt have attempted to employ theory to inform and shape performance.[7] Yet Doğantan-Dack does not discuss what can be learned from formalist analysis, or analysis in general, and why or how analysis can inform performance by providing alternative paradigms for musical awareness. It can, for example, provide a means of understanding and thence also of articulating the relationships between small and large-scale musical aspects (between motives and structure), or between voice-leading and register, which can create interpretative insight co-extensive with the investigation of melos and malleability, narrative and rhetoric, and the play with expectations that are forms of artistic research. The vital dialogue between analysis and performance aids the emergent process of listening and doing that is active, interrogatory, and, therefore, critical, and that is also a form of embodied knowledge.

Implicit in much work on the relationship between analysis and performance is what the psychoanalytic philosopher Jacques Lacan described as the position of the analyst or the 'subject [and what he or she is] supposed to know'.[8] For Lacan, desire and lack are structured by the Other, and this can be perceived through the academic turn to performance in which the libidinal allure of performance is considered as a desired form

---

5   See a digest of this in Ian Pace, 'In Defence of Analytically-Informed Performance'. Keynote Paper presented at the International Encounters on Music Theory and Analysis Conference, 6 November 2019, São Paolo, Brazil, https://openaccess.city.ac.uk/id/eprint/30386/

6   Mine Doğantan-Dack, 'Expanding the Scope of Music Theory: Artistic Research in Music Performance', *Zeitschrift der Gesellschaft für Musiktheorie*, 19/2 (2022), https://www.gmth.de/zeitschrift/artikel/1169.aspx?fbclid=IwAR26sZcGvqUEtw3s9NG5rzGdm56D3N41Z_s5HFfKZQZOGh0CbuVA_GyO3z8

7   Roger Chaffin, Gabriela Imreh, and Mary Crawford, *Practicing Perfection: Memory and Piano Performance* (New York: Psychology Press, 2002), https://doi.org/10.4324/9781410612373; Jeffrey Swinkin, *Performative Analysis: Reimagining Music Theory for Performance* (Rochester, NY: Rochester University Press, 2016), https://doi.org/10.2307/j.ctvc16ncq; Daphne Leong, *Performing Knowledge: Twentieth-Century Music in Analysis and Performance* (New York: Oxford University Press, 2019), https://doi.org/10.1093/oso/9780190653545.001.0001; and Janet Schmalfeldt, 'Who's Keeping the Score?', in *Investigating Musical Performance: Theoretical Models and Intersections*, ed. by Gianmario Borio, Giovanni Giuriati, Alessandro Cecchi, and Marco Lutzu (New York: Routledge, 2020), pp. 91–101, https://doi.org/10.4324/9780429026461-10

8   See Slavoj Žižek's discussion of this idea in his *Surplus-Enjoyment: A Guide for the Non-Perplexed* (London: Bloomsbury Academic, 2022), pp. 111–17.

and idealised benchmark of musical reality.⁹ The desire to objectify, advise, and even control performers testifies perhaps to the immanence (and also perhaps impotence) of a certain kind of musical theory. It also suggests a perceived value in the prestige (through competitions, marketing, forms of commodification, and capitalisation, for example) that can be realised through performance not necessarily through music theory. Concomitantly, there can also be a resistance to analysis from performers in conservatoires, to what (alas) can be perceived as didactic, and even as irrelevant to the skills needed for performance.

Both these extremes are unhelpful and, fortunately, are being rigorously dismantled in modern conservatoires. Artistic research can perhaps provide some form of mediation between these positions. Yet, it also must be careful not merely to reinscribe the ideological dominance of master narratives (such as analysis), or rely too heavily on abstruse intellectualisation to justify itself. There is also a debate in the artistic research community concerning its relation to other disciplines (this can be understood sometimes as form of 'special pleading' writ large through the perceived immanence of artistic research), and there is a sense also of taking refuge in gilded institutional cages under the rubric of 'research' (the issues of methodology, quality, and significance are moot especially in neo-liberal educational contexts), something that has contributed to the political understanding of artistic research.¹⁰

These issues are all perhaps symptoms of larger and laudable desires to take artistic research seriously in and out of conservatoires and to recognise it as a discipline across the arts. Lacan understood that desire is already within us, and it is an object cause of subjectivity.¹¹ Identity as a musician is bound to a desire to configure how one is understood in the world (the relationship between the 'Symbolic' and 'Imaginary'

---

9   Jacques Lacan, *Seminar XI, The Four Fundamental Concepts of Psychoanalysis*, ed. by Jacques-Alain Miller, trans. by Alan Sheridan (London: Karnac, 2004), pp. 84, 115, 180, 188, 235. The Other can be understood as superego demands or injunctions but also as the invisible and unspoken expectations placed upon thought and behaviour by society.

10 Some of these different perspectives inform the work in volume 10 of *Music & Practice*, https://www.musicandpractice.org/volume-10/. For instance, Erlend Hovland confidently asserts: 'still, its [artistic research's] main strength lies in its opposition to conventional academic research' ('Artistic Research and *Music & Practice*, unpaginated, DOI: 10.32063/1000). Yet, Anders Førisdal and Christina Sofie Kobb state: 'we do think that artistic research will benefit from adapting a practice deeply imbedded in the humanities, in which the internal criticism and 'tough' reflection regarding the use of method, theory, terminology and models is an integral part of any (scientific) standing of the research' ('Artistic Research! Where are we today?', unpaginated, DOI: 10.32063/1001). Barbara Lüneberg, in 'Knowledge Production in Artistic Research—Opportunities and Challenges', states: 'As an additional aside, disseminating findings in text form, as is typical of the Western academic research tradition, helps to make research accessible to a wider academic audience, builds in-depth knowledge of artistic research in a broader research community, and establishes an easily accessible track record as an artistic researcher' (unpaginated, DOI: 10.32063/1009). On the politics of artistic research, see Silvia Henke, Dieter Mersch, Thomas Strässle, Jörg Wiesel, Nicolaj van der Meulen, *Manifesto of Artistic Research: A Defense Against Its Advocates* (Zurich: Diaphanes, 2020). The authors recommend the emancipation of artistic research from university research (p. 5). They rehearse many of the contradictions and issues that plague this emerging field, and promote such debates as axiomatic.

11 Lacan, *Seminar XI*, p. 243.

registers for Lacan) and is connected to legitimacy—certainly a vibrant issue for artistic research. Another ramification of Lacan's thought is that human actions, whether *considered* embodied or not, are framed by this embodied desire. The creation of music theory and indeed notation (as shown below) are already forms of embodied actions.[12] The artificial separation of *Epistêmê* and *Technê*, or between the Cartesian mind and body are prima facie grounded in an embodiment and in the integration of these perceived binaries through action. The somatic educational thinker Mosche Feldenkrais (1904–1984) clearly understood the error of believing that thinking and doing are separate rather than components of a singular activity that enfolds within itself multiple modalities of thought, including agency and intention, listening and perception, and subjectivity and objectivity.[13]

Artistic research I would argue is made stronger by exposing itself and engaging with the interdisciplinarity of musicology. The continual expansion of the curriculum, the increased theoretical specificity and complexity of musical and cultural analysis (not necessarily separate), the proliferation of different forms of analysis, and the widening of repertoire, including jazz, popular, and world music offer forms of knowing that can enrich artistic research. Understanding different discourses, including analysis, speaks to the idea of differentiation that precedes integration, something that was advocated as a fundamental learning process by the Russian researcher and physician Nikolai Bernstein and by Feldenkrais.[14]

Learning, as Feldenkrais pointed out, is one of the greatest endowments that we have as human beings. Feldenkrais believed that integrating learning as embodied knowledge in action was related to our sense of pleasure.[15] He also believed that learning was best when it was embodied, and this is where I would argue that disciplines such as analysis, aural training, orchestration and arranging, and composition could be taught through the keyboard as a means of concretising kinaesthetic learning. This form of learning embraces the embodied experience advocated by Doğantan-Dack, but this chapter takes a few steps back from her purview to examine the technique and mechanism that inform a context for learning. This return to skills is an essential part of learning (at any stage) that enables a person to 'know what you are doing' so that 'you can do what you want' as Feldenkrais put it. The process or acquisition of skills,

---

12 For a recent study of embodiment and performance, see Jocelyn Ho, 'Corporeal Musical Structure: A Gestural-Kinesthetic Approach to Tōru Takemitsu's *Rain Tree Sketch II*', *Music Theory Online*, 27:4 (December 2021), https://mtosmt.org/issues/mto.21.27.4/mto.21.27.4.ho.html

13 Mosche Feldenkrais, *Thinking and Doing* (Longmont, CO: Genesis II, 2013). See also Roger Russell, 'Radical Practice: Practising Performance and Practising Oneself is the Same Activity', *The Feldenkrais Method in Creative Practice: Dance, Music, and Theatre*, ed. Robert Sholl (London: Methuen, 2021), p. 84, https://doi.org/10.5040/9781350158412

14 Nikolai Bernstein, *Dexterity and its Development*, ed. by Mark Latash and Michael Turvey (New York: Psychology Press, 1986); Dick McCaw, 'Learning through Feeling: How the Ideas of Nikolai Bernstein and Moshe Feldenkrais Apply to Performer Training', in *The Feldenkrais Method in Creative Practice*, ed. by Sholl, pp. 55–72.

15 Feldenkrais, *Embodied Wisdom: The Collected Papers of Mosche Feldenkrais*, ed. by Elizabeth Beringer (Berkeley, CA: Somatic Resources and North Atlantic Books, 2010), pp. 182–83.

through an analytical and critical process—a methodology formed of differentiations—is an essential developmental pathway to the learning of craft, which facilitates artistry.

This chapter, therefore, relies to an extent on the thinking inherent in the Feldenkrais Method, a system of somatic education. Feldenkrais believed that the goal of his Method was 'to make the impossible possible, the possible easy, and the easy aesthetically pleasurable', and this is what musicians strive to do every day through practice.[16] Feldenkrais developed group lessons that he called 'Awareness through Movement' lessons (ATMs).[17] These take a particular movement function and approach it in different ways.

This approach is implicitly adopted in this chapter, which presents a systematic focus on specific skills designed to facilitate mastery. This sense of mastery is transferrable and is something too often left to chance because curricula are often over-filled and calibrated to students who process and adapt ideas quickly with little space for experimentation or further approximations. If learning happens through feeling and sensation, as Bernstein and Feldenkrais both pointed out, then the time it to takes to listen, to feel, to sense oneself in action while making critically nuanced differentiations through judgment, is invaluable and should be understood as a vital part of conservatoire and musical education.[18]

Artistic acculturation is built on development though such time and deep listening skills, and shaped by aesthetic and sensorial feeling and judgement that creates craft; this is a form of holistic *Technê*. Artistic research is an arena in which higher levels of syntheses come into play. It is premised on knowing something, on having some 'petrol in the tank' (prior knowledge and skill), and especially on the ability to make aesthetic choices. In research terms, these choices can be construed as an interrogation of how something is done and what is done—its origins, style, and poetics.

This study, therefore, proposes a way in which this form of coming to know something—the process of what Feldenkrais calls 'integration'—can take place. It presents a form of synthesis between theory and analysis and between improvisation and composition. This is an ideal that has increasingly become the purview of jazz tutorial books which place much emphasis on blending such skills including aural training through playing.[19] There are also some excellent guides to improvisation that fold theory into discussions of harmony, shape, figuration, and form.[20] Such pedagogical books demonstrate that the often-separated elements of music and of traditions are, in fact, complementary.

---

16   Mosche Feldenkrais, 'Learning, Free Choice, Individuality', recorded lecture given at Quest Workshop, New York, [n. d.] (San Diego: Feldenkrais Resources, 1981). My transcription from programme.
17   Individual lessons are called 'Functional Integration'.
18   See McCaw, 'Learning through Feeling'.
19   For a good example of this, see Edward Sarath, *Music Theory through Improvisation: A New Approach to Musicianship Training* [book and CD] (New York: Taylor and Francis, 2010). This book works across traditions and is useful for students of jazz or western art music.
20   See Franz Josef Stoiber, *Fascination Organ Improvisation: A Study and Practice Book* (Kassel: Bärenreiter, 2018) and John J. Mortensen, *The Pianist's Guide to Historical Improvisation* (New York: Oxford University Press, 2020).

In this chapter, I treat these musical formants holistically to promote a form of literacy and fluency that is based on immersive study. Common to the study of style and technique is a process of becoming (self-)aware of our actions and calibrating these with compositional models.[21] The exercises and ideas below allow stakeholders (teachers and students) to move freely between these areas and to examine them in relation to J.S. Bach's *Goldberg Variations* (1741). Most importantly, the resulting aspects of 'integration' allow the student to develop their own sense of autonomy and pride in their achievements. This study develops a critical and reflexive method for this task. It begins by presenting a creative rethinking of species counterpoint, a foundation for thinking in Schenkerian analysis,[22] through Bach's *Goldberg Variations*.[23] This process develops a resource for pedagogy and practice. In Fig. 5.2 below, I present a layered cake of musical lines (moving from semibreves to quavers) against the figured bass of the theme as an exercise that includes various aspects of variation 1 of the *Goldberg Variations*, and then I explore the codes and ramifications of this that encourage historical sensitivity, creative development, and an embodied feeling and learning that is already a form of artistic research.

This contextualised exercise provides a stepping-stone to a discussion of Variation 4 and Variation 1 (already included in Fig. 5.2) and the development of complete variations beginning with a given 'invention' and then moving to the composition of new ideas.[24] This strategy attempts to promote an 'adaptive flexibility' in which

---

21 See David Gorton and Stefan Östersjö, 'Austerity Measures I: Performing the Discursive Voice', in *Voices, Bodies, Practices: Performing Musical Subjectivities*, ed. by Catherine Laws, William Brooks, David Gorton, Thanh Thủy Nguyễn, Stefan Östersjö, and Jeremy J. Wells (Leuven: Leuven University Press, 2019), pp. 29-79 (p. 45).

22 Kent Wheeler Kennan uses a creative adaptation of species as the basis for teaching counterpoint. His approach is a comparable to mine in that it uses 1, then 2, 3, and 4 notes against a bass, and he provides good examples from the common-practice repertoire to help students. See his *Counterpoint Based on Eighteenth Century Practice*, 3rd edn (Englewood Cliffs, NJ: Prentice-Hall, 1987). Sarath also includes a discussion of species counterpoint in Appendix 1 of his book *Music theory through Improvisation*. Kennan's goal (like Teresa Davidian's) is fugue; in her book, she moves straight from species counterpoint to fugue. See Davidian, *Tonal Counterpoint for the 21st Century Musician: An Introduction* (Lanham, MD: Rowman & Littlefield, 2015). Peter Schubert's *Modal Counterpoint, Renaissance Style* (New York: Oxford University Press, 2003) is a well-written reference source with good and clear examples that provides a very gradual way into species counterpoint. The focus in this book is more on Renaissance style, and it takes a long time to get to composition. Beth Denisch's book moves beyond species counterpoint to a wider purview of counterpoint with some application to modern contemporary styles. It includes a good online resource which helps put 'petrol' or 'gas in the tank', for the creative application of counterpoint. See Denisch, *Contemporary Counterpoint: Theory and Application* (Boston: Berklee Press, 2017). On the relationship between species counterpoint and Schenkerian analysis, see Allen Forte and Steven E. Gilbert, *Introduction to Schenkerian Analysis: Form and Content in Tonal Music* (New York: W.W. Norton, 1982), pp. 41–49, and their *Instructor's Manual for Introduction to Schenkerian Analysis* (New York: W.W. Norton, 1982), p. 18.

23 The *Goldbergs Variations* are used by Lionel Rogg in his *Improvisation Course for Organists* (Fleurier: Schola Cantorum, 1988), p. 28. For a fascinating analytical study of the variations, see Alan Street, 'The Rhetorico-Musical Structure of the 'Goldberg' Variations: Bach's 'Clavier-Übung' IV and the 'Institutio Oratoria' of Quintilian', *Music Analysis*, Vol. 6, No. 1/2 (March-July 1987), pp. 89-131.

24 On the idea of 'invention', see Laurence Dreyfus, *Bach and the Patterns of Invention* (Cambridge, MA: Harvard University Press, 1997), pp. 1–32.

students can actively and organically learn musical and technical fluency while also developing their creativity and autonomy.[25]

Bach's music, therefore, provides a structure, a model, but also a medium for both confrontation and reconciliation with the past—a template for re-imagining the levels of learning and experiment behind the score understood from a conjunction of practical, historical, and analytical perspectives. In this chapter, Bach's music is imagined as a form of questioning to the analyst-improviser-composer that asks them to reflect on their hearing, their prejudices, and their desires (for outcomes), as well as to pose contingent answers in the spirit of experimentation discussed in the introduction to this volume.

The material is written out here so that it can be re-used. Improvisation is therefore not treated as an object for study (as in much work in critical improvisation studies) but as a practice.[26] The thinking below is a method that might serve as an introduction to teaching composition or stylistic composition, and would be useful for undergraduates in their first or possibly second year of study, but it could be adapted for use in secondary school education. The material could be used in different ways, but my strong recommendation is that writing should not be separated from playing; the two activities need to co-exist to facilitate different sensations, experiences, and forms of integrated learning.

Analysis, improvisation, and composition all imply traditions, but here my concern is with creating an environment for learning in which these things intermingle as an embodied form of artistic practice. This itself has a good historical pedigree, for instance, through the *partimenti* tradition.[27] However, through the material presented in this chapter, I make a leap to another more contemporary paradigm. Artistic practice is a situated embodied practice, meaning that practice is undertaken by a body with a nervous system that is 'in a physical and social environment'.[28]

Artistic practice is a kinaesthetic practice, a practice of knowing through touching, through listening as a form of touching, that is not merely results driven but is intrinsically connected to the ways in which we use ourselves and become aware of using ourselves.[29] Those who use this material can move through it systematically or holistically and, indeed, they are encouraged to make their own variants of it. The

---

25 Esther Thelen, 'The Central Role of Action in Typical and Atypical Development', in *Movement and Action in Learning and Development: Clinical Implications of Pervasive Developmental Disorders*, ed. by Ida J. Stockman (San Diego, CA: Academic Press, 2004), p. 71.

26 See, for example, *The Improvisation Studies Reader: Spontaneous Acts*, ed. by Rebecca Caines and Ajay Heble (New York: Routledge, 2015), https://doi.org/10.4324/9780203083741, and *The Oxford Handbook of Critical Improvisation Studies*, 2 vols., ed. by George E. Lewis and Benjamin Piekut (New York: Oxford University Press, 2016), https://doi.org/10.1093/oxfordhb/9780195370935.001.0001

27 See Thomas Christensen, Robert Gjerdingen, Dirk Moelants, and Giorgio Sanguinetti, *Partimento and Continuo Playing in Theory and in Practice* (Leuven: Leuven University Press, 2010); Robert Gjerdingen, *Child Composers in the Old Conservatories: How Orphans Became Elite Musicians* (New York: Oxford University Press, 2020); and https://partimenti.org/. See also Mortensen, pp. 161–95.

28 Esther Thelen and Linda B. Smith, 'Dynamic Systems Theories', *Handbook of Child Psychology*, ed. by William Damon, 5th edn (New York: J. Wiley, 2006), pp. 287–88.

29 See Robert Sholl, 'Feldenkrais's Touch, Ephram's Laughter, Gould's Sensorium: Listening and Musical Practice between Thinking and Doing', *Journal of the Royal Musical Association*, 144. 2 (2019), 397–428, https://doi.org/10.1080/02690403.2019.1651500

material here encourages variance, experimentation, and it is this search for new solutions that can create a critical (reflective and reflexive) practice essential to learning.

Pathways to Embodied Practice as Artistic Research

For musicians, what cannot be heard cannot be controlled or shaped and, therefore, cannot be used. These are fundamental precepts that inform this study. Artistic research is nourished through a holistic approach to education. Essential to the growth of awareness and fluency is the development of an ability to perform tasks in different ways. This facilitates a feeling of control, knowledge, mastery, and craft. When a person can add (subtract, multiply, divide...) two numbers to equal six in several different ways, he or she has control of the problem through functions (theory) and working (practice). This model of learning demonstrates that mastery requires co-ordinated action through different and differentiated approaches to a problem. Flexible hands (as performers) should be accompanied by flexible brains and vice versa.[30] This study deals with a particular topic that enables this process.

The educational approach here can be simultaneously described as spiralling into an activity and widening the circumference of the spiral of material. Discerning differences and making refinements to practice are fundamental to the growth of awareness and intelligence, and what is presented here allows students the chance to develop these attributes through listening, analysis, and the putting of this awareness into artistic practice.

In this chapter, I begin with a focus on species counterpoint, often encountered in first-year courses as an introductory analytical regimen. This technique/tradition is useful for some students because it applies certain rules to music, providing seemingly sure parameters and criteria for correctness. Yet, species counterpoint is, in my view, a public-relations disaster at a conservatoire. It is fairly unexciting and disconnected from real music, even the music it is supposedly based upon, Palestrina.[31]

Some of the arguments for species counterpoint are that great composers learned from it (Mozart and Beethoven, for instance), that it is a historical method of learning the basics of craftsmanship, and that it provides a good basis for understanding Schenkerian analysis, or voice-leading in composition.[32] Another argument for it is that its abstraction from musical literature is beneficial: rules without knowledge of

---

30 Thelen and Smith state that, 'According to [the Russian physiologist Nikolai] Bernstein one of the hallmarks of skilled activity is the ability to flexibly adapt movements to current and future conditions. What constitutes skilled performance is not just a repeatable and stable pattern, but the ability to accomplish some high-level goal with rapid and graceful, but flexible solutions that can be recruited online or in anticipation of future circumstances' (p. 298).
31 Arguably, it would be better to study real sixteenth-century music (and other composers such as Orlando di Lasso, Tomás Luis de Victoria, William Byrd, Orlando Gibbons, and Clemens non Papa), especially as there are so many fine recordings of this music.
32 Felix Salzer and Carl Schachter, *Counterpoint in Composition: The Study of Voice-Leading* (New York: Columbia University Press, 1989), pp. 3–116 and 329–94.

repertoire can be followed, and reasonable results can be obtained. There is also, here, a not-so-tacit apologetics for the complexity of real music, and a certain kind of faux-patriarchal 'wisdom' and *jouissance* involved in wearing the hairshirt of such strictures.[33]

The mesmeric rules of species counterpoint seem to perplex many students. These strictures are not intended to disable the musical ear—the ear that hears line, melody, and harmony as narrative even in such exercises—but they often have this effect, hobbling these endowments along with the muse of intimate musical memory and musical history. Rather than throwing this methodology to the wind, however, I suggest here that it can be reimagined in ways that address students' musical intuition and creativity. Bach's music provides an almost inexhaustible resource and is a familiar *lingua franca* for the student of western art music. The ideas below could be used well in conjunction with other books, such as that of Thomas Benjamin on Bachian counterpoint, which is distinguished by the helpful anthology of musical examples.[34] Benjamin also emphasises the importance of rhythmic, melodic, and textural variety in composition as well as stressing the need to sing through examples and to consider expressive effects of gesture and technical devices. This is invaluable thinking that moves well beyond learning rules.

Most important is that the exercises presented in this chapter are nourished by listening to music. An internal reservoir of resources is a key aspect of successful learning, again something that takes time. Being able to turn an idealised recording on in one's mind is a vital aspect of internal hearing and musical development, and it is an essential pathway for the flexibility of choice essential to the development of craft. Craft requires guidance, and I have therefore sought to provide some general parameters rather than rules in what follows. These parameters aid stylistic rather than formalist analysis.[35] As a function of mastery, the principle that rules inscribe can eventually be altered: they become subsumed in the horizon of what is artistically possible and, in a post-Enlightenment sense, they become subject to reason and critique, but they also, crucially, become part our embodied and creaturely feeling, which is a form of knowing. The approach presented below allows different types of students to go at different speeds, and it allows them to use and explore their innate creativity in a number of different ways.

The *Goldberg Variations* are useful for my purposes because of the number of excellent recordings that exist, the possibilities to create new variations that this work may inspire, and the ways in which this work exemplifies a common but universal *lingua franca* of western music. Here is the theme as printed in the first edition:

---

33 On *jouissance*, see Dylan Evans, *An Introductory Dictionary of Lacanian Psychoanalysis* (London: Routledge, 1996), pp. 93–94 and Jacques Lacan, *Seminar VII, The Ethics of Psychoanalysis, 1959–60*, ed. by Jacques-Alain Miller, trans. by Dennis Porter (London and New York: Routledge, 1992), pp. 235–68.

34 Thomas Benjamin, *The Craft of Tonal Counterpoint with examples from the works of J.S. Bach* (New York and London: Routledge, 2003), https://doi.org/10.4324/9780203494110

35 For a guide to stylistic analysis, see Jan LaRue, *Guidelines for Style Analysis: Models for Style Analysis, a Companion Text*, 2nd edition, ed. by Marian Green LaRue (Detroit, MI: Harmonie Park, 2011).

Fig. 5.1: J. S. Bach, *Goldberg Variations* (theme in facsimile).[36]

---

36 J. S. Bach, *Clavier Übung 4e partie (Variations Goldberg) 1741*, presentation par Philippe Lescat, dir. Jean Saint-Arroman after BnF Ms 17669 (Paris: J. M. Fuzeau, 1990), unpaginated. This is available

The facsimile reproduced in Fig. 5.1 shows what this music looked like to an eighteenth-century musician, and students should be encouraged to perform from facsimile scores to broaden their understanding of such works. Doing this disrupts and refocuses habitual ways of looking (more on this below). How music is written—its cartographic disposition and organisation—changes how one reads, hears, and plays it.

It is also important to undertake a different form of embodied thinking that Bach himself learned much from but that has since fallen by the wayside.[37] Writing music out by hand is a process that develops intuition and awareness. This activity captures a way of touch, which, from an evolutionary perspective, is linked to wants, needs, desires, and survival. The experience of putting one's own mental handprints into another person's experience (from the score or from memory) is profound. This activity engages directly with a composer's uniqueness, and it enables students to feel something of the quality of the composer's thought in action. There was a moment when the *Goldberg Variations* did not exist. As a composer writes music, blank space is filled. It is worth stopping and considering the conscious and subconscious decision-making processes to appreciate that music is a human creation, an artifice that is given and constructed. The uniqueness of a composer (as a human being, like anybody else) is inscribed into the way he or she writes. Writing out music enables us to catch the breath of the age but also to sense that composition is an embodied activity created by a highly-developed nervous system and at a certain epistemic point in history.

It is important as part of this engagement with the *Goldberg Variations* to listen to a variety of recordings in and out of class. I suggest listening to

- Wanda Landowska (who made the first recording of the *Variations* in 1933 on the harpsichord)
- Trevor Pinnock on the harpsichord (1985)
- Glenn Gould (two studio recordings, piano, 1955 and 1981)
- Maria Tipo (piano, 1986)
- Murray Perahia (piano, 2000)
- Daniel-Ben Pienaar, whose (piano, 2011) recording employs techniques from early-twentieth century recordings

---

at https://s9.imslp.org/files/imglnks/usimg/2/2d/IMSLP74598-PMLP02982-Goldberg_Variations_(facsimile).pdf. All facsimiles in this chapter are from this source.

37 See, for instance, Bach's handwritten score of Nicholas de Grigny's *Livre d'Orgue: Premier livre d'orgue, édition originale, 1699, copie manuscrite de J.S. Bach, copie manuscrite de J. G. Walther* (Paris: J. M. Fuzeau, 2001).

- Chiyan Wong's recording (piano, 2021) of the composer Ferruccio Busoni's re-interpretation of the *Variations* (1915).[38]

These performances reflect considerably different visions of the work and different aesthetics of recording.

Next, it is essential to examine the structure of the theme and what makes a baroque theme useful for variations. On the keyboard, it is vital to play the chords from the figured bass or, at least, to play a two-voice reduction like that provided in Level 1 of Fig. 5.2 below. This facilitates a discussion of the function of the figured bass as enlightenment technology (defeating error and guesswork) and the way in which Bach's counterpoint is constructed to be melodic and purposeful—there is no redundancy in good art. It is then worth examining the types of figures used, including the ornamentation, types of accented and unaccented passing notes, turning patterns, neighbour-notes; how melodies are constructed and shaped (highpoints) to inflect meaning and shape structure (at cadences for example); and what makes this piece more than the sum of its parts.

Here, it is also worth drawing in some musicology, discussing the idea of rhetoric (saying something through musical figures [*Figurenlehren*]) and explaining the useful idea of 'invention' as expounded by Laurence Dreyfus.[39] It is also worth comparing this theme to other baroque themes such as Archangelo Corelli's 'La Folia' movement from his violin sonata Op. 5, No. 12, and even Pachelbel's *Canon*, all themes employed for the purposes of variation.

Bach's variations are premised on a given harmony, which can be used as a template for species-like development. So, for the purpose of this exercise, the theme has been converted from 3/4 into 4/4 time. In Fig. 5.2 and 5.7, I have left the exercise open for completion.

---

38 Busoni's version of the *Goldberg Variations* is available at: http://conquest.imslp.info/files/imglnks/usimg/6/66/IMSLP08668-Bach_-_Goldberg_Variations_(breitkopf).pdf

39 Dreyfus, pp. 1–32.

5. Artistic Practice as Embodied Learning

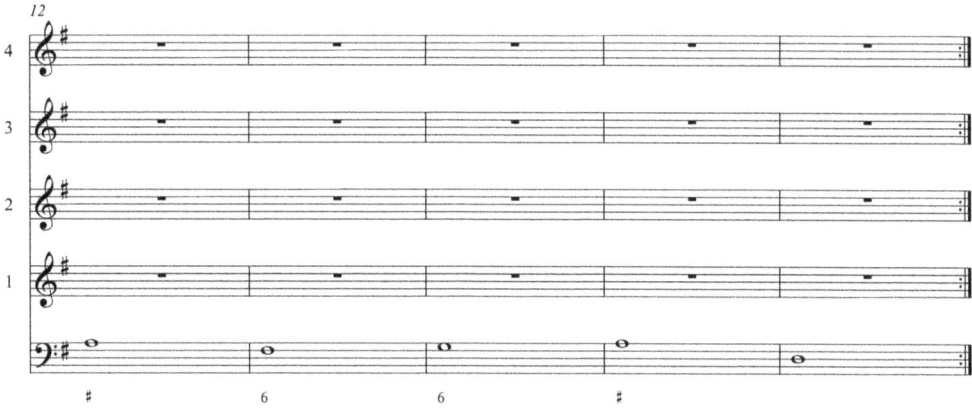

Fig. 5.2: *Goldberg* exercise.

This example presents a four-layer contrapuntal cake in which all Levels (1–4) pertain to the bass (with figures). Level 1, above the figured bass, is like 1st species (note against note), and the other lines approximate but move beyond the other species categories. Level 2 has elements of 2nd and 4th species (2 notes against 1 with suspensions). Level 3 has elements of 3rd and 5th species (4 notes against 1 and with dissonances). Level 4 develops the material further. Rather than impose the tedious rules of species counterpoint, I would give six general principles:

1. Try and write music first and check your work with points 2–4 (below) later;
2. Try and write lines that move in contrary motion as much as possible;
3. In general, do not jump off or onto a dissonance (harder to do than it is to say);
4. Check for consecutive and hidden fifths and octaves;
5. Try and have thirds, (fifths), sixths, or octaves on the strong beats; and
6. Concentrate on smooth voice-leading using scales and arpeggios.

Levels 1–4 move from longer to shorter notes, thus illustrating the principle of melodic diminution by showing the way more intricate figures can be derived from simpler ones. This enables discussions of some of the following features:

1. Melodic movement, embellishment, and diminution (this can be seen within the lines themselves);
2. Dissonance treatment (preparation and non-preparation, leaping);
3. Voice-leading (use of arpeggios and embellishment figures);
4. Cadential articulation (the shaping of highpoints, of tension and release); and
5. What happens when the number of notes fitted into the space increases (the register has to expand).

Levels 1 to 4 gradually develop and flesh out (as diminutions) the previous material: the notes of Level 2 are clearly based on Level 1, Level 3 on Levels 1 and 2, and Level 4 on Levels 1, 2, and 3. This is another aspect of this method: whatever is written at Level 1 should have a cumulative impact and relation to the other Levels. This exercise facilitates other questions such as:

1. What is being varied and how?
2. How does Bach, in his music (in Figs. 5.3 and 5.5, for examples, below), maintain a steady flow of interest for the listener? What happens in b. 5 of Fig. 5.5, for instance, and how is the invention or idea subtly changed?

and, most crucially,

3. How does the music across the Levels of Fig. 5.2 gradually come to sound like Bach? Is it, for example, the dissonance treatment, the types of melodic movement, and/or the way in which the lines rise and fall? What sustains our interest here?

To work through even one Level would take some time, and what I have offered in Fig. 5.2 is merely the beginning of one solution. Students (and instructors) should be encouraged to find their own different, yet equally valid, solutions (by beginning on a different note, for example). The exercise is structured, then, so that the rest of the variation can be created one Level at a time, and students can compare their workings.

This preliminary project employs one 'invention' with a particular 'Affekt' of musical characteristic at each level, and this is typical of Bach's practice. This observation can be sharpened by borrowing another 'Affekt', this time from Variation 4:

Fig. 5.3: Bach, *Goldberg Variations*, beginning of Variation 4 (facsimile).

Fig. 5.4a presents an adaptation of Levels 2 and 3 above (from Fig. 5.2), using the same 'invention' as Variation 4. Note that the first right-hand pitch in each bar is the same as in Levels 2 and 3 of Fig. 5.2 above:

Fig. 5.4a: Based on *Goldberg* Variation 4.

This 'invention' can be presented in the left hand. The Feldenkraisian idea of flexibility (finding different ways to approach the same 'function) is therefore instantiated in Fig. 5.4b. The right hand, here, keeps the first notes (on the strongest beat) of Level 1 from Fig. 5.2 above. Note that notes 1–4 and notes 5–8 of the right-hand part effectively form elongated ornaments (turns).

Fig. 5.4b: Based on *Goldberg* Variation 4.

The following examples (Figs. 5.4c and 5.4d), have essentially the same bass line as Fig. 5.4b. In Fig. 5.4c, a more fluid line based on level 2 and 3 (from Fig. 5.2) is added to enrich the counterpoint:

Fig. 5.4c: Based on *Goldberg* Variation 4.

In Fig. 5.4d, a still more elaborate version is created that relates to Level 4 of Fig. 5.2. In creating this counterpoint, it is important to move in a controlled manner from relative simplicity towards complexity. It is also imperative that complexity never obscures the purposefulness and transparency of the music, and that the fundamental harmony underpinning the counterpoint is always clear.

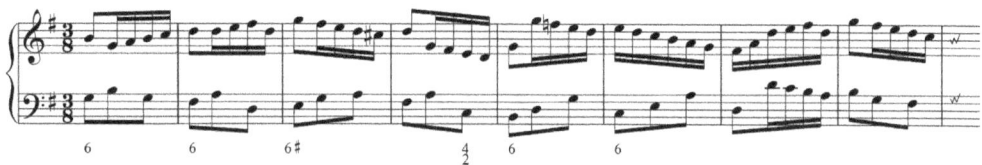

Fig. 5.4d: Based on *Goldberg* Variation 4.

These preliminary differentiations through elaborations of Variation 4 have facilitated the freeing up the bass (from Fig. 5.2), allowing it to become an integral part of the counterpoint. Variation 1 of the *Goldberg Variations* (Fig. 5.5) is useful for understanding and developing the relationships between the lines further and for making other connections and differentiations that are realised in Fig. 5.7.

Fig. 5.5: *Goldberg* Variation 1 (facsimile).

It can now be seen that what is present in Level 4 in Fig. 5.2 flows from aspects of the melodic line of Fig. 5.5. However, this observation leads to other questions about Fig. 5.5:

1. What is the rhythmic balance and contrast of melodic invention between the lines?
2. Why does the bass sound different here?
3. How do figures from one line appear in the other line?
4. How does Bach use dissonance, embellishment figures, and register, and how does this make it sound like Bach?
5. What happens when Bach swaps the figures around in b. 5, and why do these musical features do this?
6. Why does Bach use the arpeggio figure in the right hand of b. 9 and how does this relate to the opening idea?
7. How might the 'inventions' presented in the first half of the Variation recur (as further variations) in the second half?

These are complex and fascinating questions, and they go to the heart of Bach's creative engagement with his material. These questions are by no means meant as prescriptive, exhaustive, or necessarily to be taken in this order, and they can easily be transferred to other repertoire and variations. They open up other questions for discussion such as:

1. What is the function of a bass, and of the basso continuo, in baroque music?
2. On which instruments does this music sound better and why? What is 'better'?
3. Who are the main performers, and what types of traditions of performance exist for this repertoire? How can these be critically examined and compared?
4. How have the *Goldberg Variations* been extended, for example, by Robin Holloway in his *Gilded Goldbergs* Op. 86 (1992–97) for two pianos, or by the Jacques Loussier (jazz) trio?
5. What are the demonstrable differences between these variations, and, for example, Mozart's variations on *Ah, vous dirai-je maman* KV 265 (1778) or Brahms's *Variations on a Theme of Haydn* Op. 56a (1873) known as the *St Anthony Variations*?

To continue the learning trajectory from the previous examples, here are some starter 'inventions' for writing, improvising, or composing other variations that have different characters:

Fig. 5.6: Starter 'inventions' for *Goldberg* variations.

Fig. 5.6 becomes a stepping-stone to exploring the techniques and elaborations of 'inventions' in the other *Goldberg Variations*. The starter examples in Fig. 5.6 imply different speeds and are written in different meters. Already they provide material for development and variation and for continuity and narrative.

From the 'starters' given in Fig. 5.6, it is worthwhile inventing one's own 'inventions' and variations. Here, I would recommend exploring how other Bach works can be adapted. An 'invention' can be borrowed from one of the 'Passions', a Brandenburg concerto, a cantata, a violin or cello suite, or one of the organ or keyboard works (no. 11 in Fig. 5.6, for example, is borrowed from the beginning of Bach's organ Prelude and Fugue in C, BWV 547). This procedure speaks to a spiralling out from the exercises presented above to absorb other resources. It is worth creating a 'listening list' of pieces that can be used to create 'inventions' and to work through this in class. As Dreyfus shows, Bach seemed to consider some inventions to have more potential than others—*The Art of Fugue* is the *locus classicus* of this.

In this spirit of re-invention, here is a 'Goldberg' Variation created from a variant of the 'invention' at the beginning of the sprightly G major two-part invention BWV 781 (no. 6 in Fig. 5.6). Students can finish the example and then compare their findings. I have included various techniques from Variation 1 of the *Goldberg Variations* in Fig. 5.7. Note, in particular, with reference to Fig. 5.7, the way in which the right hand 'invention' in b. 1 becomes the left hand at b. 5, and the way a related figure is introduced at b. 8–9 as a form of sequential development of the 'invention'. Note also the use of contrary motion here and at b. 13, and the way the music builds to the cadence, which has a semiotically-definable form of closure. How Bach writes an ending is a feature of his music that is worthy of study in itself.

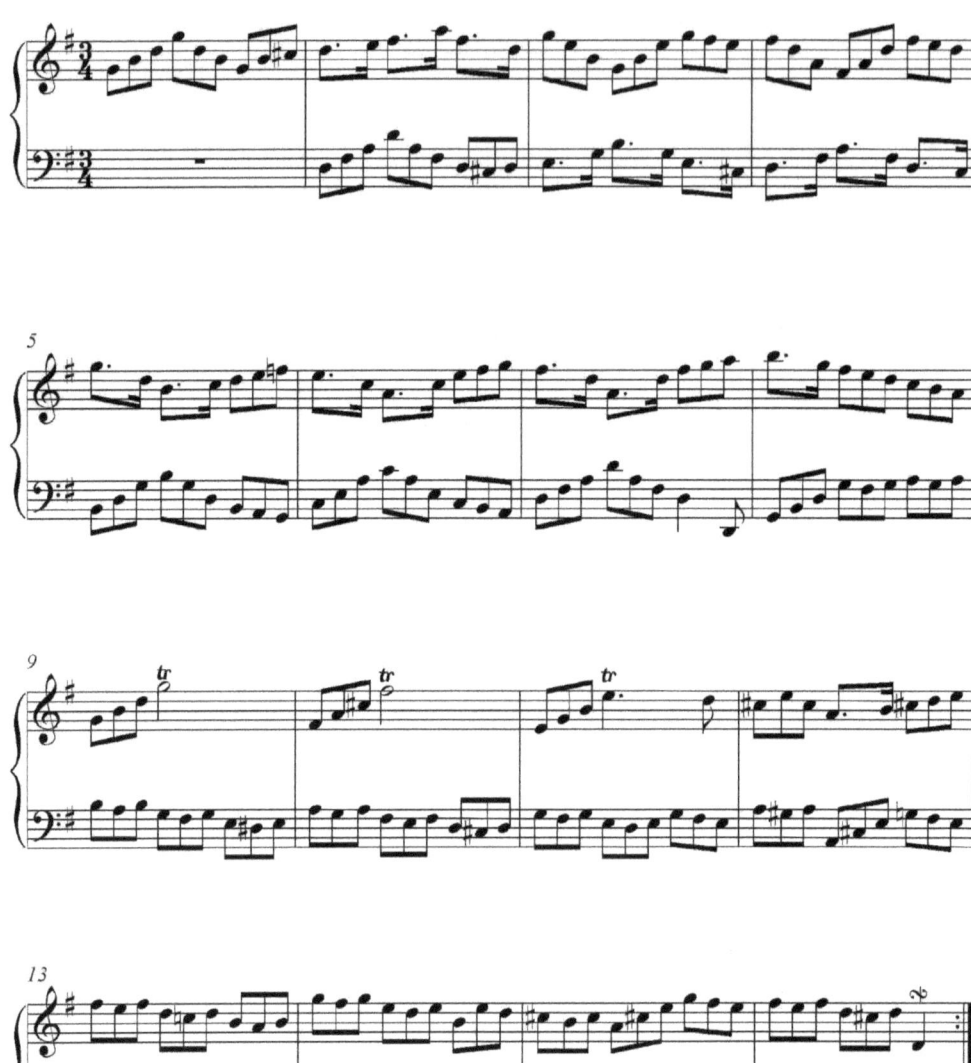

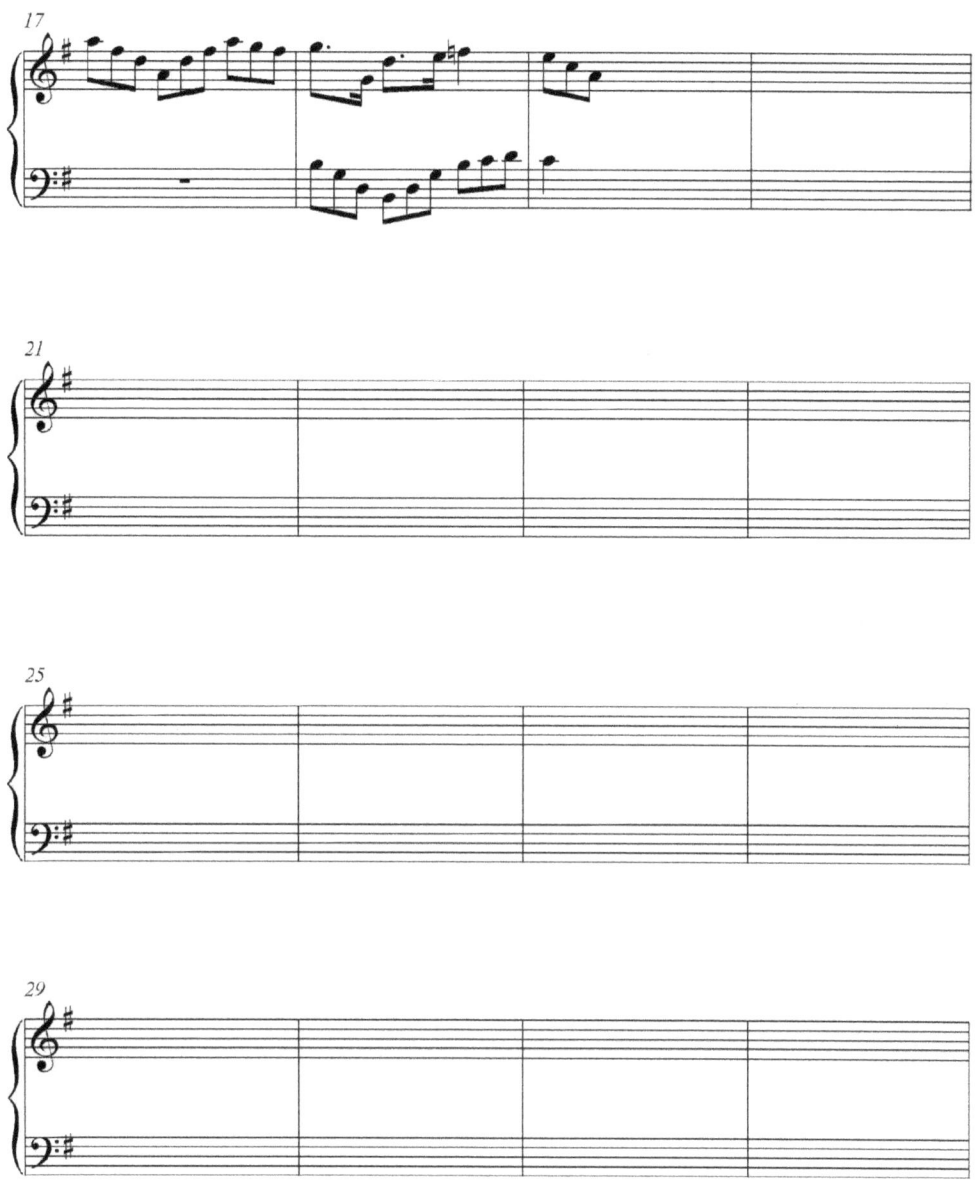

Fig. 5.7: *Goldberg* variation based on the opening of BWV 781.

Fig. 5.7 reveals some of the basic mechanisms for 'invention' and its elaboration. Figs. 5.1, 5.2, and 5.7 are all templates for improvisation. Fig. 5.2 and 5.7 can be extended, and the student can become aware of the way in which the internal listening facilitated by these examples creates different musical possibilities and solutions. Following Feldenkrais's thought, it is the finding of different solutions that facilitates choice and mastery.

Exercises for improvisation can be created through certain parameters. For instance, one deliberate 'limitation' might be that the right hand is only going to use scales and/or arpeggios belonging to the chord. For non-keyboard players, it is perfectly possible to record a bass line and then improvise on it, or, more authentically, to play these examples with a keyboard player. It is worthwhile seeing what happens when one begins a variation on different notes of the first chord (G – B – or D), with a rest, or in a different octave or register.

These are already small examples of changing focus that entail the creative decision-making fundamental to artistic research. Keyboard music is written so that the right-hand is on the top stave. This creates a certain reliable visual pattern. It is important to notice the way in which this axiomatic orthography (higher pitch = higher stave) influences the way in which we look at our hands on the keyboard, what we think of as the relationship of melody to harmony (as something derived from the bass), and how this has formed thought patterns from childhood for many musicians.[40] It is also worth considering how these precepts and our engagement with them relates to other deeper ethical, linguistic, and cultural patterns, such as the idea of right-hand dominance, the idea that heaven is up (beyond the sky) and hell is beneath the ground, or the pre-Copernican idea that the sun sets in the west.[41]

Such relationships are not set in stone. They are deep physiological and cultural patterns that can be disrupted, and that can be played with, not least in the case of Fig. 5.2 above, by crossing the hands, using different forms of articulation, or finding different fingerings. For example, one might try baroque fingering, in which the use of the thumb in passagework is minimised. I would also strongly recommend transposing the exercises, and improvising different versions of them, in at least the neighbouring keys of F and A major. It is worth examining how changing only the key causes our thought patterns and the notes we play to change. These kinds of differentiation help to build the connections between hearing, seeing, and thinking essential for 'adaptive flexibility' understood as a form of virtuosity.[42] One of Feldenkrais's discoveries was that when we change, disrupt, or build new patterns to do an activity (such as a finding non-habitual ways to interlace our fingers, for instance) the function of the habitual action is improved when we return to it—try this for yourself.

Here are some suggestions, therefore, of how to create different forms of embodied stability and instability using the material above. It is worth becoming aware of the way in which our eyes organise the movements of our hands on any instrument, not just at the keyboard. Feldenkrais became very interested in the relationship between the eyes and the hands and the ways in which altering the tonus of one creates a

---

40   See Feldenkrais, *Body & Mature Behavior: A Study of Anxiety, Sex, Gravitation & Learning* (New York: International Universities Press Inc., 1966).
41   See Chris McManus, *Right Hand, Left Hand: The Origins of Asymmetry in Brains, Bodies, Atoms, and Cultures* (London: Phoenix, 2002).
42   Thelen, 'The Central Role of Action in Typical and Atypical Development', p. 71.

change in the other.[43] Another way of thinking about this is: do we move our eyes in certain patterns at certain times in a piece (through necessity or anxiety), and how does this become habituated to and with the sounds and physical/kinaesthetic patterning imprinted through practice? Such patterns remain unnoticed until they are brought into our awareness. I would contend that such forms of play are a powerful means of developing 'adaptive flexibility' and that this in itself constitutes a form of physiological and embodied artistic research.

With this in mind, it is worth examining a number of other things in Fig. 5.2. As one moves through the different densities of information in the Levels, observe what happens to your breathing, to the tension in your face (between the eyes), or in the shoulders. Fig. 5.2 provides for an increased information density in the right hand only, a 'limitation' that allows concentration on other aspects of ourselves while playing.

Improvisation opens a space where this sense of the different levels of engagement we can make with music (technical, physical, and even spiritual) can be observed and played with. What happens if the density is increased simply by adding another note in the left hand, such as adding a minim an octave below on beat 3 of almost each bar in Fig. 5.2? Notice as you move from one Level to another what happens in the ribs, in the pelvis, or even in the right-foot. Notice the whole right-hand side of the body and how individual parts of the body on this side can be felt to participate more in the activity than those on the left. This participation, Feldenkrais has shown, leads to improved functioning.[44] The perception of these differences can be accentuated by leaning more to one side, by looking at something completely different (not your hands or the music), and, crucially, by noticing what you do and how you do it. In Fig. 5.2, attention needs to be paid to the moments leading up to and then to the change from one line of the music to the next. Is there a jump in the eyes, and can this be made smoother? Is there any noticeable change or sense of transition as one moves from written music to improvisation? How can this transition become easier, lighter, and a focus for play?

Anybody who engages in these practices will quickly discover that 'play' is fundamental to the serious business of learning – it is intense and mentally taxing. One of the things that Feldenkrais built into his 'Awareness-through-movement' lessons were breaks between differentiations. These breaks allow time for the brain to digest the experience. He discovered that integration happened in the moments when the brain was released from *doing*.[45] Stopping, I have suggested, is a powerful creative strategy in artistic practice.

Integration arrives at a point when these different forms of embodied knowledge become part of the person and can be spontaneously retrieved when circumstances

---

43 See, for instance, 'The bell hand: soft opening and closing movements of the hands' in Feldenkrais's Quest seminar.
44 See Alan Fraser, *Play the Piano with your Whole Self: Refine the Physical to Free Your Inner Musician: Biotensegrity, the Inner Conductor, & Expressively Directed Micro-Timing at the Piano* (Novi Sad: The Piano Somatics Press: 2022).
45 See Sholl, 'Feldenkrais's Touch'.

demand it. The exercises above can be used to investigate some basic mechanisms of music, moving from skills to craft. They can also aid in moving towards Feldenkrais's ideal of making flexible brains and becoming more fully aware of how to know something.

Conclusion

Feldenkrais advised some of his students: 'Be sure your intention is clearly present in your movement. The movement organises itself when your intention is clear.'[46] The question for musicians often, though, is 'how do I know that my intention is clear?' or, to return Feldenkrais's maxim at the start, 'how do I come to know what I am doing?' A straightforward answer to these questions is that experimentation—the finding of different 'solutions' to the problems posed above that are emotionally, historically, intellectually, and creatively both satisfying and contingent (awaiting other 'solutions')—is a profound way of enabling the process of knowledge acquisition that leads to craft and to artistry. This is partly why I have framed the above discussion of Bach as a mode of enquiry, more than as a schematic process. The former promotes an emergent awareness of style, knowledge, and intention though action.

The discussion above of the *Goldberg Variations* creates parameters for the development of 'self-organisation', meaning that the *'pattern and order emerge from the interactions of the components of a complex system without explicit instructions*, either in the organism itself or from the environment'.[47] This is one way of describing semi-autonomous learning that also acts as a template for creativity. Embodied cognition is too often in conservatoires understood as something implicit (merely taken for granted), or as something added to the curriculum. However, in fact, it is a primary aspect of learning that needs to be placed at the centre of everything that happens at a conservatoire. This is because it is at the centre of a musician's activities and crucial for the sustainability of a career, especially given the often-excessive demands of the music profession.

The exercises above have used the *Goldberg Variations* for the promotion of embodied learning closely aligned with awareness of technical observations. This is artistic practice in action—a burgeoning awareness of attention and intention and the critical working-through of nuance and differentiation, and of variance. These exercises meld theory and practice and help create 'knowing', an integration which Thelen and Smith describe as 'the process of dynamic assembly across multileveled systems in the service of a task'.[48]

---

46   *Dr Mosche Feldenkrais at Alexander Yanai*, ed. by Ellen Soloway, trans. by Anat Baniel (Paris: International Feldenkrais Federation, 1994), see lesson 22: 'Sitting on the Floor with the help of your hands' (p. 132).
47   Thelen and Smith, p. 259, italics in the original.
48   See Bernstein, *The Development of Dexterity*; Thelen and Smith, pp. 298, 303.

Thelen and Smith argue that '...in action and cognition, and in development, many configurations that act like programmes, stages, or structures are stable attractors whose stability limits may indeed be shifted under appropriate circumstances'.[49] This is what these researchers describe as 'soft-assembled' systems rather than 'the vocabulary of programmes, structures, modules, and schemas' that are then supplanted by 'constructs with concepts of complexity, stability, and change'.[50] From a Feldenkraisian position, such 'shifts' are desirable and, in fact, necessary to the 'behavioural development' that Thelen and Smith describe as '...a series of evolving and dissolving attractors of different stability'.[51]

Another way of thinking about this would be to say that the model presented in Fig. 5.2 above builds various levels of dependence and, therefore, stability that can be destabilised. Through improvisation, this can be thought of as an *'epigenetic developmental process* through which increasingly more complex cognitive structures emerge in the system as a result of interactions with the physical and social environment'.[52] Improvisation acts as an emergent system of finding new possibilities: new stabilities are revealed through new instabilities or, as Thelen and Smith elegantly call them, 'points of transition'.[53]

Such 'transitions' could also be applied to the move from skills to craft, which is the hallmark of artistry and artistic research. This is not merely adapting skills to future circumstances, or of 'knowing', but the ability to produce serendipitous solutions to problems through sustained engagement, and to make aesthetic choices between them.[54] This process would enable a person to 'do what you want', as Feldenkrais stated. These choices are embodied. In the words of Thelen et al., 'perception, action, decision, execution, and memory are cast in compatible task dynamics, the processes can be continuously meshed together [...] Body and world remain ceaselessly melded together'.[55]

References

Agawu, Kofi, 'How We Got out of Analysis, and How to Get Back in Again', *Music Analysis*, 23.2/3 (July–October 2004), pp. 267–86

Benjamin, Thomas, *The Craft of Tonal Counterpoint with examples from the works of J. S. Bach* (New York and London: Routledge, 2003), https://doi.org/10.4324/9780203494110

---

49 Thelen and Smith, p. 274.
50 Ibid.
51 Ibid., p. 276.
52 Ibid., p. 288. Italics in original.
53 Ibid., p. 291.
54 See Bernstein, *The Development of Dexterity*; Thelen and Smith, pp. 298, 303.
55 Esther Thelen, Gregor Schöner, Christian Scheier, and Linda B. Smith, 'The Dynamics of Embodiment: A Field Theory of Infant Perseverative Reaching', *Behavioral and Brain Sciences*, 24 (2001), pp. 1–34 (p. 2), https://doi.org/10.1017/s0140525x01003910

Bernstein, Nikolai, *Dexterity and its Development*, ed. by Mark Latash and Michael Turvey (New York: Psychology Press, 1986)

Caines, Rebecca and Ajay Heble (eds), *The Improvisation Studies Reader: Spontaneous Acts* (New York: Routledge, 2015), https://doi.org/10.4324/9780203083741

Cavett, Esther, ed and compiler, 'Valuing the Surplus: Perspectives on Julian Horton's Article "On the Musicological Necessity of Music Analysis"', with contributions by Kofi Agawu, Gurminder K. Bhogal, Esther Cavett, Jonathan Dunsby, Julian Horton, Alexandra Monchick, Ian Pace, Henry Stobart, and Simon Zagorski-Thomas, in *Music Analysis*, 32.3, 412–71, https://doi.org/10.1111/musa.12221

Chaffin, Roger, Gabriela Imreh, and Mary Crawford, *Practicing Perfection: Memory and Piano Performance* (New York: Psychology Press, 2002), https://doi.org/10.4324/9781410612373

Christensen, Thomas, Robert Gjerdingen, Dirk Moelants, and Giorgio Sanguinetti, *Partimento and Continuo Playing in Theory and in Practice* (Leuven: Leuven University Press, 2010)

Davidian, Teresa, *Tonal Counterpoint for the 21st Century Musician: An Introduction* (Lanham, MD: Rowman & Littlefield, 2015)

Denisch, Beth, *Contemporary Counterpoint: Theory and Application* (Boston, MA: Berklee Press, 2017)

Doğantan-Dack, Mine, 'Expanding the Scope of Music Theory: Artistic Research in Music Performance', *Zeitschrift der Gesellschaft für Musiktheorie*, 19/2 (2022), https://www.gmth.de/zeitschrift/artikel/1169.aspx?fbclid=IwAR26sZcGvqUEtw3s9NG5rzGdm56D3N41Z_s5HFfKZQZOGh0CbuVA_GyO3z8

Dreyfus, Laurence, *Bach and the Patterns of Invention* (Cambridge, MA: Harvard University Press, 1997)

Evans, Dylan, *An Introductory Dictionary of Lacanian Psychoanalysis* (London: Routledge, 1996)

Feldenkrais, Mosche, *Body & Mature Behavior: A Study of Anxiety, Sex, Gravitation & Learning* (New York: International Universities Press Inc., 1966).

Feldenkrais, Mosche, *Dr Mosche Feldenkrais at Alexander Yanai*, ed. by Ellen Soloway, trans. by Anat Baniel (Paris: International Feldenkrais Federation, 1994), Lesson 22: 'Sitting on the Floor with the help of your hands', pp. 131–36

——, *Embodied Wisdom: The Collected Papers of Mosche Feldenkrais*, ed. by Elizabeth Beringer (Berkeley, CA: Somatic Resources and North Atlantic Books, 2010)

——, 'Lecture: Learning, Free Choice, Individuality', *New York, Quest Workshop* (San Diego, CA: Feldenkrais Resources, 1981)

——, *Thinking and Doing* (Longmont, CO: Genesis II, 2013)

Førisdal, Anders, Christina Kobb, and Erlend Hovland (eds), *Music & Practice*, 10 (2023), https://www.musicandpractice.org/volume-10/

Fraser, Alan, *Play the Piano with your Whole self: Refine the Physical to Free Your Inner Musician: Biotensegrity, the Inner Conductor, & Expressively Directed Micro-Timing at the Piano* (Novi Sad: The Piano Somatics Press: 2022)

Forte, Allen, and Steven E. Gilbert, *Introduction to Schenkerian Analysis: Form and Content in Tonal Music* (New York: W. W. Norton, 1982)

——, *Instructor's Manual for Introduction to Schenkerian Analysis* (New York: W. W. Norton, 1982)

Gorton, David and Stefan Östersjö, 'Austerity Measures I: performing the Discursive Voice', in *Voices, Bodies, Practices: Performing Musical Subjectivities*, ed. by Catherine Laws, William Brooks, David Gorton, Thanh Thủy Nguyễn, Stefan Östersjö, and Jeremy J. Wells (Leuven: Leuven University Press, 2019), pp. 29–79

Gjerdingen, Robert, *Child Composers in the Old Conservatories: How Orphans Became Elite Musicians* (New York: Oxford University Press, 2020)

Henke, Silvia, Dieter Mersch, Thomas Strässle, Jörg Wiesel, and Nicolaj van der Meulen, *Manifesto of Artistic Research: A Defense Against Its Advocates* (Zurich: Diaphanes, 2020)

Ho, Jocelyn, 'Corporeal Musical Structure: A Gestural-Kinesthetic Approach to Tōru Takemitsu's *Rain Tree Sketch II*', *Music Theory Online*, 27.4 (December 2021), https://mtosmt.org/issues/mto.21.27.4/mto.21.27.4.ho.html

Horton, Julian, 'On the Musicological Necessity of Musical Analysis', *Musical Quarterly*, 103.1–2 (2022), 62–104

Kennan, Kent Wheeler, *Counterpoint Based on Eighteenth Century Practice*, 3rd edn. (Englewood Cliffs, NJ: Prentice-Hall, 1987)

Kerman, Joseph, 'How We Got into Analysis, and How to Get out', *Critical Inquiry*, 7.2 (Winter 1980), pp. 311–31

Lacan, Jacques, *Seminar XI, The Four Fundamental Concepts of Psychoanalysis*, ed. by Jacques-Alain Miller, trans. by Alan Sheridan (London: Karnac, 2004)

——, *Seminar VII, The Ethics of Psychoanalysis*, 1959–60, ed. by Jacques-Alain Miller, trans. by Dennis Porter (London and New York: Routledge, 1992).

LaRue, Jan, *Guidelines for Style Analysis: Models for Style Analysis, a Companion Text*, 2nd edn, ed. by Marian Green LaRue (Detroit: Harmonie Park, 2011)

Lewis, George E., and Benjamin Piekut, *The Oxford Handbook of Critical Improvisation Studies* (New York: Oxford University Press, 2016), https://doi.org/10.1093/oxfordhb/9780195370935.001.0001

Leong, Daphne, *Performing Knowledge: Twentieth-Century Music in Analysis and Performance* (New York: Oxford University Press, 2019), https://doi.org/10.1093/oso/9780190653545.001.0001

McCaw, Dick, 'Learning through Feeling: How the Ideas of Nikolai Bernstein and Moshe Feldenkrais Apply to Performer Training', *The Feldenkrais Method in Creative Practice: Dance, Music, and Theatre*, ed. by Robert Sholl (London: Methuen, 2021), pp. 55–72, https://doi.org/10.5040/9781350158412.ch-003

McManus, Chris, *Right Hand, Left hand: The Origins of Asymmetry in Brains, Bodies, Atoms, and Cultures* (London: Phoenix, 2002)

Mortensen, John J., *The Pianist's Guide to Historical Improvisation* (New York: Oxford University Press, 2020)

Pace, Ian, 'In Defence of Analytically-Informed Performance'. Keynote Paper presented at the International Encounters on Music Theory and Analysis Conference, 6 November 2019, São Paolo, Brazil, https://openaccess.city.ac.uk/id/eprint/30386/

Rogg, Lionel, *Improvisation Course for Organists* (Fleurier: Schola Cantorum, 1988)

Russell, Roger, 'Radical Practice: Practising Performance and Practising Oneself is the Same Activity', *The Feldenkrais Method in Creative Practice: Dance, Music, and Theatre*, ed. by Robert Sholl (London: Methuen, 2021), pp. 83–102

Salzer, Felix, and Carl Schachter, *Counterpoint in Composition: The Study of Voice-Leading* (New York: Columbia University Press, 1989)

Sarath, Edward, *Music Theory through Improvisation: A New Approach to Musicianship training* (New York: Taylor and Francis, 2010)

Schmalfeldt, Janet, 'Who's Keeping the Score?' In *Investigating Musical Performance: Theoretical Models and Intersections*, ed. by Gianmario Borio, Giovanni Giuriati, Alessandro Cecchi, and Marco Lutzu (New York: Routledge, 2020), pp. 91–101, https://doi.org/10.4324/9780429026461-10

Schubert, Peter, *Modal Counterpoint, Renaissance Style* (New York: Oxford University Press, 2003)

Sholl, Robert, 'Feldenkrais's Touch, Ephram's Laughter, Gould's Sensorium: Listening and Musical Practice between Thinking and Doing', *Journal of the Royal Musical Association*, 144.2 (2019), 397–428, https://doi.org/10.1080/02690403.2019.1651500

Stoiber, Franz Josef, *Fascination Organ Improvisation: A Study and Practice Book* (Kassel: Bärenreiter, 2018)

Street, Alan, 'The Rhetorico-Musical Structure of the "Goldberg" Variations: Bach's "Clavier-Übung" IV and the "Institutio Oratoria" of Quintilian', *Music Analysis*, 6.1/2 (March–July 1987), 89–131

Swinkin, Jeffrey, *Performative Analysis: Reimagining Music Theory for Performance* (Rochester, NY: Rochester University Press, 2016), https://doi.org/10.2307/j.ctvc16ncq

Thelen, Esther, 'The Central Role of Action in Typical and Atypical Development', in *Movement and Action in Learning and Development: Clinical Implications of Pervasive Developmental Disorders*, ed. by Ida J. Stockman (San Diego, CA: Academic Press, 2004), pp. 49–73

Thelen, Esther, and Linda B. Smith, 'Dynamic Systems Theories', in *Handbook of Child Psychology*, 5th edn, ed. by William Damon (New York: J. Wiley, 2006), pp. 258–312

Thelen, Gregor Schöner, Christian Scheier, and Linda B. Smith, 'The dynamics of embodiment: A field theory of infant perseverative reaching', *Behavioral and Brain Sciences*, 24 (2001), 1–86, https://doi.org/10.1017/s0140525x01003910

Žižek, Slavoj, *Surplus-Enjoyment: A Guide for the Non-Perplexed* (London: Bloomsbury Academic, 2022)

6. Working Together Well: Amplifying Group Agency and Motivation in Higher Music Education

Jacob Thompson-Bell

Introduction

It is fair to say that student-centred learning environments (SCLEs) are firmly on the agenda for higher music education (HME), at least within the United Kingdom. Calls for curricula to be responsive to the values and motivations of individual learners come not only from students themselves but also from the institutions running and promoting higher music programmes of study. In this chapter, I would like to propose that, whilst there are manifest benefits of working from a student-centred perspective, there are also blind spots or, perhaps more accurately, under-explored 'grey areas' in the ways in which SCLEs and related approaches are understood in the HME context.[1] The challenge for educators working in group teaching environments is to balance their pedagogical attention towards the learning experience of each student, whilst also attending to the needs of the overall class. This means balancing demands for both individual forms of agency, driven by 'intrinsic' motivation, and 'distributive'[2] forms of agency, which are collectively held within interdependent, yet diverse, groups of learners. As an educator with a background in both conservatoire and university settings in the United Kingdom, I am interested in how my colleagues and I can foster

---

1   For useful reviews of SCLEs, see: Susan Land and David Jonassen 'Student-centered Learning Environments: Foundations, Assumptions and Design', in *Theoretical Foundations of Learning Environments*, ed. by Susan Land and David Jonassen, 2nd edn. (New York: Routledge, 2012), pp. 3–26, https://doi.org/10.4324/9780203813799; *Shaping Higher Education with Students*, ed. By Vincent C. H. Tong, Alex Standen, and Mina Sotiriou (London: UCL Press, 2018) https://doi.org/10.2307/j.ctt21c4tcm; Crina Damşa, Monika Nerland, and Zacharias E. Andreadakis, 'An Ecological Perspective on Learner-constructed Learning Spaces', *British Journal of Educational Technology*, 50 (2019), 2075–89, https://doi.org/10.1111/bjet.12855
2   Jane Bennett, *Vibrant Matter* (Durham and London: Duke University Press, 2010), https://doi.org/10.2307/j.ctv111jh6w; Jane Bennett, *Influx and Efflux: Writing Up with Walt Whitman* (Durham and London: Duke University Press, 2020), https://doi.org/10.1215/9781478009290

a more collegiate, collective sense of agency in our students, to encourage them to recognise how their individual study goals and motivations are modulated by the co-presence of their peers, and vice versa. This is also a matter of equity, meaning, in this case, the ability of all learners not only to participate but to thrive in a study environment. Such objectives align closely with those of the REACT project, as outlined in the Introduction to this volume. Both initiatives aim to strengthen learner criticality and autonomy in HME and, thus, to reevaluate the role of teachers as transmitters of knowledge, instead understanding HME as a more complexly distributed process of shared exploration and reflection.

I will investigate these issues, firstly, by critiquing the notion of learner autonomy, which undergirds SCLEs. I will try to show how, rather than acting independently, learners can become connected in a 'distributive agential network'[3] in which the motivations and agencies of one learner cannot be fully separated from those of another, or, indeed, from those of their teacher. Next, I will offer an impressionistic vignette, inviting readers to imagine themselves as participants in a group performance workshop in a performance-class setting in order to reflect on how distributive agential networks play out in a classroom environment. The workshop will be conducted using the Critical Response Process feedback framework,[4] which I have found to be a useful model for attending both to the individual and collective agency of learners in group settings. I will try to show how this example scenario can be understood in terms of a classroom 'assemblage'[5]—a collective of networked, interleaved subjectivities making up the group teaching environment. Finally, I will consider how these ideas might have implications for equity and freedom of expression in a HME environment. Ultimately, I would like to propose that the pursuit of creative and expressive freedoms requires that careful attention is paid to the ways in which individual students and teachers can be assembled to form a learner collective.

Constructing Student-Centred Learning Environments

Before I try to deconstruct SCLEs, I should first explain what I mean by these. SCLEs are based around a Vygotskian constructivist model of perception, in which individuals build their perceptual world based on the specifics of their social and cultural position.[6] Correspondingly, the role of the teacher is not to impose their own

---

3   Bennett, *Vibrant Matter*.
4   Liz Lerman and John Borstel, *Liz Lerman's Critical Response Process: A Method for Getting Useful Feedback on Anything You Make, from Dance to Dessert* (Takoma Park, MD: Liz Lerman Dance Exchange, 2003).
5   Karen Barad, *Meeting the Universe Halfway* (Durham: Duke University Press, 2007), https://doi.org/10.2307/j.ctv12101zq; Bennett, *Vibrant Matter*; Manuel DeLanda, *Assemblage Theory* (Edinburgh: Edinburgh University Press, 2016), https://doi.org/10.1515/9781474413640
6   Monika Nerland, 'Beyond Policy: Conceptualising Student-centred Environments in Higher (Music) Education', in *Becoming Musicians: Student Involvement and Teacher Collaboration in Higher Music Education*, ed. By Stefan Gies, and Jon Helge Sætre ([n.p.]: NMH Publications, 2019), pp. 53–66

worldview on the student, since this is only one of many possible outlooks. Instead, teachers must uphold the conditions necessary for a student to undertake learning on their own terms. For HME, the designing of curricula around the study motivations and values of learners reveals a shifting sense of what we mean by 'creativity'—away from a canonical model exemplified by great 'masters' and towards a more relativistic, action-oriented approach. There is also an equity dimension to SCLEs insofar as the intention of moving away from a 'one-size-fits-all' curriculum is that a more diverse community of musicians can be represented and a more fluid understanding of music can be fostered.

SCLEs call for educators to remain open to the intentions of their students, so as to build their 'intrinsic' motivation.[7] The idea is to help students understand not only what they are studying but also why this might be important for them. Nevertheless, the openness demanded by SCLEs should not be confused with emptiness, since, in order to uphold the conditions under which students can find their own way, some pretty significant checks and balances need to be in place, likely facilitated or led by the teachers themselves. In this sense, SCLEs in HME are a process of construction in their own right, a demand to create and maintain pedagogical systems within which creativity is possible. However, individual learners do not operate in a vacuum—the identity of one person is not isolated from the identities of others but, instead, formed collectively. This is especially apparent in an institutional setting in which students and teachers work and study together, collaborating on the development of their creative practices. I have seen firsthand how the ideas and aptitudes of multiple students can mutually shape one another, so that all learners leave the class in some way changed. I think that the demand to uphold individual creativity requires a collective mindset from educators, who must hold together the multiple identities of groups of students so that points of tension and disagreement can be negotiated, if not always fully resolved.

A Question of Agency

Although de-centring teachers as the sole or even primary locus of authority can help to place more focus on student needs, there is also a risk that, as higher education becomes ever more defined through metrics of evaluation[8] (e.g. the Teaching Excellence Framework, and National Student Survey, to name two examples in the United Kingdom), the student experience becomes reduced to a simple question of individual customer satisfaction. It is, therefore, important to keep in mind the

---

7   Peter Miksza, 'A Review of Research on Practicing: Summary and Synthesis of the Extant Research with Implications for a New Theoretical Orientation', *Bulletin of the Council for Research in Music Education*, 190 (2011), 51–92, https://doi.org/10.5406/bulcouresmusedu.190.0051
8   Annouchka Bayley, 'Trans-forming Higher Education', *Performance Research*, 21 (2016), 44–49, https://doi.org/10.1080/13528165.2016.1240930.

performative, collective, dimensions of SCLEs, i.e., those aspects which keep the learning experience open and fluid, and prevent it from hardening into a commodity. As Monika Nerland reflects, teacher and student responsibilities in SCLEs are 'related and co-produced',[9] meaning that both parties share responsibility and agency for shaping, or performing, the overall learning experience.[10] This ethical and agential bond between teachers and students becomes even more apparent in group learning environments, where the learning experience is not only co-produced between teacher and student but also between fellow students, who, intentionally or unintentionally, modulate one another's motivations and capabilities. Indeed, although SCLEs are typically considered to be dialectical spaces oscillating between learner and learning environment,[11] they might be better characterised as collective ones, shaped via a collective performance of agency working towards a common sense of well-being or fulfilment, which is itself collectively and non-linearly defined in relation to the people and things assembled in a particular environment.

Thinking about learner agency as a fundamentally collective pursuit calls into question, or at least differently nuances, the dominant understanding of SCLEs as a means of strengthening learner autonomy[12] and self-efficacy,[13] since autonomy would seem to undermine the collective bonds implied by a distributive model of learner agency. Perhaps, rather than seeking to drive learner *autonomy*, SCLEs might find an alternative paradigm in the concept of 'ontonomy', a term derived from Buddhist theory to denote the interconnectedness of all beings.[14] Ontonomy means that the self exists within the other, and vice versa, so that individual actions must be understood as ontologically and ethically entangled with the others with whom, on whom, the self acts. From the perspective of SCLEs, this would mean recognising how all teachers and learners are already and always embedded within one another's unfolding educational experience. Not an 'experience' in the sense of an already defined, marketable commodity that can be given a satisfaction rating but 'experience' as a constantly shifting network of

---

9   Monika Nerland, 'Exploring Student Participation Challenges in Student-Centred Learning Environments', in *Quality Work in Higher Education*, ed. by Mari Elken, Peter Maassen, Monika Nerland, Tine S. Prøitz, Bjørn Stensaker, and Agnete Vabø ([n. p.]: Springer, 2020), pp. 97–113 (p. 99), https://doi.org/10.1007/978-3-030-41757-4_6

10 The 'performative' dimension of SCLEs is also open to critique by some commentators who consider the notion of placing obligations on students to attend classes and demonstrate engagement as a form 'presenteeism', e.g., Bruce Macfarlane, 'Student Performativity in Higher Education: Converting Learning as a Private Space into a Public Performance', *Higher Education Research and Development*, 34 (2015), 338–50, https://doi.org/10.1080/07294360.2014.956697

11 Damşa, Nerland, and Andreadakis.

12 Tong, Standen, and Sotiriou.

13 Laura Ritchie, 'Music, Research and Self-efficacy in Higher Education', in *What Is Research-led Teaching? Multi-Disciplinary Perspectives*, ed. by Alisa Miller, John Sharp, and Jeremy Strong ([n.p.]: CREST, 2012), pp. 38–45.

14 Heesoon Bai, 'Decentering the Ego-self and Releasing the Care-consciousness', *Paideusis: Journal of the Canadian Philosophy of Education Society*, 12 (1999), 5–18, https://doi.org/10.7202/1073086ar

'intra-actions' between learners, teachers, and wider ecological factors,[15] which, since it is collectively constituted, resists appropriation by any one individual. Annouchka Bayley observes that '"we" are constituted by multiple, entangled Othernesses';[16] "we" are, thus, distributive beings and the educative act is necessarily distributive, rather than bi-directional between teacher and student. It follows that one learner's agency in a group setting must be conceived of as interconnected with the agencies of other learners, rather than being autonomously held. Consequently, instead of thinking of SCLEs as based around a series of linear, dialectical exchanges between individual and separate actors (teacher and student, extrinsic and intrinsic motivation), we could understand such pedagogies as predicated on an 'ethic of care', which binds together teachers and students in a collective act.

In discussing care ethics in teaching, Dave Chang and Heesoon Bai argue against a virtue ethics theory of care (in which caring only morally improves the carer) and in favour of a relational model in which *receiving* care and *giving* care are understood as being ontologically and ethically inseparable. They propose that the virtue of care acts, such as teaching, must be understood as a continuity between multiple actors, rather than a singular, virtuous act coming from an autonomous individual.[17] In other words, approaching teaching from an ethic of care means seeking to cultivate *ontonomic* awareness in both carer and cared-for, enabling teachers and students to recognise how their learning experience binds them together, as an ethical-agential learner collective. In practical terms, this demands that learning environments are cultivated in ways that make it possible for students and teachers to collectively set educational goals and lines of communication. Therefore, whilst the learning objectives underpinning a particular SCLE might signify and specify the virtues to which such learner collectives will aspire, the agential shaping of these could be understood more like a collective reaching *towards* ideals in flux, rather than a linear process of goal-setting and self-directed learning to meet fixed objectives.

Distributing Motivation

Conventional accounts of SCLEs do not always capture this sense of agential interdependency, since they are typically constructed around the goal-directed intentions of an autonomous learner who seeks to 'appropr[iate] the world',[18] i.e., a learner who aims to take and shape resources and knowledge to their own ends. Certainly, it is quite reasonable to suppose that, from their differing subject positions,

---

15   Annouchka Bayley, 'Posthumanism, Decoloniality and Re-imagining Pedagogy', *Parallax*, 24 (2018), 243–53, https://doi.org/10.1080/13534645.2018.1496576
16   Ibid., p. 244.
17   Dave Chang and Heesoon Bai, 'Self-with-other in Teacher Practice: A Case Study through Care, Aristotelian Virtue, and Buddhist Ethics', in *Ethics in Professional Education*, ed. by Christopher Martin and Claudia W. Ruitenberg (Routledge, 2019), https://doi.org/10.4324/9781315121352
18   Damşa, Nerland, and Andreadakis, p. 2079.

individuals can find inspiration and drive for themselves (intrinsic motivation) and teachers are able to validate this through sensitive critique (extrinsic motivation). However, we also need to account for the *distributive* motivation students (hopefully) build with their peers and teachers on the programme; that is, their collective ontonomy. I have argued elsewhere that this can be expressed as a kind of 'intratrinsic' motivation, based on the 'mutually impactful dynamic between individuals within a class'.[19] This means that the collective development of motivation for students happens in some sense within one another, simultaneously, rather than one student's input leading to the other in a simple causal relationship.

From a pedagogical perspective, an agential network can be expressed in a multi-dimensional model of student motivation, based around intrinsic (student), extrinsic (teacher-to-student), and intratrinsic (student-to-student-to-teacher-to-teacher) dimensions.[20] For educators, cultivating intratrinsic motivation is a case of shaping learning not only inter-personally but also *intra*-personally. This means to become aware of the ways in which agency is distributed across the classroom but also to consider how whole-group agency interacts with the relationships being built in smaller settings, with other tutors and students, or through more direct relationships with individual students in the educational environment. For example, a momentary dialogue with one student in a classroom requires teachers to blend consideration of the individual student's perspective (intrinsic motivation) with an assessment of how their response as a teacher will help to shape the student's developing agency (extrinsic motivation) as well as how the exchange will drive the overall collective capacity of the class (intratrinsic motivation).

This is similar to Jane Bennett's idea of 'impersonal affect', a collective feeling or desire, which 'requires that one is caught up in it' rather than fully in control of one's own actions.[21] Elsewhere, Bennett characterises this in terms of 'influx/efflux', by which she means the tendency of bodies to take in and send out influences[22] and, thus, to partake in one another's intentions and actions. Bennett makes the related point that 'If we think we already know what is out there, we will almost surely miss much of it'.[23] She draws on Walt Whitman's belief that poets must develop a 'sensitive cuticle',[24] that is, be open to influence and responsive to the constantly shifting field of agencies with which, with whom, one's own subjectivity is entangled. Design for learning could be thought of as a similar effort on the part of teachers to develop a sensitive cuticle, thereby to remain open to the ways in which distributive learner agencies are manifest

---

19 Jacob Thompson-Bell, 'Student-centred Strategies for Higher Music Education: Using Peer-to-peer Critique and Practice as Research Methodologies to Train Conservatoire Musicians', *British Journal of Music Education*, 2022, 1–14 (p. 3), https://doi.org/10.1017/S0265051722000080
20 Ibid.
21 Bennett, *Vibrant Matter*, p. xv.
22 Bennett, *Influx and Efflux*.
23 Bennett, *Vibrant Matter*, p. xv.
24 Bennett, *Influx and Efflux*, p. 39.

between multiple students and other teachers within SCLEs. Our job, as educators, is not only to help students develop skills they have identified but to help them create futures for themselves that they may not yet have considered. Furthermore, given the ethical and agential bonds being woven in SCLEs, we have a responsibility to look beyond purely teacher-centred or student-centred learning trajectories to collectively imagine new creative possibilities.

A Vignette: Critical Response Process

In order to illustrate how distributive agential networks play out in practice, I would like to offer a pedagogical example, conveyed in the form of an impressionistic vignette[25] adapted from sessions I have led for MA students. The vignette is based on my experience over a period of eight years facilitating peer-to-peer feedback sessions with students across musical performance, composition, and production practices. It describes a peer-to-peer feedback class, conducted using the Critical Response Process (CRP). This is a pedagogy designed by choreographers Liz Lerman and John Borstel to allow for constructive feedback on creative work in group settings.[26] The shape of the session and the attitudes expressed by the characters in the vignette are based on existing data on student perceptions of Critical Response Process, which I have explored elsewhere.[27] Therefore, although what follows is but one example, it is an example which synthesises many similar instances. For this CRP session, the learners are working in a multidisciplinary group, bringing together musicians from many different genres, traditions, and disciplines. Some of the students in this group might identify most with classical music, or perhaps with jazz or popular music styles. They might be concerned with how to develop their understanding and performance of traditional music or to innovate new experimental approaches to sound design or multimedia practice.

I invite you now, as a reader, to imagine yourself as a student within this learning environment, a peer-to-peer feedback session in which you and your fellow students will share work with and provide feedback to one another. Looking around the room, you see musicians inhabiting different identities, equipped with differing levels of professional experience and, perhaps, divergent values, assumptions, and beliefs driving their practice. Dotted amongst the class are teachers—with similarly diverse backgrounds and musical cultures. One of these teachers stands or sits at the front of the room; beside them, an empty chair, and an array of uninhabited instruments: a drum kit and piano on standby, cables snaking from microphones raised on stands.

---

25 John Van Maanen, *Tales of the Field: On Writing Ethnography* (Chicago: University of Chicago Press, 1988).
26 Lerman and Borstel.
27 Thompson-Bell.

The room itself is a performance space, used for public recitals and lectures when not occupied by this class. On one wall, a projector screen hangs, blank, awaiting input.

The teacher at the front speaks up: 'Welcome everyone, let's get started...'. They invite the first presenter to come forward, causing one of your fellow students to rise and tread, a little nervously, down the aisle between the chairs, before sitting down at the piano.

You review the steps of the Critical Response Process in your head whilst you wait.

- Step One: statements of meaning. The presenting student will showcase their work in progress, and the facilitator will then ask the 'responders' (that's you and the others seated here and waiting to hear the work in progress) to comment on the aspects of it that they found noticeable or memorable, in order to gauge the first impressions elicited by the work.

- Step Two: artist as questioner. The presenting student will need to pose their creative challenges as questions for the group, hopefully keeping them open, so as to draw on the range of expertise and experience in the room.

- Step Three: neutral questions from responders. You'll be expected to find open-ended, neutral ways of asking questions about what you've just heard. The challenge is to avoid being too opinionated and, instead, to help the artist find their own creative solutions.

- Step Four: permissioned opinions. This is exactly what it sounds like: asking the artist if they want to hear your opinion. They can say no, and you won't be offended. After all, it might not be right time, or the same themes and issues could already have come up earlier in the process.

It is useful to have a structure, but remembering the specific steps can be difficult, and holding unsolicited opinions back until the end can be challenging, especially if you really like the work. Or don't like it...

'Is there anything you'd like to tell the group before you play?', the teacher asks.

Actually, it would better to call this teacher a 'facilitator', since they are not exactly instructing students on what to do or what to think. They might not even say much at all. They might leave feedback up to the students in the class. Sometimes the facilitator steps in to steer things a little, to bring conversation back into the feedback structure. Other times, they offer more specific feedback to students presenting their work in progress. But they are not a teacher in the traditional sense.

'Not really...this is a new composition...actually, it's a song about what it feels like to get stood up at the cinema. My ex did that to me once. So, I wrote this song about it...Hope you like it.'

Lights down. Piano stool pulled up. Everyone quiet. The music begins.

As you listen, you think about how they use their voice, the way they play the piano. Loose, simple chords, placed around a natural vocal. No microphone. Some grit. Perhaps a wry sense of humour coming across. This is pretty good, you think. I wonder if I'm that good. But I also wonder how much more they can do with this song.

Applause. Lights up. The presenter stands and moves to sit next to the facilitating teacher. It looks like an interview, but the student seems to be asking the questions. They have a notebook in front of them with topics for discussion.

The facilitator invites statements of meaning from you and the other responders. People offer general observations. One person recalls an evocative chord, another the lyrical play of words. Another person says, 'I noticed how you kept the chords really simple and how that complemented the voice.' A few more observations, then the group waits.

'What questions do you have?', the facilitator asks, turning to the presenting student. Leafing through their notebook, the presenter picks out a first question to ask their responders: 'How well do you think the arrangement supported the lyrical narrative?'

Amongst the responders, a few hands tentatively go up. The facilitator nods encouragingly to one person who has their hand raised. They say,

> I liked the simplicity of the harmony, and I thought the use of root position chords to support the immediacy of the lyric worked really well...but I did think there was, maybe, some scope to develop the chords a little more. You could think about whether the lyrical narrative grows or resolves somehow...or maybe...it might work well to use some different chord voicings after the first verse and chorus, just to expand the dramatic scope a bit and keep things moving.

Even though this is an opinion, it is coming directly in response to the artist's question, so they are ready to receive it. It is important not to add extra opinions onto these answers—the artist does not suddenly want to hear what anyone thinks about their voice or piano playing. At least, not yet.

The presenter nods, noting down the comments in their notebook. 'Yeah, I did wonder if that might be a good idea. But I wanted it to sound like someone just feeling their way through...not too contrived.'

More responses. More questions from the presenter.

Next, discussion moves onto neutral questions from the responders. Since the presenter is not leading these questions, any responder opinions will need to be neutralised within broader and more open-ended questions so that the presenter can make their own judgments. The challenge, at least for now, is to help the artist do what they do best, and by identifying their own solutions, not just to tell them what you would do.

'Do you plan to expand the instrumentation for this song, or to keep things as they are?'

'I'm not too sure actually...do you have any ideas? I usually add some strings, maybe a little backing-vocals on a studio version. What do you think?'

More questions. More responses from the presenter.

Finally, the facilitator asks, 'Who would like to offer an opinion?'. They gesture towards a raised hand.

'I have an opinion about instrumentation', one person says. 'Would you like to hear it?'

This is Step Four—a hallmark of CRP. Responders have to be prepared to offer an opinion, and presenters get to say no if they would prefer not to have more feedback on a particular topic. Hardly anyone ever refuses, though...

The presenter agrees to hear the opinion. 'I think additional instrumentation would change the context in which the music is heard', the responder says. 'I think any further instrumentation needs to match the introspective character of the song. Adding full strings might make things less intimate.'

More opinions. In each case, the opinions link back to discussion the presenter has already had, so the topics do not come as a surprise, even if they had not anticipated the specific ideas. The presenter accepts them all. They will have to choose which ones to follow up, though, since some are contrasting, contradictory even.

The facilitator thanks everyone and calls the session to a close. The presenter closes their notebook, now filled with different views, proposals, observations, and ideas. People slowly leave the room, impromptu breakout conversations, here and there, continue the discussion more informally.

You reflect on some of the topics raised. How do they relate to *your* practice? How would *you* meet the creative challenges discussed? You leave the room without having played a note. But you have a lot more questions. Questions about your own practice, questions about the music of your peers, curiosity about how it will change and develop in response to feedback.

Classroom Assemblages

What is going on here? One answer is that we are observing a classroom assemblage at play. An assemblage can be defined as a network of non/human phenomena which mutually modify the behaviour and possible associations of one another, and thereby work beyond the sum of their parts.[28] Any system, from organisms to weather, can be thought of as an assemblage, enacted across agential networks linking constituent phenomena in mutually impactful, 'intra-active' relationships.[29] Taken as an assemblage, a classroom is not simply a meeting of teachers and students but a

---

28   Gilles Deleuze and Félix Guattari, *A Thousand Plateaus: Capitalism and Schizophrenia*, trans. by Brian Massumi (Minneapolis, MN: University of Minnesota Press, 1987); Bruno Latour, *Pandora's Hope: Essays on the Reality of Science Studies* (Cambridge, MA: Harvard University Press, 1999); Bennett, *Vibrant Matter*; DeLanda.

29   Karen Barad, 'Posthumanist Performativity: Toward an Understanding of How Matter Comes to Matter', *Signs: Journal of Women in Culture and Society*, 28 (2003), 801–31, https://doi.org/10.1086/345321

site of 'distributive agency',[30] implicating the learning resources, musical instruments, room acoustics, degree programme learning objectives, institutional strategy, political concepts, and the bodies and accumulated beliefs of the people assembled. Moreover, the constituent elements work differently and move towards different goals when they act together. The concept of the assemblage might help educators to make sense of their students' identities as emergent, interlinked, processes, because it provides a model for understanding the ways in which different people and things in a classroom situation can become agentially distributed, entangled, and thereby mutually enable or obstruct one another in unpredictable ways. In other words, assemblages help to show how subjective 'ontonomy' (i.e., self-with-other bonds) can emerge amongst groups of learners.

Returning to the vignette of CRP sketched above, we can observe precisely this kind of distributive agential network in which the questions asked by responders are modulated by the comments and queries of their peers. This engenders a pedagogical environment focused both on the individual voice of the presenting student and the collective identity of the wider student group. By withholding unsolicited responder opinions on the work until the end, and then allowing the presenting artist to decline to hear them, CRP establishes a collective mindset through which students seek to negotiate a range of creative approaches with their peers. It is not necessarily that the group collaboratively defines a way forward but that they work to sustain differences of opinion and to capture the range of possible outcomes for the work in progress afforded by the dynamic flow of subjectivities within the group. This could be understood as a form of 'reflection-in-practice' (a principle explored in greater depth by Richard Fay, Daniel Mawson, and Nahielly Palacios in Chapter 8 of this volume), challenging students and teachers to play with their own established ideas and viewpoints by refracting them through the agential network, which is to say, exploring them in relation to the different people assembled in the classroom setting. This is a clear case of intratrinsic motivation building through mutually impactful dialogue within a group teaching situation. Not only is the presenting student extrinsically motivated through teacher and peer commentary on their work, but all members of the classroom assemblage (including teachers) are afforded the opportunity to develop intra-actively with one another. In doing so, they render new, further opportunities for intrinsic and extrinsic motivation to grow. To the notion of *embodied* cognition, explored by Robert Sholl in Chapter 5 of this volume, CRP highlights the sense in which learning is also *embedded*, meaning that thinking happens not only through our bodies but also between them. The hope is that students will take forward this mindset beyond their studies, adopting a similarly open comportment towards their

---

30   Emily Jean Hood and Amelia M. Kraehe, 'Creative Matter: New Materialism in Art Education Research, Teaching, and Learning', *Art Education*, 70 (2017), 32–38, https://doi.org/10.1080/00043125.2017.1274196

collaborators and colleagues, in order to allow unexpected ideas and solutions to emerge in response to collectively defined problems.

It is important to add that, although the theory of assemblages characterises agency in a distributive sense, as being enacted between people and things, this does not entirely efface the force of individual agency within a class. Agency will not be evenly or stably distributed at all times; it might be volatile, temporarily concentrated around some actors more than others, such as in the constantly shifting dynamic between a teacher and student. Within any assemblage it is quite possible, perhaps even probable, that smaller, more localised, networks will emerge, much like eddies and whirlpools can form within the flow of a river. In this sense, educators should not overlook how individual students might experience their learning, especially where there might be differences in these experiences from an equity perspective. In practice, this requires the adoption of transparent, collaborative pedagogical frameworks, so that everyone, teacher and students included, understands how they are being called upon to engage with, and perhaps alter, the classroom situation. For example, within a CRP framework, individuals have their respective roles to play (as facilitators, presenters, or responders), and individual students must be sensitive to the ways in which their questions and responses could offer encouragement to their peers. I am reminded of Mariam Kharatyan's account in Chapter 7 of this volume of how her students learned about their performance practice through gaining 'access to their own vulnerability'. Adapting Kharatyan's phrase, we could say that CRP gives learner groups access to a form of collective vulnerability and, thus, to an openness to the possibilities of the classroom assemblage. The point is that intrinsic, extrinsic, and intratrinsic motivations are linked, braided together in an agential network with both individual and collective capacities.

CRP helps the teacher and presenter not only to prepare the ground for intratrinsic forms of motivation to emerge but also helps the responders to offer moments of extrinsic motivational support for their fellow students. The point is that intrinsic, extrinsic, and intratrinsic motivations are linked, braided together in an agential network with both individual and collective capacities.

Correspondingly, educators should make efforts to remain sensitive to the character of individual students in terms of their capacity to resonate both with and against other actors within the classroom assemblage. This has implications for the ethical responsibilities of students and teachers towards one another as well as of students towards their fellow learners. Education cannot simply be a case of pursuing individual goals, perhaps in search of employability, but must instead be a matter of recognising how to instigate relationships which are mutually agencifying, i.e., which amplify the capacities of distributive networks linking them with their colleagues within and beyond their institution. In other words, educators must support their learners to partake fully in the influx and efflux[31] between their sense of subjectivity and the people and resources with whom, with which, they are assembled.

A Matter of Equity

Recently, I have spoken informally with one or two students who have questioned whether their freedom of expression is being limited by tools such as neutral questioning in CRP. These students felt that learners should simply be allowed to say whatever they liked about one another's work, since to place checks and balances on this would be a restriction on free speech. I see this as a matter of equity, concerning the relative balance between competing views, values, and agencies within a student group. Whilst the number of dissenting students has been very small, with most reflecting positively on their experiences through CRP,[32] I think that, given the times we live in, and the attack, at least in the United Kingdom, on 'woke' culture and the very principle of 'equity', it makes sense to briefly discuss these issues by way of a conclusion. This is, not least, because academic institutions are traditionally regarded as being bulwarks against incursions on freedom of expression.

The kind of distributive agency fostered through CRP and similar pedagogies is, in my view, a means of working towards equitable systems of learning and teaching in which marginalised voices can be better heard. This is because CRP helps to maximise the possible fluidity of intra-actions between individuals, and across traditions and disciplines, assembled within a classroom group. We could think of the student group as being a temporary assemblage, operational for the duration of a session or programme of study. To work equitably within such a classroom assemblage requires that individuals recognise and acknowledge their interdependence (i.e. their ontonomy) and demands individual expression be understood in relation to the expressive capabilities of other members of the group. Therefore, distributive approaches to learning and teaching must clearly outline for students how they are being asked to behave, and how incursions on the freedom of one person by another might be defined and negotiated.

Furthermore, there can be no presumption of neutrality in any pedagogical space, since there is always some form of structure or agency through which the space is sustained. Nor can there be any assumption about how individuals will want to work and how they will engage with their peers and teachers. Students do not enter educative spaces as neutral, impersonal actors but as opinionated people with values, assumptions, and very likely prejudices, about one another. As Bayley argues, 'Intra-action means that "I" am always-already marking bodies, producing the world and thus responsible for the choices that matter through knowledge-making'.[33] SCLEs thus

---

31 Bennett, *Influx and Efflux*.
32 See Thompson-Bell.
33 Bayley, 'Trans-forming Higher Education', p. 47.

need to move beyond purely individualistic models so as not to overlook the inevitable imbalances of power found both in teacher-student relationships and within classroom groups.[34] What is required of both teachers and students is really a form of democratic competency; that is, an ability to participate sensitively and actively in collective social life and to be responsive for one's fellow citizens.

This is akin to Paulo Freire's notion of 'critical pedagogy',[35] in which students are empowered to recognise, think through, and perhaps reimagine, the political structures that guide their epistemological outlook and worldview.[36] Henry Giroux summarises one aspect of Freire's stance as being 'to teach students to inhabit a particular mode of agency',[37] and this is precisely what is at stake in SCLEs: how teachers can enable students to cultivate forms of agency which are democratically and ethically sound. It is not enough for SCLEs to repair the agential cut between teacher and student; they must also attend to the distribution of agency between students. Without this critical dimension, there remains the risk in group settings that learners will replicate existing power structures that exclude certain people or find themselves undermining one another's individual efforts towards (expressive) freedom. This requires both self-knowledge, in the sense of recognising the idiosyncrasies of one's own subjective position, and an ethic of care bonding teachers and students into a learner collective or assemblage.

Thus, to design a SCLE in a critical way is to invite learners not only to appropriate learning resources to their own individual ends[38] but, perhaps more importantly, to encourage them to form agential collectives which enable them to recognise self-with-other and to embrace diversities of outlook. Accordingly, SCLEs must support learners and educators to co-create multiple and mutual paths to learning with and through one another. In other words, they must nurture impactful student-teacher, student-student, and, perhaps, teacher-teacher intra-actions. In doing so, SCLEs might cultivate a sense of ontonomy (i.e. collective agency and togetherness) in participating teachers and students, founded on shared convictions and collectively-defined rules of engagement. In my view, CRP is an example of how such a system of intra-action can be transparently, and ethically, defined.

In conclusion, and returning to the vignette sketched above, by attending to the connections between individual and collective forms of agency, CRP acts to enable and shepherd freedom of expression rather than to constrain it. This is because the

---

34　Bayley, 'Posthumanism, Decoloniality and Re-imagining Pedagogy'.

35　Paulo Freire, *Pedagogy of the Oppressed*, 50th Anniv edn, trans. by Myra Bergman Ramos (London and New York: Bloomsbury Academic, 2018).

36　Ronualdo Marques, Talita Fraguas, and Rosicler Maria Alchieri, 'Theoretical and Methodological Aspects of Paulo Freire's Pedagogy: A Pedagogical and Dialogic Possibility in the Teaching and Learning Process', *Conjecturas*, 22 (2022), 190–99, https://doi.org/10.53660/CONJ-1990-MP12

37　Henry A. Giroux, 'Rethinking Education as the Practice of Freedom: Paulo Freire and the Promise of Critical Pedagogy', *Policy Futures in Education*, 8 (2010), 715–21 (p. 718), https://doi.org/10.2304/pfie.2010.8.6.715

38　Damşa, Nerland, and Andreadakis.

process de-centres individual perspectives, thus fostering an equitable space in which a diversity of viewpoints can be heard and critically evaluated together. Far from inhibiting individual freedom of speech, the obligation to neutralise opinions and to entertain alternative viewpoints enables differences of outlook to be collectively held and observed, rather than allowing disagreements to become distracting or obstructive. Drawing together the subjectivities of individual learners into a productive classroom assemblage therefore requires a collective mindset to be established through an ethic of care between students and teachers. This involves not only enabling students to uncover their own agency as individuals but also encouraging them to guarantee the agency of their peers. In doing so, SCLEs can create networks which amplify the agency of everyone, whilst affirming new and unexpected opportunities for collective learning to take place.

References

Bai, Heesoon, 'Decentering the Ego-self and Releasing the Care-consciousness', *Paideusis: Journal of the Canadian Philosophy of Education Society*, 12 (1999), 5–18, https://doi.org/10.7202/1073086ar

Barad, Karen, *Meeting the Universe Halfway* (Durham, NC: Duke University Press, 2007), https://doi.org/10.2307/j.ctv12101zq

——, 'Posthumanist Performativity: Toward an Understanding of How Matter Comes to Matter', *Signs: Journal of Women in Culture and Society*, 28 (2003), 801–31, https://doi.org/10.1086/345321

Bayley, Annouchka, 'Posthumanism, Decoloniality and Re-imagining Pedagogy', *Parallax*, 24 (2018), 243–53, https://doi.org/10.1080/13534645.2018.1496576

——, 'Trans-forming Higher Education', *Performance Research*, 21 (2016), 44–49, https://doi.org/10.1080/13528165.2016.1240930

Bennett, Jane, *Influx and Efflux: Writing up with Walt Whitman* (Durham and London: Duke University Press, 2020), https://doi.org/10.1215/9781478009290

——, *Vibrant Matter* (Durham and London: Duke University Press, 2010), https://doi.org/10.2307/j.ctv111jh6w

Chang, Dave, and Heesoon Bai, 'Self-with-other in Teacher Practice: A Case Study Through Care, Aristotelian Virtue, and Buddhist Ethics', in *Ethics in Professional Education*, ed. by Christopher Martin and Claudia W. Ruitenberg (London and New York: Routledge, 2019) https://doi.org/10.4324/9781315121352

Damşa, Crina, Monika Nerland, and Zacharias E. Andreadakis, 'An Ecological Perspective on Learner-constructed Learning Spaces', *British Journal of Educational Technology*, 50 (2019), 2075–89, https://doi.org/10.1111/bjet.12855

DeLanda, Manuel, *Assemblage Theory* (Edinburgh: Edinburgh University Press, 2016), https://doi.org/10.1515/9781474413640

Deleuze, Gilles, and Félix Guattari, *A Thousand Plateaus: Capitalism and Schizophrenia*, trans. by Brian Massumi (Minneapolis: University of Minnesota Press, 1987)

Freire, Paulo, *Pedagogy of the Oppressed*, 50th Anniv edn, trans. by Myra Bergman Ramos (London and New York: Bloomsbury Academic, 2018)

Giroux, Henry A., 'Rethinking Education as the Practice of Freedom: Paulo Freire and the Promise of Critical Pedagogy', *Policy Futures in Education*, 8 (2010), 715–21, https://doi.org/10.2304/pfie.2010.8.6.715

Hood, Emily Jean, and Amelia M. Kraehe, 'Creative Matter: New Materialism in Art Education Research, Teaching, and Learning', *Art Education*, 70 (2017), 32–38, https://doi.org/10.1080/00043125.2017.1274196

Land, Susan, Michael Hannafin, and Kevin Oliver, 'Student-centered Learning Environments: Foundations, Assumptions and Design', in *Theoretical Foundations of Learning Environments*, ed. By Susan Land and David Jonassen, 2nd ed. (New York: Routledge, 2012), pp. 3–26, https://doi.org/10.4324/9780203813799

Latour, Bruno, *Pandora's Hope: Essays on the Reality of Science Studies* (Cambridge, MA: Harvard University Press, 1999)

Lerman, Liz, and John Borstel, *Liz Lerman's Critical Response Process: A Method for Getting Useful Feedback on Anything You Make, from Dance to Dessert* (Takoma Park, MD: Liz Lerman Dance Exchange, 2003)

Macfarlane, Bruce, 'Student Performativity in Higher Education: Converting Learning as a Private Space into a Public Performance', *Higher Education Research and Development*, 34 (2015), 338–50, https://doi.org/10.1080/07294360.2014.956697

Marques, Ronualdo, Talita Fraguas, and Rosicler Maria Alchieri, 'Theoretical and Methodological Aspects of Paulo Freire's Pedagogy: A Pedagogical and Dialogic Possibility in the Teaching and Learning Process', *Conjecturas*, 22 (2022), 190–99, https://doi.org/10.53660/CONJ-1990-MP12

Miksza, Peter, 'A Review of Research on Practicing: Summary and Synthesis of the Extant Research with Implications for a New Theoretical Orientation', *Bulletin of the Council for Research in Music Education*, 190 (2011), 51–92 https://doi.org/10.5406/bulcouresmusedu.190.0051

Nerland, Monika, 'Beyond Policy: Conceptualising Student-centred Environments in Higher (Music) Education', in *Becoming Musicians: Student Involvement and Teacher Collaboration in Higher Music Education*, ed. By Stefan Gies, and Jon Helge Sætre, n.p.: NMH Publications 2019:7, pp. 53–66

——, 'Exploring Student Participation Challenges in Student-Centred Learning Environments', 2020, pp. 97–113, https://doi.org/10.1007/978-3-030-41757-4_6

Ritchie, Laura, 'Music, Research and Self-efficacy in Higher Education', in *What Is Research-Led Teaching? Multi-Disciplinary Perspectives*, ed. By Alisa Miller, John Sharp, and Jeremy Strong ([n.p.]: CREST, 2012), pp. 38–45

Thompson-Bell, Jacob, 'Student-centred Strategies for Higher Music Education: Using Peer-to-peer Critique and Practice as Research Methodologies to Train Conservatoire Musicians', *British Journal of Music Education*, 2022, 1–14, https://doi.org/10.1017/S0265051722000080

Tong, Vincent C. H., Alex Standen, and Mina Sotiriou (eds), *Shaping Higher Education with Students* (London: UCL Press, 2018), https://doi.org/10.2307/j.ctt21c4tcm

Van Maanen, John, *Tales of the Field: On Writing Ethnography* (Chicago: University of Chicago Press, 1988)

7. Score-Based Learning and Improvisation in Classical Music Performance

Mariam Kharatyan

Introduction

When I was a student at the Yerevan State Conservatory, Armenia, it was typical to think of the performance of a scored piece of music as a task to reproduce the composer's intentions. Even after the collapse of the Soviet Union (USSR) and the country's regaining of its independence as the Republic of Armenia, authoritative teaching methods continued to dominate. The master-apprentice model, for example, demanded a complex classical repertoire and a high level of technical and musical proficiency in every performance. Even though I had improvisation lessons as part of the classical piano performance curricula at the Yerevan State Conservatory, the common practice was score-based learning. Continuing my performance education in Norway unfolded many new possibilities. I was given more space for reflection and musical freedom, and yet, the core concepts in classical music education and performance practice that I experienced in Norway were still mainly anchored in score-based learning.

The REACT *Stakeholders Requirement Report* identified how the teaching of western art music performance in most Higher Music Education Institutions continues to rely on nineteenth-century values, standards, and practices. It is largely focused on the reification of scores by concentrating on reconfiguring/realizing the composer's intentions.[1] Indeed, throughout decades of classical music education, performance traditions have continuously been anchored consciously or subconsciously in *Werktreue*,[2] as well as in stereotypical understandings of established Classical/

---

1   Jorge Correia and others, REACT–Rethinking Music Performance in European Higher Education Institutions, *Artistic Career in Music: Stakeholders Requirement Report* (Aveiro: UA Editora, 2021), p. 3, https://doi.org/10.48528/wfq9-4560
2   The term *Werktreue* (Being True to the Work, an approach which puts the score at the centre of performative interpretation) was coined by E. T. A. Hoffmann at the beginning of the nineteenth

Romantic performance traditions. The continued influence of these two dominant strands highlights the need to explore new approaches to classical music education, seeking ways in which neither the letter of the score, nor the legacy of performance traditions, shall inhibit the potential for individual creativity in each student. Performers' individual musical expression—the whole spectrum of musical shaping through timing, timbre, colours, and nuance—reaches far beyond what any score can possibly indicate. I share my reflections on developing new approaches to classical music interpretation and performance through improvisation, using the departure point of my artistic research doctoral project *Armenian Fingerprints* (2019) and the ongoing artistic research project *Armenian Crossroads*, as well as an improvisation session with students presented through quotations from semi-structured interviews.

Creative Crossroads

I became aware of the impact of *Werktreue* in my piano playing during the four years of my artistic research fellowship project, *Armenian Fingerprints*, an exploration of Komitas's and Aram Khachaturian's piano music in the light of Armenian folk music. When playing the music of these two composers, I felt a deep confusion, as well as a gap between what the written score indicated and what my imagination and interpretations sought to express. I had to delve deeper into the music beyond the written scores, to find the missing lines that connect the letter of the score with hidden aspects of those compositions. This brought me closer to the inspirational sources of the composers and sometimes to the original source of a particular peasant song/folk tune/folk dance melody. The scores in European music notation appeared as if they were an attempt at poor translations of what, in live performance, the music could sound like—with its large palette of expressiveness and the rich cultural traditions and layers of contrast that Komitas's and Khachaturian's music could unfold. Different aspects of improvisation—as well as the improvisational timing of music—have been a vital part of the Armenian folk music tradition from which these two composers received massive inspiration, often basing entire compositions on peasant and folk tunes. Without going into too much detail, I would like to emphasise that one of the major findings from my exploration of Komitas's and Khachaturian's music and its interplay with folk-music aesthetics has been that the improvisational timing of music, *rubatos*, and agogics have been often inspired by the art of folk musicians and troubadours—*ashughs* and *gusans*. When approaching these composers' scores, it was obvious to me that many layers of the music remain dormant, locked within the limitations/restrictions of the notation. I have observed in my piano playing, since that work, that I not only play their music with many nuances not indicated

---

century (Lydia Goehr, *Being True to the Work*, The Journal of Aesthetics and Art Criticism, 47. 1 (Winter, 1989), p. 57, https://doi.org/10.2307/431993

in scores—such as agogics, articulations, dynamics, timbres, pedalling, phrasing, and timing—but I also subconsciously add ornaments and other elements as well. This practice is seemingly a result of my response to the folk instruments' sounds and aesthetics. These elements, especially the improvisational timing of the music, gave me a feeling of liberation from scores and bar lines, a freer flow, and a new expression of music. This is particularly the case when playing Komitas's songs and folk dances, with their roots in Armenian peasant songs, dance songs, and instrumental music that the composer collected from rural regions of Armenia, first notated them in the Armenian notation system and later translated them into European notation through his compositional work, presenting his versions of these folk tunes.[3] Komitas, in his research, highlighted the limitations that European notation bears when notating a folk melody, along with the problems of bar-accent and the emphasised syllables in relationship with the downbeat and strongest beat of the bar. The notated, so-called 'finished', or written form of a folk song is entirely uncharacteristic of the nature of folk music, which is created and shaped during improvisation, developing into multiple versions of the same melody.

Improvisational timing and elements of the performance practices of traditional music were vital throughout my four-year study of Komitas's and Khachaturian's music. These experiences led naturally to a further questioning of the boundaries of the written text in my performances, a freer approach to the scores, and eventually to improvising on the piano in response to a particular melody or a composition, as well as exploring free improvisation.

In 2022, I started a new artistic research project, *Armenian Crossroads*, within which the aspect of (free) improvisation as a response to composed and written music are vital elements. It was both an implicit and explicit need in me to embrace music improvisation again. The project involves both explorations through my solo piano playing but also includes a collaborative aspect where classical musicians and students studying at the Department of Classical Music and Music Education and the Department of Popular Music at the University of Agder (UiA) are involved. I grew up playing music by ear and improvising on folk, urban, and pop tunes, all this in parallel with my professional studies of classical music. However, as briefly mentioned earlier in this chapter, improvising in my path as a classical pianist has been strongly suppressed by many years of focus on strictly classical repertoire under the impact of *Werktreue*. During the last few years, my return to a pattern of improvising on piano in parallel with my professional classical music performances has felt as if the withheld expression accumulated throughout the years has found release through the artistic research projects *Armenian Fingerprints* and *Armenian Crossroads*. During my improvisation sessions, I experience the feeling of musical timing transforming

---

3   Mariam Kharatyan, *Armenian Fingerprints* ([n.p.]: Norwegian Artistic Research Programme, 2019), https://www.researchcatalogue.net/view/650083/650084

and becoming unrecognizable to me as if entering an unknown and mystical territory. Unpredictability dominates as I find myself discovering hidden angles of music, its shades fading, illuminating, and flowing. All these elements are also present when improvising with others, which creates a new musical space through Listening, Transforming, Responding, and Musicking together—a territory for exploration and experimentation. Silence becomes a vital part of music; it is sounding and expressive, condensed and, at the same time, airy. Just being there and being part of music is a completely different way of being than that experienced during a classical music performance. In the moment, new expressions and timbres are born from within, from the subconscious, from the performer's true self, intertwining with everything and everyone around.

One of the melodies I had as my musical points of departure during my improvisation sessions was *Oror*, an Armenian folk song, a lullaby from Akna, a historical Armenian region. The melody of *Oror* was written down in Armenian notation by Komitas and published as ethnographic material in 1895 in Ejmiatsin (Vagharshapat, located in today's Republic of Armenia). The second melody I had as my inspiration was a tenth-century resurrection hymn *Havun, Havun* by the Armenian poet, musician, and philosopher Grigor Narekatsi (Gregory of Narek (951–1003). Having the nineteenth-century folk melody *Oror* and the medieval spiritual hymn [*tagh* in the Armenian language] *Havun, Havun* [Bird, Bird] as the initial seed and playing through them, I developed these melodies through improvisation. Inspired by and responding to their motives and intonation patterns, I began to transform their rhythms, intertwining the two songs eventually in free improvisation with the two flautists, vocalist, and live electronics. This felt as if I was at a crossroads of the past, present, and future, where the fundamentally different musical traditions—medieval, folk, classical, and contemporary—meet in interplay, intertwined and transformed, reborn in a new creative breath and force.

As I felt the urge to experiment and integrate the improvisation on my piano performance practice, it was also evident for me that there is much to explore by including students in my artistic research exploration processes. This could be understood as an attempt to provide the students with alternatives to the *Werktreue* ideals which typically characterise their approach to performance. I will, in the following, discuss two improvisation sessions that were held in 2022, in which I played the piano with live electronics and vocals in collaboration with students from the UiA's Department of Popular Music. During one of the sessions, two flute students joined the same ensemble, participating in the session as part of their studies entitled 'In-depth course: Classical music improvisation' at the Department of Classical music and Music Education at the UiA. After the improvisation session, I carried out semi-structured interviews with the two flautists, transcribed the audio recording of the interviews into text, and analysed the data. In the interview, they were asked to elaborate on questions such as how they feel when listening to the recording of their improvised playing, how they feel playing in an improvisation session with no preparation or no scores, and what such experiences of improvisation might contribute to their musicianship. They were also asked to reflect on aspects of their playing, their musical thinking, or their techniques, and on the way they listen when improvising. I invited their reflections on how the improvisation session could transform their playing of classical music. Finally, I asked if they thought that improvisation should be part of all classical students' curricula. The interviews had many interesting moments. The flautist with a Norwegian background observed that playing by ear was considered a positive thing while she was growing up but that she never had an opportunity to try any sort of training in the art of improvisation until enrolling on the 'Classical Music Improvisation' course. In the following quotations, she underlines the fear of making mistakes in playing scored music, which is a very common psychological and behavioural pattern among classical musicians conditioned through *Werktreue*. However, she noticed that, through improvisation, new performative possibilities unfolded and a transformation took place:

> I was scared of improvisation, but after being involved in several projects I feel more relaxed, free, and comfortable, with no mistakes and fear of mistakes as it would be from playing written music. You are you, the true yourself kind of reveals through improvisation. My personal expression comes forward more naturally. When I am back to classical compositions, I feel my performance becomes better also here, freer and I can express myself more. My listening has completely transformed, it is easier now for me to listen to others with who I play, and the way I interact with others also has transformed.
>
> When I listen to myself playing improvised, I feel more relaxed, because when I listen to the written music I play, I always scan for mistakes, right or wrong notes, but when listening to improvised music I play, it feels very free and easier to immerse myself into different vibes of music.

The second flautist, who has a Hungarian background, explained that she had previously improvised with electronics and could relate to my tunes and folk-inspired intonations during the improvisation session because she also gravitates toward folk music from her country of origin when improvising:

> I dare to do more and express much more now. I find more musical details and approach the score more creatively and even improvise over the score, daring to add to the scores. The improvisation changes my perspective. It also feels like me more productive way of working with music, because when I am back from experimenting it gives me more progress in my playing, on the contrary if I would have stayed focused on perfection, repetition, and exact reproduction of the written text. However, I do not dare yet to add improvisation into the written scores during my performances at the concert, I am not yet there, but I feel the urge of experimenting during my practice.
>
> Many classical friends do not like even to talk about improvisation, they are stuck in the system and completely depend on scores, they do not even like to listen to improvised music, because they are thinking it is not real music, not beautiful, and in my opinion, it comes from the fear of the unknown. I think that improvisation should be part of classical studies

because it gives so much. Improvisation is like learning about yourself, like a mirror to look into, which makes you naked in front of yourself and others, which is such a vulnerable, intimate and can be a very hard thing to feel such way during playing, but so important.

After reflecting on data from interviews with the two classical flute students about their experience of improvised music playing, I recognised several positive aspects. They reported changes in their performance practice, including heightened creativity, the broadening of their musical perspectives, and accepting their own vulnerability and fears. Both also noted the transformation of their acts of listening, how improvisation sharpened their presence and communication during music-making sessions with other players.

The 'Transparent Performer' and Resistance through Improvisation

With the establishment of the Conservatory of Mendelsohn in 1843, the notion of the 'transparent performer'[4] spread throughout Europe. This entailed being true to the work, adding nothing of oneself, in complete obeyance to the letter of the written score. Not only did this affect leading musicians and performance venues of the time, but it has continued to shape many decades of teaching and learning of music performance. In his chapter 'The Transparent Performer', Bruce Haynes questions the predominant paradigmatic 'untouchability'[5] of the score—a strict notion of performance aesthetics that continues to be fostered in today's music teaching—by pointing out that it was not always the dominant approach; composers and performers in earlier epochs followed different performance traditions. These open a wide space for modern-day discussions in classical music concerning improvisation and exploration and the way these have been implemented as a naturally anticipated aspect of music performance. For instance, in most baroque compositions, the ornaments were widely left to the musical taste and artistry of the performer. Also, parts of large compositions were modified and performed according to the concert situation, or entirely new parts were added by the performer into the composition. A similar tradition can be seen in the concerto genre during the classical period: with the rise of the soloist, players in this role would add entire cadenzas, which, in many cases, were improvised. Singers of the Baroque and Romantic periods, too, had lots of freedom in adding entirely new details, ornaments, passages, and cadenza-like parts in their roles in different operas. Moreover, opera singers were expected to shape the main roles of operas with great artistic freedom and imagination. It thus follows that composers had to tolerate such creative interpretations of the music they composed and the scores they provided. It is known that famous composer Gioachino Rossini did not recognize his own aria 'Una voce poco fa' as performed by opera singer Adelina Patti. After complimenting

---

4   Bruce, Haynes, The End of Early Music, A Period Performer's History of Music for the Twenty-First Century (Oxford University Press, 2007), p. 93.
5   Ibid.

the singer's impressive rendition, he asked curiously, 'who wrote the piece you just performed?'[6]

Haynes further argues that 'Where seventeenth- and eighteenth-century musicians had a casual view of written music, and no doubt "improved" pieces regularly, a modern performer usually feels a definite constraint about altering anything'.[7] The idea of 'improving' the musical compositions that Haynes introduces here, or, in other words, the very practice of altering freely the written scores as performing musicians undoubtedly did a couple of centuries ago, is equally relevant today in the trajectory of music performance education. It is relevant to the discourse and epistemic perception of musical work and performance practice.

> Some improvisers believe that it is impossible to transcribe improvisations. But then, the best performers of written music give the illusion that they are improvising (since to read mechanically is the kiss of death). Besides, composing is often a matter of repeating a good invention, often enough to be able to remember it and get it down on paper. The act of writing down the notes is actually a mechanical process that consists of documenting an idea that already exists. The creative moment has already taken place when the invention or inspiration occurred to the composer while performing or practicing.[8]

The ability to improvise and add spontaneous details to a written composition is an approach to written music which has been a vital part of the performance traditions and aesthetics of classical music up until the nineteenth century. 'By the twentieth century, improvisation was virtually purged from Classical music and "untouchability" was the rule'.[9]

An important parallel in the context of the 'untouchability' of scores came with technological developments and the huge impact of the recording industry. Performance traditions and approaches to written compositions have been heavily influenced by 'text fetishism' and allowed it to firmly dominate classical musicians' attitudes, consciously or subconsciously. A normality of the last two centuries of classical music, one that all classical musicians continue to face, is the need for multiple, almost-identical recording 'takes' in the classical recording process. Further editing the body of music—collecting those 'takes' and representing them as an interpretation of classical works—is part of this practice. Many performers strive to play different takes during the recording as similarly as possible in order to facilitate their editing and assembly. This practice is especially prevalent during the challenging recording processes of chamber music played by different ensembles and of symphonic music played by large orchestras. In those situations, precision is of the utmost importance: in each take, every note by every musician must be sounded almost mechanically

---

6   Quoted in Clive Brown, cited in Haynes, p. 208.
7   Haynes, p. 207.
8   Ibid., p. 209.
9   Ibid.

and tempos are strictly automated. The score-based playing and performance of the composition must remain uniform.

Haynes suggests an alternative approach:

> A score might also be seen as a gene map of series of potential performances, each differing by individual traits. A gene map is not in itself any single living creature; it is merely an abstraction of what is common between groups of living things. In the same way, a piece of music can be defined as the musical content that is shared in all its performances.[10]

This mindset towards written music, if implemented in a classical music study process, opens enormous possibilities for creativity among students, allowing them to be more vocal regarding their understanding of the piece. Additionally, the students can express a strong connection to their musical ideas through the music they play, instead of maintaining a distanced and detached attitude while reproducing already-existing interpretations and performances of the same composition. This, also, would allow them to escape the mechanical repetitions during practising and provoke an evolution from technical perfection towards musical expressiveness, spontaneity, and a strong sense of presence during playing. It is important, here, to shed light on the imperfection of music notation. Stanley Boorman says, that 'no practical notation has been (or has been devised to be) comprehensive or precise. Each notation, and each source using it, assumes a series of understandings on the part of the reader'.[11] It is notable that different performers, even if they do not alter a single note from the written score, can produce very different renditions of the exact same musical composition. There are clear limitations in the relationship between notation and a piece itself and between the composition and the performer that, from an epistemic point of view of music, need to be addressed. It is also important to mention the allusive aspect of music notation. As Boorman puts it, the notation only alludes to the music's composition, as well as to aspects of performance: 'It specifies little or much and leaves the rest to the performer. Given the performer's experience and training, the allusive aspects of notation will readily stimulate certain responses, and thereby extend the hold of the text over a performance'.[12]

The importance of addressing these limitations of European music notation from an early stage of music education could bridge many knowledge gaps that later occur among classical musicians. Being constrained by the written text via our classical musical education directly affects students' approach and their ability to interpret different compositions freely and place themselves in a broader artistic and creative context—skills that are crucial for becoming emancipated, free-thinking performers with distinct musical and artistic voices. Implementing improvisation as well as improvisational

---

10 Ibid., p. 88.
11 Stanley Boorman, 'The Musical Text', in *Rethinking Music*, ed. by Nicholas Cook and Mark Everist (Oxford University Press, 1999/2001), pp. 403–23 (p. 408).
12 Ibid., p. 411.

thinking and improvisational timing of music in their performance education will nurture an ability to approach the scores as a map to discover the music beyond the written notation.

Improving Scores, Improvising

During the *Armenian Crossroads* artistic research project, I experimented with integrating my own cadenza during a performance of *Lousadzak* [Coming of Light], a concerto for piano and string orchestra, written in 1944 by the American-Armenian composer Alan Hovhaness (1911–2000). This performance took place in March 2023 with the string students at the University of Agder.[13] Having the *Lousadzak* score as a departure point, I not only added my own cadenza but also experimented with responding to the piece through several solo improvisations on piano. Seeking to share my musical ideas and include the string students in artistic research and experimentation, I carried out five improvisation sessions with them, including during the live concert. I have attempted to immerse the students in experimenting with the idea of response-improvisations, creating soundscapes inspired by certain sections of *Lousadzak*, as well as exploring the possibilities of microvariations, effects on the drone notes inspired by the *dam* tradition in Armenian folk music. The students explored the possibilities of expanding the techniques for using their instruments, discovering new sounds, timbres, and expressions in an intense communication that the group-improvisation experience unfolded. We also used musical motives from *Lousadzak* to experiment with the idea of 'improving' the score. Contrary to *Werktreue* and the notion of 'transparent performers' who are supposed to add nothing of themselves to the performance of music compositions, Haynes mentions that performers of the past centuries often modified, added, edited, and significantly transformed the music they performed in such a manner that it was perceived at the time as part of the tradition, as well as an inseparable element of the performance 'language'. It is in Haynes's use of the word 'improving', in reference to the scores, that I find a possible bridge from *Werktreue* to improvisation. From the perspective of epistemic phenomena, if the 'improvement' of scores—through the addition of ornaments, cadenzas, *rubatos*, and articulation not indicated in them—is implemented as a norm in students' everyday musical performance practice, it can act as an antidote to *Werktreue* and help students to develop their ability to improvise. In other words, a freer approach to scores that allows for the incorporation of creative musical elements during playing and into the written scores themselves could take the students closer to improvisation. This would

---

13 For a recording of the piece, see https://soundcloud.com/armenian-crossroads/sets. ALAN HOVHANESS (1911–2000), *LOUSADZAK/COMING OF LIGHT* Concerto for Piano and Strings, op. 48 (1944), Mariam Kharatyan, piano; Tanja Orning, cello; Helge Kjekshus, conductor The String Ensemble at the University of Agder; The String Students from the Talent Development Programme at the UiA; Recorded live at Sigurd Køhns Hus; University of Agder, Kristiansand, Norway, 31 March 2023.

improve their ability to freely communicate in their performance practice with or without scores, strengthen their connections to the music as performed, and help them to master complex technical, musical, and aspects related to the development of their instruments/voice.

José A. Bowen suggests that each performance of a piece of music is bridging the past and the future.[14] The performer becomes part of shaping the tradition of the interpretation of the work in each performance. Further, the shaping allows the possibility of innovation, as resonances of the present are often subconsciously manifested in the 'accent' of the musical 'language'. The performance practice inherent in the performer's time thus transfers to following generations, especially keeping in mind the role technology plays in music creation and transmission. Fostering this idea in today's music performance practice and teaching of music could nurture the ability of students to own their education and to consciously embrace the idea that they are part of a historical trajectory. The essential game-changers in music performance practice would be accessible and their performances could reach far beyond repetitions of what was before them, while unfolding their own potential through a reconfiguring and a reinventing of the past and present, and a reimagining of the musical reality of today and tomorrow. Bowen says:

> While each performance attempts to mediate between tradition and innovation, it in turn becomes part of the remembered tradition. It is easy for an interpretive or accidental quality to become an essential quality of the work for later generations, especially since the advent of recording technology. That is what happens when the novice imitates [any] sample ornamentation exactly. The boundary between interpretive and essential qualities can and does change, and the new boundary is then enforced by tradition. Tradition is, therefore, the history of remembered innovation, and it defines a set of normative assumptions or essential qualities about the work which can change over time. Each performance, therefore, looks both backwards and forwards in time. In other words, each performance is simultaneously both example and definition of the musical work.[15]

While seeking to expand my perspectives on the interpretation of *Lousadzak*, it occurred to me that the process itself is filled with distinct ambiguity. Yet, it offers potential for discovering myself as pianist from angles unknown to me, both through solo and group/ensemble improvisations. By actively using the approach of 'improving' the scores and creating my own response-improvisations, I have transformed my piano performance practice. This result, in turn, motivated me to explore further how tradition and innovation can be combined in performance practice.

---

14 José A. Bowen, 'Finding the Music in Musicology: Performance History and Musical Works', in *Rethinking Music*, ed. by Nicholas Cook and Mark Everist (Oxford: Oxford University Press, 1999/2001), pp. 424–51.

15 Bowen, p. 427.

Reconfiguring, Reflecting

Reconfiguring the traditions of classical music performance through innovation involves the potential of interweaving these two aspects. The process is a constant stimulus for reflection and, importantly, fuels my musical creativity. When reflecting on the *Lousadzak* concerto and the two different approaches of interpretation that I have created—one with my own cadenza and one with the cadenza written by the composer—I felt as if I was at a crossroads, negotiating between the pianistic performance traditions and innovation. The integration of an entire section of music into the written composition raised many questions for me about the relationship between composer and performer, not least in what ways does improvising within the composition affect the overall interpretation of the work? This activates notions of co-composing and co-creativity through improvisation within scored music, and it plays an important part in the reconfiguration of tradition. Such a reconfiguration may enable a teacher to address the limitations of learning an instrument merely through European staff notation from an early stage of music education and, by acknowledging these issues, could bridge many gaps. For example, it could help to address the inability to improvise in classical music performance practice that later occurs among classical musicians. Integrating improvisation in my performance of classical music has been crucial and transformative; improvisation has functioned as a tool and method for emancipation from *Werktreue* constraints. I have felt the importance of sharing these insights with students through improvisation sessions and various other techniques in the hope of creating a safe space for them to develop and find their way to becoming emancipated, free-thinking performers with distinct musical and artistic voices.

The students observed in themselves several important responses to playing in the improvisation sessions: (i) it stimulated their musical creativity; (ii) it broadened their horizons of musical thinking; (iii) it made them aware of listening, responding, and communicating through music; (iv) it gave them access to their own vulnerability; (v) it gave them new insight into sound, its colour and timbre, and into the technical and musical possibilities of their instruments; and, lastly, (vi) it increased their focus and ability to be present in the moment of performance.

Score-based learning and improvisation are two parallel perspectives that are both crucial to classical music performance practice. It is of the utmost importance for instructors to guide students to an understanding of the complexity of these two approaches to performance, their correlation, and their impact on forming the identity of a musician. This entails a rethinking of (and, indeed, reacting to) the teaching and learning of classical music performance and the importance of critical thinking and student autonomy. As a concluding note, this chapter suggests that the implementation of improvisation and improvisational thinking in music students' performance education nurtures their ability to think of scores as maps—mere tools for discovering the music beyond them. The approach of 'improving' the scores/notes of compositions opens enormous possibilities within music interpretation and music performance practice for students. In addition, this practice can shape their artistic creativity in beneficial ways, both as future performing artists and educators as well as in the many complex socio-cultural roles these musicians may occupy in our society.

It is pertinent to mention that the University of Agder already has integrated improvisation into the curricula of classical students from 2021. This implementation includes consistent and long-term projects that immerse students into the processes of improvisation and different aspects related to it, giving them a possibility for deeper understanding and knowledge within this field. The official name for the newly implemented curriculum is 'In-depth field: Classical music improvisation', and its description on the webpage of the Department of Classical Music and Music Education explains what instigated the need for the implementation of improvisation in students' studies:

> As notation became more detailed and elaborate in the 19th century, a greater distinction arose between composer and performer, and these roles became better defined. Respect for the score, the Urtext, and the composer's intention (Werktreue), have led the performance tradition down a narrower track, where the performer's creativity has been subordinated and even stifled under the idea of the Work-concept.[16]

Classical music improvisation at the UiA aims to cultivate musical individuality and freedom, as well as to develop creativity among students and an interest in playing their own music. Students are encouraged to explore different types of improvisation in classical music through the use of historical examples as departure points, improvisation within existing compositions and structures, as well as contemporary music improvisation and various forms of free improvisation. The learning and explorations within improvisation are carried out through one-to-one music sessions and through solo and ensemble playing. Listening is emphasised as the fundamental basis of music improvisation practice. The practitioners in this field seek to

> provide students with knowledge and skills via a variety of methods, techniques and strategies for practising and performing improvisation, and the confidence to improvise independently on their main instrument, developing their expressive vocabulary.[17]

In an interview held in November 2022, professor Jørn Eivind Schau, the Head of the Music Performance Programmes at UiA, reflected on the role of improvisation in the curriculum development in the Department for Classical Music and Music Education. He noted, in particular, how the programme may respond to today's challenges and opportunities:

> Today's job market for musicians is complex, largely international, and rapidly developing. A learning outcome in our courses is that the students will develop their personal expression and artistic profile as musicians. Our department continuously seeks to strengthen its prerequisites to develop and improve a diverse way of sustaining performance education in classical music. Here, during recent years – classical music

---

16 The University of Agder, In-depth field Classical music improvisation, https://www.uia.no/en/studies2/classical-music-performance/in-depth-fields/in-depth-field-classical-music-improvisation
17 Ibid.

improvisation within early music and contemporary music has become important. The work on improvisation is implemented as an instrumental main area on bachelor's, as a performance in-depth field on master's, and in regular projects for students across instruments, programmes, and genres and in chamber music and different ensembles.[18]

Even though improvisation has only been integrated in the curricula of classical performance music at the UiA for only a couple of years, the positive impact of such an approach is already manifesting. The students feel more and more comfortable with each new project related to improvisation and are unfolding their musical potential more fully. Meanwhile, we need to accept that such a significant change is not easy to implement in larger HMEIs and their established curricula.

To summarize the findings from semi-structured interviews with the two flute students that joined the improvisation session performing with me and the electronic music students at the UiA (as part of my ongoing artistic research processes), it is pertinent to highlight that the students recognised such important moments as (i) the improvisation stimulated them towards a more daring and creative approach in their musical practice; (ii) it provided broader horizons of artistic and musical thinking; (iii) it promoted active listening and interaction with other players; (iv) it demanded that the performers accept their vulnerability and fears; (v) it provided new musical insights; (vi) it increased their focus and sense of presence. It is important to allow the students from a very early stage of musical education to deviate from the established pedagogical routine. The educational process anchored in score-based learning is crucial, but so is helping students dare to play music by ear as well, thus giving space to more creative and artistic thinking from an early age. The process of improvisation and experimentation is perhaps the most important aspect, avoiding the one-sided, narrow, conservative approach to music. Regardless of which direction students prefer to take in further performance practice, the improvisation sessions create space that broadens their perspectives and horizons of understanding in music, as well as offering a deeper perception of all aspects that are connected to performance practice and music interpretation.

References

Berkowitz, L. Aaron, *The Improvising Mind, Cognition and Creativity in the Musical Moment* (Oxford University Press, 2010), https://doi.org/10.1093/acprof:oso/9780199590957.001.0001

Boorman, Stanley, 'The Musical Text', in *Rethinking Music*, ed. by Nicholas Cook, Mark Everist (Oxford University Press, 1999/2001), pp. 403–23, https://doi.org/10.1093/oso/9780198790037.003.0019

Bowen, José A., 'Finding the Music in Musicology: Performance History and Musical Works', in *Rethinking Music*, ed. by Nicholas Cook, Mark Everist (Oxford University Press, 1999/2001), pp. 424–51, https://doi.org/10.1093/oso/9780198790037.003.0020

Correia, Jorge, Gilvano Dalagna, Clarissa Foletto, Ioulia Papageorgi, Natassa Economidou Stavrou, Nicolas Constantinou, Heidi Westerlund, Mieko Kanno, Guadalupe López-Íñiguez, Stefan Östersö, Carl Holmgren, Randi Eidsaa, Tanja Orning, REACT–Rethinking Music

---

18   Jørn Schau, personal communication, November 2022.

Performance in European Higher Education Institutions, *Artistic Career in Music: Stakeholders Requirement Report* (Aveiro: UA Editora, 2021), https://doi.org/10.48528/wfq9-4560

Crispin, Darla and Bob Gilmore (eds), *Artistic Experimentation in Music, An Anthology* (Leuven University Press, 2014), https://doi.org/10.2307/j.ctt14jxsmx

Clarke, Eric, F. and Mark Doffman (eds), *Distributed Creativity: Collaboration and Improvisation in Contemporary Music* (New York: Oxford University Press, 2017), https://doi.org/10.1093/oso/9780199355914.001.0001

Gyodakyan, Georgi, *Ejer Hay Yerjshtutyan Patmutyunic* [Pages from the History of Armenian Music] (Yerevan: HH GAA 'Gitutyun' Hratarakchutyun, 2009)

Cook, Nicholas, *Music as Creative Practice* (Oxford University Press, 2018), https://doi.org/10.1093/oso/9780199347803.001.0001

Goehr, Lydia, *The Imaginary Museum of Musical works, An Essay in the Philosophy of Music* (Oxford, Clarendon Press, 1992/2002)

——, *Being True to the Work, The Journal of Aesthetics and Art Criticism*, 47.1 (Winter, 1989), pp. 55–67, https://doi.org/10.2307/431993

Haynes, Bruce, *The End of Early Music, A Period Performer's History of Music for the Twenty-First Century* (Oxford University Press, 2007), https://doi.org/10.1093/acprof:oso/9780195189872.001.0001

Kharatyan, Mariam, *Armenian Fingerprints* (Norwegian Artistic Research Programme, 2019), https://www.researchcatalogue.net/view/650083/650084

——, 'Aspects of Interpretation with Multicultural Performers', in *Music E-ducation in XXI-st century: New challenges and perspectives*, ed. by Mikolaj Rykowski (Wydawnictwo Miejskie Posnania: Akademia Muzyczna im. I. J. Paderewskiego w Poznaniu, 2021), pp. 209–20

Huber, Annegret, Doris Ingrisch, Therese Kaufmann, Johannes Kretz, Gesine Schröder, and Tasos Zembylas (eds), *Knowing in Performing, Artistic Research in Music and the Performing Arts* (Bielefeld: Transkript Verlag, 2021)

Rink, John, Helene Gaunt, and Aaron Williamon (eds), *Musicians in the Making, Pathways to Creative Performance* (New York: Oxford University Press, 2017), https://doi.org/10.1093/acprof:oso/9780199346677.001.0001

Östersjö, Stefan, 'Thinking-Through-Music, On Knowledge production, Materiality, Embodiment, and Subjectivity in Artistic Research', in *Artistic research in Music: Discipline and Resistance*, ed. by Jonathan Impett (Leuven: Leuven University Press, 2017), pp. 88–107, https://doi.org/10.2307/j.ctt21c4s2g.6

——, *SHUT UP 'N' PLAY! Negotiating the Musical Work* (Lund: Malmö Academies of Performing Arts, Lund University, 2008)

Pahlevanyan, Alina, 'Komitas and the Problems of Armenian Music Folkloristics', in *Komitas Museum-Institute Yearbook, Volume V*, ed. by Tatevik Shakhkulyan (Yerevan, Berlin, Halle: Publication Komitas Museum-Institute, 2020), pp. 252–61, https://arar.sci.am/dlibra/publication/295147/edition/270882/content

Small, Christopher, *Musicking: The Meanings of Performing and Listening* (Middletown, CT: Wesleyan University Press, 1998/2012)

University of Agder, 'In-depth: field Classical music improvisation', course description, website, https://www.uia.no/en/studies2/classical-music-performance/in-depth-fields/in-depth-field-classical-music-improvisation

8. Intercultural Musicking: Reflection in, on, and for Situated Klezmer Ensemble Performance

Richard Fay, Daniel J. Mawson, and Nahielly Palacios

Introduction

This chapter focuses on the reflective performer practices embedded in the Klezmer Ensemble Performance (KEP) module at The University of Manchester, UK. To set these reflective performer practices in context, we first outline how, as non-Jewish music educators,[1] we understand—and seek to develop our students' understandings of—the cultural, historical, and other complexities of the music culture (or set of cultures) now referred to as *klezmer*. The module is situated by these understandings through which we seek to encourage a respectful and informed cultural appreciation of klezmer whilst remaining attentive to the risks of cultural appropriation.[2] The chapter then introduces the university context for our klezmer teaching with a focus on the performance opportunities available during 2020–21 academic year (when the COVID-19 pandemic-related social-distancing measures were in place). We then introduce the reflective performer frame we promote with our klezmer ensemblists and examine their performance of reflection through the texts they generated to accompany their actual assessed performance, i.e., the texts through which they situate their informed performance intentions. Finally, we conclude with our emerging thinking regarding the value of reflective performer practices in HME.

---

1. 'We', here and throughout the chapter, refers primarily to the first and second authors who teach the KEP module. The third author is an Education colleague whose reflective-practice expertise has guided the reflective performer frame discussed in this chapter.
2. Richard Fay and Daniel J. Mawson, 'Appropriate, No Appropriative, Methodology: (Online) Klezmer Ensemble Performance as Intercultural Musicking', ISSME2021 Conference, online 21–24 June 2021, https://youtu.be/KXliY-3Rnsg

Our Understanding of Klezmer

The term *klezmer* comes from the Hebrew כְּלֵי זֶמֶר (*k'léi zémer*) meaning 'vessel of song', and it originally referred to a musician rather than to a particular music culture. In the (translated) words of the Yiddish proverb, 'a wedding without a klezmer is worse than a funeral without tears'.[3] These musicians—or *klezmorim* (the plural form of *klezmer*)—were essential for the wedding celebrations of the largely Yiddish-speaking Ashkenazi Jewish communities in the Pale of Settlement of the Russian Empire, and in Eastern Europe more generally. The fortunes of this Jewish music culture, which dates back to the Middle Ages, has waxed and waned. It is a music culture that has been shaped variously by the interplay between religious practices and social life in these communities; the persecution, pogrom, and genocide experienced by those communities; an extensive migratory history and the establishment of new diaspora communities (in the USA for example); the experience of musical-cultural assimilative influences (for example, the influence in the early-middle part of the twentieth century of swing on klezmer in the USA and tango in Argentina); the decline of klezmer's popularity as the twentieth century progressed; and the USA-driven klezmer revival of the 1970s/80s.[4] That revival has generated substantial interest in, and a growing literature about, klezmer.[5] Today, klezmer can be seen, amongst other things, as a thriving, globally-distributed world music genre. Not without controversy,[6] it is now performed more widely and with changed/ing functions.

Klezmer is now, as it was previously, a dynamic and developing musical practice. For us, in Manchester in 2024, it is one being shaped most immediately by the

---

3   Yale Strom, *The Book of Klezmer: The History, The Music, The Folklore* (Chicago: Chicago Review Press, 2011), p. xiv.
4   Tamara Livingston, 'Music Revivals: Towards a General Theory', *Ethnomusicology*, 43 (1999), 66–85, https://doi.org/10.2307/852694; Tamara Livingston, 'An Expanded Theory for Revivals as Cosmopolitan Participatory Music Making', in *The Oxford Handbook of Music Revival*, ed. by Caroline Bithell and Juniper Hill (Oxford: Oxford University Press, 2014), pp. 60–69, https://doi.org/10.1093/oxfordhb/9780199765034.013.018; Hankus Netsky, 'Klez Goes to College', in *Performing Ethnomusicology: Teaching and Representation in the World Music Ensembles*, ed. by Ted Solis (Oakland: University of California Press, 2004), pp. 189–201, https://doi.org/10.1525/california/9780520238749.003.0011 .
5   See, for example, Walter Zev Feldman, *Klezmer: Music, History and Memory* (Oxford: Oxford University Press, 2016), https://doi.org/10.1093/acprof:oso/9780190244514.001.0001; Hankus Netsky, *Klezmer: Music and Community in Twentieth Century Philadelphia* (Philadelphia, PA.: Temple University Press, 2015); Seth Rogovoy, *The Essential Klezmer: A Music Lover's Guide to Jewish Roots and Soul Music - From the Old World to the Jazz Age to the Downtown Avant-garde* (Chapel Hill, NC.: Algonquin Books, 2000); Henry Sapoznik, *Klezmer Music 1910–1942* (1981), https://folkways.si.edu/klezmer-music-1910-1942-recordings-from-the-yivo-archives/judaica/music/album/smithsonian; Henry Sapoznik, *Klezmer! Jewish Music from Old World to Our World* (New York: Schirmer Trade Books, 1999); Mark Slobin, *Fiddler on the Move: Exploring the Klezmer World* (Oxford: Oxford University Press, 2000); Mark Slobin, *American Klezmer: Its Roots and Offshoots* (Oakland: University of California, 2002), https://doi.org/10.1525/california/9780520227170.001.0001; Strom.
6   See, for example, Magdalena Waligórska, *Klezmer's Afterlife: An Ethnography of the Jewish Music Revival in Poland and Germany* (Oxford: Oxford University Press, 2013), https://doi.org/10.1093/acprof:oso/9780199995790.001.0001

students' diverse characteristics and those of their audiences, but shaped, too, by the students' responses to the archive and contemporary resources available to them. These local particularities are important for the KEP module—thus, it is situated in Manchester (rather than London, or New York, or Kraków, for example); it is in proximity with, but not embedded in, Manchester's Jewish communities; and it is surrounded by a cultural milieu in which Yiddish and klezmer cultural practices feature very little, now or previously. There are only tantalising references to the klezmer-oriented repertoire of the Jewish wedding bands in Manchester in the early twentieth century.[7] Despite Manchester's substantial Jewish communities, klezmer here rarely fulfilled the earlier wedding and celebratory function of music. The revival of the 1970s/80s began in the USA but also generated interest elsewhere. Thus, in Manchester, there were klezmer pub sessions from the early 1990s. But, by the time the university klezmer ensemble was established in 2011, these revivalist pub sessions had largely ceased. Interest had waned, and when we first approached the Manchester Jewish Museum in 2012 with a proposal for a klezmer-based Chanukah concert, the response was cautious: the CEO commented, 'we've tried klezmer before but there doesn't seem to be much of a market for it'. Since then, a market has been relocated, or generated, and klezmer performances and teaching now have a stable footing in the university and beyond.

Given the almost invisible imprint of klezmer in Manchester's immigrant Jewish communities of the early twentieth century, we can say that klezmer has gained popularity locally through the revival surge, rather than being revived through that surge. It is now being performed largely because the students (and a small local community of musicians) are there to play it. As they do so, they create new spaces and new audiences beyond both the academic and local Jewish contexts. Through these spaces, they experience the developing functions of klezmer in twenty-first-century Manchester: for entertainment, traditional dancing, celebrating cultural heritage, and as a vehicle for audiences to connect with their own memories or cultural identity.

Our Klezmer Education Context

The KEP module

The small (10-credit) KEP module was introduced in 2011 as an elective course within the 360-credit undergraduate curriculum in the music department at The University of Manchester. It recruits music students in their second or third (and final) year of study

---

[7] For example, in Oral History Transcript J3 held by the Manchester Jewish Museum, Harold Abrams remembers playing trumpet and cello in the Manchester Jewish Brass Band, which was active until the start of WW1: 'I played for all the yiddisher weddings in Manchester, me. We used to call it a quadrille band in those days. No jazz. I used to love it and play for all the weddings.'

on a programme which has 'Western' music theory and practice at its core as built on the three mutually-supporting areas of musicology, performance, and composition. The programme has, however, become more diverse in recent years. Thus, whereas the KEP module was initially an outlier along with Gamelan in focusing on non-canonical Western music cultures, it now forms part of a cluster of such performance modules with a focus on musics other than 'Western Classical'.

These academic aspects are also important for anchoring the module: it is based in a university (rather than a conservatoire); it forms part of an undergraduate music programme (rather than contributing to a more interdisciplinary programme); it is assessed with a focus on ensemble performance of klezmer rather than on individual competence or virtuosity in klezmer (although the latter forms part of the requirements of the former); it is designed for students who are highly-competent both musically and academically; and the majority of the students it attracts have no Jewish affiliation or heritage. Acknowledging these anchors, a distinctive methodology has developed for the module over the last decade.[8]

Cultural Translation and Intercultural Musicking

Waligórska considers klezmer performance to be in its *afterlife* in Germany and Poland especially. Following her lead, we conceptualise the ensemble's performances not as 'an impoverishment of the culture of origin', but more as informed, respectful, skilful cultural translation enabling 'new modes of encountering the other and expressing the self'.[9] Here, the focus is less on '*who* is making use of the culture text' [i.e., klezmer] and more on '*how* they are doing it'. Thus, we encourage our mostly non-Jewish music students to develop historically-, culturally-, and functionally-informed understandings of klezmer's complexities, but also to situate their performances of it within an appreciation of how the klezmer as a music culture is evolving in our local context and how it might develop in their own portfolio of practices.

Whilst the ensemble is located and performs in an academically-oriented music department, the students also perform the music for Chanukah concerts in the Manchester Jewish Museum, for well-being and reminiscence sessions in the local Jewish residential homes, for gatherings of the Association of Jewish Refugees (Holocaust survivors and their families), and for Muslim-Jewish Forum events. We see these klezmer performance opportunities and experiences as sites of 'intercultural musicking'.[10] This is an extension of Christopher Small's term 'musicking', which captures the idea that 'music is not a thing [...] but an

---

8 Richard Fay, Daniel J. Mawson, and Caroline Bithell, 'Intercultural Musicking: Learning through Klezmer', *Languages & Intercultural Communication*, 22 (2022), 204–220, https://doi.org/10.1080/14708 477.2022.2029467
9 Waligórska, p. 8.
10 Fay, Mawson, and Bithell.

activity, something that people do' as they 'take part, in any capacity, in a musical performance, whether by performing, by listening, by rehearsing or practicing [sic], by providing material for performance (what is called composing), or by dancing'.[11] Through the term 'intercultural musicking', we bring Small's process-oriented approach to music together with understandings—such as Adrian Holliday's—of the intercultural as process-oriented and emergent rather than static.[12] Following Marshall H. Singer, we see our ensemblists not as being fixed in their cultural and music culture identities, but rather being culturally (and musically) complex and unique.[13] Small's understanding, and our extension of it, are underpinned by a 'verbing' move evident in other coinages such as language → languaging, that is, the way in which people use language to make sense of their world and, indeed, help to shape it.[14] While not following the name noun+ing format, this process-oriented perspective is also evident in Holliday's proposal that the word 'culture' be attached not to regional or national reference points but, rather, small social groupings or activities wherever there is cohesive behaviour.[15] With this in mind, we like to think of the emergent culture of our klezmer ensemble and not simply focus on the origins of klezmer.

The klezmer module also provides opportunities for 'performing ethnomusicology'.[16] For almost all the KEP students concerned, the module represents an encounter with musical Otherness, an encounter which seeks not only to develop their awareness of other musics but also to enrich their intercultural awareness through music. It is an encounter mediated by us, their tutors. We, too, first experienced klezmer as a musical Other. Thus, the KEP module represents, for both students and tutors, a space for developing what Mantle Hood termed 'bi-musicality', analogous perhaps with being bi-lingual.[17] Bi-musicality has been critiqued for its somewhat static view of the music cultures in question, that is, this music plus that music.[18] The complexity of, and diversity within, music cultures might be better understood to be polymusical.[19] As such, musicians need what

---

11 Christopher Small, *Musicking: The Meanings of Performing and Listening* (Middletown, CT.: Wesleyan University Press, 1998), pp. 2–9.
12 Adrian Holliday, 'Small Cultures', *Applied Linguistics*, 20 (1999), 237–64, https://doi.org/10.1093/applin/20.2.237
13 Marshall H. Singer, *Perception and Identity in Intercultural Communication* (Yarmouth, ME.: Intercultural Press, 1998).
14 Alison Phipps and Mike Gonzalez, *Modern Languages: Learning and Teaching in an Intercultural Field* (London: Sage, 2004), p. 167, https://doi.org/10.4135/9781446221419
15 Holliday.
16 Solis.
17 Mantle Hood, 'The Challenge of Bi-Musicality', *Ethnomusicology*, 4 (1960), 55–59, https://doi.org/10.2307/924263
18 See, for example, Bruno Deschênes, 'Bi-Musicality or Transmusicality: Viewpoint of a Non-Japanese Shakuhachi Player', *International Review of the Aesthetics and Sociology of Music*, 49 (2018), 275–94. https://www.jstor.org/stable/26844647
19 Bruno Nettle, *The Study of Ethnomusicology: Thirty-one Issues and Concepts* (Champaign, IL.: University of Illinois Press, 1983/2005), p. 58.

John S. Bailey terms 'intermusability', which Henry Stobart notes, 'suggests the possibilities of overlaps and continuities in skills, competences, and other forms of musical experience'.[20] We understand the KEP module to be less a meeting place for two static music cultures, and more a space for developing transmusicality, by which we mean students' musically-complex and musically-unique engagement with the musical resources in their musically-complex environment.

Situated Performance

The KEP module is framed by a focus on situated performance, that is, performer attentiveness to the particularities of each klezmer ensemble performance. Thus, we encourage the ensemblists to think about the ways in which each performance is situated:

- in *time* (e.g. a lunch-time vs. an evening concert),
- in *space* (e.g. in the Manchester Jewish Museum vs. in the department concert hall),
- in *purpose* (e.g. for Chanukah party vs. departmental concert),
- in *relationship* (e.g. for city dignitaries vs. klezmer aficionados),
- in *function* (e.g. for reminiscence sessions in care home vs. entertainment),
- in *logistical possibilities/constraints* etc (e.g. for a quintet rather than the full ensemble), and
- in *music cultures* (e.g. for an Old World wedding vs. klezmer swing in the New World).

Using these and similar parameters, each year we invite the ensemblists to consider what aspects of the environment in which the performance is taking place may be shaping how the performance develops. We do so through prompts of different types, such as:

- **chrono-topical:** Given the rich history and development of klezmer as a music culture, what are the implications and possibilities for, and responsibilities when, performing klezmer in Manchester in the twenty-first century?

---

20   John S. Bailey, 'Ethnomusicology, Intermusability, and Performance Practice', in *The New (Ethno) Musicologies*, ed. by Henry Stobart (Lanham, MD.: Scarecrow Press, 2008), pp. 117–134 (p. 58); Henry Stobart, 'Unfamiliar Sounds: Approaches to Intercultural Interaction in the World's Musics', in *Music and Familiarity: Listening, Musicology and Performance*, ed. by Elaine King and Helen M. Prior (London: Routledge, 2016), pp. 111–36 (p. 128).

- **socio-political:** Given the politics swirling around klezmer as a music culture, what are the implications for, and responsibilities of, the ensemble performing klezmer for/in particular performance contexts?
- **contextual-performative:** Given the contrasting characteristics of the performance opportunities available, what are the implications for, and affordances of, performing klezmer for each of these performance contexts?

Each cohort of ensemblists is divided in to small groups with each group taking responsibility for leading the ensemble's arrangement of a piece for the ensemble's assessed performance. Explicit in the instructions for this activity are the contextual and functional parameters. For assessment purposes, we ask them to imagine (and articulate) what situation their arrangement is intended for and what function the performance would have.

The 2020–21 Cohort and its Performance Opportunities

The 2020–21 academic year was much impacted by the global Covid-19 pandemic. In previous and subsequent years, student performance opportunities arose through onsite concerts in diverse venues, including the annual Chanukah party in the old synagogue which forms the centre-piece of the Manchester Jewish Museum, and the assessed performance in the concert hall in the music department. However, because of the social-distancing measures in place in 2020–21, all performance opportunities were based on the practice of online presentation of filmed performances that had been curated in advance. These were as listed in Table 8.1.

1	an online Chanukah party for the Muslim-Jewish Forum (MJF) in November 2020[21]
2	a spot in the online KlezmerKabaret at KlezNorth (KN) in March 2021[22]
3	online contributions to an Intercultural Musicking symposium hosted by The University of Manchester in April 2021

Table 8.1. Performance opportunities for the 2020–21 cohort of the KEP module.

21　Michael Kahan Kapelye, 'Odessa Bulgar - Michael Kahan Kapelye - Muslim Jewish Forum Performance', YouTube, uploaded by Callum Batten-Plowright Music, 6 December 2020, https://www.youtube.com/watch?v=KaeS6rbYC_c&list=PL1D469599FFE5C9DE&index=20

22　Michael Kahan Kapelye, 'The Michael Kahan Kapelye ensemble plays "Odessa Bulgar"', YouTube, uploaded by Music Department, University of Manchester, 17 March 2021, https://www.youtube.com/watch?v=J2531LXz7PQ&list=PL1D469599FFE5C9DE&index=24

Performance 1: The Muslim-Jewish Forum

The first 'curated video' performance was developed for an online Chanukah party as organised by the Muslim-Jewish Forum (MJF) of Greater Manchester in late November 2020. This was quite a serious, formal occasion, and two Lord Mayors, a local MP, and local councillors were amongst the 35 present. Many of the attendees were either Jewish or Muslim; few, if any, were musicians in a professional sense; and few, if any, had a detailed understanding of klezmer as a music culture. This event occurred quite early in the module when the ensemblists' knowledge and experience of klezmer were still at an initial stage. They did not attend the Zoom-based party itself so did not experience their curated video performance being viewed by the attendees. Their task—as shaped by the organisers—was to provide an enjoyable, upbeat musical ending to the proceedings. To meet this remit, the group chose the lively 'Odessa Bulgar' from the material they had already begun to play together. For this video performance, the ensemblists had to individually record their part in the piece and film themselves playing this part. Other tasks divided across the team included arranging the piece (a process scaffolded by us), organisational matters (such as arranging rehearsals, resource distribution, etc), audio editing, video editing, and speaking roles. The hope was that each ensemblist took on some responsibility (usually linked to an existing skill-set and/or preference) and that no-one was overburdened—as we reiterate every year, 'the first rule of klezmer ensemble is that we look after each other'.

Performance 2: KlezNorth Kabaret

The second performance took place in March 2021 towards the end of the module, that is, when the ensemblists' knowledge and experience of klezmer had substantially increased and assessment loomed. This was for an online Kabaret night as part of the KlezNorth (KN) weekend immersion in the worlds of klezmer (with talks, workshops, concerts, etc.). Here, the audience were all klezmer aficionados, albeit with differing levels of experience and expertise and different passions (some were dancers, others musicians, other Yiddish learners, and others cultural ambassadors).

In preparation for Performance 2, a revised performance of 'Odessa Bulgar', the ensemblists collectively and individually reflected on the experience of Performance 1 (that is, the MJF video performance) and considered what might reasonably be changed given the new audience as well as their increased experience of, and developing competence in, klezmer performance. They individually took responsibility to make changes (to their own musical performance, video appearance, etc). As with Performance 1, other tasks, including audio and video editing, team communications/organisation, liaising with the KN team, and public speaking, were equitably divided across the ensemble. The revised version was shown to the Kabaret zoom audience of 60+ people. The ensemblists all attended, and the compère invited them to share their klezmer trajectories and learning with the audience.

Assessment and Reflection

For the assessment of their KEP learning, the students had to develop a portfolio of work that, in addition to the curated video performances, also included a written element: their Reflective Notes. Here, they reflected on the tasks of: a) developing a performance situated for the MJF event; then b) revising that performance for the situated KN Kabaret; and then c) looking ahead to the future klezmer performances—most immediately, their assessed performances in April 2021. These texts have a dual status. In and through them, the ensemblists verbalised their performance-related reflections and their thoughts looking ahead to future performances. Thus, the texts function as the verbal manifestation of the reflective performer stance that the module seeks to inculcate. But the texts also have an assessment purpose and can, therefore, also be understood as the performance of reflection. In our experience, reflective processes are reasonably common in the university but are not especially foregrounded. Our ensemblists were, thus, aware of reflection as an activity type but not necessarily well-supported for, or experienced in, articulating such reflections (this remains an aspect of our teaching which we seek to strengthen). Our concern here is less with the form of the reflections than with their content and with what we can learn from these performances of reflection vis-à-vis students' developing KEP confidence, competence, and purposefulness.

Reflection on Situatedness

We now return to the earlier discussion of situated performance as we illustrate these reflective assessment texts. From this 2020–21 cohort, we have a data-set comprising the reflective texts (each being up to 1,000 words) produced by the eleven klezmer students for their assessment portfolio. The students followed our instructions that these texts should not conform to the more usual academic conventions (for example, by including literature citations); the texts are, therefore, somewhat idiosyncratic. Below, we focus on the sections of the students' reflective texts where they drew attention to a number of situating aspects of their performances:

The Historical
When creating our arrangement for the Muslim-Jewish Forum's event we had to consider the historical background of the tune, and how we would retain elements of this in our arrangement while making the performance individual to our ensemble. (Student H)

The Functional
The function of our video for KlezNorth being for the Kabaret evening helped us decide that each one of us needed to adapt an element of their audio or video to appear more animated. (Student F)

The Technical
The online curated nature of our performance impacted the ecology of both productions: Recording via multitrack allowed us as performers to take as many takes as we want before submitting, which is not really in line with the distinct live nature of Klezmer music. Necessities such as performing to a metronome also limited the ensemble's performance, as live there would have been natural tempo fluctuation. (Student M3)

The Particular (Performance 1)
We intended to present a more formal version of this tune for the Muslim Jewish Forum due to the nature of the event having an organising committee and links with the political scene in Manchester. (Student F)

The Contrastive (Moving from Performance 1 to Performance 2)
The kabaret we participated in had a very casual, all-inclusive feel. It certainly wasn't a formal performance space, like the Muslim-Jewish Forum which was more of an academic environment. The main purpose of the kabaret was for everyone to have fun and to strive to create a sense of community over zoom, like the environment that would've been experienced in-person. Our video therefore had to reflect this. (Student B)

The Reflective Frame for the KEP Module

Starting Points

Our thinking is primarily informed by two writers: Donald A. Schön, who, as a musician himself, was able to illustrate his reflective processes with reference to musicians;[23] and Thomas S. C. Farrell, a second-language teacher educator with whose work we are familiar through our roles as educators as well as musicians.[24] With Farrell, we share

---

23 Donald A. Schön, *The Reflective Practitioner: How Professionals Think in Action* (London: Routledge, 1983); Donald A. Schön, *Educating the Reflective Practitioner* (San Francisco: Jossey-Bass, 1987).
24 Thomas S. C. Farrell, *Reflective Practice in Action* (Thousand Oaks, CA: Corwin Press, 2004); Thomas S. C. Farrell, *Reflective Language Teaching: From Research to Practice* (London: Bloomsbury Academic, 2015).

an interest in the role of the reflective process in professional development.[25] For us, the professionals concerned are musicians-in-training or, more accurately, performers-in-the-making. Whilst the reflective processes we explore may have value for other ensemble performance development, we are concerned most directly with students' reflective practices in their development as klezmer ensemblists. Our aspiration is that the way in which reflection is embedded in their KEP module will support them as they make sense of their developing experience of KEP itself, and their competence and confidence in it.

Knowing–in–action

Schön argued that professionals' knowledge is implicit in their action, and that this 'knowing-in-action' is the distinctive mode of 'ordinary practical knowledge'.[26] He illustrates this musically:

> When good jazz musicians improvise together, they also manifest a 'feel for' their material and they make on-the-spot adjustments to the sounds they hear [...]. As [they] feel the direction of the music that is developing out of their interwoven contributions, they make new sense of it and adjust their performance to the new sense they have made.[27]

In this case, the musicians are performing their knowing-in-action through their feel for the music. We want our students, as becoming-professionals, to value their knowing-in-action or what we term their 'knowing-in-performance'. We hope that, through the reflective processes of the module, their knowing-in-performance can become the ordinary practical knowledge of their klezmer performance practice. However, to a large extent, this aspect of their development as klezmer ensemblists remains unknowable through the assessment-oriented reflective performer practices of the module.

Following Schön, our belief is that klezmer ensemblists come to be experts in their professional performance role as they experience certain performance situations. Thus, they develop expectations and techniques, learning what to look for, and how to respond to what they encounter, both in and with/through the ensemble. For Schön, a unique situation involves circumstances that are uncertain, unpredictable, and interesting. It makes professionals become aware of the experienced situation, think of it, and act upon it. Unique situations are both puzzling and relevant to professionals' practice. Again, applying this to our context, we work on the understanding that, when our student klezmer ensemble performers experience particular ensemble performances, they are likely at some points in the performance to engage in what we

---

25 Nahielly Palacios, Zeynep Onat-Stelma, and Richard Fay, 'Extending the conceptualisation of reflection: making meaning from experience over time', *Reflective Practice: International and Multidisciplinary Perspectives*, 22 (2021), 600–13. https://doi.org/10.1080/14623943.2021.1938995
26 Schön, *The Reflective Practitioner*, p. 54.
27 Ibid, p. 55.

term 'reflection in klezmer ensemble performance'. During a performance, they may experience situations where they become aware of the need to adjust their performance to continue making sense of the direction of the music that is developing and the materials they have. For example, the electric bass player may adjust the volume settings on their amp after sensing that their part was insufficiently present, or the flute player might decide not to persevere with the switch to their alto flute because they are aware of intonation issues. In such cases, the ensemblists—in keeping with other professionals—are 'reflecting-in-practice',[28] at least to some degree.

Unique situations thus provide individuals with opportunities to reflect upon their own tacit knowing-in-action, their own practice, and the particular context in which they work. Klezmer ensemble performances—especially those away from our departmental concert hall, for example Chanukah festivities in the local Jewish community—can often take our students out of their performance comfort zone, providing them with not only new musical experiences but also encounters with 'Otherness' and opportunities for intercultural learning.[29] Such situations can indeed be uncertain, unpredictable, and interesting, and also puzzling and relevant to the ensemblists' KEP practice. For example, ensemblists in previous years have commented on the disconcerting experience of playing in very close proximity to the audience at the Jewish Museum. In these performances, they became intimately aware, in ways unfamiliar from their previous concert hall performances, of individual audience responses to the emerging music, for example the changing breathing through excitement, the teary eyes of emotion, and the animated glances to other audience members as they recognised the opening of a familiar tune. As ensemblists, our students feed off this audience response, and they fine-tuned their performance accordingly; they 'played to the gallery' once they felt the audience's appreciation of the performance.

Reflection-in-Action

Schön further explained that reflection-in-action is a spiral process that begins when professionals experience a unique situation. It has three stages: appreciation, action, and reappreciation. In the *appreciation* stage of the spiral, professionals draw on their 'familiar repertoire' to compare the experienced unique situation with previous relevant experiences. For Schön, 'familiar repertoire' refers to all the experiences that someone has lived so far, experiences carrying the 'overarching theories, by which individuals make sense of phenomena'.[30] By drawing on previous relevant experiences, professionals can describe the experienced unique situation in terms of a familiar one,

---

28 Palacios et al., p. 606.
29 Fay, Mawson, and Bithell.
30 Simona Marchi, 'Participatory and Appreciative Action and Reflection in Adult Learning: Transformation as Appreciative Reflection', in *Encyclopedia of Information Communication Technologies and Adult Education Integration*, ed. by Victor K. Wang (Hershey, PA.: IGI Global, 2011), pp. 723–39 (p. 728), https://doi.org/10.4018/978-1-61692-906-0.ch043

thereby developing an initial understanding of it.³¹ We see a parallel as our klezmer ensemblists compare the unique klezmer performance to relevant experiences in their familiar musician's repertoire. This is a comparison between the new performance and all and anything that helps them make sense of that new performance experience. It is one which helps them explain that new experience in terms of old/familiar musician frames of reference, thereby giving them an initial understanding of the new performance experience.

The utility and adequacy of such appreciation is discovered in the stage of *action*.³² This is where professionals think of ways in which they can approach the unique situation and operationalise the action that they think will help them to satisfactorily deal with it. In this stage, klezmer ensemblists think of ways in which they can approach the new performance situation and also operationalise such ways with the objective of satisfactorily dealing with the new performance context. When professionals develop further meanings of the unique situation, they enter the stage of *reappreciation*. The outcome of this stage is a 'new theory' that comprises the professionals' practical knowledge as emergent from experience.³³ In this stage, klezmer ensemblists develop further meanings (that is, new theory) of the particular performance. Thus, their practical klezmer-ensemblists' knowledge emerges from further action. Nahielly Palacios, Zeynep Onat-Stelma, and Richard Fay, informed by their own work and by Farrell's ideas on reflection, argue that the formulation and operationalisation of the new emerging theory is an additional stage of the spiral process of reflection-in-action developed by Schön.³⁴ They refer to this stage as *further action* as it involves purposeful planning and operationalisation of the emergent new theories. For the purposes of this chapter and to avoid confusion between what has become commonly known as reflection-in-action (following the interpreters of Schön's work, see section below), we refer to the spiral process of reflection-in-action described by Schön as *the reflective spiral*.

Reflection in, on, and for Action

Schön further argued that reflection-in-action may not be very rapid because it is bound to the *action-present* which can 'stretch over minutes, hours, days, even weeks or months'.³⁵ This idea is that professionals can engage in the stages of reflection-in-action over a period of time. Schön suggests that professionals can reflect on their knowing-in-practice 'in the relative tranquillity of a post-mortem' when they think back on '… a situation they have lived through, and they explore the understandings they have brought to their handling

---

31 Schön, *The Reflective Practitioner*.
32 Ibid.
33 Ibid.
34 Farrell, *Reflective Practice in Action*; Palacios et al., p. 607.
35 Schön, The Reflective Practitioner, p. 62

of the situation'.[36] Based on this statement, interpreters of his work suggest that there are two different moments in time in which reflection can occur, namely:[37]

1. while experiencing a unique situation (*reflection-in-action*); and
2. after having experienced a unique situation (*reflection-on-action*).

Putting this together, we identify two different moments in time in which performance-related reflection can take place for our klezmer ensemblists:

1. while experiencing a particular performance unique situation (or what we term *reflection-in-performance*); and
2. after having experienced a particular performance unique situation (or what we term *reflection-on-performance*).

Based on the interpreters of Schön's work, reflection-in-action has been understood as thinking about experience whilst that experience is occurring.[38] The phrases 'thinking while doing something' and 'thinking on your feet' are frequently used when scholars talk about this mode of reflection.[39] In our adapted understanding, reflection-in-performance can be understood as thinking about performing whilst that performance is occurring (that is, 'thinking while performing'). Reflection-on-action has been understood as the retrospective analysis and thoughtful consideration that professionals perform with the purpose of preparing themselves for future practice.[40] Again, by extension, reflection-on-performance can be understood as the retrospective analysis and thoughtful consideration that klezmer ensemblists engage with in order to prepare themselves for future practice. This understanding overlaps to some extent with the next idea.

Later, Farrell introduced the notion of 'reflection-for-action' to indicate the relevance of thinking about future actions which can help improve teachers' practice.[41] This mode of reflection involves thinking proactively with the purpose of developing a plan of action that includes what to do, why, how, and when. For us, *reflection-for-performance*

---

36   Ibid.
37   For example, see Gillian Bolton, *Reflective Practice: Writing and Professional Development* (Thousand Oaks, CA: Sage, 2005); David K. Boud, Rosemary Keogh, and David Walker, *Reflection, Turning Experience into Learning* (London: Routledge, 1985); Linda Finlay, 'Reflecting on "Reflective Practice"', *Practice-based professional learning*, Paper 52 (Milton Keynes: The Open University, 2008); Robert B. Kottkamp, 'Means for Facilitating Reflection', *Education and Urban Society*, 22 (1990), 182–203, https://doi.org/10.1177/0013124590022002005 ; Karen F. Osterman, 'Reflective Practice: A New Agenda for Education', *Education and Urban Society*, 22 (1990), 133–52, https://doi.org/10.1177/001312459002200 2002
38   Delia Fish and Collin Coles, 'Towards a Re-Vision of Professional Practice', in *Developing Professional Judgement in Health Care: Learning through the Critical Appreciation of Practice*, ed. by Delia Fish and Colin Coles (Oxford: Butterworth-Heinemann, 1998), pp. 3-75; Jennifer Greenwood, 'Reflective Practice: A Critique of the Work of Argyris and Schön', *Journal of Advanced Nursing*, 18 (1993), 1183–87, https://doi.org/10.1046/j.1365-2648.1993.18081183.x
39   Finlay, p. 3
40   Ruth Leitch and Christopher Day, 'Action Research and Reflective Practice: Towards a Holistic View', *Educational Action Research*, 8 (2000), 179–93, https://doi.org/10.1080/09650790000200108
41   Farrell, *Reflective Practice in Action*; Farrell, *Reflective Language Teaching*.

can be understood as prospective thinking about future actions which can help improve the ensemblists' performance, a mode of reflection involving thinking proactively with the purpose of developing a plan of action that includes what to do, why, how, and when with regard to performance.

All in all, it is our understanding that the three modes of performer reflection above may involve all or some of the stages of the reflective spiral described by Schön. For example, when performers engage in reflection-in-performance (that is, thinking while doing something) and are able to develop an initial understanding of the unique situation, act upon it, develop new theories and plan for future similar encounters right on the spot, they will be engaging in all of the stages of the reflective spiral. However, following Schön's rationale, it could also be the case that professionals might engage in some, rather than all, of the stages of the spiral while doing something. For instance, in rehearsal when developing suitable musical arrangements, KEP students may remain stuck in the *appreciation* stage, repeatedly looking at moment from different angles or perspectives, and trying to problem-solve without really dealing with it in action and not arriving at a new understanding of it (that is, they talk about potential options rather than trying them out and seeing what happens in order to hone the arrangement). From observation, they may also get stuck in the *action* stage: for instance, within a session scenario, a non-klezmer-playing cajon player may hear the group performing a *zhok*, a klezmer dance-type in triple time, and draw upon their previous knowledge of triple-time percussion playing and provide a waltz-like accompaniment, unaware that the *zhok* has a distinctive omission of the second beat; if the cajon player were to continue playing a waltz rhythm while the more klezmer-literate musicians around them play a *zhok* rhythm, they would be stuck in the *action* stage and never reach the *reappreciation* stage. Further, when professionals engage in reflection-on-performance (that is, retrospectively analysing a situation), the assumption is that they will be able to go through all of the stages of the reflective spiral as they will have the time to deeply analyse it. Finally, when performers engage in reflection-for-performance, they will be able to purposefully plan for subsequent similar unique situations (for example, playing 'Odessa Bulgar' for a dance, not for a concert), devise the action possibilities (for example, removing conventional arrangement features that de-emphasise the driving bulgar rhythm that is important for articulating the dance) and wait for the further understandings of them (that is, new theory). Hence, they will be engaging with some of the stages of the reflective spiral.

Overview of the Reflective Performer Process

For the ensemblists' first two performances (see above), the actual playing was not assessed; rather, it was the reflections (of various kinds) about these performances which were assessed. Because our focus in this chapter is on reflective processes rather than actual performance and its assessment, we have chosen not to focus on the reflection (also contained in the students' submitted assessment portfolio) regarding their third video performance. The process of reflection for this generation of klezmer ensemblists involved the stages listed below (see Table 8.2). These build upon the sense of situated performance emphasised in the module as well as on the reflective spiral and other reflective aspects discussed above.

Stage of the reflective spiral	The klezmer ensemblists ...
Reflection-for-performance: Appreciation	reflected orally (through group discussion at the start of the module) on what they brought to the klezmer module.
Reflection-for-Performance: Action Preparation for Performance 1	decided as an ensemble how to collectively and individually prepare for the first curated video performance context (MJF), i.e. foregrounded situatedness.
Reflection-in-performance Students might engage in all of the stages of the reflective spiral	individually reflected in the process of developing their video performance—for example, by getting a feel for their material, making on-the-spot adjustments to the sounds they hear, making further sense of the developing music, re-recording their part in response to how they felt each iteration had captured what they intended, and also through their collaborative comments to each other as the recording developed.
Reflection-on-performance: Going through all of the stages of the reflective spiral	individually and collectively reflected on Performance 1 as a starting point for Performance 2.
Reflection-for-performance: Appreciation	took stock of what they now knew and had experienced regarding klezmer, and considered how to channel this into the task of developing the second situated performance (KN Kabaret).
Reflection-for-performance: Action Preparation for Performance 2	decided as an ensemble how to collectively and individually revise the earlier curated video performance as now directed for the new context (KN Kabaret).
Reflection-in-performance Students might engage in all of the stages of the reflective spiral	individually reflected in the process of their developing video performance and reflected on their performance as they experienced it being viewed by the KN Kabaret participants.
Re-appreciation / Reflection-on-performance	reflected individually and collectively on Performance 2 as a starting point for their upcoming assessed video performance.

Reflection-on-performance 2: All stages of the reflective spiral	reflected (through the reflective note in the first part of the written component of their assessment portfolio), on what they now knew and had experienced re klezmer and considered how to channel this into plans for specific and more general future performances.

Table 8.2. Performances emphasised in the KEP module.

We next consider two ensemblists who exemplify the kind of reflective trajectory achieved through the Reflective Notes submitted as part of the assessment portfolio.

Ensemblist Reflections

Case 1 (Student B)

Given that these comments were for assessment purposes and were generated some time after the performance itself, it is unsurprising that Student B's text presents both thinking subsequent to the performance (that is, reflection on their performance) as coupled to more forward-looking considerations (reflection for performance). Her assessment text does not present any meaningful moments of reflection during the performance itself (reflection-in-performance).

Reflecting on, and Looking Forward from, the MJF performance

Looking back on the experience of creating a curated video performance for the MJF event, Student B can see 'many aspects of my performance that I would have changed … mostly these are to do with my technical abilities and my playing'. Recognising her insecurity with the genre at that early stage in her encounter with it, she reflects on her 'relatively limited' and 'bare-minimum' playing:

> For example, I kept my *sekund* [i.e. accompaniment] very consistent and unvaried throughout as it took me a while to get to grips with the chords and different rhythmic patterns I was following in each section, as well as the *misheberakh* mode. Therefore, I tended to alternate between two or three notes in a repeated pattern rather [than] moving fluidly between different notes in the triad. I also didn't double-stop, a technique which, in retrospect, would have been effective as it is characteristic of klezmer string playing. In terms of my *primash* [i.e. melody] playing, I experimented with playing down the octave in places, especially in the string sections to add some variety (as I am the only viola player). However I did not attempt any counter melodies - something I think would have added more depth to the performance.

She also commented on the wider range of ensemble roles including video/audio editing that, 'given the uncertainty of the future of the pandemic', she would be keen to develop in the future. For us, this is important, providing evidence that she has taken to heart our guidance regarding the full range of roles needed for ensemble performance (of klezmer). Most of the students would not have expected such skills development as learning outcomes when they signed up for the module. This can be seen in a related evaluative comment made by Student M1:

> My experience in these different roles in the ensemble experience, from public speaking, to liaising and being able to explore all of the different roles in an ensemble, really made me realise how versatile one must be in a klezmer ensemble. There's a lot of trust that must be put in fellow ensemble members to fulfil their own role which in the end only brings an ensemble closer together.

Student B notes that the ensemble as a whole learned from this MJF experience too: 'we were proud of what we had created - especially of the arrangement in particular, since we had had very little time to play together as an ensemble'. Taking stock (through reflection on this performance), she notes that 'we all felt that the performance lacked something. [... W]hat we needed was to find the spark that we were missing by not being able to perform live'.

Reflecting on, and Looking Forward from, the KN Kabaret Performance

The headline learning from this next stage of reflection was the ensemble's recognition of the 'visibly large step up between our original video and the KlezNorth adaptation', and mostly this step was achieved through 'the spark' of the performance being enhanced through attention to the video aspects of the performance. Student B identifies the original issue: 'in our original recording, a lot of us were focussing hard on keeping up with the click track and remembering the structure of the piece without the support of other players around us'; and, as a result, 'a lot of our individual videos lacked character and "fun" [...]. I was certainly a culprit for this, not smiling or really appearing to "get into" the music as I was very much preoccupied with keeping in the right place'.

Whilst the playing back of a curated video performance is substantially different from a more conventional live performance, it is, we believe, a performance nonetheless. The ensemblists performed and took professional care with the quality of their performance; it was situated for a particular event and a known audience, and it had an audience who collectively experienced the online performance. As they reflected on this first performance, some of the ensemblists decided to re-record parts of their performance to better capture their developing sense of what klezmer could sound like. Others, like Student B, attended to wider aspects of the performance such as their stage presence. Student B, thus, reports how the ensemble sought to resolve the stage-awkwardness of the first performance by re-recording their videos: 'We either reused our original audio or sent new audio in separately, ensuring that the main focus in our new videos was appearing enthusiastic and engaged'. Focusing on her own contribution here, she writes: 'I re-recorded my video and was much happier with how it came across [. ... W]ithout having to focus on my sound while I recorded, I was able to concentrate on making my visual performance more "fun"'.

At many points in this pandemic-affected year, the students and tutors struggled with a sense of the limited, second-best character of the online experience of KEP. The status given in her reflections to the curated video performances is interestingly different in this regard:

> We were lucky that we were able to create a video like this as everyone else at the Kabaret performed live over zoom, so generally had to play solo music. While this was still very enjoyable, I think the audience appreciated our ensemble performance and the layers we were able to add: it certainly felt like a somewhat 'authentic' experience of klezmer. In fact, many people at the Kabaret commented that our performance felt like a small return to normality.

By the end of her performance of reflection regarding this second online performance, Student B reported being pleased that they had 'worked particularly hard in the arranging process to create a wide variety of textures in the performance as this really highlighted the ensemble "feel" of our performance'. Her Reflective Note ends with a strong statement of reflection-for-performance:

> My final reflection from this project is that I would like to get more comfortable with straying from what I have been explicitly taught in klezmer playing. In other words, I wish to feel able to create counter melodies and perhaps to add more intricate rhythms in my *sekund* playing which fit into the rhythmic pattern but are not the base rhythms I have been taught specifically. I think these things will come with more experience of the music and familiarity with the modes.

Case 2 (Student M3)

Reflection on Performance 1

This student was succinct, forensically evaluative in his reflections on the first performance (MJF event):

> Elements of the ensemble performance lacked Klezmer essence: many of the videos looked flat.

> ... due to the trouble of coordinating remotely, things like melodic fills in between phrases (perhaps by a soloist or equally by tenor-voice/*Sekund*) were absent, and this absence was audible.

> Some sections became out of time; some 'bum' notes were left in (myself included).

My [trumpet] solo did outline the melody, but not as subtly as it could have done. It also lacked in melody ornaments [other] than some basic semi-quaver trills.

Furthermore, I could have worked better with the chord changes beneath, anticipating and accentuating them, rather than playing as if I were catching up.

Reflecting for Performance 2

Here, Student M3 noted that 'the key difference between the audience of KlezNorth and that in the forum was that this audience knew a lot about klezmer'. He also took stock of how his deepening understandings of klezmer and detailed preparation for his role informed his revised performance:

> More playing experience, discussion and listening aided my revision of [my opening solo]. I learnt specifically from the *Doyna* form for inspiration

His preparation for the improved solo gives a good sense of the 'informed performance' the module encourages:

> My most listened to klezmer band at this point had been Frank London (and his Klezmer Brass all-stars). This seemed a natural place for me to listen as I am a brass player and London and his crew really showcase the capabilities of klezmer brass, with virtuosity, big heterophony and charismatic loud playing.

But, he notes, 'this listening might be too far away from the slow, quiet introduction that was needed for [Performance 2]'. He has come to recognise that his listening so far of mainly post-revival klezmer performers 'did not have much in common with our ensemble'. This realisation took him on an exploratory journey back into the older, archive recordings of *Doynas* and other introductions. Here, he found 'a perfect example ... Kleftico Vlachiko', which he then partly transcribed in order 'to fit my part around the melody of [the tune in our arrangement]'.

While a close listening of the two curated video performances is needed to gauge the full impact of this reflection and the detailed preparation it stimulated, such a listening does support our sense that the reflection is of value in his developing KEP awareness, competence and confidence.

Final Reflections

In this chapter, we have outlined our KEP module focus on situated performance as supported by a reflective-performer frame. We exemplified this in action with a particular cohort of klezmer ensemble students. As we have reviewed the Reflective Notes that these ensemblists produced for their assessment portfolios, we can see that there are reflective areas present that we had not expected. For example, we had invited their reflections for specific upcoming performance (the move from the MJF event to KN Kabaret), but we also found reflection for future performance more generally (see, for example, the final quote from Student B above). Further, we had focused the reflective lens on the ensemblists' experiences of performance but their notes extended also to reflections on the course experiences. For the 2020–21 cohort, this included online participation in KlezNorth teaching sessions and a chance to reflect on the value of expert scaffolding for future performance:

> However, my performance in both of these videos reflects the more limited klezmer knowledge that I had before KlezNorth, whilst after KlezNorth I felt noticeably more confident with klezmer style. I stuck strictly to roles of *primash* and *sekund* in Odessa Bulgar, and did not feel confident exploring counter melodies and adding melodic embellishments, as I did later on in *Misirlou*, thanks to the enriching sessions at KlezNorth. The lessons from Ilana Cravitz were particularly valuable in developing my style as a klezmer violinist, as after KlezNorth I felt confident with adding slides and ornaments to create a klezmer sound. (Student E)

> After attending multiple events at KlezNorth, including the jam sessions, a session with Ilana Cravitz on bringing melodies to life, and a transcription session, I feel I could add even more to my performance in the video. I would like to add some counter melodies when I am playing *sekund* to complement the melody, and I have more ideas for how to embellish the melody, such as varying the way I play held notes and experimenting more with *krekhtsn*. (Student H)

> The lessons from Ilana Cravitz were particularly valuable in developing my style as a klezmer violinist, as after KlezNorth I felt confident with adding slides and ornaments to create a Klezmer sound. (Student E)

The diversity of reflective foci similarly surprised us. There were reflections, variously, on the technical (including arrangement aspects), the technological, and group/ensemble aspects, as well as on performativity and situatedness (historical, event-specific, immediate constraints/affordances, function/purpose). There was also an intriguing mix of individually-focused and group-focused reflections. For example, Student D commented:

> In general, the individual videos that we submitted for the project did not convey our collective sense of enjoyment and comradery to the extent that we would have liked. To address this ....

> On reflection, my cajon playing in the original video could have been more varied and did not sufficiently emphasise the syncopated bulgar rhythm in the loudest sections. Therefore, to improve the use of percussion for the KlezNorth version, we added a drum kit and tambourine alongside a re-recorded cajon part which enables the percussion section to continually drive the piece forward using 'forward motion'.

Similarly, Student C noted how:

> As a group we thought we could improve on our initial video by engaging more with the camera to make the performance more active. Individually I wanted to provide more variation in my *Primash* playing in the first A section adding in mordents and note bends to make it more idiomatic of klezmer.

Further, we can see that these Reflective Notes are clearly functioning as a demonstration of the students' credit-worthy commentary, that is, they are an assessment-focused performance of reflection, but they are also articulating something more immediate, raw, and relevant to the developing-performer process. As we listened in on their reflection-informed discussions as an ensemble between the first and second curated video performances, their desire to improve their performance was clearly evident. This discussion was no box-ticking exercise to please their tutors. Rather, their contextual attentiveness and increased understandings of klezmer were to the fore. We could see how the reflective-performer practices we hoped to instil in them were already leading to the kind of performance outcomes for which the module aimed. We are encouraged by the ways in which their reflections seem to be functioning as a vehicle for expressing their contextual knowledge about klezmer as well as being a means for them to improve their KEP most immediately but also their transmusicality more generally.

We are realising that reflective thinking that focuses on the situatedness of klezmer seems to create a connectedness to the modern living tradition and practice of klezmer, and, relatedly, foregrounds something historical and intrinsic to the lives of earlier klezmorim. The benefits of the former orient the KEP module as a practical 'extra string to your bow' of a modern working musician, since the students are having to think about music as functional—as *for* someone and/or something. Forging connections between the ensemblists and the living local tradition as well as emphasising reflective skills to navigate that music culture, enables (we believe) students to more easily continue this tradition beyond their 10-credit module. Perhaps this is part of our own agenda—as klezmer aficionados cultivating this music culture—but it does give students skills that may often be regarded as extraneous within music degrees in a university setting (as opposed to the industry 'training' you might find more commonly at conservatoires) and highlights our emergent, non-static approach to klezmer culture (or set of cultures).

The Zoom cohort of 2020–21 forced us to rethink our methodology; there were both constraints on what we could do but also new affordances. The latter included the foregrounding of reflection as linked to the curated videos performances. The need to create performance artefacts in lieu of a live performance meant students were able to more critically reflect on something tangible rather than having to remember key moments of the live performance. While the immediacy of reflection-in-performance was of a different kind with curated performances than it would have been with live ones, this enforced performance practice enabled a more structured approach to reflection, one for which we as examiners also had more tangible reference points.

Foregrounding reflection enabled us to turn these enforced changes and frustratingly limited opportunities into something more positively framed for that group of students. But, as we move beyond the pandemic era, we are encouraged as educators to be more attentive, structured, and purposeful as we embed reflective-performer practices into the KEP experience. For example, we now explicitly task the ensemblists to create arrangements with a particular situatedness in mind. We are also exploring recording/filming sessions, the results of which may be used both as artefacts for the students to reflect-on-/for-performance and, potentially, as assessment material for us. We are giving thought, also, to how we can best support these music students in the academically located practice of reflection: how might reflective writing differ from what they are otherwise used to? How might we advise them on the balance of reflective performer thinking and the performance of reflection for assessment? How can we most effectively 'sell' the idea of structured reflection to them alongside all the other learning domains within this small-scale KEP module? As we consider such matters, we retain a sense that the idiosyncratic character of the reflections to date may actually be helpful. Reflection is not a homogenised, commodified part of the module and the playing of the assessment game; it is a highly individualised space and a set of practices for which our vague instructions may be more helpful than a set of polished reflective instruments. As happens so often with the students' own arrangement thinking, we need to work with what is realistically achievable as we select from all the ideas we have about what may be possible regarding reflection in our music-education practices.

References

Bailey, John S., 'Ethnomusicology, Intermusability, and Performance Practice', in *The New (Ethno) Musicologies*, ed. by Henry Stobart (Lanham, MD.: Scarecrow Press, 2008), pp. 117–134

Bolton, Gillian, *Reflective Practice: Writing and Professional Development* (Thousand Oaks, CA: Sage, 2005)

Boud, David K., Rosemary Keogh, and David Walker, *Reflection, Turning Experience into Learning* (London: Routledge, 1985)

Deschênes, Bruno, 'Bi-musicality or Transmusicality: Viewpoint of a Non-Japanese Shakuhachi Player', *International Review of the Aesthetics and Sociology of Music*, 49 (2018), 275–94

Farrell, Thomas, S. C. *Reflective Practice in Action* (Thousand Oaks, CA.: Corwin Press, 2004)

——, *Reflective Language Teaching: From Research to Practice* (London: Bloomsbury Academic, 2015)

Fay, Richard, and Daniel J. Mawson, 'Appropriate, No Appropriative, Methodology: (Online) Klezmer Ensemble Performance as Intercultural Musicking', *ISSME2021* Conference, online, 21–24 June 2021, https://youtu.be/KXliY-3Rnsg

Fay, Richard, Daniel J. Mawson, and Caroline Bithell, 'Intercultural Musicking: Learning through Klezmer', *Languages and Intercultural Communication*, 22 (2022), 204–20

Feldman, Walter Zev, *Klezmer: Music, History and Memory* (Oxford: Oxford University Press, 2016)

Finlay, Linda, 'Reflecting on "Reflective Practice"', in *Practice-based Professional Learning* (paper 52) (Milton Keynes: The Open University, 2008).

Fish, Delia, and Collin Coles, 'Towards a Re-Vision of Professional Practice', in *Developing Professional Judgement in Health Care: Learning through the Critical Appreciation of Practice*, ed. by Delia Fish and Colin Coles (Oxford: Butterworth-Heinemann, 1998), pp. 3–75

Greenwood, Jennifer, 'Reflective Practice: A Critique of the Work of Argyris and Schön', *Journal of Advanced Nursing*, 18 (1993), 1183–87

Holliday, Adrian, 'Small cultures', *Applied Linguistics*, 20 (1999), 237–64

Hood, Mantle, 'The Challenge of Bi-Musicality', *Ethnomusicology*, 4 (1960), 55–59

Kottkamp, Robert B., 'Means for Facilitating Reflection', *Education and Urban Society*, 22 (1990), 182–203

Leitch, Ruth, and Christopher Day, 'Action Research and Reflective Practice: Towards a Holistic View', *Educational Action Research*, 8 (2000), 179–93

Livingston, Tamara, 'An Expanded Theory for Revivals as Cosmopolitan Participatory Music-Making', in *The Oxford Handbook of Music Revival*, ed. by Caroline Bithell and Juniper Hill (Oxford: Oxford University Press, 2014), pp. 60–71

Livingston, Tamara, 'Music Revivals: Towards a General Theory', *Ethnomusicology*, 43 (1999), 66–85

Livingston, Tamara, 'An Expanded Theory for Revivals as Cosmopolitan Participatory Music Making', in *The Oxford Handbook of Music Revival*, ed. by Caroline Bithell and Juniper Hill (Oxford: Oxford University Press, 2014), pp. 60–69

Marchi, Simona, 'Participatory and Appreciative Action and Reflection in Adult Learning: Transformation as Appreciative Reflection', in *Encyclopedia of Information Communication Technologies and Adult Education Integration*, ed. by Victor K. Wang (Hershey, PA.: IGI Global, 2011), pp. 723–39

Netsky, Hankus, 'Klez Goes to College', in *Performing Ethnomusicology: Teaching and Representation in the World Music Ensembles*, ed. by Ted Solis (Oakland, CA.: University of California Press, 2004), pp. 189–201

——, *Klezmer: Music and Community in Twentieth Century Philadelphia* (Philadelphia, PA.: Temple University Press, 2015).

Nettl, Bruno, *The Study of Ethnomusicology: Thirty-one Issues and Concepts* (Champaign, IL.: University of Illinois Press, 1983/2005)

Osterman, Karen F., 'Reflective Practice: A New Agenda for Education', *Education and Urban Society*, 22 (1990), pp. 133–52

Palacios, Nahielly, Zeynep Onat-Stelma, and Richard Fay, 'Extending the Conceptualisation of Reflection: Making Meaning from Experience over Time', *Reflective Practice: International and Multidisciplinary Perspectives*, 22 (2021), 600–13

Phipps, Alison, and Mike Gonzalez, *Modern Languages: Learning and Teaching in an Intercultural Field* (London: Sage, 2004)

Rogovoy, Seth, *The Essential Klezmer: A Music Lover's Guide to Jewish Roots and Soul Music - From the Old World to the Jazz Age to the Downtown Avant-garde* (Chapel Hill, NC.: Algonquin Books, 2000)

———, *The Essential Klezmer: A Music Lover's Guide to Jewish Roots and Soul Music - From the Old World to the Jazz Age to the Downtown Avant-garde* (Chapel Hill, NC.: Algonquin Books, 2000)

Sapoznik, Henry *Klezmer Music 1910-1942* (1981), https://folkways.si.edu/klezmer-music-1910-1942-recordings-from-the-yivo-archives/judaica/music/album/smithsonian

Sapoznik, Henry, *Klezmer! Jewish Music from Old World to Our World* (New York: Schirmer Trade Books, 1999)

Schön, Donald A., *The Reflective Practitioner: How Professionals Think in Action* (London: Routledge, 1983)

———, *Educating the Reflective Practitioner* (San Francisco: Jossey-Bass, 1987)

Singer, Marshall H., *Perception and Identity in Intercultural Communication* (Yarmouth, ME.: Intercultural Press, 1998)

Slobín, Mark, *Fiddler on the Move: Exploring the Klezmer World* (Oxford: Oxford University Press, 2000)

———, *American Klezmer: Its Roots and Offshoots.* (Oakland: University of California, 2002)

Small, Christopher, *Musicking: The Meanings of Performing and Listening* (Middletown, CT: Wesleyan University Press, 1998)

Solis, Ted, *Performing Ethnomusicology: Teaching and Representation in the World Music Ensembles* (Oakland: University of California Press, 2004)

Stobart, Henry, 'Unfamiliar Sounds: Approaches to Intercultural Interaction in the World's Musics', in *Music and Familiarity: Listening, Musicology and Performance*, ed. by Elaine King and Helen M. Prior (London: Routledge, 2016), pp. 111–36

Strom, Yale, *The Book of Klezmer: The History, The Music, The Folklore* (Chicago: Chicago Review Press, 2011)

Waligórska, Magdalena, *Klezmer's Afterlife: An Ethnography of the Jewish Music Revival in Poland and Germany* (Oxford: Oxford University Press, 2013).

Links/Resources

Michael Kahan Kapelye, 'Odessa Bulgar - Michael Kahan Kapelye - Muslim Jewish Forum Performance', YouTube, uploaded by Callum Batten-Plowright Music, 6 December 2020, https://www.youtube.com/watch?v=KaeS6rbYC_c&list=PL1D469599FFE5C9DE&index=20

Michael Kahan Kapelye, 'The Michael Kahan Kapelye ensemble plays "Odessa Bulgar"', YouTube, uploaded by Music Department, University of Manchester, 17 March 2021, https://www.youtube.com/watch?v=J2531LXz7PQ&list=PL1D469599FFE5C9DE&index=24

PART III

CHALLENGES AND OPPORTUNITIES OF MUSIC PERFORMANCE EDUCATION IN SOCIETY

Introduction to Part III

Helen Julia Minors

A wider societal perspective on artistic practice is essential for developing a considered understanding both of the subjectivity of individual musicians and how musicianship is shaped through collaboration and interaction, and, further, to identify the potential impact of musical practices in contemporary society. Music Performance in society is a core part of artistic research and practice as our work is disseminated in public with diverse audiences. Part III shares four case studies, each of which helped to inform the REACT model (see Introduction). The chapters here necessarily engage with all spheres within the model because, if students are being taught to share their work (lower sphere) and to apply their artistic research in all practice, including their learning, they must first have understood the context of their artistic world. This understanding must precede students' exploration of their artistic voice, as it will help them to develop their own new practices, to build creative relations, and to then work across musical traditions and to grow their own innovations. The following chapters show how teaching, including the embedding of employability skills and questions of intersectionality, can facilitate students to develop their confidence, resilience, and engagement, as well as the skills to contextualise, explore, and share their artistic research through their intended art world.

The case studies in this Part offer four different teaching perspectives from different institutions, followed by Conclusions. Chapters 11 and 12, by, respectively, Sarah-Jane Gibson and Helen Julia Minors, are both examples from the UK that embed employability skills and emphasise graduate outcomes. These chapters also include discussion of issues of race, identity, intersectionality, and relationships. Both authors now work at the same institution and have developed their research into pedagogy across a decade, having taught and assessed in various countries, including India, Ireland, South Africa, Sweden, and the UK. As such, their development research applied through pedagogy here shares work that was in process and has been built over many years. As such, the longitudinal nature of the examples has helped formulate the multi-shared approach of the REACT model, which was developed following the various research activities presented in this present volume. This is a real genuine benefit to the field, as the model, to be shared with others in the sector, has been informed by international experience over many years.

The importance of terminology to inform practice is significant in managing student expectations and in sharing research to broaden and improve our collective sector practices. It is also therefore pertinent to why we have created the model, and to its future application within more institutions. As such, Odd T. Furnes's chapter, 'The Musical Object in Deep Learning', Chapter 9, is crucial to defining and broadening our understanding of deep learning. Deep learning is important as it shows how there are many ways in which we as researchers and practitioners approach our work. It is pertinent that each of the Part III authors' aims are articulated through research and applied in practice, as the hope is that these case studies may inspire similar work elsewhere. Definitions of process and reference to learning outcomes, module guides, and our institutional processes are also included to ensure there is transparency of Higher Education Institution process and practice. Readers will see that each chapter cites both institutional policy and develops to include the authentic student voice in feedback, focus groups, and so on, in order to learn from and with our students, how the pedagogy has been successful, and where developments are still needed. Each of the authors offers examples of how the co-construction of content with students ensures a student-centred approach. This is vital as the projects aim to improve graduate outcomes and students' ability to move smoothly into the creative industries, and, by so doing, to influence societal change for the better. Chapter 10, by Randi Eidsaa and Mariam Kharatyan, specifically questions how we teach performance through a contemporary societal lens. This chapter looks at the beginning of the REACT project with case studies which are specifically part of the development nature of the funded work.

As this volume addresses the need and appetite for developing performance education in a higher education context, spanning the continent of Europe, it is important here that the voices, experiences, and case studies are diverse. To that effect, the notion of intercultural practice underpins these chapters, in exploring how connections between cultures, and exchanges across cultures are significant (see especially Chapters 11 and 12). Through questioning the intercultural aspects of this artistic research in pedagogic practice, the authors reflect on their practice, much as in

Part II, to detail not only what they have done but also how the process has benefited their students, in providing new experiences and challenging students (and staff) to look beyond their own experience to that of others. In essence, questioning the interculturality of the work we co-create encourages us all, as artistic researchers, to consider the relationality and intersectionality of the process and final artwork.[1]

It speaks to the model's adaptability that each of the case studies in Part III references the model to illustrate how the work, completed prior to the model, has been reflected in it. The model, therefore, is a result of a longitudinal project. It is founded on many years of pedagogic research and practice that, though it predates the network, has been brought together and consolidated through REACT.

---

1   Helen Julia Minors, 'Opera and intercultural musicology as modes of translation', in *Opera in Translation. Unity and Diversity*, ed. by Adriana Şerban and Kelly Kar Yue Chan (Amsterdam: John Benjamins, 2020), pp. 13–33, https://doi.org/10.1075/btl.153.01min

9. The Musical Object in Deep Learning

Odd Torleiv Furnes

Introduction: Redesigning Education

In 54 BCE, Caesar invaded Britain. The campaign had fought its way from Rome using horses and wooden carriages for transportation. Over a millennium later, in 1510 CE, Martin Luther travelled from Germany to Rome using the exact same technology—one that remained virtually unaltered for a further 300–400 years. If we fast forward, the variety in means of transportation today has exploded and so has the advance in all other forms of technology. The kind of education where the students are set to copy skills and facts from yesterday to handle the jobs of tomorrow has rapidly become more and more irrelevant and outdated. Andreas Schleicher, director for Education and Skills in the Organization for Economic Cooperation and Development (OECD), puts it like this: 'We live in a fast-changing world, and producing more of the same knowledge and skills will not suffice to address the challenges of the future'.[1] Such insight has forced a change in education, and the solution has been turning towards the so-called twenty-first-century skills. With these skills, we look to the future: 'We are preparing students for jobs that don't yet exist'.[2] In Norway, one answer to these challenges was to replace the national curriculum for primary, lower secondary and upper secondary education. In the new curriculum, introduced in 2020, the renewal of subjects and competencies is aimed at equipping students with the necessary knowledge and competencies to handle the unknown challenges of tomorrow. Competence, a central concept in the curriculum, is thus defined as 'the ability to acquire and apply knowledge and

---

[1] Andreas Schleicher, 'The case for 21st-century learning', Organization for Economic Cooperation and Development, 14 June 2012, OECD Web Archive, https://web-archive.oecd.org/2012-06-14/61660-thecasefor21st-centurylearning.htm

[2] Maruan El Mahgiub, 'Education: Preparing Students for Jobs that Don't Yet Exist', TEDxIEMadrid, YouTube, uploaded by TEDx Talks, 4 September 2019, https://www.youtube.com/watch?v=uGR4eJmNI90

skills to master challenges and solve tasks in familiar and unfamiliar contexts and situations'.³ The concept of deep learning (in-depth learning) has also been given a central place, alongside competence, in the new curriculum. There are varying definitions of the concept. Deep learning is said to provide room for the students to 'develop understanding of key elements and relationships in a subject'.⁴ Other definitions are 'to learn something so well that you understand relationships and can apply what you have learned in new situations' or 'gradually developing knowledge and lasting understanding of concepts, procedures and relationships in the subject and between subject areas'.⁵

The turn towards twenty-first-century skills and deep learning represents a break with traditional pedagogy, replacing the acquisition of facts and concrete, isolated skills—often referred to as surface learning—with that of understanding concepts, seeing relationships, and applying knowledge in new contexts.⁶ We can interpret this as a shift from obtaining a certain defined amount of knowledge to, instead, grasping the structure of knowledge.⁷ Here, memorising isolated facts and procedures is considered of less value than understanding how the different elements are interrelated and structured. The new emphasis on structural understanding, in turn, allows for the recognition of similarities in structure between seemingly unrelated problems and challenges—a skill that enables the transfer of knowledge. This may seem a logical response to the unforeseen challenges of the twenty-first century, but there are some issues that need to be addressed. Although deep learning is partly defined as an understanding of concepts, the concept of deep learning itself is not necessarily easy to understand, and its application to the subject of music is, perhaps, even less obvious. One main objective of this chapter is to clarify how deep learning in music can be understood and facilitated.

---

3   Utdanningsdirektoratet, 'Core curriculum: Competence in the subjects', 2019, para 3 of 7, https://www.udir.no/lk20/overordnet-del/prinsipper-for-laring-utvikling-og-danning/kompetanse-i-fagene/?lang=eng
4   Ibid., para 6 of 7.
5   Utdanningsdirektoratet, 'Dybdelæring', 13 March 2019, para 1 and 2 of 4 (my translation), https://www.udir.no/laring-og-trivsel/dybdelaring/
6   Sawyer, R. Keith, 'Introduction: The New Science of Learning', in *The Cambridge Handbook of the Learning Sciences*, ed. by Keith Sawyer (Cambridge: Cambridge University Press, 2014), pp. 1–16. See Table 9.1.
7   Michael Schneider and Elsbeth Stern, 'The cognitive perspective on learning: Ten cornerstone findings', in *The Nature of Learning: Using Research to Inspire Practice*, ed. by Hanna Dumont, David Istance, and Francisco Benavides (Paris: OECD Publishing, 2010), pp. 69-90, https://doi.org/10.1787/9789264086487-5-en

Deep Learning	Traditional Learning
Deep learning requires that learners look for patterns and underlying principles.	Learners memorize facts and carry out procedures without understanding how or why.
Deep learning requires that learners integrate their knowledge into interrelated conceptual systems.	Learners treat course material as disconnected bits of knowledge.
Deep learning requires that learners relate new ideas and concepts to previous knowledge and experience.	Learners treat course material as unrelated to what they already know.
Deep learning requires that learners reflect on their own understanding and their own process of learning.	Learners memorize without reflecting on the purpose or on their own learning strategies.

Table 9.1. Deep learning vs traditional learning.

Musical Knowledge and Meaning

To define the concept of deep learning in music, different aspects of meaning and knowledge become central to the discussion. I will pursue two strands of reasoning: the ontological question regarding the source of musical knowledge, and the epistemological question of how we can attain musical knowledge. In terms of musical ontology, the notion of the musical object as the source of musical knowledge can be contrasted to the situated view that musical knowledge is created within the social, relational musical activity. The epistemological strand investigates our ability to perceive, process, and understand music as sound and follows the discourse between analytical or verbal (language-based) knowledge and intuitive, experiential, somatic, and non-verbal knowledge. Upon inspection, we can find signs of both an ontological and an epistemological perspective in the definition of deep learning. Following these two strands, I start with the question of musical ontology.

Source of Musical Meaning

In search of the source of musical knowledge, we cannot escape the question of meaning. Traditionally, there have been two diametrically opposite stances regarding in what musical meaning is grounded. Some believe that the source of musical meaning can be found within the musical object (for example, in the performed and/or broadcast sound in performance, or in the score as written by the composer). Others think that music is given meaning through extra-musical references. Leonard B. Meyer, in his book *Emotion and Meaning in Music* (1956), described this difference of opinion as being:

between those who insist that musical meaning lies exclusively within the context of the work itself, in the perception of the relationships set forth within the musical work of art, and those who contend that, in addition to these abstract, intellectual meanings, music also communicates meanings which in some way refer to the extramusical world of concepts, actions, emotional states, and character. Let us call the former group the 'absolutists' and the latter group the 'referentialists'.[8]

The absolutist stance is further divided into the positions of formalism and expressionism. Formalists believe that 'the meaning of music lies in the perception and understanding of the musical relationships set forth in the work of art and that meaning in music is primarily intellectual'.[9] The Austrian music critic and formalist Eduard Hanslick (1825–1904) exemplifies this stance when stating: 'Music consists of tone successions, tone forms; these have no content other than themselves'.[10] Then, there are absolute *expressionists* who do not think that the meaning of music lies in an intellectual understanding of musical form but in the musical *experience* excited by those forms without the need for any extramusical reference. Another type of expressionism takes the view that 'emotional expression is dependent upon an understanding of the referential content of music'.[11] This gives us the following notions of musical meaning: the formalist, the absolute expressionist, and the referential expressionist. Note that Meyer describes two forms of absolutism—the formalist and the expressionist—but only one type of referentialism. He states that 'almost all referentialists are expressionists',[12] but he is not clear about an alternative to referentialism that is not directly related to expressiveness. One candidate for covering the non-expressive, referential side could be so-called conceptual art. Here, the artistic object is of less importance than the extramusical idea or concept that the spectator can detect through thoughtful reflection. Conceptual art has even been described as anti-aesthetic.[13] Another candidate, although it is not explicitly non-expressive, is the discipline of musical semiotics. In *Signs of Music*, Eero Tarasti describes the discipline in this way:

> No object or thing has any existence for us unless it means or signifies something. Music thus mediates between values be they aesthetic, ideological, or whatever—and fixed, ready-made objects. In fact, music as a sign provides an ideal case of something meaningful and communicative, and thus of something semiotical par excellence.[14]

---

8 Leonard B. Meyer, *Emotion and Meaning in Music* (Chicago: University of Chicago Press, 1956), p. 1.
9 Ibid., p. 3.
10 Eduard Hanslick, *On the Musically Beautiful*, trans. by L. Rothfarb and C. Landerer (Oxford: Oxford University Press, 2018 (1854)), p. 109.
11 Meyer, p. 3.
12 Ibid.
13 Arthur P. Shimamura, *Experiencing Art: In the Brain of the Beholder* (Oxford: Oxford University Press, 2013), p. 25.
14 Eero Tarasti, *Signs of Music: A Guide to Musical Semiotics* (The Hague: De Gruyter Mouton, 2002), p. 4, https://doi.org/10.1515/9783110899870

In musical semiotics, the claim is that music gains meaning through non-musical references. These non-musical references can be related to gestures, gender, biology, intertextual connotations, etc. Thus, for music to be meaningful, one must see and understand what the music signifies. Although there could be an intuitive, experiential component involved, this can be seen as a matter of conceptualising relationships between the realms of the musical and the non-musical.

With conceptual art and the conceptual side of musical semiotics, we may have completed the picture drawn by Meyer: musical meaning emerges through a) the *expressive* dimension, where the source of emotional expression is either within the musical object itself or in the referential, non-musical associations; or b) the *conceptual*, intellectual logic detected within the musical object itself or in the referential, non-musical denotations. In other words, when focusing on the musical object as the source of knowledge, meaning can arise through an intellectual and conceptual discovery of relationships between the musical elements (formalism) or through an intuitive, emotional response to the unfolding music (absolute expressionism). On the referential side, music can attain meaning through emotional reactions caused by associations between the music and non-musical objects or actions (referential expressionism) or through a more intellectual detection of a conceptual connotation between musical signs pointing to a non-musical reality (conceptual art and musical semiotics). It all boils down to whether musical meaning is reliant on the musical object or on non-musical denotations and to whether meaning emerges through emotional responses or conceptual, abstract thinking. Other disciplines that treat musical meaning as referential are sociology of music and parts of educational philosophy and music education. These disciplines provide the strongest opposition against the absolute view of art and music.

Absolutism under Attack

Formalism and absolute expressionism have been under attack from both sociological and philosophical sides. A significant voice was John Dewey, who critiqued the art object as being detached from real life. In his book *Art as Experience* (1939), he said the following:

> When an art product once attains classic status, it somehow becomes isolated from the human conditions under which it was brought into being and from the human consequences it engenders in actual life-experience. When artistic objects are separated from both conditions of origin and operation in experience, a wall is built around them that renders almost opaque their general significance, with which esthetic theory deals.[15]

According to Dewey's pragmatism, music loses significance and value when it is removed from actual life experience. We might say it also loses meaning. In an attempt

---

15   John Dewey, *Art as Experience* (Berkley, CA: Berkley Publishing Group, 2005 (1934)), p. 1.

to distance music and musical meaning from the musical object, Christopher Small coined the term 'musicking', which put emphasis not on music as an object but as action: 'There is no such thing as music. Music is not a thing at all but an activity, something people do'.[16] David J. Elliott and Marissa Silverman adopt a similar perspective in *Music Matters*, stating that:

> musical values are not intrinsic; they are not 'fixed-in' sonic forms or captured in notated scores. Musical values are socially assigned to sounds according to how sounds are used, experienced, and understood as being 'good' or 'right' for various purposes in musical, personal, and ethical social life. [...] Musics can only be understood and experienced in relation to contexts of socio-musical contexts. From Dewey's pragmatic perspective, and from our praxial perspective, musics have meaning only in relation to, and in recognition of, distinct human aims and needs.[17]

Their term 'musics' refers to all forms of making music, and 'musicing' (Elliott and Silverman's parallel to Small's 'musicking') includes performing, improvising, composing, arranging, conducting, and recording. However, it also 'always includes listening because music makers of all kinds listen to what they do in acts of musicing and because listening is, in itself, a form of musical-social-participation'.[18] Elliott and Silverman, by stressing that listening is a part of music making and a form of social participation, seem to understate listening as an independent activity oriented towards the aesthetic properties of the musical object. This can be seen as an attempt to build a case against both the idea of a musical object and an aesthetic form of listening because both concepts have historically been ignorant of human concerns:

> [...] the aesthetic work-concept defines music listening via a negative norm: to listen aesthetically is *not* to connect musical sounds to other human concerns. In the jargon of aesthetics (and 'music education as aesthetic education'), our dispositions as listeners must be 'disinterested' and 'distanced'.[19]

Elliott and Silverman may be right that the concept of aesthetics has been interpreted according to the philosopher Immanuel Kant's idea of disinterestedness, which urges the listener to 'forget' about personal interests and concerns and direct his or her attention directly towards the musical work. In 2015, when their book was published, however, the idea of 'disinterestedness' did not have a monopoly on how to define the concept of aesthetics. Furthermore, when they argue against the notion of the 'work-concept', they build their case on ideas that were more prevalent 200 hundred years ago than they are today:

---

16   Christopher Small, *Musicking: The Meanings of Performing and Listening* (Middletown, CT.: Wesleyan University Press, 1998), p. 2.
17   David J. Elliott and Marissa Silverman, *Music Matters: A Philosophy of Music Education*, 2nd edn. (Oxford: Oxford University Press, 2005), p. 103.
18   Ibid., p. 16.
19   Ibid., p. 67, emphasis in original.

> The elements-based work-concept of music, which reached maturity around 1800 [...] institutionalized the false but widespread assumption that 'musical meaning' resides inside musical form and exists only for listeners' intellectual contemplation, not *felt* enjoyment.[20]

They seem to make a case against both aesthetic listening and the musical object due to an association with what we recognise as a formalist notion of musical meaning. While they acknowledge that many aesthetic philosophers refer to feelings, Elliott and Silverman claim that this does not refer to actual *felt* emotions. There is some historic validity to this accusation, but the rhetoric drives them into an apparent wholesale rejection of both the musical work and aesthetics in terms of musical meaning. As a consequence of their reasoning, they arrive at a definition of music as something completely dependent on social function: 'sound is deemed to be music according to the personal, social, and cultural functions it serves'.[21]

What could be seen as an attempt to marginalise the importance of individual listening outside of the activities of music-making fits the socio-constructivist paradigm that treats meaning and knowledge production as a shared social and cultural activity. Consequently, there is less of both valuable meaning and knowledge to be found for the individual attending to the aesthetic properties of the musical object than in how we use the objects for our common good.

Traces of the perspectives described above can be found in the Norwegian curriculum. One of the core elements in music claims that 'The meaning of music is created when music is used in social contexts'.[22] Such a stance may be seen to oppose what has been considered somewhat elitist attitudes within absolutism and formalism—attitudes that, according to Dewey, render the general significance of the artistic object opaque.[23] This dissociation from art as an object does not just seem to bury the notion of absolute formalism and expressionism; it also makes us question the idea of aesthetic learning *per se*: if musical meaning is treated as a socially defined symbolic language under relativistic and pragmatic terms, what is the status of the individual's perceptual experience of music as sound? Is there nothing in the sound itself that may give rise to perceptual and emotional experiences that are not socially pre-defined, functional, or pragmatic?

Many of us have experienced so-called 'guilty pleasures'. Kris Goffin and Florian Cova describe the phenomenon like this:

> In everyday language, the expression 'guilty pleasure' refers to instances where one feels bad about enjoying a particular artwork. Thus, one's experience of guilty pleasure

---

20   Ibid., p. 68, emphasis in original.
21   Ibid., p. 102.
22   Utdanningsdirektoratet, '(MUS01-02) Curriculum for Music: Core elements', 15 November 2019, https://www.udir.no/lk20/mus01-02/om-faget/kjerneelementer?lang=eng
23   See, for example, Elliott and Silverman's discussion on aesthetic objects as 'highbrow', for the socially privileged, educated, and 'classy' people, p. 96.

seems to involve the feeling that one should not enjoy this particular artwork and, by implication, the belief that there are norms according to which some aesthetic responses are more appropriate than others.[24]

In the case of guilty pleasures, is the meaning of music 'created when music is used in social contexts'? Or, how does this fit with the claim from Elliott and Silverman, quoted above, that 'Musical values are socially assigned to sounds according to how sounds are used, experienced, and understood as being "good" or "right" for various purposes in musical, personal, and ethical social life'?[25] If social values determine our norms for 'good' and 'bad' music, despite our personal and private experience, we are removing the aesthetic aspect from music listening and are left with just another social activity. The very existence of the phenomenon of guilty pleasures shows that musical meaning has more to it than just being the outcome of a socially constructed process. In fact, a guilty pleasure can be seen as a response to musical expressions that is the opposite of being pragmatic and social.

In discussions about the ontology of music wherein claims are made about the true source of musical meaning, we find that social sciences generally have rejected ideas of music as an object, of musical autonomy, and of formalism. Such ideas have been replaced with socio-cultural and pragmatic paradigms claiming that musical meaning is socially constructed. Anyone suggesting that musical meaning resides in the musical object risks being labelled as outdated or elitist. The debate around musical ontology has been rather unconstructive and has resulted in an entrenchment on both sides of the discussion. A more fruitful path to understanding the phenomenon of music and musical meaning might be found by turning to the epistemological side of things. Next, I explore what we know about our perceptual system and emotional responses to music.

The Aesthetic Experience

As we have seen, the concept of aesthetics is not considered neutral but, rather, is laden with philosophical ideas around the ontology of the arts. These range from defining aesthetics as the philosophical study of beauty and taste (via the aesthetic as a disinterested experience) to the study of art forms.[26] Let us try to refrain from arriving at an irrefutable philosophical definition of aesthetics and instead approach the aesthetic from a more basic point of view—our sensory system and emotional responses. In doing this, we are closer to the etymological origin of aesthetics, the Greek *aisthetis*, which means 'sensation and perception'. This notion is positioned in contrast to *noesis*, which refers to intellectual knowledge. The following gives an overview of

---

24   Kris Goffin and Florian Cova, 'An empirical investigation of guilty pleasures', *Philosophical Psychology*, 32/7 (2019) (p. 1129–55).
25   Elliott and Silverman, p. 103.
26   T. Munro, et al., 'Aesthetics', *Encyclopedia Britannica*, https://www.britannica.com/topic/aesthetics

the basic elements of the biological or innate side of sensation and perception as well as the mechanisms involved in our emotional responses to the perceptual input.

Sensation

The sensation of seeing, hearing, or smelling is caused by external stimulation of our sense organs. Even if the dictionary entry of 'sensation' refers to a mental process,[27] much of our experience of sensation can be ascribed to physical factors and processes. In the case of hearing, the anatomy and physiology of our auditory pathways[28] define what we are able to detect from the incoming fluctuations in sound pressure that hits our outer ear. Due to both the structure of our head and to how our outer and inner ear are constructed, the hearing abilities of humans differ from those of animals.[29] The basilar membrane in the cochlea has a tonotopic organisation, meaning that different parts of the membrane have different physical sensitivity corresponding to different sound frequencies. The physical construction of the human basilar membrane defines our hearing range from 20 to 20000 Hz. We also find that the membrane has a limited resolution for simultaneous frequencies: two pitches that appear at the same time within the same critical band[30] will interfere with each other, creating the sensation of beating or roughness. This is referred to as 'perceptual dissonance'.[31] Perceptual dissonance can be naturally produced by the close frequencies that occur, for example, in a bear growl, a rockfall, or in a thunder roll. It has been found that experiencing perceptual dissonance is linked with a brainstem reflex[32] that makes us alert or afraid, something that has served us well in trying to survive in a threatening environment. Perceptual dissonance occurring in music can trigger the same reflex.

After the sound waves have been registered as frequencies and converted into electric signals in the cochlea, the electric signals are sent up the cochlear nerve into the brain where it is further processed in the auditory cortex. Although there is not a clear-cut division between the two, we may refer to the physical process happening in the cochlea as sensation and the psychological processing done in the brain as perception.

---

27 'Sensation', *Merriam-Webster Dictionary*, 2022, website, https://www.merriam-webster.com/dictionary/sensation
28 James O. Pickles, 'Auditory pathways: anatomy and physiology', *Handbook of Clinical Neurology*, 129 (2015), 3–25, https://doi.org/10.1016/B978-0-444-62630-1.00001-9
29 Kerry M. Walker, Ray Gonzalez, Joe Z. Kang, Josh H. McDermott, and Andrew King, 'Across-Species Differences in Pitch Perception are Consistent with Differences in Cochlear Filtering', *Elife*, 8 (2019), https://doi.org/10.7554/elife.41626
30 'Critical band', *APA Dictionary of Psychology*, online edn, 19 April 2018, https://dictionary.apa.org/critical-band
31 Albert Bregman, *Auditory Scene Analysis: The Perceptual Organization of Sound* (Massachusetts: MIT Press, 1990); David Huron, 'Tone and Voice: A Derivation of the Rules of Voice-Leading from Perceptual Principles', *Music Perception*, 19/1 (2001), 1–64, https://doi.org/10.1525/mp.2001.19.1.1; Ernst Terhardt, 'The Concept of Musical Consonance: A Link between Music and Psychoacoustics', *Music Perception*, 1/3 (1984), 276–95, https://doi.org/10.2307/40285261
32 Patrick N. Juslin, *Musical Emotions Explained: Unlocking the Secrets of Musical Affect* (Oxford: Oxford University Press, 2019).

Perception

Our auditory environment is created by numerous sources. A main task of perception is to organise and interpret the auditory signal and group the sensory inputs into separate and coherent streams according to their respective sources. This is done through a combination of bottom-up and top-down processing. Albert Bregman, author of the book *Auditory Scene Analysis*, describes the difference between the bottom-up and top-down processes like this:

> Primitive grouping is considered a 'bottom-up' process because it operates on the perceptual data at the input or 'bottom' of the perceptual-cognitive system [...]. Bottom-up processing involves only the immediate present (echoic and short-term memory). This is in contrast to 'top-down' processing that usually operates on the data after primitive grouping has taken place, and involves long-term memory. The grouping that is the result of top-down processing with long-term memory constitutes the second kind of grouping effects, called 'learned' or 'schema-driven grouping effects'.[33]

When Bregman is talking about primitive grouping, he refers to the 'laws of perceptual organisation' outlined by the German gestalt psychologists Kurt Koffka, Wolfgang Köhler, and Max Wertheimer at the beginning of the twentieth century. The theory 'stresses that we perceive the environment with respect to its inherent organisational and relational properties, and that we tend to perceive holistic, cohesive, meaningful forms'.[34] To sort the sensory input into coherent and meaningful groups, perception operates according to laws like proximity, similarity, symmetry, good continuation, and closure. They all follow the fundamental law of Prägnanz: 'Of several geometrically possible organisations that one will actually occur which possesses the best, simplest and most stable shape'.[35] Bregman demonstrated that the laws of gestalt perception also apply to auditory grouping: 'They include such things as frequency proximity, spectral similarity, [and] correlations of changes in acoustic properties'.[36] The factors involved in auditory grouping follow the assumption that sounds have a physical source and that the task at hand is to determine things like the location, movement, size, and origin of the sound's source. We find, for example, that sounds which start and stop at the same time, come from the same direction, and are similar in timbre and pitch are assumed to come from the same physical source and are, therefore, grouped into the same auditory stream. The laws or principles of gestalt perception have also been demonstrated within musical perception and have played a major role in the theories

---

33 Bregman, p. 32.
34 Michael W. Eysenck and Mark T. Keane, *Cognitive Psychology: A student's handbook* (Philadelphia: Psychology Press, 2000), p. 26.
35 Kurt Koffka, *Principles of Gestalt psychology* (London: Routledge, 1999), p. 138.
36 Bregman, p. 401.

of researchers like Leonard B. Meyer, Eugene Narmour and E. Glenn Schellenberg.[37] We shall not go into detail on these theories but just give a few examples of some of the basic principles for grouping in music:

- sequential pitches that are close in time, frequency and timbre group together and form motives and melodies;
- pitches that appear simultaneously group together and forms a single harmony;
- simultaneous melodies moving in the same direction with similar intervals and pitch-duration (homophony, correlation of changes) are perceived as one 'thickened melody';
- simultaneous melodies moving in opposite direction with different intervals and pitch-duration are grouped into separate streams and perceived as independent melodies (counterpoint).

The fundamental principle in auditory perceptual grouping is that it is object-oriented. The same goes for grouping in music perception. The difference between auditory perception of natural sounds and music is that music does not originate from a single source but from multiple sound sources that usually correlate on one or more auditory dimensions. When there is no such correlation, we might be experiencing aleatoric music, or something that we would have trouble categorising as music. Due to the correlation between different sound sources on different dimensions, music has been compared to the mythological 'chimera', a creature which was a lion, a goat, and a snake in the same body. Elvira Di Bona has described this phenomenon in music as 'chimericity':

> It is the property of hearing as a unified whole a melody or a harmony that does not belong to any single sound source but instead consists of the assembling of melodic or harmonic fragments coming from different sources. Chimericity is not reducible to the low-level audible properties of pitch and loudness; it is cognized at the perceptual level thanks to the auditory mechanism of primitive grouping.[38]

The chimericity of music may be seen as a product of the combination of low-level, bottom-up grouping and top-down, learned patterns. When there is low-level 'evidence' of multiple sound-sources that, to a greater or lesser degree, correlate and create compound and multidimensional patterns, we are 'forced' to interpret these as one multidimensional object. The factors involved in sensation and perception point to the fundamental task of interpreting sensory input so that we can detect objects in

---

37 Eugene Narmour Meyer, 'The Top-down and Bottom-up Systems of Musical Implication: Building on Meyer's Theory of Emotional Syntax', *Music Perception*, 9/1 (1991), 1–26, https://doi.org/10.2307/40286156; E. Glenn Schellenberg, 'Simplifying the Implication-Realization Model of Melodic Expectancy', *Music Perception*, 14 (1997), 295–318, https://doi.org/10.2307/40285723.

38 Elvira Di Bona, 'Hearing chimeras', *Synthese*, 200/3, 257 (2022), 1-20, https://doi.org/10.1007/s11229-022-03721-y

our surroundings. This is also a fundamental aspect of auditory perception and is a necessary factor in music perception as well. What we have seen seems to undermine Small's statement quoted earlier: 'There is no such thing as music. Music is not a thing at all but an activity, something people do'.[39] We might not talk about sounds *as* objects, but we certainly associate sound *with* objects. The difference between *seeing* a lion and *hearing* a lion, for example, is barely a philosophical one: both forms of sensory input make us conclude that 'it is a lion'. As visual perception is oriented at identifying objects in our surroundings, so is auditory perception. What is special about music is that it is perceived as a multidimensional object, or a chimeric 'thing'.

So far, I have dealt mainly with the so-called bottom-up aspect of primitive grouping. We shall turn to research on our emotional responses to music, where other bottom-up as well as top-down aspects of learning play a prominent role.

Emotional Mechanisms

In *Musical Emotions Explained*, Patrik N. Juslin gives a broad review of research on musical emotions. One main focus is a set of evolved mechanisms that account for music-evoked emotions. The overview of the mechanisms presented below will cast light on the discussion of whether musical meaning is reliant on the musical object or on non-musical denotations in terms of emotional experience.

Brainstem Reflex

As touched upon earlier, brainstem reflexes can be caused by dissonant sounds. Juslin suggests that this is because 'sensory dissonance is suggestive of "danger" in a natural environment'.[40] Brainstem reflexes can also be caused by sounds that are very sudden, loud, or have a fast or accelerating tempo.

Rhythmic Entrainment

It is assumed that we are equipped with perceptual rhythms that can entrain to rhythmic patterns in our environment.[41] This entrainment can affect our inner bodily rhythms (for example, the heart rate) as well as result in visible, synchronised bodily movement. Entrainment to slow rhythms can be a source of a feeling of calmness, while entrainment to fast rhythms can induce excitement and heightened arousal, and in general can being in 'sync' with music be a source of pleasure.[42]

---

39 Small, p. 2.
40 Juslin, p. 267.
41 Mari Riess Jones and Marilyn Boltz, 'Dynamic Attending and Responses to Time', *Psychological Review*, 96/3 (1989), 459–91, https://psycnet.apa.org/doi/10.1037/0033-295X.96.3.459
42 Juslin, p. 283.

Contagion

When we spend time with someone who is uplifted and happy, we may feel uplifted, and when a person smiles at us, we find it very hard not to smile back. This kind of emotional contagion can also happen through conversations with people who are sad or depressed. It is assumed that our tendency to mimic the expressions of feelings stems from our ability for emotional empathy. This mimicry not only involves a visible physical reaction but also a mirrored emotional response. We do not only automatically react to visible cues like a smile but also to the character of the human voice. Research has shown that the same effect can be found through music. Music with a slow tempo, dull timbre, and with low pitch and sound level may be experienced as sad, while music with a bright timbre, high pitch, fast tempo, and strong sound level tends to be experienced as happy.[43]

Evaluative Conditioning

If you often spend time at a friend's house and they always play a certain kind of music in the background, hearing this music outside of this context may bring back the good feeling associated with being with your friend. This connection often occurs outside of our awareness. Juslin explains:

> Evaluative conditioning refers to a process whereby an emotion is aroused by a piece of music just because this stimulus has been paired, repeatedly, with other positive or negative stimuli, which are not necessarily logically connected to the music in any way.[44]

Thus, contrary to the first three mechanisms, evaluative conditioning may create an emotional response to music that has little to do with the actual musical content. Because evaluative conditioning belongs to our subconscious procedural memory of learned associations, we are often unaware of the link between a stimulus and an associated emotional response, and we may not be able to explain why we have a certain feeling when hearing a specific piece of music.

---

43 Ibid., p. 187; Patrick N. Juslin, and Erik Lindström, 'Musical Expression of Emotions: Modelling Listeners, Judgements of Composed and Performed Features', *Music Analysis*, 29/1-3 (2010), 334–64, https://doi.org/10.1111/j.1468-2249.2011.00323.x

44 Juslin, p. 304.

Episodic Memory

As with evaluative conditioning, episodic memory also involves an association between a stimulus and memory. The difference between the two mechanisms is that, in episodic memory, the association is made with a specific memory. In the case of music, if we hear a song during our first kiss, hearing the same song years later may invoke the memory of that specific kiss. As with evaluative conditioning, a positively valenced episodic memory 'infects' our emotional response to the associated music. We can also have strong episodic musical experiences that make us remember a specific context; when thinking of the context, we can relive the specific episode and the emotional musical experience.

Visual Imagery

We have the ability to imagine scenes that have never happened. We do this by combining memory fragments of things we have experienced, seen, or heard about. Visual imagery involves a process where the listener invokes emotionally laden inner images while listening to music. Juslin refers to three different ways in which images come about: 1) 'Mental imagery may occur when listeners conceptualise the musical structure through a non-verbal mapping between the metaphorical "affordances" of the music and image schemata grounded in bodily experience'.[45] A melody gradually rising in pitch may for example invoke the image of flying higher and higher. 2) Imagery invoked by myths or knowledge about the creation of the music (for example, 'Tears in Heaven' by Eric Clapton or Mozart's Requiem[46]). 3) The listener creates images based on how the music appears to comment or mirror certain aspects of the listener's current life experience. This happens through a metaphorical projection based on musical structures.

Musical Expectancy

Juslin refers to musical expectancy as

> a process whereby an emotion is aroused in a listener because a specific feature of the music violates, delays, or confirms the listener's expectations about the continuation of the music. Every time you hear a piece of music your expectations are raised, based on music you have heard before.[47]

---

[45] Juslin, p. 331; George Lakoff and Mark Johnson, *Metaphors we live by* (Chicago: University of Chicago Press, 2003).

[46] Clapton wrote 'Tears in Heaven' in memory of his son, Conor, who died tragically at the age of 4. When Mozart was commissioned to write a requiem mass, he had deteriorating health. He was convinced that he wrote the requiem for his own funeral.

[47] Juslin, p. 344.

Juslin leans on Leonard B. Meyer's theory of emotional arousal based on inhibited or delayed expectations. According to Meyer, musical expectation is a product of a) primitive perceptual processes, which are the aforementioned gestalt laws of perceptual organisation, and b) expectations based on learned 'schemata'. These schemata include aspects like tonality and structural regularities in specific genres.

Consequences for Discussions on Aesthetics and Musical Meaning

Together with perspectives from sensation and perception, the factors involved in creating musical emotions cast light on our discussion on aesthetics and musical meaning. Contrary to what we have learned about the perceptual and emotional mechanisms involved in an aesthetic experience, Elliott and Silverman, among others, choose to downplay the importance of listening to music as sound. One reason for this can be found in their opposition towards absolutism, as with Elliott and Silverman's attack on the aesthetic work-concept. By associating aesthetics with formalism, intellectualism, and elitism, they seem at the same time to make a wholesale rejection of aesthetics in music education. Instead of seeking musical meaning through an aesthetic attention to the sounding object, they understand musical meaning as something solely socially constructed. This is reflected in the statement referred to earlier: 'Musics can only be understood and experienced in relation to contexts of socio-musical contexts'.[48] Based on what we have learned about emotional mechanisms like evaluative conditioning and episodic memory, there is an obvious problem with giving social context an exclusive role in defining musical meaning; the emotional mechanisms that emphasise social context can create an emotional response that stands in opposition to both the innate and schematic responses that take their input from the sounding object (brainstem reflex, rhythmic entrainment, contagion, visual imagery,[49] musical experience). In accordance with Juslin, emotions stemming from contextually dependent mechanisms 'are not necessarily logically connected to the music in any way'.[50] Hence, when Elliott and Silverman discourage taking an aesthetic attitude towards music and claim that music can only be understood in relation to a socio-musical context, their account of musical meaning is not only flawed but could turn out being musically irrelevant.

The seven emotional mechanisms discussed above work in an interrelated manner where bottom-up, primitive processes meet top-down, learned, schematic processes. Together, they create a rich, compound emotional musical experience. To account for this, we should strive to take a broader, synergistic approach when trying to

---

48   Elliott and Silverman, p. 103.
49   This is a compound mechanism, but the aspect of perceptual affordance in this mechanism points to a strong element of a bodily anchored metaphorical projection that is shared across individuals, and to a certain extent across cultures.
50   Juslin, p. 304.

understand the nature of musical meaning and knowledge. The late American music educator Bennett Reimer upheld the importance of taking a synergistic position in music education philosophy. In *A Philosophy of Music Education*, he quotes Paul G. Woodford and his thoughts about this matter:

> What gets many contemporary critics and theorists into trouble, I think, are their monolithic and dogmatic assertions that all authority is arbitrary and, therefore, suspect, and that absolutely everything is socially constructed [...]. A more reasonable proposition is that we are both processes and products of some complex, even chaotic, mix of biological nature and lived experience.[51]

We know that in the workings of perception, bottom-up and top-down processes interact in the attempt to organise sensory inputs, and we know from the overview of emotional mechanisms in music that both innate and learned factors are involved in creating what we perceive as emotional, meaningful musical experiences. When we assign social construction exclusive rights to define musical meaning, we have a problem.

Although Reimer asks for a synergetic approach, due to a long-lasting view where listening is treated as valid only as a subsidiary of performing and making music,[52] he seeks to bring attention to the importance of aesthetic listening. In fact, he considers the construction of musical meaning as primarily originating from an aesthetic engagement which produces musical feeling:

> Experiencing music as an 'affecting presence'—as a source of meanings gained through feeling—is a primary end of being involved with music [...] musical feeling becoming musical meaning. Music immerses us in the raw reality of feeling—its naked, subtle, exquisite truth, the truth of conscious being. This accounts for its charm and joyousness, and also its profundities and awesomeness—the entire spectrum of aware undergoing. That primal experience of the affecting presence of sounds is what I call 'knowing within' music.[53]

When we turn to the aspect of deep learning in music, we shall bring with us the perspective given by Reimer: it is the affecting presence of sounds that allows for 'knowing within' music.

---

51   Paul G. Woodford, qtd. in Bennett Reimer, *A Philosophy of Music Education: Advancing the Vision*, 3rd edn. (London: Prentice Hall, 2003), p. 75
52   Ibid., p. 110.
53   Ibid., p. 186.

Towards a Deeper Understanding of Music[54]

Structure of Knowledge

The concept of deep learning refers originally to computers and machine learning where the attempt has been to 'mimic the human brain'.[55] Ed Burns, Kate Brush, and Alexander S. Gillis compare deep learning to how a toddler learns the meaning of the word 'dog':

> Deep learning is a type of machine learning and artificial intelligence (AI) that imitates the way humans gain certain types of knowledge. [...] Deep learning enables a computer to learn by example. To understand deep learning imagine a toddler whose first word is *dog*. The parent says, 'Yes, that is a dog,' or, 'No, that is not a dog.' As the toddler continues to point to objects, he becomes more aware of the features that all dogs possess. What the toddler is doing, without knowing it, is clarifying a complex abstraction: the concept of dog. They are doing this by building a hierarchy in which each level of abstraction is created with knowledge that was gained from the preceding layer of the hierarchy.[56]

Christian Janiesch and colleagues describe the essence of the process involved in deep learning like this: 'machine learning seeks to automatically learn meaningful relationships and patterns from examples and observations'.[57] This is similar to what psychologist Keith Sawyer describes as one aspect of deep learning: 'Deep learning requires that learners look for patterns and underlying principles'.[58] It is interesting to note that the American psychologist, Jerome Bruner, already back in the 1960s stressed the importance of students gaining an understanding of the structure of a subject matter:

> Grasping the structure of a subject is understanding it in a way that permits many other things to be related to it meaningfully. To learn structure, in short, is to learn how things are related.[59]

Ironically, this is analogous to what Michael Schneider and Elsbeth Stern, fifty years later, describe as the need for a paradigm shift in education today: 'from the amount of knowledge to the structure of knowledge'.[60] We have seen that the perspectives taken in the new curriculum resemble this, where an interpretation of the concept of deep

---

54 Parts of the discussion are elaborations and developments of some of the perspectives presented in my book about deep learning in music: O. T. Furnes, *Dybdelæring i musikk - musikalsk forståelse gjennom sansning, følelser og begreper* (Oslo: Universitetsforlaget, 2022).
55 IBM, 'What is Deep Learning?', IBM website, n.d., https://www.ibm.com/topics/deep-learning
56 Ed Burns, Kate Brush, and Alexander S. Gillis, 'Deep Learning', *Tech Target Network* website, 2023, https://www.techtarget.com/searchenterpriseai/definition/deep-learning-deep-neural-network
57 Christian Janiesch, Patrick Zschech, and Kai Heinrich, 'Machine Learning and Deep Learning', *Electronic Markets*, 31/3 (2021), 685–95.
58 Sawyer, p. 4.
59 Jerome Bruner, *The Process of Education* (Boston: Harvard University Press, 1990), p. 7.
60 Schneider and Stern, p. 71

learning is to 'develop understanding of key elements and relationships in a subject'.[61] Another aspect involved in definitions of deep learning is that of conceptual learning: 'Deep learning requires that learners integrate their knowledge into interrelated conceptual systems'.[62] An equivalent to this in the Norwegian national curriculum is 'gradually developing knowledge and lasting understanding of concepts, procedures and relationships in the subject and between subject areas'.[63]

If we try to translate all of this to the teaching of music, some will be opposed to deeper learning in music as something that seems to place emphasis on a formalistic and intellectual approach to musical understanding—a conceptual and theoretical knowledge of musical structure. Since Reimer sees musical feelings as the key to 'knowing within' and to musical meaning, he does not support conceptual learning as an end in itself. He does, however, emphasise the role played by 'knowledge about' and 'knowledge why' to enhance 'knowing within'.

> All those learnings (knowing about and knowing why) serve a purpose—the purpose of enhancing the quality of the direct engagement with the sounds of music themselves—of knowing within music. Knowing about and knowing why are means. The end is enhanced knowing within music (and knowing how) in direct, immediate musical experiences.[64]

Knowledge can enhance the perceptual sensitivity,[65] and we know that learned schemata interact with bottom-up, sensory inputs, so when Reimer claimed that knowledge can provide for a richer musical experience, he was on to something. Accordingly, if the aesthetic experience can be enriched and deepened through knowledge, conceptual understanding becomes a factor in musical meaning: 'Teaching for musical meaning requires the use of language as a means to enhance musical experience'.[66]

Deep Learning through Aesthetic Attending

The emphasis on conceptual understanding and learning structure by educators, psychologists, and researchers like Bruner, Sawyer, Schneider, and Stern turns attention toward the key elements in music as a source for acquiring a deeper understanding of music. In terms of conceptual learning, this should not be approached through memorising definitions but can be achieved through implicit learning. This kind of learning involves a process of 'acquiring knowledge about the structure of the environment without conscious awareness, or the non-intentional acquisition of

---

61 Utdanningsdirektoratet, Core curriculum: Competence in the subjects.
62 Sawyer, *The New Science of Learning*, p. 4.
63 Utdanningsdirektoratet, 'Dybdelæring', para 1 and 2 of 4.
64 Reimer, Bennett, *A Philosophy of Music Education: Advancing the Vision*, 3rd edn (London: Prentice Hall, 2003), p. 187.
65 Rasha Abdel Rahman and Werner Sommer, 'Seeing What we Know and Understand: How Knowledge Shapes Perception', *Psychonomic Bulletin and Review*, 15/6, 1055–63, https://doi.org/10.3758/PBR.15.6.1055
66 Reimer, A Philosophy of Music Education, p. 257.

knowledge about structural relations between objects or events'.[67] One kind of implicit learning of concepts is described by cognitive linguists such as Mark Johnson and George Lakoff as part of their theory on embodied cognition.[68] One aspect of this is that meaning arises from bodily experience and is a prerequisite for conceptual understanding: 'Meaning traffics in patterns, images, qualities, feelings, and eventually concepts and propositions'.[69] Johnson further emphasises the bodily component of meaning: 'Meanings emerge "from the bottom up" through increasingly complex levels of organic activity'.[70] Furthermore, he warns against intellectualising conceptual learning:

> I will be using the terms embodied meaning and immanent meaning to emphasize those deep-seated bodily sources of human meaning that go beyond the merely conceptual and propositional. Structures and dimensions of this immanent meaning are what make it possible for us to do propositional thinking. But if we reduce meaning to words and sentences (or to concepts and propositions), we miss or leave out where meaning really comes from. We end up intellectualizing human experience, understanding, and thinking, and we turn processes into static entities or properties.[71]

Inherent in the theory of embodied cognition, as laid out by Lakoff and Johnson, is the role metaphors play in translating bodily experience into conceptual understanding: 'Our ordinary conceptual system, in terms of which we both think and act, is fundamentally metaphorical in nature'.[72] Given that 'metaphor is understanding and experiencing one kind of thing in terms of another',[73] understanding key elements and relationships in music need not be an intellectual and formalised enterprise but can be accomplished through experience translated into images or everyday concepts. The emotional mechanism of visual imagination described earlier is an example of a metaphorical projection from music to visual objects and actions. Juslin explains that 'mental imagery may occur when listeners conceptualise the musical structure through a non-verbal mapping between the metaphorical "affordances" of the music and image schemata grounded in bodily experience'.[74] Thus, in terms of understanding the key elements in music, we can perceive pitch as a physical location in altitude, rhythm as a horizontally moving object, dynamics as the size of an object, or melody as a movement in vertical and horizontal physical space. When listening to the music

---

67 J. S. Freund, 'Learning', in *Encyclopedia of Gerontology*, 2nd edn., ed. by James E. Birren ([n.p.]: Elsevier, 2007), https://doi.org/10.1016/B0-12-370870-2/00106-2
68 George Lakoff and Mark Johnson, *Metaphors we live by* (Chicago: University of Chicago Press, 2003).
69 Mark Johnson, *The Meaning of the Body: Aesthetics of Human Understanding* (Chicago: University of Chicago Press, 2007), p. 9.
70 Ibid., p. 10.
71 Ibid., p. 11.
72 Lakoff and Johnson, p. 3.
73 Lakoff and Johnson, p. 4.
74 Juslin, p. 331.

as one multidimensional object, elements like melody, rhythm, dynamics, and timbre interact in creating rich visualisations of imaginary scenes.[75]

The American philosopher Jerrold Levinson talks about aesthetic attending and appreciation of music and our tendency to hear music as movements:

> we hear motion or movement, of an imaginary or perhaps metaphorical sort, in music: we hear music rising, falling, soaring, plunging, expanding, shrinking, advancing, retreating, rushing, lingering, trudging, leaping, swelling, subsiding, and so on.[76]

Descriptions such as these can be used both to describe gestures both as expressions of musical content and meaning. Levinson even compares aesthetic appreciation to a kind of 'latent dancing':

> musical understanding is itself essentially a kind of latent dancing, whereby one moves with musical movement, but on a psychic or imaginary plane.[77]

Using language to describe music as gestural movements gives us access to our intuitive experience of music and musical expressions. Through metaphorical descriptions, we can communicate both musical movement, expressions, and perceived emotional content (note that there is a difference between perceiving and feeling emotional content).[78]

The Musical Object as a Metaphor

Our discussion has shown that there are ample reasons for talking about music as an object and that this is not an intellectualised, formalised, isolated object deprived of real-life significance. On the contrary, the musical object, as we have discussed here, is essential both to sensation, perception, and emotion and to the construction of musical meaning. Furthermore, if deep learning is to understand key elements, see patterns and relationships, and to acquire a conceptual understanding of the subject's basic structures, then attending to the musical object, its expressive qualities and its multidimensional construction, seems central to a deeper knowledge and an enhanced experience of music. Talking about music as a metaphorical object in terms of size, speed, gestural expressions, etc., we gain an increased understanding of the musical multidimensional object as well as of our perception and interpretation of the music. Both in music education and in artistic research, this kind of aesthetic attention and conceptual interpretation builds knowledge of music, not primarily as a scientific,

---

75 For a more in-depth description of possible metaphors for musical movement and structure, Steve Larson's book *Musical Forces: Motion, Metaphor, and Meaning in Music* (Bloomington: Indiana University Press, 2012) is a suggested starting point.
76 Jerrold Levinson, *Musical Concerns: Essays in Philosophy of Music* (Oxford: Oxford University Press, 2015), 23, https://doi.org/10.1093/acprof:oso/9780199669660.001.0001
77 Ibid., p. 29.
78 Juslin.

formalised object, but as a human expression of ideas and emotions of real life expressed through a metaphorical multidimensional object.

A scientific description of the musical object and its expressed content should therefore be grounded both in the intuitive experience and on experiential and metaphorical descriptions of perceived force, size, and gestural movements. This would help us keep music research and discourse relevant to human experiences. Furthermore, with this as the foundation, when we extend musical research to investigate social and cultural impact, and social construction of musical meaning, we are grounded in an embodied, aesthetic approach to music as sound. A grounding of musical discourse in the embodied, aesthetically perceived, also allows for extending the concept of aesthetics to pragmatist or relational aesthetics, and gives added meaning to concepts like 'musicing', or even the idea of conceptual art.

Understanding the musical object as emerging from our attempt to interpret our auditory surroundings, constructed through gestalt perception, perceived emotional content and as a movement of gestural expression, leaves little room for old accusations; this object is not elitist, intellectual, or opaque to general significance. On the contrary, attending to the musical object in the way described in this chapter, provides for an embodied and aesthetic experience that is perceived as meaningful. Furthermore, when our aesthetic attending is done with an awareness of the movements and gestural, expressive qualities of the different interrelated musical dimensions, we gain a deeper understanding of the structure of music as a multidimensional object. Through language, first with metaphorical descriptions and later with musical terms and concepts, our conceptual understanding of music deepens. Verbal descriptions may in turn enhance our perceptual discrimination and give added depth to our aesthetic experience. This approach answers to definitions of deep learning given in the Norwegian national curriculum: develop 'understanding of key elements and relationships' or 'understanding of concepts, procedures and relationships'.[79]

Deeper Learning in Music for the Future

With deep musical learning, we do not associate 'aesthetics' with a philosophical discourse but with our sensations in meeting with the unfolding musical object together with an attempt to verbalise and conceptualise this experience. This resembles one central point in Chapter 12 in this volume, where Helen Julia Minors encourages us to break down the barriers between critical analysis and performance, and to see aesthetic understanding and performance as integrated curricular elements. The presented perspective on deep learning in music, with its emphasis on combining aesthetic awareness with verbal conceptualisations, may also be one way to remedy Stefan Östersjö's concern regarding the need for to artistic research to enable movement

---

79 Utdanningsdirektoratet, 'Core curriculum', para. 3 of 4.

'between different forms of knowledge [which] is a factor in artistic research that remains in its infancy'.[80]

Deepening our aesthetic awareness together with conceptual insight provides us with important tools for lifelong learning, including the ability to reflect upon our perception and performance. This has been emphasised by Eva Georgii-Hemming et al.: 'Reflection is at the core of lifelong learning and linked to action'.[81] The aspect of lifelong learning is also a central point for Minors when she emphasises 'self-awareness, self-assessment, self-learning and self-branding'[82] as important outcomes of a curriculum that combines aesthetic awareness with critical reflection. Furthermore, with a deepened aesthetic understanding we will be better equipped to meet new and unfamiliar musical expressions, not with judgement, but with curiosity and interest. This can serve as a means for intercultural understanding and assist in reducing Western cultural hegemony in higher music education, a central theme in Sarah-Jane Gibson's chapter, Chapter 11, in this publication.

When discussing lifelong learning and the challenges of the twenty-first century, we need to take the increasing influence of artificial intelligence (AI) into account. We already have AI-powered tools for musicians and producers that can serve as guidance—for example, in practice or mixing. We also see that AI is capable of both composing, producing, and playing sound. The AI output can serve as a starting point for creative discovery or generate a complete musical output on its own. AI already surpasses humans in storing knowledge, and the latest trends in AI research attempt to equip machines with emotions—something that can be tracked in the recent call for abstracts within the theme 'Emotions and Artificial Intelligence' by the journal *Frontiers*. Here we find that the research 'intends to help in the creation of future AIs that are more responsive, empathetic, and intuitive in their interactions with humans'.[83] While this might seem disturbing to both artists and others, we can assume that this 'empathy' at best is recognition and mimicking of human emotions, not actually feeling them. Facing a future where AI is infiltrating our society, our responsibility both as artists, researchers, and teachers for the coming generations involves working along three main strands: 1) While artificial intelligence might surpass humans in 'hard', factual knowledge, we should not fall to the temptation to off-load all cognitive tasks to artificial intelligence and to blindly follow its instructions. Doing this could result in reducing our conceptual understanding of the world around us, including music. Therefore, we need to deepen our embodied conceptual understanding of the

---

80   Stefan Östersjö, 'Art Worlds, Voice and Knowledge: Thoughts on Quality Assessment of Artistic Outcomes', *Online Journal for Artistic Research*, 3/2 (2019), p. 71, https://doi.org/10.34624/impar.v3i2.14152

81   Eva Georgii-Hemming, Karin Johansson, and Nadia Moberg, 'Reflection in Higher Music Education: What, Why, Wherefore?', *Music Education Research*, 22:3 (2022), 245–56, https://doi.org/10.1080/14613808.2020.1766006

82   Helen Julia Minors in Chapter 12 of this volume

83   *Frontiers*, 'Emotions and AI', call for submissions, para 2 of 5, https://www.frontiersin.org/research-topics/56458/emotions-and-artificial-intelligence

structure and inner workings of music as a tool for creative and artistic expression. 2) Machines might be able to mimic human emotions. However, unlike machines, humans have the ability to express actual felt emotions. Thus, upcoming composers and musicians should go beyond reproducing and mimicking genres and expressions of others and turn to an aesthetic awareness and deeper understanding of the music. This allows for making personal aesthetic interpretations that can result in subjective, creative, and artistic expressions of felt emotions. 3) Although artificial intelligences are superior in collecting data and imitating reality, they do not do well in interpreting data in a larger context. This is partly because machine learning systems do not have access to the world of physical, social, and cultural interactions like we do. This should be an incitement to see our role as artists in a broader context as interpreters and communicators of human emotions, relationships, cultures, values, concepts, and ideas. This is where we tap into concepts like 'musicking' and 'relational aesthetics' discussed in this and other chapters in this book.[84]

Since deep learning, as I have discussed it here, seeks to deepen our conceptual understanding, aesthetic awareness, and expressive abilities, it may provide the foundation for lifelong learning for students, artists, researchers and teachers facing both known and unknown challenges throughout the twenty-first century.

References

Abdel Rahman, Rasha, and Werner Sommer, 'Seeing What we Know and Understand: How Knowledge shapes Perception', *Psychonomic Bulletin and Review*, 15/6 (2008), 1055–63, doi.org/10.3758/PBR.15.6.1055

Bregman, Albert, *Auditory Scene Analysis: The Perceptual Organization of Sound* (Massachusetts: MIT Press, 1990)

Bruner, Jerome, *The Process of Education* (Boston: Harvard University Press, 1990)

Burns, Ed, Kate Brush, and Alexander S. Gillis, *Deep Learning*, https://www.techtarget.com/searchenterpriseai/definition/deep-learning-deep-neural-network (2023)

Critical band, *APA Dictionary of Psychology* (American Psychological Association: no date).

Dewey, John, *Art as Experience* (Berkley, CA: Berkley Publishing Group, 2005 (1934)).

Di Bona, Elvira, 'Hearing chimeras', *Synthese*, 200/3, 257 (2022), doi.org/10.1007/s11229-022-03721-y

El Mahgiub, Maruan, *Education: Preparing Students for Jobs that Don't Yet Exist*, TEDxIEMadrid, Madrid, uploaded by Tedx Talks, 4 September 2019. YouTube, https://www.youtube.com/watch?v=uGR4eJmNI90

Elliott, David J., and Marissa Silverman, *Music Matters: A Philosophy of Music Education*, 2nd edn (Oxford: Oxford University Press, 2005)

---

84 See Chapter 10 and Chapter 12.

Eysenck, Michael W., and Mark T. Keane, *Cognitive Psychology: A Student's handbook* (Philadelphia: Psychology Press, 2000)

Freund, J. S., 'Learning', in *Encyclopedia of Gerontology*, 2nd edn, ed. by James E. Birren ([n. p.]: Elsevier, 2007), pp. 23–33, https://doi.org/10.1016/B0-12-370870-2/00106-2

Frontiers, 'Emotions and AI', call for submissions, para 2 of 5, https://www.frontiersin.org/research-topics/56458/emotions-and-artificial-intelligence

Furnes, Odd T., *Dybdelæring i musikk - musikalsk forståelse gjennom sansning, følelser og begreper* (Oslo: Universitetsforlaget, 2022)

Goffin, Kris, and Florian Cova, 'An Empirical Investigation of Guilty Pleasures', *Philosophical Psychology*, 32/7 (2019), 1129–55, doi.org/10.1080/09515089.2019.1646897

Hanslick, Eduard, *On the Musically Beautiful*, trans. by L. Rothfarb and C. Landerer (Oxford University Press, 2018 (1854))

Georgii-Hemming, Eva, Karin Johansson, and Karin Moberg, 'Reflection in Higher Music Education: What, Why, Wherefore? *Music Education Research*, 22:3 (2020), 245-256, doi.org/10.1080/14613808.2020.1766006

Huron, David, 'Tone and Voice: A Derivation of the Rules of Voice-Leading from Perceptual Principles', *Music Perception*, 19/1 (2001), 1–64, https://doi.org/10.1525/mp.2001.19.1.1

IBM, 'What is Deep Learning?', IBM website, n.d., https://www.ibm.com/topics/deep-learning

Janiesch, Christian, Patrick Zschech, and Kai Heinrich, 'Machine learning and deep learning', *Electronic Markets*, 31/3 (2021), 685–95, doi.org/10.1007/s12525-021-00475-2

Johnson, Mark, *The Meaning of the Body: Aesthetics of Human Understanding* (Chicago: University of Chicago Press, 2007)

Jones, Mari and Marilyn Boltz, 'Dynamic Attending and Responses to Time', *Psychological Review*, 96/3 (1989), 459–491, doi.org/10.1037/0033-295x.96.3.459

Juslin, Patrick N., *Musical Emotions Explained: Unlocking the Secrets of Musical Affect* (Oxford: Oxford University Press, 2019)

Juslin, Patrick N., and Erik Lindström, 'Musical Expression of Emotions: Modelling Listeners, Judgements of Composed and Performed Features', *Music Analysis*, 29/1-3 (2010), 334–64, doi.org/10.1111/j.1468-2249.2011.00323.x

Koffka, Kurt, *Principles of Gestalt psychology* (London: Routledge, 1999)

Lakoff, George and Mark Johnson, *Metaphors We Live By* (Chicago: University of Chicago Press, 2003)

Larson, Steve, *Musical Forces: Motion, Metaphor, and Meaning in Music* (Bloomington: Indiana University Press, 2012)

Levinson, Jerrold, *Musical Concerns: Essays in Philosophy of Music* (Oxford: Oxford University Press, 2015), doi.org/10.1093/acprof:oso/9780199669660.001.0001

Meyer, Leonard B., *Emotion and Meaning in Music* (Chicago: University of Chicago Press, 1956)

Munro, T. et al, 'Aesthetics', in *Encyclopedia Britannica*, https://www.britannica.com/topic/aesthetics

Narmour, Eugene, 'The Top-down and Bottom-up Systems of Musical Implication: Building on Meyer's Theory of Emotional Syntax', *Music Perception*, 9/1 (1991), 1–26, doi.org/10.2307/40286156

Pickles, James O., 'Auditory pathways: anatomy and physiology', *Handbook of Clinical Neurology* 129 (2015), 3–25. doi.org/10.1016/B978-0-444-62630-1.00001-9

Reimer, Bennett, *A Philosophy of Music Education: Advancing the Vision*, 3rd edn (London: Prentice Hall, 2003)

Sawyer, R. Keith, 'Introduction: The New Science of Learning', in *The Cambridge Handbook of the Learning Sciences*, ed. by Keith Sawyer (Cambridge: Cambridge University Press, 2014), 1–16, doi.org/DOI:10.1017/CBO9780511816833.002

Schellenberg, E. Glenn, 'Simplifying the Implication-Realization Model of Melodic Expectancy', *Music Perception*, 14 (1997), 295–318, doi.org/10.2307/40285723

Schleicher, Andreas, *The Case for 21st-century Learning*. OECD.org. (2022) https://www.oecd.org/general/thecasefor21st-centurylearning.htm

Schneider, Michael and Stern, Elsbeth, 'The Cognitive Perspective on Learning: Ten Cornerstone Findings', in *The Nature of Learning: Using Research to Inspire Practice* OECD, ed. by O. f. E. Co-Operation & Development (2011), 69–90

'Sensation', *Merriam-Webster Dictionary*, 2022, website, https://www.merriam-webster.com/dictionary/sensation

Shimamura, Arthur P., *Experiencing Art: In the Brain of the Beholder* (Oxford: Oxford University Press, 2013)

Small, Christopher, *Musicking: The Meanings of Performing and Listening* (Middletown, CT: Wesleyan University Press, 1998)

Tarasti, Eero, *Signs of Music: A Guide to Musical Semiotics* (The Hague: De Gruyter Mouton, 2002), doi.org/10.1515/9783110899870

Terhardt, Ernst, 'The Concept of Musical Consonance: A Link between Music and Psychoacoustics', *Music Perception*, 1/3 (1984), 276–95, doi.org/10.2307/40285261

Utdanningsdirektoratet, 'Core Curriculum: Competence in the Subjects', 2019, https://www.udir.no/lk20/overordnet-del/prinsipper-for-laring-utvikling-og-danning/kompetanse-i-fagene/?lang=eng

Utdanningsdirektoratet, '(MUS01-02) Curriculum for Music: Core elements', 15 November 2019, https://www.udir.no/lk20/mus01-02/om-faget/kjerneelementer?lang=eng

Utdanningsdirektoratet, 'Dybdelæring', 13 March 2019, https://www.udir.no/laring-og-trivsel/dybdelaring/

Walker, Kerry M., Ray Gonzalez, Joe Z. Kang, Josh H. McDermott, and Andrew King, 'Across-Species Differences in Pitch Perception are Consistent with Differences in Cochlear Filtering', *Elife*, 8 (2019), doi.org/10.7554/elife.41626

Woodford, Paul G., 'Living in a Postmusical Age: Revisiting the Concept of Abstract Reason', *Philosophy of Music Education Review*, 7/1 (1999), 3–18

Östersjö, Stefan, 'Art Worlds, Voice and Knowledge: Thoughts on Quality Assessment of Artistic Outcomes', *Online Journal for Artistic Research*, 3/2 (2019), 60–89, doi.org/10.34624/impar.v3i2.14152

10. Rethinking Music Performance Education Through the Lens of Today's Society

Randi Margrethe Eidsaa and Mariam Kharatyan

This chapter aims to shed light on perspectives that emerged through the data collection and analysis conducted by the Norwegian team of the Erasmus+ Project REACT (Rethinking Music Performance in European Higher Education Music Institutions). The team gathered data within a series of small-scale studies which includes REACT-network activity at the University of Agder and the Academy of Music in Oslo, conversations with a group of fourteen music students at the University of Agder, Kristiansand, and a report analysis after the students had participated in a creative ensemble project. In the introduction, we also refer to a small curriculum study at the University of Agder which dealt with some of the educational demands that emerged from the extensive research on music performance curriculum and pedagogy in Higher Music Education in the early, mid, and late 2010s.[1]

In the second section, data from the stakeholder interviews in June 2021 will be discussed to shed light on our two main research questions: 1) in what way could the music education curricula be strengthened to support students entering their professional music careers, and (2) in what way could we expand students' musical thinking and prepare them to become contributors in society.

The third section exemplifies how issues related to the research questions were explored when music students from the University of Agder participated in the

---

1 Rosie Perkins, 'Rethinking career for Music Students. Identity and Vision', in Dawn Bennett, *Life in the Real World. How to Make Music Students Employable* (Champaign, IL: Common Ground Research Network, 2012), pp. 11–25; Dawn Bennett and Ruth Bridgestock, 'The Urgent Need for Career Preview: Expectation and Graduate Realities in Music and Dance', *International Journal of Music Education*, 33/3 (2014), 263–77; Tony Woodcock, 'REVIEW External Evaluator Report', Association Européenne Music des Conservatoires, Academies de Musique et Musikhochschulen, Jorn Schau and Randi Margrethe Eidsaa, 'Higher Music Performance Education in a Changing World: Towards a New Curriculum?', in *Music Education in XXI-st Century. New Challenges and Perspectives*, ed. by Mikolai Rikovsky, Poznan: Akademia Muzyczna im. I. J. Paderewskiego w Poznaniu, 2021), pp. 195–208.

interdisciplinary and socially engaging project *Music for Microsculptures* in 2020. The project was presented to the students as a curriculum component in the Year 1 course module *Musical Communication* in the bachelor's programme in Music Performance at the University of Agder. The students' reflections on the practice experience illuminate results from the analysis of the stakeholders' interviews and aspects often commented on in research on music performance curricula in Higher Education.

In the concluding section, we connect our findings of the REACT Report,[2] and in particular we return to the outcomes of the Norwegian study and related it to essential issues which have emerged in international research on music performance education during the last decades and were recognized as central values of the Erasmus+ project REACT–Rethinking Music Performance in European Higher Education Institutions. We highlight how novel approaches to music performance, such as community-based perspectives, creative ensemble collaborations, and improvisation in students' music educational activities, address challenges that occur on the students' path when entering professional careers in music today.

Background

During the last decades, music performance programmes in Western Classical Music in several higher education institutions in Europe have been revised to include a broader perspective on music performance. The traditional music conservatoire model, which highlighted performance skills on the student's main instrument, has been challenged.[3] Revisions have added new components to the curricula, such as creative music-making in ensembles, collaborations with outside campus groups, digital approaches to musical presentations and composition, multidisciplinary, multimodal performance concepts, and business and entrepreneurial knowledge.[4] Through the

---

2   Jorge Correia and others, REACT–Rethinking Music Performance in European Higher Education Institutions, *Artistic Career in Music: Stakeholders Requirement Report* (Aveiro: UA Editora, 2021), p. 20, https://doi.org/10.48528/wfq9-4560

3   Perkins, 'Rethinking career for Music Students', 2012; June Boyce-Tillman, 'The Complete Musician: The Formation of the Professional Musician', in *Musician–Teacher Collaborations. Altering the Chord*, ed. by Christophersen, Catharina, Kenny, Ailbhe (New York: Routledge, 2018), pp. 108–20; Jon Helge Sætre, Stefan Gies, Anna Maria Bordin, Lars Brinck, Karine Hahn, Siri Storheim, Stabell van Els Susanne, and Ellen Mikalsen, 'The Music Performance Student as Researching Artist? Perspectives on Student-Centeredness in Higher Music Education', in *Becoming Musicians: Student Involvement and Teacher Collaboration in Higher Music Education*, ed. by Stefan Gies and Jon Helge Sætre ([n. p.]: NMH publications, 2019), pp. 173–96.

4   Pamela Burnard, and Elizabeth Haddon, 'Introduction: The Imperative of Musical Creativities in Academia and Industry', in *Activating Diverse Musical Creativities* (Bloomsbury Collections, 2015), pp. 3–18; Woodcock, 'External Evaluator Report'; Stefan Gies, 'How Music Performance Education became Academic: On the History of Music in Higher Education in Europe', in *Becoming Musicians: Student Involvement and Teacher Collaboration in Higher Music Education*, ed. by Stefan Gies and Jon Helge Sætre ([n. p.]: NMH publications, 2019), pp. 31–51; Schau and Eidsaa, 'Higher Music Performance Education in a Changing World: Towards a New Curriculum?' in *Music E-ducation in XXI-st Century. New Challenges and Perspectives*, ed. by Mikolaj Rykowski (2021) Poznan: Akademia Muzyczna im. I. J. Paderewskiego w Posnaniu, 2021), pp. 195–208.

development of digital communication, contemporary society has become increasingly complex, in ways that also affect the art worlds in which institutions and individual artists develop their practices,[5,6,7] and these developments have caused a shift in the nature of job opportunities in the music industry. In response to these challenges, HME must challenge their students to develop a wide portfolio and to embrace diverse skills that allow them to engage in new and a wider range of musical practices.[8] Based on this understanding, students in higher music performance education should be challenged to explore their future careers as musicians from a starting point where they recognize the complex challenges and opportunities of the performing arts in a context of turbulent global change.[9]

In 2015, one of the authors and two colleagues at the Faculty of Fine Arts at the University of Agder established a module within a three-year bachelor programme to highlight a broader conceptualization of music performance than the traditional music conservatoire model. The members of the groups had a critical approach to the main instrument focus in the curriculum. Among the sources of inspiration were Christopher Small's concept of 'musicking',[10] the notion of 'community music',[11] 'relational aesthetics',[12] and collaborative and creative approaches to composition.[13] The students were exposed to ensemble collaborations, creative orientations in

---

5   Anne Bamford, *The Wow Factor Global Research Compendium on the Impact of the Arts in Education* (Münster: Waxman Verlag GmbH, 2006).

6   Nic Beech, Stephen Broad, Ann Cunliffe, Celia Duffy, Charlotte Gilmore, 'Development in organization theory and organizing music', in *Organising Music. Theory, Practice, Performance*, ed. by Nic Beech and Charlotte Gilmore (Cambridge, Cambridge University Press, 2015), pp. 1–24.

7   Matthew Doran Thibeault, 'Music Education in the Post-Performance World', in *The Oxford Handbook of Music Education*, 2 vols, ed. by Gary E. McPherson and Graham Welch (Oxford: Oxford University Press, 2012), ii, pp. 517–30.

8   Dawn Bennett, and Ruth Bridgestock, 'The Urgent Need for Career Preview: Expectation and Graduate Realities in Music and Dance', in *International Journal of Music Education*, 33/3 (2014), 263–77; Margarita de Reizábal, Gomés Lorenzo, Manuel Benito, 'When Theory and Practice Meet: Avenues for Entrepreneurship Education in Music Conservatories', in *International Journal of Music Education*, 38/3 (2020), 352–69; Helena Gaunt, Celia Duffy, Ana Čorić, Isabel R. Gonzáles Delgado, Linda Messas, Oleksandr Pryimenko, and Henrik Sveidahl, 'Musicians as Makers in Society: A Conceptual Foundation for Contemporary Professional Higher Music Education', in *Frontiers in Psychology*, 12 (2021), 1–20.

9   Gaunt and others, 'Musicians as Makers', p. 1.

10 Christopher Small, *Musicking: The Meanings of Performing and Listening* (Middletown, CT.: Wesleyan University Press, 1998).

11 Lee Higgins, 'The Community within Community Music, in *The Oxford Handbook of Music Education*, 2 vols., ed. by Gary E. McPherson and Graham Welch (Oxford: Oxford University Press, 2012) ii, pp. 104–19; Kari Veblen, 'Emerging Trends in Community Music', in *The Oxford Handbook of Music Education*, 2 vols, ed. by Gary E. McPherson and Graham Welch (Oxford: Oxford University Press, 2012), ii, pp. 203–20.

12 Nicholas Bourriaud, *Relasjonell estetikk* (Oslo: Pax, 2007).

13 Anna Craft, *Creativity in Schools. Tensions and Dilemmas* (Oxon: Routledge, 2005); Martin Fautley and Jonathan Savage, *Creativity in Secondary Education* (Exeter: Learning Matters, 2007); Bernadette Colley, Randi Margrethe Eidsaa, Ailbe Kenny, Bo Wah Leung, 'Creativity in partnership practices', in *Creativities, Technologies, and Media in Music Learning and Teaching. An Oxford Handbook of Music Education*, 2 vols, ed. by Gary E. McPherson and Graham Welch (Oxford: Oxford University Press 2018), ii, pp. 95–112.

music-making, participatory performance models, interdisciplinarity concepts, and cultural entrepreneurship.[14]

In 2018, the bachelor's programme was revised based on the students' and teachers' evaluations as well as insight from the international field of research in music performance education. The importance of, for example, preparing students for graduate realities by teaching entrepreneurship and multiple roles,[15] introducing creative ensemble projects and collaboration strategies,[16] and developing contextual competence,[17] were the starting points for the curriculum revision at the University of Agder.

One of the sources of inspiration was the Erasmus+ Project for Strategic Partnership RENEW–*Reflective Entrepreneurial Music Education World Class*. This project analysed the data of recent graduates, exploring what careers graduates went into and what form those careers took, notably that portfolio careers for performers were now the most common graduate outcome from performers from UK Conservatoires. In a review of the project, Tony Woodcock questions the musician's role in the contemporary world, asking which skills are needed for a musician to function in society and if the students are given these skills through our bachelors' and masters' programmes.[18] Woodcock argues that a more integrated learning approach could be redefined as 'contemporary skills' (Chapter 12 of this book also tackles these questions, referencing the 'Future Skills' programme presented to the UK Government by Kingston University). He mentions:

> ensemble playing, the ability to play in any genre from pop, hardcore, contemporary to early music staging and production, story creation, ear training and planning, music history, click tracks, etudes, and creative writing, duos, and technology.[19]

Corresponding issues are discussed by Sætre et al., who focused on the need to involve the students in improvisation, composing, the use of digital technology, contextualising music in broader fields of theory, and looking for new ways of working and understanding in and with the arts.[20]

---

14 Jorn Schau and Randi Margrethe Eidsaa, 'Higher Music Performance Education in a Changing World: Towards a New Curriculum?', in *Music Education in XXI-st Century. New Challenges and Perspectives*, ed. by Mikolai Rikovsky (Poznan: Akademia Muzyczna im. I. J. Paderewskiego w Poznaniu,, 2021), pp. 195–208.
15 Bennett and Bridgestock.
16 Sawyer; Burnard and Haddon.
17 Boyce-Tillman.
18 Woodcock, p. 12.
19 Ibid., p. 7.
20 Sætre et al., 'Higher Music Performance Education', p. 27.

Methods and Design

This chapter draws on analysis of a series of smaller case studies as part of the REACT Training School. Data was collected using a series of different approaches: interviews related to the initial stage of the REACT project resulting in the Stakeholders Requirements Report;[21] interviews with the student participants in the REACT Training School; an analysis of the same students' reflexive reports after taking part in the creative, interdisciplinary ensemble project *Music for Microsculpture* in September 2020. Below, we provide details of the design of each case study and outline who the stakeholders and students for these were.

In June 2021, the Norwegian partners of the REACT team interviewed fourteen stakeholders to investigate perspectives on Higher Music Education Institutions (HMEIs) in Norway. The interviews were conducted as a sub-project in the frame of the first phase of the REACT project (see the Introduction to this book). The empirical data includes qualitative semi-structured interviews with fourteen stakeholders—music performance students, alumni, composers, course directors, representatives for funding, and teachers in higher music education. These stakeholders' ages range from twenty-five to sixty-five years, and several stakeholders have multiple professional roles including teaching, leading, managing and administering. The list below provides detailed information about participants and their roles related to music performance and education:

- Two music performance students (female, Masters' programme, in data marked as S1 and S2)
- Two teachers (female and male, involved in relevant subjects/modules in Music Performance Education, T1 and T2)
- Two teachers (male, course director, involved in curriculum development in Music Performance Education, T3 and T4)
- One alumnus (female, established as teacher and freelance musician, A)
- Two music career coaches/teachers (male, director at Cultural School; female, teacher, MC1 and MC2)
- Two funding establishment professionals (female, director at a Cultural Funding Board, F1); female, representative of funding and freelance musician, F/M2)
- One concert production manager (male, working within Music Performance Education, established concert production company, as well as teacher and concert producer, CPM)

---

21 Jorge Correia and others, REACT–Rethinking Music Performance in European Higher Education Institutions, *Artistic Career in Music: Stakeholders Requirement Report* (Aveiro: UA Editora, 2021), https://doi.org/10.48528/wfq9-4560

- Two composers (male, teacher in Music Performance Education and musician at a Symphony Orchestra; and female, teacher in Music Performance Education and freelance musician, C1 and C2).

This chapter also builds on data collected from qualitative interviews with twelve students in the second year of the Bachelor programme during and after they participated in the first REACT Training School, which took place at the University of Agder in December 2021. The interviews were conducted as focus-group interviews in December 2021 and February 2022. The data that has been collected in the frame of REACT training school in Norway are stored and available upon request, as well as reviewed by the Research and Innovation Department at the University of Agder and The Research Dean at the Faculty of Fine Arts. All answers of participants were presented anonymously, and the participants had the right to withdraw at any time, without any further explanation. Furthermore, we have included an analysis of the same student group's practice reports that reflect on experiences from the project *Music for Microsculptures*. In addition to being a mandatory curriculum component, the project was connected to the University of Agder programme 'Students in Research Projects 2020'. The participants were informed that their reflection reports would be included as empirical data in a research project exploring novel approaches to musical presentations in the Bachelor programme in classical music performance. The students were invited to comment on the lecturers' data collection and analysis including photos and video recordings and presented their written consent to our use of their data.

The REACT Project and the Stakeholder Interviews

In this section, we show the results of our analysis of the stakeholder interviews, illustrating what challenges to music performance education were identified. The team's point of departure was the realisation that musicians in the twenty-first century need a broader set of skills than those traditionally offered through existing courses and curricula to flourish in diverse working contexts.

The informants were involved in studying, performing, teaching, or producing music, focusing on Western Classical music. Based on the analysis of these interviews, several essential aspects emerged related to the development of students' musical and artistic skills and skills that are directly related to the role of the musician in society: 1) the need to prepare and maintain music students' high-performance level/skills on their main instruments, and meanwhile, implementing flexible creative approaches into teaching practices that include ensemble performance and interdisciplinary collaboration; 2) rethinking today's music performance education to enhance our understanding of its relationship to employability skills for a contemporary society (also discussed in Chapter 12); 3) students developing communication competencies/skills in digital technology in Higher Music Education Institutions (HMEIs).

While programmes in HME aim to provide the students with solid musical and technical performance skills and knowledge, several challenges were identified in the interviews; the increasingly competitive music industry. A course director, responsible for curriculum development in HMEIs (T3), identified the main challenges in the contemporary music performance context as:

> One challenge is to get through with music as a 'product' in a market that consists of many employers, when the offerings to potential target and audience groups are rapidly growing, and where the complexity of music, art, and cultural life is increasing. Educational institutions in classical music usually cultivated performer traditions and instrumental skills with the need within the traditional producing art institutions (symphony orchestra, opera, etc.) or for traditional solo activities. The master/apprentice tradition and the principle of reproduction that have been the basis for generations still prevail.

Another stakeholder, who is a teacher and course director (T4), mentioned the decreasing number of positions in classical music's labour market, and stated that:

> The number of performing positions in traditional producing art institutions such as orchestras and operas, etc. is declining concerning the fact that the number of performing music education is continuously increasing. In a global labor market in classical music, competition for institutional jobs is fierce. At the same time, we see that the openness, job opportunities, and thus the need associated with the free field of art and music increase in complexity and size. An increasing number of musicians will need a broader and more updated orientation than what we offer today if the goal is for them to make a living from music. Concerning the actual labor market and the further development of this—it will be a challenge for many performing musicians to enhance their competencies to more and new types of musical performing and artistic tasks and work situations.

The informants highlighted the importance of introducing students to cross-disciplinary practices and critical thinking. According to one of the stakeholders (a music career coach and teacher, marked as MC2 in the data) 'the student's educational path seems to be too narrow concerning the work-life that they face after graduation'.

An example of ensuring cross-disciplinary practices can be seen in the bachelor's programme in music performance at the University of Agder which offers the choice between one main instrument and two other music subjects. These can be other instruments, composition, conducting or classical music improvisations or similar combinations. Additional opportunities for the students' development can come from closer collaboration with music organisations through, for example, professional internships, work placements, that could assist to create a smoother transition for students from apprenticeship into the professional industries.

One of the students (S1) underlined the importance of not compromising the level of technical skills, which, according to her, could happen when incorporating novel approaches into the curriculum such as cross-disciplinary collaborations. The student argued that 'there is the clear need for finding new ways of thinking within the institutions for a greater degree of collaborating across disciplines, however, the requirements for instrumental technical skills cannot be weakened'. A contrasting view was put forth by another student (S2) who noted the need to 'teach the ability to tailor their outstanding artistic performance to the time, place, and social context, and to learn how to produce concerts and delegate responsibilities and build teams around them so they can function in ensembles'.

Many students were concerned about how the embedding of employability skills would impact their music education, considering their main focus is that of instrumental practice wishing to preserve traditional teaching practices: 'The educational institutions are cultural libraries that preserve the tradition and should not let go of these music traditions, but balance between the old culture and the new innovative concepts', said one of the master students (S2). Another student, however, argued for the need to revise the traditional conservatory model since the needs of musicians and society have changed.

Nearly every respondent, in one way or another, voiced the need for closer contact between the professional musical industries and the music performance education institutions. Several stakeholders criticised music performance programmes in HMEIs for not promoting a holistic approach to music. One commented that 'too many musicians are trained with the same, somewhat limited and directional competence', and identified two significant issues, firstly that 'the institutions prepare the upcoming musician for working in traditional producing art institutions' and secondly that the instrument teachers highlight the 'solo performance' as the pertinent performance concept. The curricula should offer subjects that prepare students for their future professional career. A stakeholder observed how, in the classical music industry:

> The perspective of craftsmanship is still stronger than the artist's perspective, which gives much focus on instrumental, technical perfection, and the globalized standard of excellence. There are few conversations about how to develop as an artist in an educational trajectory, an artist who has something in mind, who has a voice and can contribute with artistic utterances, create space, and place, and create a movement in the world.[22]

Our research on professional careers in music in Norway holds similarities with international researchers' reports highlighting upcoming musicians' need to be prepared for portfolio careers.

One of the stakeholders refers to Christophers Small's key concept of 'musicking' (also discussed in the preceding chapter) and its critique of the concert-hall tradition, contrasting the latter's socially constructed nature. The stakeholder, a teacher in HME (T1) also claimed that:

> They (the students) need competencies about how music is used as a tool in different contexts and institutions, for example in hospitals and old people's homes. We need more of a 'community music' mindset, for example, more knowledge about music and health. Future musicians need to have flexibility as their core skill.

---

22   Representative for funding/musician, F/M2.

This comment is valuable since it voices many neglected aspects which have not traditionally been part of the conservatoire curriculum. It is important that the innovative curriculum engages with placements in: elderly people's care centres, asylum centres, orphanages, and young or adult people in prisons and correctional centres. The point of this, in response to the stakeholder interviews, is that our students are encouraged to engage with wider audiences which reflect contemporary societal needs. These perspectives resonate with Gaunt et al. who underlined that:

> Musicking refocuses attention to the social, interactive, and actively participatory nature of music-making in diverse contexts, and is particularly valuable in that it may equally apply to music- making in concert venues and to music-making for example in informal workshop settings. Thus, it offers a powerful foundation from which to bring the continuum of art for art's sake through to art for social purpose into focus within HME.[23]

One of the alumni (A) voiced a serious issue that was present in their music educational experience:

> Those who need to speak are not allowed to do so. There are small adjustments that allow you to get in touch with your inner core as a musician, and then the moment you are in touch with it, you understand why you play. Then you can take ownership of your education. A twenty-year-old student should not be able to answer big questions, but being asked questions at the right time is quite crucial.

The issue here is the lack of engagement with the student voice (as discussed in this part) and the need for teachers in HME to work in more collaborative ways. In other words, the changes we are hoping to achieve within our student body must also be achieved amongst the staff. The change in music teaching approaches is not easy to achieve at the institutional level, but personal pedagogic changes can be made by all HME teachers.

One of the stakeholders emphasised that if we want creative and reflective performers, their teachers also need to develop their critical thinking. Music performance education has been too much focused on instrumental skills. A representative for funding and a professional musician (F/M2) emphasises: 'they must sharpen their thinking to practice their music with a greater awareness of their own choices and communicate the context in which they stand. The 'neutrality' that musicians claim they have through the 'autonomy of music' does not exist'.[24] This stakeholder further emphasised the need for developing music students' ability to contextualise their music performance practice, which demands the integration of wider sociological and philosophical perspectives in students' education. Another stakeholder challenged the limited curricula for performance education, and the main challenge is what is *not* offered—the importance of building bridges between education and society's professional demands. Some students graduate, after six years of executive education, without having outside practice projects

---

23 Gaunt et al., p. 6
24 Representative for funding and professional musician (F/M2).

and insight into music and cultural life as an industry. A teacher and course director responsible for curriculum and development at HMEI (T3) says:

> The students lack qualifications of social knowledge, insight into financing opportunities, and how they can work in society. Unfortunately, these elements are not strong enough to be integrated into compulsory subjects. Thus, there is a shortage in the current performance education.

When it comes to communication competencies, it is not only crucial for students to have the ability to connect the different disciplines and placing own music practice into a larger context and cross-disciplinary settings, but also it is crucial to have skills within digital technology, its impact on the music industry and gain knowledge and necessary skills within music digitalization. In light of the COVID-19 pandemic and the flourishing of online concerts streaming, music teaching, and even ensembles and choirs practising together, teachers became experts in using the technology for their music teaching and lectures in a very short time. Those active implementations of the digital/online possibilities (with all its limitations as well) underline that it is time to make a solid space in curricula of classical music students and give them the necessary skills to survive in the digital realm of today's society. As one of the stakeholders, a concert producer and teacher (CPM), mentioned:

> We need to understand how to communicate in digital media with streaming. It is a case of being 'live' and present via 'streaming' to promote one's own art and music in today's world. One must face the global changes that are happening both with technology and with the industry since we are affected by the trends and economic situation in Europe. If we are to improve music education, we must address these challenges in our education and find solutions.

The Stakeholder's Requirement Report, Artistic Career in Music published in 2021 by Editora at the University of Aveiro proposes the need to be proactive in relation to the professional industries:

> It is pertinent that musicians understand the role of music and that of the musician in today's society and learn of their historical function. The learning experience should be related to the professional demands of society, social knowledge, insight into financial opportunities, and working environments. Furthermore, education should be based on a holistic learning experience, one that helps guide students toward an interdisciplinary understanding of music and other art forms and one that relates and prioritizes research and development with musical entrepreneurship. This, in turn, would allow them to become more flexible and versatile musicians/performers leading to originality and individuality.[25]

To summarise the crucial points from the interviews carried out with the Norwegian stakeholders: it is vital to nurture high-level music performance skills in students

---

25   Correia and others, p. 15.

while also embedding a creative and flexible mindset in various contexts beyond solo performance. We propose that we should rethink today's performance education and the role of music and musicians in society through the approach of a holistic learning experience.

Bachelor Students' Creative Music-Making Project in 2020

To provide some further examples of students' experiences, we will in the following section provide some results drawn from the project created at the Department of Classical Music and Music Education at the Faculty of Fine Arts, the University of Agder and called *Music for Microsculpture*. The project sought to expand the students' musical thinking and aimed to prepare them to develop more socially grounded musical practices. The students were introduced to a learning environment that demanded competencies described by June Boyce-Tillman as 'necessary for working outside the professional musical world: contextual, pedagogic, artistic/creative, research, social, project management'.[26]

As described in our chapter introduction, the Department of Classical Music and Music Education at the Faculty of Fine Arts, the University of Agder has investigated diverse musical practices as curricular activities in the Bachelor in Classical Music Performance Programme. Thus, *Music for Microsculptures* sought to create opportunities for the students and teachers to explore novel approaches to concert production and music performance beyond score-based music in traditional solo or ensemble recitals.[27]

The following section briefly explains the educational foundation for the project. Thereafter, we present empirical data, which shows how the students experienced problem-solving, dialogues, and conceptual inquiry as a methodological framework for creating a concert.[28]

In *Music for Microsculpture*, the students were responsible for creating a twenty-five-minute music performance connected to a current museum exhibition and presented the resulting performance in the exhibition hall to a kindergarten audience. For the 2020 session, the Museum presented *Microsculptures*, a collection of large insect images made by the British photographer Levon Biss, a collaborator with the Oxford University Museum of Natural History in the UK. His pictures show the specimen enlarged multiple times with colours and forms invisible to the human eye. The students were required to consider how to create an appropriate performance for the setting and for their audience. This task demanded collaboration—which entailed relational dimensions such as student-student, student-teacher, student-museum-staff, student-exhibition objects, and student-audience—as the participants searched

---

26 Boyce-Tillman, 2018, p. 108.
27 Burnard and Haddon; Boyce-Tillman; Woodcock; Hahn; Gaunt et al.
28 Hahn.

for possible relationships between the museum objects and music, investigating and developing a contextually appropriate repertoire related to the kindergarten audience.

The main objective of the project was to create a learning environment that would promote an experience of student ownership and responsibility as well as the opportunity to experiment.[29] The contextual situation (a public setting with a specific audience) demanded student collaboration, contextual awareness, communication with children, as well as a need to document the experience in a reflective and evaluative report for assessment. Most of these students were previously experienced in solo performances and ensemble work with standard classical repertoires. When confronted with the Levon Biss images and a kindergarten audience each student was expected to work beyond their prior experience of traditional performance of repertoire. *Music for Microsculptures* demanded a contextual approach and personal authenticity to work toward an effective performance.[30]

The quotations below are selected from the students' reflective reports in order to show how they engaged with the project. Some students used traditional classical music repertoire as a point of departure for the project work, while others perceived the image colours and shapes as inspiration for improvisation:

> Bright colors contrast with the dimmed light and dark background, all while carrying a theme of insects. Some of the first ideas were obvious, we were thinking about just a repertoire based around animals, forests, bugs, and playing.

> The first thing that came to my mind when I searched for repertoire for the *Microsculptures* exhibition was fast music, such as Flight of the Bumblebee. I thought that the music should include cheerful and fun elements to bring out the animals' pleasure of living, running, and flying around.

While the quotations above mirror students' knowledge of the classical music canon, we also distinguish a contextual approach considering both ecological elements and connections between various aesthetic expressions:

> *Microsculpture* made me envision new ways to use the instruments. I would try to imitate the sound I imagined the insects made, to recreate the moods the picture gave me or a combination of these two.

Instead of choosing a composition based on 'music alone',[31] this student was inspired to explore the instrument's possibility as a tool for communicating imaginative impressions. Another student used the images as signposts for his compositional process. He describes his creative process as follows:

> By looking at the detailed insects, many associations popped into my head. I filmed the insect I was thinking about while I said aloud what I associated it with. I could look at it

---

29 Sætre et al., p. 22.
30 Ibid., p. 23.
31 Boyce-Tillman.

later and use the association as inspiration for a composition. As an example, one of the insects made me think about Vikings, and another made me think of a Chinese woman.

One of the students was fascinated by the image colours and details, which became her source of inspiration:

> The artist's eye for detail inspired me to prepare for the project. This gave me many ideas on how we could implement the focus on details in our project. This and the striking colors that were such a nice contrast to the overall black were decisive for how I approached the project.

The students' comments above indicate how the Levon Biss images served as elements from which they picked up information to create the result, which ended up as a fairytale-like narrative presented in between the instrumental pieces *Morning Mood* (Grieg), *Waltz* from Jazz suite No 2 by Shostakovich, and *Prelude no 4 for Guitar* by Villa-Lobos, snippets from three well-known children's songs with re-written lyrics, and three instrumental improvisations. The students moved to various positions in the exhibition hall while inviting the children to follow.

Fig. 10.1: Jewel Longhorn Beetle and double bass (used with permission from the photographer, McKnox.no).

We recognize the stakeholder's term 'community music mindset' as a reference to a value shift that has become evident in research in music performance education during the last decades (discussed in Chapter 11). The notion of the musician as a 'maker in society', opens up to a mindset understanding music as an inclusive practice, as Gaunt et al. promoted:

> diverse ways for example into programming and engaging with audiences or incorporating improvisatory dimensions as well as new composition into performance; equally it opens up completely different ways of engaging with communities, collaborating or co-creating with them, and evolving practices organically. The "musician as a maker" foregrounds the importance of developing a relationship, individually and collectively as a community of practice, both with musical traditions and with the possibilities and demands of contemporary situations.[32]

In recent decades, music education researchers have discussed relationships and music performance.[33] *Music for Microsculptures* offered a performance setting in which relational skills could be developed. One student exposed uncertainty about finding a repertoire to 'match with the venue and the target audience'. Such concerns for how the performance might eventually communicate with the children audience was evident in several student reflections:

> When I first got the assignment, I must admit that I was not particularly inspired. I thought it would never work. When we talked together in small groups, I experienced that the ideas came flowing.

> When we started, I was worried that the story we had created was too complicated and that the children would not understand what was going on. When performing for such a young audience as we did, it is important to choose music that does not demand specific skills to enjoy.

The *Music for Microsculptures* project was intended as an arena for experiencing collaborative activities and community music perspectives, as articulated by one of the students:

> We strived to provide a group of five-year-olds with a pleasant experience of how beautiful and musical nature is, with the opportunity to experience the various instruments' unique sounds, shapes, and qualities. Eventually, everyone found a segment where they could feel that they were contributing, transcribing, arranging music, moderating brainstorming processes, being in front, or having an interacting role.

This student also comments on ensemble relationships and a concern for the children's aesthetic experience.

---

32   Gaunt et al., p. 12.
33   R. Keith Sawyer, 'Group Creativity: Musical Performance and Collaboration', in *Psychology of Music*, 34/2 (2006), 148–65, https://doi.org/10.1177/0305735606061850; Pamela Burnard and Elizabeth Haddon, *Activating Diverse Musical Creativities* (London: Bloomsbury Academic, 2015); Kari Holdhus and Magne Espeland, 'Music in Future Nordic Schooling. The Potential of the Relational Turn´, *European Journal of Philosophy in Arts Education*, 2/2 (2017), 84–117; Tony Woodcock, 'RENEW – External Evaluation Report', in RE-new Reflective Entrepreneurial Music Education World Class 2018 in Association Européenne des Conservatoires, Academies de Musique et Musikhochschule.

Fig. 10.2:. Pleasing Fungis Beetle and guitarist (used with permission from the photographer Kristin Joyce Knox, McKnox.no).

The student feedback after *Music for Microsculptures* shows that the students had a valuable experience directing their musical performance to a new setting.[34] They could not rely on the 'music alone', but, through exploration, they discovered connections between the various elements, which Hahn refers to as 'the intergenerational dynamics'.[35] *Music for Microsculptures* was in a museum where the large insect images were a primary source of inspiration for the participants' music-making. Even if time limitations (of the performance being only 25 mins per student group) were a constraining factor during the working process, the students were in dialogue with multiple aesthetic approaches to music-making. The students were connected to societal and global issues at a micro level through their interaction with a local kindergarten and a natural science museum.

Concluding Observations

We have discussed the need for a more holistic education, through the perspectives of musicking and community music making. Findings from our exploration of the student feedback confirm the need for Higher Music Education in our context to develop curriculum design, modes of study and pedagogies to support learning for contemporary and future contexts.[36] The stakeholders' response and the music students' reflective reports mirror the change in HME thinking during the last years: the need to move towards embracing musical practices as a social process intricately connected to artistic and musical craftsmanship.[37]

In his article, 'Music Education as Craft: Reframing a Rationale', Magne Espeland underlines the need for educators to consider multiple perspectives on music, to find a balance between the 'wider aims' and 'details that ensure mastery over execution'.[38] As music educators, we continuously strive for a balance between exposing the students to explorative musical practices and encouraging their study of the Western Classical music canon.

Our second research question was related to how HMEIs may contribute to preparing students to become contributors to society. We realise the complexity and even naiveté in trying to connect curricula in Higher Music Performance to societal needs. There are no easy answers. However, we agree with Gaunt et al., who propose three essential domains within a contemporary conceptual paradigm for Higher Music

---

34 Therese Schoder-Larsen and Flavio Sefa, 'Digital dokumentasjon av prosjektet Music for Microsculptures' (University of Agder: Studenter i forskningprosjekt 8 December 2020), https://www.uia.no/

35 Karine Hahn, 'Inquiry into an Unknown Musical Practice: An Example of Learning through Project and Investigation', in *Becoming Musicians: Student Involvement and Teacher Collaboration in Higher Music Education*, ed. by Stefan Gies and Jon Helge Sætre ([n. p.]: NMH publications, 2019), p. 189.

36 Gaunt et al., p. 2.

37 Ibid., p. 16.

38 Espeland, p. 224.

Education: 1) musical craft and artistry; 2) musicians' visions and identities; and 3) the need and potential in society.[39] Student-centred and interdisciplinary activities, exemplified in this article by the museum project *Music for Microsculptures*, are one path to open the students' understanding of the multiple possibilities of making music relevant as an aesthetic expression and a comment on contemporary societal issues. Researchers have referred to various lines of action, presenting a holistic vision of the entire curriculum in which each of the following aspects are interconnected to promote a clear direction for students: the design of masters programmes; specialisation courses;[40] regular programmes of research and development projects based upon international collaboration and partnerships;[41] enhanced development in technology-oriented knowledge and digital skills.[42] These all need to expose the students to diverse music practices, community music concepts, and new forms of musical creativities.[43]

Based on the above theoretical perspectives and the interview data presented in this chapter, we believe that closer collaboration and continued dialogues between music students, teachers in HMEIs, professionals in the music culture field, and representatives for societal community institutions will be essential in order to create more holistic learning contexts for teaching and learning music performance.

References

Bamford, Anne, *The Wow Factor: Global Research Compendium on the Impact of the Arts in Education* (Münster: Waxman Verlag GmbH, 2006)

——, *Arts and Cultural Education in Norway* (Oslo: The Norwegian Centre for Arts and Cultural Education, 2012)

Beech, Nic, Broad, Stephen, Cunliffe, Ann, Duffy, Celia, Gilmore, Charlotte, 'Development in organization theory and organizing music', in *Organising Music. Theory, Practice, Performance*, ed. by Beech, Nic, Gilmore, Charlotte (Cambridge, Cambridge University Press, 2015), pp. 1–24

Bennett, Dawn, *Understanding the classical music profession: The past, the present and strategies for the future* (Farnham: Ashgate, 2008)

Bennett, Dawn, and Ruth Bridgestock, 'The Urgent Need for Career Preview: Expectation and Graduate Realities in Music and Dance', in *International Journal of Music Education*, 33/3 (2014), 263–77, https://doi.org/10.1177/0255761414558653

Bourriaud, Nicholas, *Relasjonell estetikk* (Oslo: Pax, 2007)

Boyce-Tillman, June, 'The Complete Musician: The Formation of the Professional Musician', in *Musician–Teacher Collaborations. Altering the Chord*, ed. by Catharina Christophersen and Ailbhe Kenny (New York, Routledge, 2018), pp. 108–20

---

39 Gaunt et al., p. 12.
40 de Reizabal and Gómez.
41 Woodcock.
42 Correia and others.
43 Burnard and Haddon; Hahn.

Burnard, Pamela, and Elizabeth Haddon, 'Introduction: The Imperative of Musical Creativities in Academia and Industry', in *Activating Diverse Musical Creativities* (London: Bloomsbury Collections, 2015), pp. 3–18, https://doi.org/10.5040/9781474220316.ch-001

Clarke, Eric F., *Ways of listening. An Ecological Approach to the Perception of Musical Meaning* (Oxford: Oxford University Press, 2005, https://doi.org/10.1093/acprof:oso/9780195151947.001.0001

Colley, Bernadette, Randi Margrethe Eidsaa, Ailbe Kenny, and B. W. Leung, 'Creativity in partnership practices', in *Creativities, Technologies, and Media in Music Learning and Teaching. An Oxford Handbook of Music Education*, ed. by Gary McPherson and Graham F. Welch (Oxford: Oxford University Press 2018), pp. 95–112

Correia, Jorge, Gilvano Dalagna, Clarissa Foletto, Ioulia Papageorgi, Natassa Economidou Stavrou, Nicolas Constantinou, Heidi Westerlund, Guandalope López-Íñiguez, Stefan Östersjö, Carl Holmgren, Randi Eidsaa, and Tanja Orning, REACT–Rethinking Music Performance in European Higher Education Institutions, *Artistic Career in Music: Stakeholders Requirement Report* (Aviero: UA Editora, 2021), https://doi.org/10.48528/wfq9-4560

Craft, Anna, *Creativity in Schools. Tensions and Dilemmas* (Oxon: Routledge 2005)

De Nora, Tia, *Music in Everyday Life* (Cambridge: Cambridge University Press, 2000), https://doi.org/10.1017/CBO9780511489433

Espeland, Magne, 'Music Education as Craft: Reframing a Rationale', in *Music Education as Craft Reframing Theories and Practices*, ed. by Kari Holdhus, Regina Murphy, and Magne Espeland (Cham: Springer, 2021), pp. 219–39, https://doi.org/10.1007/978-3-030-67704-6

Fautley, Martin, and Jonathan Savage, *Creativity in Secondary Education* (Exeter: Learning Matters, 2007), https://doi.org/10.4135/9781446278727

Gaunt, Helena, Celia Duffy, Ana Čorić, Izabel R. Gonzales Delgado, Linda Messas, Oleksander Pryimenko, and Henrik Sveidahl, 'Musicians as Makers in Society: A conceptual Foundation for Contemporary Professional Higher Music Education', in *Frontiers in Psychology*, 12 (2021), 1–20, https://doi.org/10.3389/fpsyg.2021.713648

Gibson, James J., *The Ecological Approach to Visual Perception* (New York and London: Laurence Erlbaum Associates, 1986)

Gies, Stefan, 'How Music Performance Education became Academic: On the History of Music in Higher Education in Europe', in *Becoming Musicians: Student Involvement and Teacher Collaboration in Higher Music Education*, ed. by Stefan Gies and Jon Helge Sætre (Oslo: NMH publications, 2019), pp. 31–51, https://hdl.handle.net/11250/2642235

Hahn, Karine, 'Inquiry into an Unknown Musical Practice: An Example of Learning through Project and Investigation', in *Becoming Musicians: Student Involvement and Teacher Collaboration in Higher Music Education*, ed. by Stefan Gies and Jon Helge Sætre (Oslo: NMH publications, 2019), pp. 173–98

Higgins, Lee, 'The Community within Community Music, in *The Oxford Handbook of Music Education*, ed. by Gary E. McPherson, and Graham Welch (Oxford University Press, 2012), pp. 104–119, https://hdl.handle.net/11250/2642235

Holdhus, Kari, and Magne Espeland, 'Music in Future Nordic Schooling. The Potential of the Relational Turn´, *European Journal of Philosophy in Arts Education*, 2/2 (2017), 84–117, https://doi.org/10.5281/zenodo.3383789

'Microsculpture. The Insect Portraits of Levon Biss'. Oxford University Museum of Natural History, website, http://microsculpture.net

Rink, John, Helene Gaunt, and Aaron Williamon (eds), *Musicians in the Making, Pathways to Creative Performance* (New York: Oxford University Press, 2017), https://doi.org/10.1017/S0265051719000111

Nerland, Monika, 'Beyond Policy: Conceptualising Student-Centred Learning Environments in Higher (Music) Education', in *Becoming Musicians: Student Involvement and Teacher Collaboration in Higher Music Education*, ed. by Stefan Gies and Jon Helge Sætre (Oslo: NMH publications, 2019:7), pp. 53–66, https://hdl.handle.net/11250/2642235

Papageorgi, Ioulia and Graham Welch (eds), *Advanced Musical Performance, Investigations in Higher Education Learning* (Aldershot: Ashgate, 2014)

Perkins, Rosie, 'Rethinking Career for Music Students. Identity and Vision', in *Life in the Real World. How to Make Music Students Employable*, ed. by Dawn Bennett (Champaign, IL: Common Ground Research Network, 2012), pp. 11–25, https://doi.org/10.18848/978-1-61229-079-9/CGP

de Reizábal, Margarita, Lorenzo, Gomés, Benito, Manuel, 'When Theory and Practice Meet: Avenues for Entrepreneurship Education in Music Conservatories', *International Journal of Music Education*, 38/3 (2020), 352–69, https://doi.org/10.1177/0255761420919560

RENEW, Reflective Entrepreneurial Music Education Worldclass. Association Europeenne des Conservatoires, Academies de Musique et Musikhochschulen (2016–2018), https://aec-music.eu/project/renew-2016-2018/

Sawyer, R. Keith, 'Group Creativity: Musical Performance and Collaboration', *Psychology of Music*, 34/2 (2006), 148–65, https://doi.org/10.1177/03057356060618

Schau, Jorn and Randi Margrethe Eidsaa, 'Higher Music Performance Education in a Changing World: Towards a New Curriculum?', in *Music Education in XXI-st Century. New Challenges and Perspectives*, ed. by Mikolai Rikovsky (Poznan: Akademia Muzyczna im. I. J. Paderewskiego, 2021), pp. 195–208

Schoder-Larsen, Therese, and Flavio Sefa, 'Digital dokumentasjon av prosjektet Music for Microsculptures' (2020), https://www.uia.no/studenter-i-forskningsprosjekt

Small, Christopher, *Musicking: The Meanings of Performing and Listening* (Middletown, CT: Wesleyan University Press, 1998)

Stepniak, Michael and Peter Sirotin, *Beyond the conservatoire model: Reimagining classical music performance training in higher education* (London and New York: Routledge, 2020)

Sætre, Jon Helge, Stefan Gies, Anna Maria Bordin, Lars Brinck, Karine Hahn, Siri Storheim, Susanne van Els, and Ellen Mikalsen Stabell, 'The Music Performance Student as Researching Artist? Perspectives on Student-Centeredness in Higher Music Education', in *Becoming Musicians: Student Involvement and Teacher Collaboration in Higher Music Education*, ed. by Stefan Gies, Jon Helge Sætre (Oslo: NMH publications, 2019:7), pp. 173–98, https://hdl.handle.net/11250/2642235

Thibeault, Matthew Doran, 'Music Education in the Post-Performance World', in *The Oxford Handbook of Music Education*, 2 vols, ed. by Gary E. McPherson and Graham Welch (Oxford: Oxford University Press, 2012), ii, pp. 517–30

University of Agder, Faculty of Fine Arts, bachelor's Programme in Western Classical Music Performance, https://www.uia.no/en/studies2/music-performance-western-classical-music2

Veblen, Kari, 'Emerging Trends in Community Music', in *The Oxford Handbook of Music Education*, 2 vols, ed. by Gary E. McPherson and Graham Welch (Oxford: Oxford University Press, 2012), ii, pp. 203–20

Weller, Janis, 'Composed and improvised', in *Life in the Real World: How to make music graduates employable*, ed. by Dawn Bennett (Champaign, IL: Common Ground, 2013), pp. 45–62

Westerlund, Heidi, and Helena Gaunt, *Expanding Professionalism in Music and Higher Music Education: A Changing Game* (London and New York: Routledge, 2021)

Windsor, W. Luke and Christoph de Bézenac, 'Music and Affordances', in *Musicae Scientiae*, 16/1 (2012), 102–20, https://doi/pdf/10.1177/1029864911435734

Woodcock, Tony, 'REVIEW External Evaluator Report', Association Européenne Music des Conservatoires, Academies de Musique et Musikhochschulen, https://aec-music.eu/project/renew-2016-2018/

11. Experience, Understanding and Intercultural Competence: The Ethno Programme

Sarah-Jane Gibson

Considering the differences between intercultural experience, understanding, and competence is relevant to anyone engaging in higher music education (HME) as we prepare our students for careers in an ever-changing industry and a global society experiencing more deeper and urgent challenges. As discussed by Randi Eidsaa and Mariam Kharatyan in Chapter 10 of this volume, it is vital that HME explore diverse music practices, however, much like Helen Minors in Chapter 12, I argue for the importance of critical reflection as part of the learning process to ensure students engage critically with music and issues within society. Gage Averill challenges music educators, saying: 'we may unwittingly indulge our student participants and our audiences in a form of concert tourism that superficially nods to multicultural diversity without challenging preconceived notions or acknowledging the noisy clash of cultures, politics, and musics in the contemporary world'.[1] It is vital that we approach intercultural engagement in such a way that we critically reflect on our epistemological understanding of music-making and the sociological effects of engaging with cultures different to our own.[2]

Ethno is a 10-day residential event for young musicians. Intercultural immersion takes place there when attendees, who come from a variety of places around the world, engage with one another through sharing and learning folk tunes and songs from each other's cultural heritage. Participants also spend time together eating meals and socialising. The Ethno Gatherings do not have a standardised approach

---

1   Gage Averill, '"Where's 'one'": Musical Encounters of the Ensemble Kind', in *Performing Ethnomusicology: Teaching and Representation in World Music Ensembles*, ed. by Ted Solis (Berkeley and Palo Alto: University of California Press, 2004), 108.
2   Robert Aman, 'Other Knowledges, Other Interculturalities: The Colonial Difference in Intercultural Dialogue' in *Unsettling Eurocentrism in the Westernised University*, ed. by Julie Cupples and Ramón Grosfoguel (Oxford: Routledge, 2019), pp. 171–86.

towards facilitated discussions surrounding issues of intercultural understanding, and not all Ethno organisers believe such time for critical reflection is necessary. Based on this perspective, I consider the following research questions: To what extent should an intercultural music programme also focus on developing intercultural understanding and competency? Is it enough for participants to have an intercultural musical experience without allowing time for facilitated discussions to develop intercultural competencies? Further to this, I consider how the Ethno approach may influence intercultural understanding in formal higher music education programmes, specifically within UK HME contexts.

After a brief description of Ethno and its pedagogical approach followed by a review of interculturality, I will explore various notions of intercultural understanding such as Gordon Allport's contact hypothesis, intercultural competence, as outlined by Darla Deardorff, and intercultural understanding through critical reflection using examples from Ethno research.[3] I argue for more time in ensemble rehearsals for critical reflection in the form of facilitated discussions so that people who engage in intercultural music-making are able to develop their intercultural competency skills.

Ethno

Ethno is a residential gathering of 10 days where young musicians teach one another songs from their folk music traditions and work towards public concerts held at the end of the event. It was founded by Magnus Bäckström, a Swedish folk musician, in 1990. The inspiration was to create a programme that provided opportunities for folk musicians that complimented the more Western classically orientated World Youth Choir and the World Youth Orchestra, all programmes facilitated by JM International (JMI), a global network of NGOs that provide opportunities for young people and children to develop through music across all boundaries.[4] Ethno became part of JMI's programmes in 2000 and has now expanded to over 40 countries around the world.[5]

Bäckström wanted to create an opportunity for young folk musicians to 'meet and play', hoping to create a space with a 'structure that gives some kind of order but still allows creative encounters to happen'.[6] The result was an event that focuses on a culturally democratic approach.[7] Peers have the opportunity to teach and share their music and their culture. An Ethno organiser describes the process of sharing

---

3   Gordon Allport, *The Nature of Prejudice* (Cambridge: Addison-Wesley, 1954); Darla Deardorff, 'Assessing Intercultural Competence', *New Directions for Institutional Research*, 149 (2011), 65–79.
4   'About JMI', JM International, website [n.d.], www.jmi.net/about
5   Sarah-Jane Gibson, Lee Higgins, Ryan Humphrey, Linus Ellström, Helena Reiss; and Lisandra Roosioja, *30 Years of Ethno: The History of Ethno* (York: York St John University, 2022).
6   Magnus Bäckström, Hugo Ribeiro, Peter Ahlbom, 'An Autobiographical History of Ethno Sweden: A Testimonial about its Origins, Underlying Ideology and Initial Goals', *ORFEU*, 4.2 (2019), 7–29 (pp. 17, 18).
7   Cultural democracy refers to supporting diverse cultures in a respectful and celebratory manner, resisting dominant ideologies and cultural hierarchies, and promoting a philosophy of empowerment

and learning tunes and songs as making 'everyone equal. Everyone has something to teach and something to learn').[8] In this sense, Ethno can be seen to epitomise a model that furthers student autonomy, lifelong learning, and musical identity in a supportive learning environment, a key concern of the REACT project.[9]

Ethno Pedagogy

Ethno Pedagogy embraces a foundational principle of 'valuing others through critical approaches to intercultural and experiential learning'.[10] Andrea Creech, Maria Varvarigou, Lisa Lorenzino, and Ana Čorić, the researchers of the Ethno Pedagogy report, concluded that Ethno works within a non-formal and scaffolded expansive learning framework using core pedagogical practices of learning by ear, peer learning, and self-directed, situated learning. They describe the residential nature of Ethno as 'shaping the pedagogical environment'.[11] This approach has led some participants to consider their Ethno experience as transformational and led towards a lifelong interest in learning music.

Two aspects of the pedagogical framework are relevant to this chapter: situated learning, which results in a level of autonomy regarding learning and an openness to exploring new ideas both within the facilitated sessions and in the non-formal and social settings of the gathering, and learning by ear.

Method

Ethno Research comprised an international team of twenty researchers led by the International Centre for Community Music at York St John University. The project was led by Professor Lee Higgins. Research findings were drawn from participant observation at 11 Ethno gatherings, over 330 interviews, online social media analysis, onsite and video observations, surveys, and questionnaires. The complete catalogue of research reports is available at www.ethnoresearch.org.

I have worked with this project since its inception in May 2019, first as a post-doctoral researcher then as a research associate until the project's completion in December 2022. The research question under discussion here is born out of a meta-analysis of all the research reports and my final research project into the global growth of Ethno, which was published in December 2022.

---

through participation. Lee Higgins, *Community Music: In Theory and in Practice* (New York: Oxford University Press, 2012), pp. 32–35.
8   Focus Group Meeting, June 2021
9   Gilvano Dalagna, Stefan Östersjö, Clarissa Foletto, and Jorge Salgado Correia, *REACT Symposium – Reflective and Critical Approaches to Teaching and Learning* (Aveiro: UA Editora, 2022).
10 Andrea Creech, Maria Varvarigou, Lisa Lorenzino, and Ana Čorić, *Pedagogy and Professional Development: Research Report* (York: York St John University, 2022), p. 12.
11 Creech et al., p. 13.

The chapter also draws upon the authors' HME teaching with a particular focus on an 'Ethno inspired' band, which I facilitated between 2019–2020 and a drumming module I currently coordinate wherein I focus on diverse percussion traditions. I have drawn upon these HME experiences to demonstrate how this research has broadened sociological and musical understandings of other cultures for music students at York St John University, an institution with a commitment to social justice and a strategic aim that embeds this value in the daily working of the university including standing up against inequality.[12]

Interculturality

Huib Schippers explains that 'in an intercultural environment conscious efforts are made to enable cultural meetings and mixing'.[13] Across the literature, there is an acknowledgement that intercultural understanding is a constant process that involves both awareness of one's own culture as well as a knowledge and respect for different cultures.[14] The value of intercultural understanding in a global community is that it can support 'peace and tolerance building between different communities and cultures across the globe'.[15]

Where intercultural understanding refers to an awareness of and respect for one's own culture and different cultures, intercultural competence extends interculturality to include a particular outcome within intercultural situations. Deardorff highlights the need for greater intercultural competency as society becomes more diverse; however, she acknowledges that there is no consensus surrounding intercultural terminology across academic disciplines.[16] She defines intercultural competence as 'any who interact with those from different backgrounds, regardless of location' with a desired outcome of *'effective* and *appropriate* behaviour and communication in intercultural situations'.[17]

Roger Mantie and Pedro Toroni suggest that interculturality within Ethno could be theorised through Allport's contact hypothesis or intergroup contact theory, which proposes that interpersonal contact, under certain conditions, can promote tolerance and acceptance between minority and majority groups.[18] This is most effective when

---

12 York St John University, 'Strategy 2026 Refresh' (York: York St John University, 2021), p. 3.
13 Huib Schippers, *Sharing Songs, Shaping Community* (York: York St John University, 2022), p. 12.
14 Mark Heyward, 'From International to Intercultural: Redefining the International School for a Globalized World', *Journal of Research in International Education*, 1.1 (2002), 9–32; Ian Hill, 'Student Types, School Types and their Combined Influence on the Development of Intercultural Understanding', *Journal of Research in International Education*, 5.1 (2006), 5–33; Debra Williams-Gualandi, 'Intercultural Understanding: What Are We Looking For and How Do We Assess What We Find?', *International and Global Issues for Research* (2015), https://www.bath.ac.uk/publications/department-of-education-working-papers/attachments/intercultural-understanding-what-are-we-looking for.pdf
15 Gibson et al., p. 39.
16 Deardorff, p. 65.
17 Ibid., p. 66,
18 Roger Mantie and Pedro Toroni, 'Marvelling at the Ethnoverse: Intercultural Learning through Traditional Music', in *Ethno Music Gatherings*, ed. by Sarah-Jane Gibson and Lee Higgins; Allport.

groups 'share similar status, interests, and tasks and when the situation fosters personal, intimate intergroup contact'—as Ethno does.[19] Mantie and Toroni suggest that Ethno offers an example of how 'intercultural' success in breaking down stereotypes and negative assumptions may be dependent upon the mode or mechanism of interaction: music. They argue that 'music's ubiquity as a cultural practice makes it exceptionally powerful as a form of interaction with the potential for mediating intercultural differences'.[20] This is a similar position to that found in the 'White Paper on Intercultural Dialogue'. In this White Paper, it is recognised that:

> Cultural activities can provide knowledge of diverse cultural expressions and so contribute to tolerance, mutual understanding and respect. Cultural creativity offers important potential for enhancing the respect of others. The arts are also a playground of contradiction and symbolic confrontation, allowing for individual expression, critical self-reflection and mediation. They thus naturally cross borders and connect and speak directly to people's emotions.[21]

JMI draws their conception of intercultural dialogue from the Council of Europe definition: 'Intercultural dialogue is understood as an open and respectful exchange of views between individuals and groups with different ethnic, cultural, religious and linguistic backgrounds and heritage on the basis of mutual understanding and respect'.[22] Regarding interculturality, Ethno organisers believe that they create the space for intercultural dialogue through informal jamming and discussions where participants speak about their culture and political situations amongst themselves.[23] They write:

> at the root of intercultural understanding lies intercultural curiosity, which is stimulated by entering into contact with different cultures (for example during an Ethno camp). The curiosity sparked at/by an Ethno camp inspires musicians to learn more when they return home, sometimes driving lifelong interests and/or involvement in a new musical culture/genre.[24]

Both intercultural understanding and competency definitions suggest the need for active facilitation or critical reflection which results in an awareness of cultural differences or in developing effective patterns of behaviour in intercultural situations. This statement of the Ethno organisers suggests that Ethno does focus more on a contact hypothesis approach: putting diverse cultures in a space together, but not actively developing intercultural competency or understanding. Contact hypothesis

---

19   Thomas Pettigrew and Linda Tropp, 'A Meta-Analytic Test of Intergroup Contact theory', *Journal of Personality and Social Psychology*, 90.5 (2006), 751–83 (p. 752).
20   Mantie and Toroni, 112.
21   Council of Europe, Ministers of Foreign Affairs, 'White Paper on Intercultural Dialogue: Living Together as Equals in Dignity, 7 May 2008, p. 109, https://www.coe.int/t/dg4/intercultural/source/white%20paper_final_revised_en.pdf
22   Ibid.
23   Focus group meeting, 2021.
24   Ethno Research Key Questions, Feedback, 2021.

could thus be comparable to an intercultural experience where people meet different cultures, but do not necessarily develop deeper understandings or competencies.

In the following sections, I shall explore how these three approaches relate to the experiences of participants at Ethno Gatherings and how some of these concepts have been explored in the HME setting at York St John University (YSJU).

Intercultural Experience

As Mantie and Torino argue, musical engagement can be seen as an effective tool for people from different cultural backgrounds to engage with one another from an interpersonal, contact hypothesis perspective.[25] The primary requirement appears to be bringing people from diverse or conflicting backgrounds into a space together to enable engagement or an intercultural experience. For example, a memory shared by an Ethno participant named Keon describes a pivotal, interpersonal contact moment at Ethno that he felt was transformational. It was in 2005 at a time when the impact of the Kosovo war was still felt in Europe.[26] The participant paints a picture of two musicians jamming late into the night at an Ethno gathering, whilst at the same time also describes a conversation that he is hearing next to him. Whilst in a heightened state of music-making he is hearing another person share their experiences of being a solider in the Kosovo war:

> He'd been a soldier in the Kosovo war, and his father being a soldier there as well. And every family in Serbia, there is at least one or a few male members of the family who one way or the other would've been involved in [...] the Kosovo war. And how that war is really, also in Serbia, a national trauma. And he was [...] at all talking about like, 'Oh, yeah. It's a shame that we lost' or whatever it was. It was nothing about making the Serbians heroes, or making the international community into villains [...] He was really only talking about the human aspects of being in a war. And to hear that from… Because, I mean in Western media, or the Swedish media, the Serbians were really… Kind of… Everyone knew that the Serbians were the bad guys, and the Kosovo were the kind of… The ones that needed protection. I was hearing snippets of this conversation that gave me a really, really strong experience of: 'Yes, of course! They are also human beings, they were on the other side, but they were also human beings. And it's something that affected them really strongly as well.' And I think THAT experience, THAT moment is something that's changed me. I think that very experience made me definitely more humble. Towards life in general, and towards… Understanding that there are always, there's always a different side. There's always another side of things. And also, we're all humans with the will to protect our lives and our families.[27]

---

25   Mantie and Toroni.
26   The Kosovo war was an armed conflict between Serbians and Albanians between 1998–1999. Kosovo was seeking independence from Yugoslavia, and Serbia responded by the persecution of Albanians. The conflict ended through a NATO intervention of air strikes. Yugoslavia withdrew their forces. The area remains a contested space. Tamara Kovacevic, 'Kosovo: Why is Violence Flaring between Ethnic Serbs and the Albanians?', BBC News (2023), https://www.bbc.co.uk/news/62382069
27   Keon, Interview, 2020.

Keon is describing a situation where a new understanding is developed in an unmediated manner. There was no facilitation, rather the experience occurred during an informal situation. In his description, it does not appear that he is engaging with the Serbian participant through conversation or music-making. Rather, he is listening to a conversation. The content of the discussion and sincerity of the Serbian's story resulted in a realisation that became transformational for the participant. What is striking about this experience is that there appears to have been no personal engagement between Keon and the Serbian he overheard. The experience occurred because they were in close proximity to one another and in a residential setting.

The Ethno committee emphasise that their decision not to facilitate sessions on intercultural understandings is 'intentional and does not undermine the effectiveness of the experience'.[28] The encounter described above was enabled due to the residential nature of the Gathering, something that Elise Gayraud argues is essential for 'sufficient intercultural immersion' at Ethno.[29] It happened because people were in constant engagement with one another, an approach identified as a successful method of connecting diverse people.[30]

Participants attend Ethno Gatherings with the expectation of sharing music from their cultural heritage and learning music that their fellow participants have brought with them from their musical cultures, thus Ethno Gatherings are perceived by participants as a learning opportunity. I would like to suggest that it was the particular learning environment created at the Ethno Gatherings that enabled this encounter.[31] The facilitation during sharing sessions encouraged an attitude of 'respectful musical exchange'.[32] This attitude embeds the core pedagogical value which may have created a space safe enough for the Serbian participant to share his personal experiences of the Kosovo war and for Keon to be in a receptive position. The sense of openness that had been cultivated throughout the gathering allowed for the opportunity to be open to a differing perspective, enabling a transformational experience.

The need for conversation in diverse cultural settings is noted as extremely important in intercultural settings.[33] Yet, HME settings do not always allow for space

---

28   Ethno Research Key Questions, Feedback, 2021.
29   Elise Gayraud, *Towards an Ethnography of a Culturally Eclectic Music Scene* (Durham: Durham University, 2015), p. 119.
30   Peter Block, *Community* (San Francisco: Berret-Koehler, 2009); Deardorff.
31   Sarah-Jane Gibson, 'Case Study: Ethno Sweden. A Catalyst for Change, in *Ethno Research Pilot Case Studies* (York: York St John University, 2019).
32   Lee Higgins, 'Case Study: Ethno Portugal: Crossing the Threshold', in *Ethno Research Research Pilot Case Studies* (York: York St John University, 2019).
33   Block; Benjamin Brinner, *Playing Across a Divide: Israeli-Palestinian Musical Encounters* (New York and Oxford: Oxford University Press, 2009); Pamela Burnard, Valerie Ross, Laura Lis Hassler, and Lis Murphy, 'Translating Intercultural Creativities in Community Music: Introducing the Role of Interculturality in Community Music Practice', in *The Oxford Handbook of Community Music*, ed. by Brydie Bartleet and Lee Higgins (New York: Oxford University Press, 2018), pp. 44–70; Deardorff; Sarah-Jane Gibson, *Community Choirs in Northern Ireland: Reimagining Identity through Singing* (Bristol: Intellect, 2023); Juliet Hess, *Music Education for Social Change: Constructing an Activist Music Education* (New York: Routledge, 2019).

for conversation and relationship building in musical ensembles. Spaces around the peripheral of musical engagement allow for moments to become familiar with the social context of fellow musicians. Through conversations, new understandings can be expanded upon, opening a door towards intercultural competence.

Making space for conversation was one of the challenges of the 'Ethno inspired band' that I facilitated at YSJU. I incorporated 'check-ins' before we began each session, where participants expressed how they were feeling. Each person in the group brought a piece of music to share, and I encouraged participants to share their abilities and skills, thinking about what they could contribute to each piece we were learning. Feedback from the students was that some of them wanted even more detail about each participant and more time to get to know each other's abilities, emphasising academic findings of how much time is needed for conversation in such spaces.[34] As students began to share their musical backgrounds and cultural heritage, it became striking how diverse the students were. Further feedback from students is that they value the bonding moments and believe it can lead to more successful performances.

Providing space for dialogue and discussion within intercultural environments is vital in bringing awareness to issues of cultural dominance and appropriation. It also enables the opportunity to work together to resolve any concerns members from ethnic minorities may have. This complexity needs to be constantly reflected upon, and in doing so, will lead to intercultural experiences that are meaningful, respectful, and promote social change.[35]

Intercultural Competence

Deardorff points out that intercultural experts agree on one aspect of intercultural competence: that of seeing from others' perspectives.[36] This is evident in Keon's reflection in the previous section. He was able to see another perspective, one that was not being promoted by the media surrounding the Kosovo war. This realisation of there being 'another side of things' led to a moment that he describes as transformational. Ethno appears to be particularly effective in developing the attitudes of respect, openness, and curiosity which are a further basis for developing intercultural competence.[37] However, Deardorff emphasizes that intercultural competence is ongoing, arguing that critical thinking skills are vital in acquiring knowledge. Critical thinking skills are an

---

34 Jing Yeo, 'The Methods to Intercultural Musical Engagement and the Effects on Musical Performance Practice' (unpublished BA (Hons) Dissertation, York St John University, 2019).
35 Solis, Introduction; Bob White, 'The Promise of World Music: Strategies for Non-Essentialist Listening,' in *Music and Globalization: Critical Encounters* ed. by Bob White (Bloomington: Indiana University Press, 2012), pp. 189–218; Brydie-Leigh Bartleet, 'How Concepts of Love can Inform Empathy and Conciliation in Intercultural Community Music Contexts', *International Journal of Community Music*, 12/3 (2019), 317–30; Gibson, *Community Choirs*; Hess.
36 Deardorff, p. 68.
37 Deardorff.

area that some Ethno participants felt were lacking, as one, Olivia, explained in 2014, '[We needed] Activities to communicate better and develop the understanding apart from music because...you learn, you play and you rehearse it. And that is (it). It's not that hard. That's the easy part, the hardest part is developing the real understanding behind the cultural difference'.

This issue of cultural difference is stressed by Robert Aman who writes that there may be 'unequal positions from which participants in an intercultural dialogue may encounter each other'.[38] Aman is referring to the power dimensions that come into play due to globalisation and colonisation in particular. He stresses the importance of the 'geopolitical dimension of knowledge production',[39] concluding that 'part of the challenge in achieving an intercultural dialogue [...] involves understanding the social-historical power relations that imbue knowledge production'.[40] This is particularly interesting when considering how we teach and learn music. Often assumptions can be made that students all learn music through the same cognitive processes. However, Deborah Bradley argues that we need to 'approach all music, and all philosophies of music education, with an understanding of their contextually situated nature'.[41]

This is highlighted in relation to the Ethno approach by Mio Yachita in their analysis of Ethno Cambodia. Yachita noted an interesting response to the use of learning by ear in which musicians who learned orally in their everyday practice resorted to using notation to aid their learning of Ethno songs.[42] The feedback from these musicians was that they felt they did not have enough time to learn the music effectively by ear during the workshops, so they used their own notation systems as a memory aid. The musicians' understanding of how and why they learn by ear and appeared to be conceptually different to the way it was being used in Ethno. Yachita argues that '"learning music by ear" is at the core of the Ethno programme because it allows musicians to escape from formal western training',[43] which is rooted in reading a musical score. For some of the musicians in Cambodia, learning by ear was considered a 'formal' approach, thus becoming a challenge for them in the non-formal situation of Ethno. Yachita notes that fundamental concepts such as 'learning by ear'[44] may need to be reconsidered when 'bringing Ethno into the non-Western world'.

---

38 Robert Aman, 'Other Knowledges, Other Interculturalities: The Colonial Difference in Intercultural Dialogue', in *Unsettling Eurocentrism in the Westernised University*, ed. by Julie Cupples and Ramón Grosfoguel (Oxford: Routledge, 2019), pp. 171–86 (p. 172).
39 Aman, p. 184.
40 Ibid.
41 Deborah Bradley, 'Good for what, Good for whom? Decolonising Music Education Philosophies', in *The Oxford Handbook of Philosophy in Music Education*, ed. by Wayne Bowman and Ana Lucia Frega (New York: Oxford University Press, 2012), pp. 409–33 (p. 429).
42 Mio Yachita, 'An analysis of Ethno Cambodia 2019: Youth, Tradition and the Unavoidable Issue of Ethnicity in Asia' (unpublished paper 2019).
43 Ibid., p. 10.
44 Ibid.

Meki Nzewi, Israel Anyahuru, and Tom Ohiaraumunna explain: 'most ethnomusicologists have come to accept that the standard theories about the music of one human society are often inadequate for a cognitive understanding of the music of another, culturally differentiated society'.[45] This suggests that everyone views music from a particular cultural lens, including how we understand and conceptualise music-making. Thus, while intercultural music-making may be a successful starting point for contact hypothesis and reducing prejudice, it fails to recognise deeper conceptual differences. Acknowledging such difference in perception may prevent Eurocentric dominance in intercultural music-making processes such as those that occur at Ethno and may lead to greater intercultural competence.

It is within this context that formal education, and in particular HME, may complement a non-formal residential gathering, or, where lectures may supplement the learning that takes place during world music ensembles. This is an approach taken in a module that explores world drumming traditions at York St John university. Workshops are alternated with lectures. During the lectures, time is spent exploring and reflecting on the contextually situated nature of the music students are learning in their workshops, allowing them to critically reflect on their learning and to develop their intercultural competence when engaging with music from different cultures.

Critical Reflection

Gibson et al. consider 'understanding in terms of conceptual knowledge brought about through critical and reflective thinking'.[46] Higgins notes that, for some participants, the Ethno experience becomes a 'critical thinking tool', meaning that some at Ethno were actively utilising the experience as 'a lens through which to think and reflect on both current contemporary affairs and broader aspects of personal life'.[47] In this sense, they were choosing to engage in critical thinking as a tool for helping them process their experiences at Ethno. Opportunities for such discussion between participants currently occur between the scheduled musical rehearsals at the gathering. These were not facilitated discussions or sessions enforced upon participants. Critical reflection can result in profound intercultural understanding, as one participant, Carina, experienced in her first Ethno in 2014:

> The first Ethno I went to I shared a lot with an Indian singer [...]. And I remember that she asked the crew of the Ethno to open the woman's bathroom in the nights only for her because in the morning when we used to go to take a shower, we were naked [..] and all of us together and that wasn't comfortable for her. I always remember that because it is

---

45 Meki Nzewi, Israel Anyahuru, and Tom Ohiaraumunna, *Musical Sense and Musical Meaning: An Indigenous African Perception* (Pretoria: UNISA Press, 2008), p. 1.
46 Gibson et al., '30 Years of Ethno', pp. 76–77.
47 Higgins, 'Case Study: Ethno Portugal'.

important to have the comprehension that we have to be empathic with another person because they can require different things and not every person feels the same.

Carina was able to critically reflect on the needs of her fellow participant, which led to a new comprehension of empathy for people who may have different circumstances to her own. Her intercultural competence developed towards a recognition that some people have different needs that need to be met.

In another situation, an Ethno participant was able to critically reflect on his encounters in a transcultural music group called the Världens band, which comprised people who had 'aged out' of the Ethno Gatherings:[48]

> This is the dangerous thing with Ethno because it started in Europe, with European values and ideas, in music as well. When you go to an Ethno, most of them are based on having a melody, accompaniment and rhythm and we always talk music theory in Western terms. There's this big risk that it's Western culture being implied on other cultures and being told this is the right thing. I started realising these things [...] because of Ethno.[49]

This participant is recognising the Eurocentric nature of the structure of music-making during Ethno as well as the ideology behind the gathering. Interestingly, he comments that it was because of his attendance at Ethno that he became aware of the dominance of European musical approaches in world music settings. He continues with an example of an experience that occurred early on in the Världens band:

> I have a very concrete example with our first singer [in our multicultural band]. He was playing the mbira and he had his way of tuning it which didn't work together with our own instruments. We were young and not conscious of how different music cultures are. And we said, 'why can't you just change the tuning?'. And he said, No, it will lose the African spirit'. And we were like, 'come on, that's not a real thing' – but of course it is and when you read about it more [...] it was tuned in a [...] natural harmonic series, so [it] would vibrate and sound in a certain way, which it doesn't in equal temperament.[50]

This musical group, the Världens band, acknowledge that they need to use a harmonic and tonal system in part to be accessible to their largely Euro-American audiences.[51] Balosso-Bardin argues, however, that 'commercial compromise [...] is different from intercultural compromise which encourages the musicians both to make their music intelligible to their audience and to find a common ground in order

---

48   The Världens band visited YSJ in November 2019 as part of the University's strategic aims to engage our students with research at YSJ. The band provided workshops for our students and then gave a performance at the University. Our students were able to perform alongside the band by playing the tunes they had learned at the workshops. The intention of the visit was to allow students to experience some of the collaborative learning practices that the band engage in when learning folk music and to enable our students to perform alongside a professional touring group.
49   Världens band member G, focus group, 2019.
50   Ibid.
51   Cassandre Balosso-Bardin, '#No Borders. Världens Band: Creating and Performing Music across Borders', *The World of Music*, 7.2 (2018), 81–105.

facilitate musical collaboration'.[52] Balosso-Bardin is recognising a tension: using harmony from outside the Western tonal system may alienate their audience, thus losing them revenue. They have therefore come to compromises, such as agreeing to resist singing any English lyrics.

In these examples, we observe a comprehension of what the participants have experienced. They are able to articulate their experience explaining a realisation that not everyone thinks in the same way that they do, or that not everyone has the same needs as they may have. Their critical reflection enabled intercultural understanding. What we need to consider is the value of the understanding behind the experience; the praxial and embodied versus the cognitive processing, or, being able to articulate what one has just learned. This is a point that Deardorff emphasises regarding study abroad programmes, suggesting that students need to be given preparation prior to their journey 'in order to articulate the learning that occurs'.[53] Brydie-Leigh Bartleet, Catherine Grant, Charulatha Mani, and Vanessa Tomlinson also acknowledge that 'global mobility programmes can become powerful sites for embodied learning and understanding'; however, they also note that students who wish to 'readjust their prior acquired artistic schema' successfully need to reflect and explore 'action-based processes'.[54] Through data gathered from our interviews, the Ethno research team have identified that most participants already attend Ethno with an openness and curiosity to learn about different cultures. The challenge is how to encourage further critical reflection upon their learning once they return home and how this may then influence both their musical practice and social interactions in intercultural settings. This challenge could be met within HME if critical reflection is incorporated into the learning that takes place in intercultural ensembles.

Conclusions

In this chapter, I have interrogated the differences between intercultural experience, competency, and understanding. Using the narratives of Ethno participants as examples, I have related intercultural experience to interpersonal contact theory. I have argued that intercultural experience is effective due to the residential nature of the gathering, which can enable a 'reduction of prejudice' due to the learning environment and constant interaction participants have with one another. This is an example where non-formal immersion into music cultures can complement learning in formal HME. I have also argued for the value of more time within intercultural ensembles for conversation within HME, to further develop understanding and

---

52 Ibid., p. 98.
53 Deardorff, p. 71.
54 Brydie-Leigh Bartleet, Catherine Grant, Charulatha Mani, and Vanessa Tomlinson, 'Global Mobility in Higher Education: Reflections on how Intercultural Music-Making can Enhance Students' Musical Practices and Identities', *International Journal of Music Education*, 38.2 (2020), 161–77 (pp. 173, 174).

competency, as feedback from students at YSJU suggest that they believe deeper understanding and connections within their ensemble can strengthen their performances.

I have suggested that intercultural music programmes could enhance their participants' experience by developing intercultural competency, particularly regarding musical transmission. Developing awareness of the dominance of Western musical systems can better allow musicians to engage with world music in a more equitable manner and further enhance their own understanding of their music-making practice. This may be an area where formal HME can complement learning in world music ensembles with lectures. This is vital if HME aims to challenge dominant hegemonies.

Finally, I reflected on the value of critical reflection for intercultural music engagement. I argue that this is a vital element to the practice of intercultural music-making. Participants at Ethno reflect on how their intercultural experience is 'the easy part' but feel that there is value in developing this experience towards a better understanding of how different cultures engage with the world and music. Critical reflection can support students in better understanding their experience of an intercultural encounter, enabling them to apply their learning in different situations and perhaps better engage with people from different cultures in future encounters.

Patrick Kabanda suggests that 'we need to ask how we should recalibrate and sharpen our tools of engagement. We need to take time to understand cultural activities and how they can play a meaningful role in building a more secure and peaceful world amidst modern globalisation'.[55] The development of intercultural competence may not just happen through learning about other countries' backgrounds or because persons from differing backgrounds are in the vicinity of one another or even interacting with each other. Contact hypothesis may be an important starting place as it brings people together, but intercultural competence occurs when people experience a transformation of their understandings. It is here where HME has the potential to develop intercultural understanding through deeper critical reflection. Whilst students are engaging in intercultural music-making in their musical ensembles, providing spaces that challenge and acknowledge dominant epistemologies of music-making and encourage critical reflection can lead to deeper intercultural understanding.

---

55 Patrick Kabanda, *The Creative Wealth of Nations* (New York: Cambridge University Press 2018), p. 41.

References

About JMI, JM International, website, www.jmi.net/about

Allport, Gordon, *The Nature of Prejudice* (Cambridge: Addison-Wesley, 1954)

Aman, Robert, 'Other Knowledges, Other Interculturalities: The Colonial Difference in Intercultural Dialogue' in *Unsettling Eurocentrism in the Westernised University*, ed. by Julie Cupples and Ramón Grosfoguel (Oxford: Routledge, 2019), pp. 171–186

Averill, Gage, '"Where's 'one'": Musical Encounters of the Ensemble Kind', in *Performing Ethnomusicology: Teaching and Representation in World Music Ensembles*, ed. by Ted Solis (Berkeley and Palo Alto: University of California Press, 2004), pp. 93–111

Bäckström, Magnus, Ribeiro, Hugo, Ahlbom, Peter, 'An Autobiographical History of Ethno Sweden: A Testimonial about its Origins, Underlying Ideology and Initial Goals', *ORFEU*, 4/2 (2019), 7–29

Balosso-Bardin, Cassandre, '#No Borders. Världens Band: Creating and Performing Music across Borders', *The World of Music*, 7/2 (2019), 81–105

Bartleet, Brydie-Leigh, 'How concepts of love can inform empathy and conciliation in intercultural community music contexts', *International Journal of Community Music*, 12/3 (2019), 317–30

Bartleet, Brydie-Leigh; Catherine Grant, Charulatha Mani, and Vanessa Tomlinson, 'Global Mobility in Higher Education: Reflections on how Intercultural Music-Making can Enhance Students' Musical Practices and Identities', *International Journal of Music Education*, 38/2, 161–77

Block, Peter, *Community* (San Fransisco: Berrett-Koehler Publishers, 2009)

Bradley, Deborah, 'Good for what, Good for whom? Decolonising Music Education Philosophies', in *The Oxford Handbook of Philosophy in Music Education*, ed. by Wayne Bowman and Ana Lucia Frega (New York: Oxford University Press, 2012), pp. 409–33

Brinner, Benjamin. E., *Playing Across a Divide: Israeli-Palestinian Musical Encounters* (New York, Oxford: Oxford University Press, 2009)

Burnard, Pamela, Valeria Ross, Laura Hassler, Lis Murphy, 'Translating Intercultural Creativities in Community Music: Introducing the Role of Interculturality in Community Music Practice', in *The Oxford Handbook of Community Music*, ed. by Brydie Bartleet and Lee Higgins (New York: Oxford University Press, 2018), pp. 44–70

Council of Europe, Ministers of Foreign Affairs, 'White Paper on Intercultural Dialogue: Living Together as Equals in Dignity, 7 May 2008, https://www.coe.int/t/dg4/intercultural/source/white%20paper_final_revised_en.pdf

Creech, Andrea, Maria Varvarigou, Lisa Lorenzino, and Ana Čorić, Ana, *Pedagogy and Professional Development: Research Report* (York: York St John University, 2022)

Dalagna, Gilvano, Stefan Östersjö, Clarissa Foletto, and Jorge Salgado Correia, *REACT Symposium – Reflective and Critical Approaches to Teaching and Learning* (Aveiro: UA Editora, 2022)

Deardorff, Darla, 'Assessing Intercultural Competence' in *New Directions for Institutional Research*, 149 (2011), 65–79

Gayraud, Elise, *Towards an Ethnography of a Culturally Eclectic Music Scene. Preserving and Transforming Folk Music in Twenty-First Century England* (unpublished PhD Thesis, Durham University, 2015)

Gibson, Sarah-Jane, 'Ethno on the Road and Varldens Band: Beyond the Ethno Gatherings' (York: York St John University, 2022)

——, 'Case Study: Ethno Sweden. A Catalyst for Change', in *Ethno Research Pilot Case Studies* (York: York St John University, 2019)

——, *Community Choirs in Northern Ireland: Reimagining Identity through Singing* (Bristol: Intellect, 2023)

Gibson, Sarah-Jane, Lee Higgins, Ryan Humphrey, Linus Ellström, Helena Reiss, and Lisandra Roosioja, *30 Years of Ethno: The History of Ethno* (York: York St John University, 2022)

Hess, Juliet, *Music Education for Social Change: Constructing an Activist Music Education* (New York: Routledge, 2019)

Heyward, Mark, 'From International to Intercultural: Redefining the International School for a Globalized World', in *Journal of Research in International Education*, 1:1 (2002), 9–32

Higgins, Lee, *Community Music: In Theory and in Practice* (New York: Oxford University Press, 2012)

——, 'Case Study: Ethno Portugal: Crossing the Threshold', in *Ethno Research Pilot Case Studies* (York: York St John University, 2019)

Hill, Ian, 'Student Types, School Types and their Combined Influence on the Development of Intercultural Understanding', *Journal of Research in Education*, 5.1 (2006), 5–33

Kabanda, Patrick, *The Creative Wealth of Nations* (New York: Cambridge University Press, 2018)

Kovacevic, Tamara, 'Kosovo: Why is Violence Flaring between Ethnic Serbs and Albanians?', *BBC News* (2023), https://bbc.co.uk/news/62382069

Mantie, Roger and Toroni, Pedro, *Marvelling at the Ethnoverse: Intercultural learning through traditional music* in *Ethno Music Gatherings* ed. by Lee Higgins and Sarah-Jane Gibson (Bristol: Intellect, 2024) pp. 96–113

Nwezi, Meki, Israel Anyaharu, and Tom Ohiaraumunna, *Musical Sense and Musical Meaning: An Indigenous African Perception* (Pretoria: UNISA Press, 2008)

Pettigrew, Thomas and Linda Tropp, 'A Meta-Analytic Test of Intergroup Contact Theory', *Journal of Personality and Social Psychology*, 90.5 (2006), 751–83

Shippers, Huib, *Sharing Songs, Shaping Community* (York: York St John University, 2022)

Solis, Ted, 'Introduction. Teaching What Cannot be Taught: an Optimistic Overview', in *Performing Ethnomusicology: Teaching and Representation in World Music Ensembles*, ed. by Ted Solis (Berkeley and Palo Alto: University of California Press, 2004), pp. 1–19

White, Bob, 'The Promise of World Music: Strategies for Non-Essentialist Listening,' in *Music and Globalization: Critical Encounters*, ed. by Bob White (Bloomington: Indiana University Press, 2012), pp. 189–218

Williams-Gualandi, Debra, 'Intercultural Understanding: What Are We Looking For and How Do We Assess What We Find?' *International and Global Issues for Research* (2015), https://www.bath.ac.uk/publications/department-of-education-working-papers/attachments/intercultural-understanding-what-are-we-looking-for.pdf

Yachita, Mio, 'An Analysis of Ethno Cambodia 2019: Youth, Tradition and the Unavoidable Issue of Ethnicity in Asia' (unpublished paper, 2019)

Yeo, Jing, 'The Methods to Intercultural Musical Engagement and the Effects on Musical Performance Practice' (unpublished BA (Hons) dissertation, York St John University, 2019)

York St John University, 'Strategy 2026 Refresh', 2022, https://www.yorksj.ac.uk/media/content-assets/news-and-events/documents/YSJ-Strategy-Refresh-2026-(PDF-22MB).pdf

12. Employability Skills within an Inclusive Undergraduate and Postgraduate Performance Curriculum in the UK

Helen Julia Minors

In aspiring to integrate employability skills[1] into the music curriculum of both undergraduate and postgraduate music students, while, at the same time, working to develop an inclusive curriculum (whereby students can see themselves, their culture, their identity, and their desired career aspirations reflected), I worked on two parallel projects which culminated in two revised modules: one at undergraduate level adding performance to an analytical module, and one at master's level to reflect on the personal performance brand of individuals. Both projects embody the skills outlined in the REACT model, notably requiring the contextualisation of the societal and subject relevance of the skills before exploring those skills practically and before one can share those skills through the dissemination of the project work. Due to the relevance of these projects to the model, I was given a visiting professorship at Luleå University of Technology, Sweden, where the project discussed below have been used both in the doctoral research methods course and in research dissemination as part of the REACT project. Notable for this project is the centre of the model: every learning in the below modules linked directly to the programme outcomes, which were designed to enable students to gain theoretical and practical knowledge and skills that they could apply in their own artistic research and artist practice, enabling them to develop their own artistic voice. Similarly to Chapter 10, this chapter relies on diverse practices within the music degrees, and, similarly to the project described in Chapter 11 (written by my co-worker), the ones discussed here embed critical reflection as part of the entire process.

---

1 Kingston University, 'Future Skills' (Kingston University, 2022), https://www.kingston.ac.uk/aboutkingstonuniversity/future-skills/

Modification of the curriculum has taken time and research, over more than a decade, leading to revised approaches to module content development that integrate students as partners and peers in the learning journey. I question: how can the curriculum embed employability skills in an authentic manner? In other words, how do I embed employability skills alongside performance technique, aesthetic understanding, and analytical ability? How can these embedded skills be developed in an authentic manner to support students' learning? As both module changes concerned performance, it is important to ask, within the performance curriculum specifically, what might an inclusive curriculum look like?

This chapter explores, first, the challenges in Higher Music Education (HME) and the inclusive-curriculum concerns that led to two interconnected curriculum changes: 1) the funded project 'Taking Race Live' (2014–2018) and the project's associated second year (Level 5) module, 'Aural and Analysis' which became 'Aural, Analysis and Improvisation'; 2) Developing from the lessons learnt from 'Taking Race Live', a concern to advance an inclusive approach in the postgraduate performance curriculum led to module change from 'The Aesthetics of Musical Performance' to a revision entitled 'Critical Aspects of Musical Performance'. Integrating the student as an equal partner and peer in the learning process was important to me. Why? Much research had identified that some students were not seeing themselves reflected among university staff or in the reading lists: for example, critical questions concerning, 'Why isn't my professor Black?'.[2] Or, as one student commented via mid-module review in my class, 'Music and Motion' (a third-year module exploring the interrelations of music and dance): 'that's the first time I've seen someone who looks like me in class'. I had shared an example of Yo Yo Ma, the cellist playing the famous 'The Swan' by Saint-Saens, performing with Lil Buck, a hip hop dancer, to explore connections which are beyond genre limitations.[3] The latter example also, like Chapter 11, ensures we foster broader intercultural experiences and dialogues. And also, that the level of anxiety and wellbeing concerns were increasing and continue to increase amongst young people within the UK.[4] I also wanted to embed approaches to help performers in the module to manage their anxiety.

As such, this chapter is a self-reflection that charts how the lessons learned from both projects informed a revised curriculum development and approach to teaching and learning. I reflect on the curriculum changes and the teaching and learning approaches I developed to support, nurture, encourage, and guide both undergraduate and postgraduate performance students to develop their confidence and resilience; to develop their performance brand, marketing, and confidence; and to advance their

---

2   Mariya Hussain, 'Why is My Curriculum White?', NUS News, 11 March 2015, http://www.nus.org.uk/en/news/why-is-my-curriculum-white/; Winston Morgan, 'Why is My Professor Still Not Black?', *Times Higher Education*, 14 March 2016, http://www.timeshighereducation.com/blog/why-my-professor-still-not-black

3   Lil' Buck and Yo Yo Ma, 'Yo Yo Ma and Lil' Buck Do "The Swan" in Beijing', YouTube, uploaded by Flatone, 7 Nov 2014, https://www.youtube.com/watch?v=qfEYjKWJ56E

4   See Johann Hari, *Lost Connections: Why You're Depressed and How to Find Hope* (London: Bloomsbury, 2018)

critical self-reflection, in a context where they were aware of their wellbeing and had tools to help support anxiety. The chapter is written from the voice of a module leader and lecturer, while I was, at the same time, the School Head of Department and active performer (trumpet/voice) and researcher simultaneously.

HEI Challenges and Models of Inclusion and Performance in the Curriculum

An inclusive curriculum needs to ensure that all students see themselves represented. This part of the practice needs to be embedded in all dimensions of the REACT model (see the Introduction of this volume). Building the curriculum from their starting point means integrating their culture, their experiences, and their background. But most music courses had been largely limited by genre barriers; modules explored traditional and largely Western concepts. But moreover, courses often taught performance and theory separately: assessments on live performance were often in one module and assessments exploring critical reflection and analysis are often in another, creating a perceived barrier between the two. The relationship between the critical dimensions of the curriculum in theory and practice is often delineated. As Jerrold Levinson outlined, the interpretation of music is divided between the pure critical and performative.[5] Stefan Östersjö clarifies that the 'distinction between the two rests on the relation between verbal interpretation as an act of translation, which characterizes "critical" interpretation, while a "performative" interpretation takes shape within the artistic domain and therefore evades translation'.[6] As I note elsewhere, if every act of musical interpretation is a form of translation, then translation is never evaded, but how we enact the process changes.[7] In other words, one is spoken and written, the other is embodied and lived through the performative act. In a teaching context, therefore, it is imperative that we encourage students to know and be critical in both a thoughtful and practical manner, through speaking/writing and through making/doing. These multiple literacies are the core of our experience as musicians. And we should be approaching music students as future performing musicians, training them for the professional music industries. Indeed, as Östersjö extends: 'The ability to move between different forms of knowledge is a factor in artistic research that remains in its infancy'.[8] Nevertheless, many have asserted the need to disseminate knowledge in the art world,

---

5   Jerrold Levinson, 'Performative vs. Critical Interpretations in Music', in *The Interpretation of Music*, ed. by M. Krausz (Oxford: Clarendon Press, 1993), pp. 33–60.
6   Stefan Östersjö, 'Art Worlds, Voice and Knowledge: Thoughts on Quality Assessment of Artistic Outcomes', *Online Journal for Artistic Research*, 3/2 (2019), 60-89 (p. 64).
7   Helen Julia Minors, 'Introduction', in *Music, Text and Translation*, ed. by Helen Julia Minors (London: Bloomsbury, 2013), pp. 1-6 (p. 1).
8   Östersjö, p. 71.

through the applied practice, as a fundamental part of the research.[9] This approach, whereby knowledge is demonstrated through performance and not only through text, is vital to enabling students and artists to enact criticality in their art world. It is a principle which became core to the module changes I made and which I discuss below.

There is a liminal space between the learning outcomes of a module within an institution and the art world outside the institution (illustrated under Sharing, in the REACT model, see Introduction) whereby artistic practice is situated. Indeed, as Megan McPherson has shown, the 'university studio prepares art students for the art worlds' that are in industry and that are important to art cultures.[10] Indeed, these art studio practices are detailed in validation documents for degree programmes, represented through learning outcomes (or, put another way, what students will have achieved and demonstrated when they pass the module) and programme handbooks (which detail programme level learning outcomes, which include a detailed summary of the skills and qualities students gain and develop throughout the acquisition of the degree). Recently, in the UK, employability skills in particular have been legitimised institutionally via the graduate attributes that are declared by each UK institution. During this research, those attributes were named as positive and aspirational 'future skills' at Kingston University, as we piloted and embedded these employability skills into the Music Technology undergraduate degree. I, as the head of department, and course leaders met to rewrite all the learning outcomes for modules to ensure they were cohesive, consistent, and utilised the language of the graduate attributes, to ensure both module leader and student could see exactly where these skills were to be taught and supported, and also to generate a consistent language to articulate those skills which are often transferrable.[11] The resulting work saw first-year students discussing their learning: 'it's very important knowing your worth … it's all about networking, knowing how to talk to people in the right sort of way … how can I overcome [anxiety]?'. The career adviser noted that students 'being able to talk about the wider career world and also about themselves' is important.[12] The Vice Chancellor, Stephen Spier, hosted a delegation of local MPs to share the work of students and careers staff. He noted that the 'future skills report clearly shows what businesses say they need to meet the challenges of the future'.[13] This report is one strategic output from many years of work at Kingston University, with colleagues

---

9   *Artistic Research in Performance through Collaboration*, ed. by Martin Blain and Helen Julia Minors (Basingstoke: Macmillan, 2020).

10 Megan McPherson, 'In-Between Practice and Art Worlds', in *Creativities in Arts Education, Research and Practice: International Perspectives for the Future of Learning and Teaching*, ed. by L. R. de Bruin., P. Burnard, and S. Davis (Leiden and Boston: Brill Sense, 2018), pp. 33-45 (p. 35).

11 For more on this revision, called 'Navigate', see Kingston University, 2022, 'Kingston University's Navigate programme to prepare students for career success by embedding future skills across curriculum', https://www.kingston.ac.uk/news/article/2747/16-nov-2022--kingston-universitys-navigate-programme-to-prepare-students-for-career-success-by-embedding-future-skills/

12 Kingston University, 'Lib Dem MPs visit Kingston University to hear how Future Skills are being embedded into curriculum', YouTube, uploaded by Kingston University, 14 Nov 2022, https://www.youtube.com/watch?v=f8gy54op2FE

13 Ibid.

working to develop their inclusive curriculum framework and working with industry to reflect on how to modernise a curriculum.[14] It has, undoubtedly, been integral to my own development as my own work was within and in parallel to this context.

These graduate attributes are refined and unique to each institution, setting out their unique selling points, but essentially, they all show the skills which students need and should acquire as part of their degree to best support their progression into graduate employment. The graduate attributes at my present institution are vital for artists working in the art worlds, but they are equally transferable qualities for all, and are certainly pertinent to this volume. The attributes are under the following headings: 'confident', 'authentic', 'resilient', 'enterprising', and 'professional'.[15] For an institution with a social justice remit in all we do, York St John University encourages everything we do to follow the same approach as the inclusive curriculum: to include all, to make a positive change, and to support the future change needed to align learning to industry needs. In other words, we are making our graduates into self-sufficient lifelong learners, critical thinkers, problem solvers, and creative collaborators.

Since first becoming a degree-programme director (2008, Roehampton University), I started to consider how music was not only used *as* the curriculum, but that—in schools, colleges and university—it was also used *in* a broader curriculum; music was used to teach research skills and personal skills *through* practice. Indeed, the faculty at the time were exploring how music was used in education *as an* education, and even *for* education, as part of their working in school music education.[16] It is significant that these prepositions were also central to Christopher Frayling as he defined the categories of arts research in his seminal report of 1993: 'research into art and design, research through art and design and research for art and design'.[17]

University programmes have been adapting their courses to ensure they prepare their students for employment. In UK Higher Music Education departments and institutions, there is a priority to ensure that graduate outcomes are strong. The outcomes consist of the data regarding the kind of employment students go into and their earnings. These metrics feed league tables and are used politically to argue for the value of certain degrees. We want the best for our students. Alongside this, it is imperative that we work to make the curriculum inclusive and accessible, and that we support the

---

14 Kingston University, 'Inclusive Curriculum Framework', 2023, https://www.kingston.ac.uk/aboutkingstonuniversity/equality-diversity-and-inclusion/our-inclusive-curriculum/inclusive-curriculum-framework/
15 York St John University, 'Graduate Attributes', 2022, https://www.yorksj.ac.uk/careers-and-placements/graduate-attributes/
16 R. Purves, N. A. Marshall, D. J. Hargreaves, G. Welch, 'Teaching as a Career? Perspectives From Undergraduate Musicians in England', *Bulletin of the Council for Research in Music Education*, 161/162 (2004), 1–8.
17 Christopher Frayling, 'Research in art and design', Royal College of Art Research Papers Series, 1/1 (1993), pp. 1–9 (p. 5).

inclusion of collaborative working and digital technologies.[18] Indeed, the most recent Quality Assurance Agency (QAA) 'Benchmark Statement for Music', against which all music degrees are validated, notes that: 'Music graduates develop transferable skills of analytical thinking, problem-solving, leadership, cooperation and communication'.[19] In charting the subject knowledge and skills, the benchmark also notes that: 'All music graduates are expected to be able to engage with music critically, confidently and creatively'.[20] The wording aligns closely to Kingston University's institutional graduate attributes. Interestingly, the benchmark does not refer to equality at all, and, when diversity is mentioned, it concerns the diversity of courses and provision, and of the 'diversity of approach' with the degrees, but there is no requirement to specifically embed teaching and outcomes which reflects the students' diversity.[21]

There have been pressures to expand genres, styles, and multiple literacies (and rightly so), but the issues and challenges have been how to do so within a single degree. As Celia Duffy and Joe Harrop have shown in their exploration of academic studies for performers, there have been 'recent moves to unite distinct strands of musical study within a single curriculum'.[22] Combining multiple literacies and approaches for performers means that we must enable students to develop their own approaches, their own specialisms, and, therefore, as academics, we must build into programmes the ability for students to make their own choice (of modules, of assessment types, of specialisms) which enables them to meet the learning outcomes on their personalised journeys. Only by supporting their needs, their career aspirations, and journeys, in parallel with offering a range of technical, critical, reflective and applied skills, will students be able to create their own authentic journeys which are meaningful to them.

Pedagogic Aims and Roles—Applying the Models

Lived experience is vital to the educational process for performers. Feeling, hearing, understanding, and sensing the artistic knowledge in all forms ensures that the knowledge spreads across the performative act: in doing the performance, in the art world, through engagement with the instrument (the genre, the setting, the venue), and through thinking about the context, background, and theories applied in the practice. Many art scholars have iterated this in the ways they model education in relation to the art world (notably,

---

18 For an overview of these drivers, see H. Gaunt, C. Duffy, G. Delgado, L. Messas, P. Oleksandr, and H. Sveidahl, 'Musicians as "Makers in Society": A Conceptual Foundation for Contemporary Professional Higher Music Education', *Frontiers in Psychology*, 12/713648 (2021), 1–20 (see p. 2).

19 QAA (Quality Assurance Agency for UK Higher Education), 'Subject Benchmark Statement: Music', December 2019, p. 6, https://www.qaa.ac.uk/docs/qaa/subject-benchmark-statements/subject-benchmark-statement-music.pdf?sfvrsn=61e2cb81_4

20 Ibid., p. 10.

21 Ibid., p. 17.

22 Celia Duffy and Joe Harrop, 'Towards Convergence: Academic Studies and the Student Performer', in *Musicians in the Making: Pathways to Creative Performance*, ed. by John Rink, Helena Gaunt, and Aaron Williamon (Oxford: Oxford University Press, 2017), p. 271.

the aspect of Sharing, in the REACT model is particularly pertinent to my case studies and to the UK pedagogic approach to embedding employability). They refer to the ways in which we are 'thinking-in-art'[23] and 'thinking-through-art'[24] but also to how we are 'doing-thinking'[25] as art practitioners and as educators. These different prepositions reveal the ways in which we need to consider how we teach performance. Educating music performance relies on all the senses and, so, for an authentic experience and understanding that is relatable to the art world, the learning and, in turn, assessment must be embodied.

The aim for these two modules and their associated projects, discussed below, was to ensure that students can see themselves reflected in the curriculum and see themselves as part of the art world in a way which is meaningful to their career aims, to their experiences. The objective included enabling students to expand their knowledge and experiences, and so to ensure the learning is embodied in the art practice. As such, it was imperative that the learning environment, the learning outcomes, and the assessment facilitated a process whereby, in performance classes and practical music-making sessions, 'tacit knowledge can be translated into discursive knowledge'.[26] This aim meant that I needed to identify where students could not see themselves represented, where barriers existed in the curriculum, but also, in cases where assessment used traditional forms of writing and reflection, how I could ensure that learning was also embodied. Integration was and is central: the curriculum now integrates critical-thinking skills (REACT model, Contextualization), applied music-making skills, cultural and societal awareness into a 'deeply interconnected ecology'.[27]

Project 1: 'Taking Race Live', Integrating Soundpainting into an Inclusive Undergraduate Curriculum

Taking Race Live (2014–2018) was a four-year funded project that aimed to utilise performance experiences[28] of race, ethnicity, identity, culture (in an intersectional

---

23   Maurice Merleau-Ponty, *Signs*, trans. by Richard McCleary (Evanston: Northwestern University Press, 1964).

24   Stefan Östersjö, 'Thinking-through-Music: On Knowledge Production, Materiality, Embodiment, and Subjectivity in Artistic Research', in *Artistic Research in Music: Discipline and Resistance: Artists and Researchers at the Orpheus Institute*, ed. by Jonathan Impett (Leuven: Leuven University Press, 2017), pp. 86–107.

25   Robin Nelson, *Practice as Research in the Arts: Principles, Protocols, Pedagogies, Resistances* (Basingstoke: Palgrave, 2013), p. 3.

26   David Gorton and Stefan Östersjö, 'Austerity Measures I: Performing the Discursive Voice', in *Voices, Bodies, Practices*, ed. by C. Laws, W. Brooks, D. Gorton, T. T. Nguyên, S. Östersjö, and J. Wells (Leuven: Leuven University Press, 2019), pp. 29-82 (p. 38).

27   Duffy and Harrop, p. 72.

28   H. J. Minors, P. Burnard, C. Wiffen, Z. Shihabi, Z., and J. S. van der Walt, 'Mapping Trends and Framing Issues in Higher Music Education: Changing Minds/Changing Practices', *London Review of Education*, 15/3 (2017), 457–73. Helen Julia Minors, 'From Women's Revolutions Per Minute through Taking Race Live to Co-Founding Equality, Diversity and Inclusion Music Studies Network', in *Routledge Companion to Women and Musical Leadership: the nineteenth century and beyond*, edited by Laura Hamer and Helen Julia Minors (London and New York: Routledge, 2024), pp.624–633.

approach) to develop an inclusive, equitable curriculum, with a specific aim of removing the awarding gap (the gap between the attainment of UK White domicile students, and student from Black, Asian Ethnic Minority Backgrounds) in that curriculum.[29] Alongside this, I had hosted the International Soundpainting Think Tank and developed an extra-curricular ensemble whereby we were testing our own creativity in an improvisatory setting to see how we could create music between stylistic boundaries.[30] These two experiences led to questions about the implementation of societal-change-informed pedagogic approaches. In order to develop the aims of 'Taking Race Live', my research collaborators and I linked the research to second-year level 5 modules in our associated subject (in music, sociology, dance, media, drama). Ultimately, the project aimed to remove the awarding gap between the different performance achievements of different demographics of students, to ensure equity of experience and opportunity. As such, I chose to link this to the module 'Aural and Analysis' for two reasons: 1) The awarding gap was the widest of the modules I led, and 2) the mid-module review had shown that, although students were enjoying the classes, they could not see the module's relevance to their future careers. 'Taking Race Live' recruited students' partners, who were paid, to lead meetings, to lead the end-of-year symposium, and to work with colleagues as peers in reassessing the ways in which our lived experience could be utilised in learning. Through discussion with students, it was clear they wanted to do something, to make things, and to use their performance skills. As such, I choose to consider how we might bring improvisation into the module and its assessment, as a way to bring in individual voices, experiences, cultures, and preferences into learning about structure, form, style, and how to discern those facets aurally.

In making the assessment work inclusively, I needed to find a way to integrate their critical thinking through writing and talking, as much as through the creative work in their art world[31]—that of making music. As such, the module changes, shown in Table 12.1 below, moved the learning outcomes from rigid recognition of small- and large-scale structure to a more open approach in order to understand a range of structural attributes that are relevant to different musics, thereby expanding the potential for a wider number of musical genres to be included. Different improvisation approaches were included in the class, including Soundpainting, Conduction, free improvisation, and improvising over a figured bass/ground bass/groove.

To integrate improvised performance approaches, I decided to apply a guided method—one which emphasised coaching students into finding their own performance voice and facilitating them in listening to each other and co-constructing music in

---

29 S. Sharma, E. Catalano, H. Seetzen, H. J. Minors, and S. Collins-Mayo, 'Taking Race Live: Exploring Experiences of Race through Interdisciplinary Collaboration in Higher Education', *London Review of Education*, 17/2 (2019), 193–205.

30 Helen Julia Minors, 'Soundpainting: A Tool for Collaborating during Performance', in *Artistic Research in Performance through Collaboration*, ed. by M. Blain and H. J. Minors (Basingstoke: Macmillan, 2020), pp. 113–38.

31 Östersjö, 'Art Worlds'.

the moment. I was aware this would mean introducing a new musical approach and another musical literacy, that of Soundpainting. Students already were reading scores, reading tab, using graphic notation, using various software (Logic and Protools mainly), so they had different forms of musical literacies. I chose to add another, which was embodied and physical. Multiple literacies, or perhaps it is best described as a 'communal meta-language',[32] I saw it as a benefit for musical education as it encourages the student to see, hear, feel, understand, and critique the many aspects of what is happening. The senses work in combination to make the learning applied.

The approach taken was collaborative in that no student was asked to perform alone. By using guided methods, through the signed coded gestures of Soundpainting, the entire class could experiment together to find their sound and to find a way this could work for them. The importance of the individual was central to developing the inclusive framework, which asks, among other things: 'Are a diverse range of assessment styles (including choice) used to reduce the need for reasonable adjustments and ensure that the assessment medium reflects their own strengths and educational backgrounds?'.[33] By offering choice in assessment, students could explore within one-to-one tutorials and in groups, according to their preferences. They could utilise peer support and dialogue. Moreover, in working as a group, I was hoping to reduce anxiety in assessment through art-world application by giving the opportunity for group, and not only solo, performance. As such, I hoped that I met the inclusive curriculum aim of 'involv[ing] in real-world tasks that demonstrate meaningful application of essential knowledge and skills'.[34] In other words, I wanted students to use problem solving, creative tools, dialogue, collaboration, and their individual instrumental performance skills to create a coherent piece of music in the moment. Interestingly, despite the option for group or solo improvisation, only one student across four annual iterations of the module chose a solo performance to improve over a ground bass; all other members of these cohorts choose, as a group, to create a Soundpainting. Mid-module feedback from 2014–2015 was that, as the creation was 'guided', it 'enabled everyone to have a voice and a sound', it gave 'freedom of style' and it was 'open to any mistake being revised in the moment – essentially, you could create to avoid a musical error'.

The central aim was for students to be critically aware of the structure, style, rhythm, melody, and harmony of the work and to offer a creative performance in which they co-constructed the development of the piece. My approach was similar to Duffy and Harrop's in that the learning outcomes and aims of the module revision defined a creative performance as: 'one that is somehow independent, individual, challenging, thoughtful, risky, enlightening and disturbing, offering new light on the music'.[35] Similar qualities are listed in the QAA benchmark, in fact, for exploring performance

---

32 Ibid., p. 46.
33 Kingston University, 'Inclusive Curriculum Framework'.
34 Ibid.
35 Duffy and Harrop, p. 272.

skills, ensuring collaborative performance, enabling interpretative performance, and discerning new music in different settings.[36] With this agenda set in the module, we listened and created music each week, varying approaches. But, on a weekly basis, the module group listened to new music, were introduced to different analytical approaches, and created music on their chosen instrument.

McPherson's definition of an art space within education is what this module and the associated changes achieved and aspired to: 'The creative ecology generated in higher education art schools is in space and place, with matter and mattering that position artists in, with and outside boundaries, borderlands and the in-betweens of creative practices'.[37] Or, phrased in line with the REACT model, the educational spaces need to encourage the learner to be a confident and resourceful artistic researcher and practitioner through their learning, by engaging across the intersectional dimensions of the model (see Introduction). Through encouraging individual performance approaches to guide critical listening and creativity, individuals were shown as valuable. Through 'Taking Race Live', the students had the opportunity, additionally, to engage with guest talks, pop-up performance events, and focus groups, to explore how their learning had been supported. One student partner, in reflecting on the module and the project summed it up as: 'it was an amazing opportunity for everyone to voice their experience'. In response to specific requests for self-reflection about how the module had expanded their experiences, another student said: 'I developed a talent that I'm trying to express myself through music ... as part of a culture ... [while] trying to analyse, from outside, what we do'. This response is directly related to the revised learning outcomes, which, as Table 12.1 shows, requires students to analyse and critically reflect on music through analytical models and through improvisation. As referred to elsewhere,[38] the second-year modules associated with 'Taking Race Live' all removed the former awarding gap, showing that equity of opportunity had, at the time, been achieved.

But how had these activities responded to the inclusive-curriculum framework set out by Kingston University, within which the project 'Taking Race Live' was hoping to develop meaningful learning and research? The framework 'promotes a universal approach to course design intended to improve the experience, skills and awarding of all students'.[39] As such, it offers guidance but allows the subject experts to create the content. Three key aims are issued: 'Create an accessible curriculum; Enable students to see themselves reflected in the curriculum; Equip students with the skills to positively contribute to and work in a global and diverse world'.[40] One student partner reported that the approach helped them to develop a 'refreshed enjoyment' of their studies,

---

36   QAA, UK Quality Code for Higher Education: The Frameworks for Higher Education Qualifications of UK Degree-Awarding Bodies, October 2014, https://www.qaa.ac.uk/docs/qaa/quality-code/qualifications-frameworks.pdf
37   McPherson, p. 34.
38   Minors et al.; Sharma et al.
39   Kingston University, 'Inclusive Curriculum'.
40   Ibid.

creating a sense of belonging in the group and in their cohort. In equipping students to work independently in the future, it was noticeable that, in the focus groups, student partners referred to their future. One was convinced that 'it's definitely going to help in the future because of that personal development'.

Guided by critical questions to help the module leader and course leader to question the subject-specific needs, the inclusive curriculum framework supported an open approach to reflecting on curriculum design that avoided and managed unconscious bias. For example, 'Have you checked all the content is accessible to different groups of students and materials adhere to best practice for disabled students and students with a learning difference?'.[41] Interestingly, in the focus groups in 'Taking Race Live', the participants recognised that 'it was about me'.

Original Module	Aural and Analysis (as revised in 2011) (This module had also been revised in 2014 to include an arrangement but this was lasted only the year as this skill was moved into its own module)
Original Learning Outcomes	With respect to music from a variety of genres, identify aurally both large-scale and small-scale structures and patterns, as well as instrumentation and stylistic characteristics;
	Interrogate musical scores in order to discern structure, use of compositional devices and deployment of instrumental forces;
	Present clearly their own analysis of a piece using world and diagrams.
Original Assessment	A listening test, 50%;
	A portfolio of short analyses, 50%.
Modified Module	Aural, Analysis, and Improvisation (revised in 2014).
Modified Learning Outcome	To further develop students' skills in critically listening to music and in reading, writing and analysing it;
	To introduce students to analytical methodology;
	To enable the students to understand the philosophies underpinning a variety of different approaches to improvisation;
	To enhance creativity through the exploration of a variety of improvised techniques and styles.
Modified Assessment	Aural test and improvisation (practical), 70% assessment—consisting of aural awareness and understanding test (30%) and an improvisation (40%) (the style and manner of which is chosen by the student;
	Analysis folio (30%) (students choose the music to analyse from a prepared selection).
Level FHEQ (2014, Online)	Level 5, second year of a full time three undergraduate year degree).

---

41 Ibid.

Identifying significant curriculum content change	Introduction of applied learning through creating music through guided improvisation; considering analysis through listening, writing, reading, and doing; offering choice within the assessment whereby students chose which form of improvisation to use from those introduced, and where students choose which pieces/styles to analyse; a change to assessment weighting to bring in the practical art world experience of creating music into the assessment through performance with an audience, removing the notion of the exam.

Table 12.1. Aural, Analysis, and Improvisation, second-year module.

Project 2: Developing an Inclusive Postgraduate Performance Curriculum

An outward facing approach to research, practice, and teaching is important. In other words, the institution, within which the work is being created and the ideas being taught, cannot close itself off from the wider art world. The pedagogic practice needs to encourage a student to look outwards to that art world, and inwards to their own response and approach to it. As Marina Cyrino asked for her own PhD studies and her institution, it is necessary to remember to ask oneself: 'what does artistic research ... have to say?'.[42]

The challenges of integrating a personality into the interpretation of music, of helping students' find their personal voice, was outlined by Janet Ritterman. She was aware that there is a balance between personal voice, technical knowledge, and performance practices being taught within specific cultures: 'young performers need to be helped to acquire this knowledge gradually and to wear it lightly: it cannot be a substitute for musical instinct, or become so weighty that it silences the personal voice'.[43] In reflecting on how to develop an inclusive curriculum for the postgraduate music performance students, I was clear that it needed to go beyond performance and include critical, analytical, and reflective skills. These had always been part of the longstanding Master's in Music Performance at Kingston, but the aesthetic module, which I had been teaching since 2010, had been written to largely look at Western, classical traditions. It struck me during 'Taking Race Live' that the reading and examples were limited and not inclusive. So, alongside the above module, I decided to work with colleagues in developing my master's module, which had been entitled 'The Aesthetics of Musical Performance'. This was retitled 'The Critical Presentation of Performance' (see Table 12.2) to acknowledge that its scope included the students'

---

42 Marina Cyrino, 'An inexplicable hunger – flutist)body(flute (dis)encounters', PhD Dissertation (University of Gothenburg, 2019), p. 25, https://gupea.ub.gu.se/handle/2077/59147
43 Janet Ritterman, 'On Teaching Performance', in *Musical Performance: A Guide to Understanding*, ed. by John Rink (Cambridge: Cambridge University Press, 2002), pp. 75-88 (p. 84).

own experiences, their voice, their futures, and their need to develop explicit and tangible employability skills.

As Table 12.2 shows, the module wording was also changed to become more inclusive by avoiding specific reference to any styles or genres, removing the debates which had benefitted those more confident speakers and had prompted much anxiety in the cohort (as reported in end-of-year module reviews). By integrating the students' own performance aims and career goals, I was able to retain a focus on aesthetics but relate this directly to their chosen instrument, style, genre, and skills. Additionally, the graduate attributes concerning confidence, resilience, development, and wellbeing were supported by developing personal SWOT (strengths, weaknesses, opportunities, threats) analyses.

Original Module	The Aesthetics of Musical Performance (revised 2013)
Original Learning Outcomes	Demonstrate awareness and understanding of a range of issues relating to the study of the aesthetics of musical performance;
	Evaluate and assess a range of texts and other materials from an aesthetic standpoint;
	Engage in debate on the roles, values and practices of musical performers in a critical and informed manner;
	Express arguments relating to the aesthetics of musical performance in an appropriate academic written format.
Original Assessment	2 Debates, 30% (formed from 50% written and presented component and 50% active participation in the debate);
	Essay, 70%, *c.* 2,500 words.
Modified Module	Critical Aspects of Musical Performance (revised 2018)
Modified Learning Outcome	To develop in students an awareness of psychological issues relating to musical performance;
	To enable students to develop positive mental performing beliefs and strategies;
	To develop skills of critical and analytical thought in relation to the aesthetics of musical performances;
	To develop professional promotional strategies and materials throughout the year.
Modified Assessment	Critical reflection on a musical performance on video, 60%;
	Folio of promotion materials (including website, social media channels, SWOT analysis and marketing brief) 40%.
Level FHEQ (2014, Online)	Level 7, postgraduate 1 year degree programme (full time, or 2 year part time study)

Identifying significant curriculum content change	Removal of debates and replaced with an individual, personally bespoke critical development and reflection on their own performance brand and a development of a professional folio which includes website and social media channels;
	Essays on aesthetics replaced by an analysis of a performance which applied aesthetic understanding, bringing the performance to the centre of the activity.

Table 12.2. The Critical Presentation of Performance, master's module.

SWOT analysis involves a self-assessment of one's own strengths and weaknesses in order to explore learning needs, but it also encourages students to be authentic and honest with themselves as they start to plan the next steps of their professional careers. As Aaron Williamon advises in his research into musical excellence, all teachers and students in performance should 'carry out a realistic assessment of individual strengths and weaknesses in skill'.[44] As part of the revised module, I gave models for how to do a SWOT analysis, both on the virtual learning environment, with templates for completion, and also in class for group discussion, with large sheets of paper for small groups to work on, to reflect on the strengths and weaknesses that need to be considered. The peer observation and peer feedback seemed most helpful, with students regularly asking others for thoughts on their own ideas.

The module fundamentally changed how students explores the aesthetic. Instead of analysing an essay of others' examples, an activity students had verbally described as being 'abstract', the revisions brought into focus self-awareness, self-assessment, self-learning, and self-branding. Interestingly, by moving the essay to the analysis of a video recording and allowing students to choose (with guidance) the performance to analyse, almost all chose a video related to their own instrument. They fed back that the choice would 'inform' their own work, 'be supportive' of their listening, and 'broaden' their experience.

Importantly, though, to ensure this module engaged with graduate attributes in a meaningful way, the revised content now included advice and approaches for mental practice. It included discussions about Mikhail Csikszentmihalyi's notion of flow[45] and his ideas that one's creativity and performance intersect with the cultural context. By raising these topics, we discussed the points at which students' began to feel anxious during the preparation for performance and during the performances themselves. We discussed and practised breathing techniques. During the Covid-19

---

[44] Aaron Williamon, 'A Guide to Enhancing Musical Performance', in *Musical Excellence: Strategies and Techniques to Enhance Performance*, ed. by Aaron Williamon (Oxford: Oxford University Press, 2004), pp. 3–18 (p. 13).

[45] Mikhail Csikszentmihalyi, *Creativity: Flow and the Psychology of Discovery and Invention* (New York: Harper Collins Publishers, 1997).

pandemic when we were in a national lockdown and teaching online, I supplemented weekly classes with online rehearsals, whereby anyone could join to say hello, touch base, and, while on mute, rehearse in their own homes with the knowledge that others were also rehearsing at the same time. This idea I took from my own orchestra, the Aldworth Philharmonic Orchestra, where we often meet online to rehearse, to generate a community of support to encourage practice. Knowing someone else is there and committing to someone else was a good driver in encouraging practice. Considering that some of the top 10 future skills identified by employers and businesses[46] include resilience, adaptability, digital skills, and creativity, it was important for me as a lecturer to embed these qualities into my teaching.

As such, I guided these students in how to create their own performance websites, including social-media channels and with a complete marketing brief—a first step in helping them establish their professional portfolio for the future. And it had a hidden bonus I had not anticipated. To these websites, they uploaded videos of performances, events, rehearsals, blogs, vlogs, and even TikTok videos, creating a one-stop archive of their performance work and a location, for those who were ready, to promote their teaching, their live events (though these were paused during the Covid-19 pandemic), and their album launches. As one student noted by email, following graduation: 'I'm still using my website we created for assessment, it's set me up well for being a freelance musician'. By encouraging students to perform self-analysis as well as analyses of others, they were constantly encouraged to reflect on their place in their art world, within the industry of their performance mode of study. One benefit of working in lockdown during the Covid-19 pandemic was that, with the reduced time spent commuting, students began to engage more with online platforms, and we used the virtual learning environment's discussion board to share videos of performances individuals found significant. The additional discussion positively impacted peer-to-peer learning and support. Though it is difficult to refer to metrics regarding the issue of confidence at the end of that 2020–2021 academic year (the one most impact by online learning), everyone in the class had reported in module feedback an improvement in confidence and resilience.

Concluding Reflections

In essence, what I have discussed above is an approach to teaching, learning, and assessment that aligns with Small's idea of 'musicking'[47]—that is, in whatever we are creating, doing, and making, we are part of the musical activity in various ways. All aspects of our work link to it. We are doing music, and specifically, we are doing music

---

46 Kingston University, 'Future Skills'.
47 Christopher Small, *Musicking: The Meanings of Performing and Listening* (Middletown, CT: Wesleyan Press, 1998).

in the space of the art world as much as possible, not only in the synthetic context of the classroom.

To say this again, in relation to the REACT model (see Introduction), the learning process ensures critical thinking at every stage in order to enable students to develop new practices in full awareness of their own subjectivities. It facilitates students in exploring and experimenting to create their own individual artistic voice, while recognising the need to do so in a way which is ready and fit for their artistic world, to ensure they will be able to disseminate and share their work professionally in the future. The model is important in illustrating the intersections between all aspects of the learning process, and, also, though in different terms, it shows the integration of employability skills. This latter is so vital in the UK pedagogic practice for undergraduate degrees, as these are assessed on their outcomes in terms of graduate salary fifteen months after graduation. The model speaks in terms that are transferable across the continent of Europe (the setting of the project) and beyond. The inclusive language of the model and of the project are deliberate to ensure we ourselves share the practice within the art world and the educational world.

The quality of the student's work in each module and each assessed project was paramount: ensuring they could meet the learning outcomes and that they could develop their understanding in a critical way, which would benefit their future employment, making then autonomous and lifelong learners, was central to the changes being made in these projects. Embedding the graduate attributes in an explicit way was important to reveal where these skills were being taught, as previously they had seemed implicit, and students could not always see the relevance of what was being asked of them. Although the assessments in performance courses are held in higher education institutions for the purposes of grading, we must make the assessment practice as authentic as possible, to replicate the art world outside the institution. To this extent, many institutions, including Kingston, supported students in performing externally to the university and encouraged them to do so as part of their performance modules. This was particularly revealing in the students' websites, as they shared images of the venues, or the programmes and marketing material for all the work they were creating in the art world, for the purposes of academic assessment. As Östersjö concludes in his research, the artistic quality must be understood 'within its art world'.[48] Assessing a performance in a venue and with an audience is a priority. Creating and enabling an in-person and virtual audience for the music is so important in today's global music-streaming context. Music is the topic of their chosen degree course. The ideas and experiences are lived in practice, 'thought through music'.[49] The 'through' part of this process is integral, and this is why the assessment in both modules focussed on the process and the application in both the learning outcomes and in the choice of assessment. Or, as Gaunt and colleagues noted in their research,

---

48   Östersjö, 'Art Worlds', p. 82.
49   Cyrino, p. 26.

integrating musicking into Higher Music Education learning is 'a partnering of artistic and social values in order to enable HME to respond dynamically to societal need, and to continue to engage with the depth and integrity of established musical transitions and their craft'.[50]

To ensure participation and inclusion of all, there needs to be a starting point which is aligned to the cohort and the individual students. Each student needs to develop critical awareness of not only the subject matter but also their own performance skills and approaches, with an understanding of their own strengths and weaknesses and with a plan to develop personal quality through practice, testing, sharing, reflection, feedback, and support. Advocating for a regular peer-to-peer dialogue was one way of supporting students outside as well as inside the classroom. Higher Music Education is, like all areas of higher education, 'characterized by fast moving change, the imperative for networking and innovation, and the necessity of being able to negotiate cultural differences'.[51] This is vital to a learning environment which includes global concerns. Changing the wording of validation documents, learning outcomes, and assessments to declare more clearly the employability skills being trained is vital to support students' understanding and to guide everyone through their personal journeys to reach their potential. Embedding discussions on wellbeing, self-awareness, resilience and coping strategies, can help build confidence. Being authentic in teaching is also about sharing personal experiences and to offer advice beyond the theoretical and enable students to test out ideas.

References

Blain, Martin and Helen Julia Minors (eds), *Artistic Research in Performance through Collaboration* (Basingstoke: Macmillan, 2020)

Buck, Lil and Yo Yo Ma, 'Yo Yo Ma and Lil' Buck Do "The Swan" in Beijing', YouTube, uploaded by Flatone, 7 Nov 2014, https://www.youtube.com/watch?v=qfEYjKWJ56E

Bull, A., D. Bhachu, A. Blier-Carruthers, A. Bradley and S. James, 'Slow Train Coming? Equality, Diversity and Inclusion in UK Music Higher Education', *Equality, Diversity and Inclusion in Music Studies Network* (2022) https://edims.network/report/slowtraincoming/

Östersjö, Stefan, 'Art Worlds, Voice and Knowledge: Thoughts on Quality Assessment of Artistic Outcomes', *Online Journal for Artistic Research*, 3/2 (2019), 60–89

Cyrino, Marina, 'An inexplicable hunger – flutist)body(flute (dis)encounters', PhD Dissertation (University of Gothenburg, 2019), https://gupea.ub.gu.se/handle/2077/59147

Csikszentmihalyi, Mikhail, *Creativity: Flow and the Psychology of Discovery and Invention* (New York: Harper Collins Publishers, 1997)

---

50 Gaunt et al, p. 1.
51 Helena Gaunt and Heidi Westerlund, *Collaborative Learning in Higher Music Education* (London: Routledge, 2016). p. 1.

Duffy, Celia and Joe Harrop, 'Towards Convergence: Academic Studies and the Student Performer', in *Musicians in the Making: Pathways to Creative Performance*, ed. by John Rink, Helena Gaunt, and Aaron Williamon (Oxford: Oxford University Press, 2017), pp. 271–87

Frayling, Christopher, *Research in Art and Design: Royal College of Art Research Papers Series*, 1/1 (1993)

Gaunt, H., C. Duffy, G. Delgado, L. Messas, P. Oleksandr, and H. Sveidahl, 'Musicians as "Makers in Society": A Conceptual Foundation for Contemporary Professional Higher Music Education', *Frontiers in Psychology*, 12/713648 (2021), 1–20

Gaunt, Helena and Heidi Westerlund, *Collaborative Learning in Higher Music Education* (London: Routledge, 2016)

Gorton, David and Stefan Östersjö, 'Austerity Measures I: Performing the Discursive Voice', in *Voices, Bodies, Practices*, ed. by C. Laws, W. Brooks, D. Gorton, T. T. Nguyễn, S. Östersjö, and J. Wells (Leuven: Leuven University Press, 2019), pp. 29–82

Hari, Johann, *Lost Connections: Why You're Depressed and How to Find Hope* (London: Bloomsbury, 2018)

Hussain, M., 'Why is My Curriculum White?', *NUS News*, 11 March 2015, http://www.nus.org.uk/en/news/why-is-my-curriculum-white/

Kingston University, 'Future Skills', 2022, https://www.kingston.ac.uk/aboutkingstonuniversity/future-skills/

Kingston University, 'Kingston University's Navigate programme to prepare students for career success by embedding future skills across curriculum', 2022, https://www.kingston.ac.uk/news/article/2747/16-nov-2022--kingston-universitys-navigate-programme-to-prepare-students-for-career-success-by-embedding-future-skills/

Kingston University, 'Inclusive Curriculum Framework', 2023, https://www.kingston.ac.uk/aboutkingstonuniversity/equality-diversity-and-inclusion/our-inclusive-curriculum/inclusive-curriculum-framework/

Kingston University, 'Lib Dem MPs visit Kingston University to hear how Future Skills are being embedded into curriculum', YouTube, uploaded by Kingston University, 14 Nov 2022, https://www.youtube.com/watch?v=f8gy54op2FE

Levinson, Jerrold, 'Performative vs. Critical Interpretations in Music', in *The Interpretation of Music*, ed. by M. Krausz (Oxford: Clarendon Press, 1993), pp. 33–60

McPherson, Megan, 'In-Between Practice and Art Worlds', in *Creativities in Arts Education, Research and Practice: International Perspectives for the Future of Learning and Teaching*, ed. by L. R. de Bruin, P. Burnard, and S. Davis (Leiden and Boston: Brill Sense, 2018), pp. 33–45

Merleau-Ponty, Maurice, *Signs*, trans. by Richard McCleary (Evanston, IL: Northwestern University Press, 1964)

Minors, Helen Julia (ed), *Music, Text and Translation* (London: Bloomsbury, 2013)

Minors, Helen Julia, 'From Women's Revolutions Per MInute through Taking Race Live to Co-Founding Equality, Diversity and Inclusion Music Studies Network', in *Routledge Companion to Women and Musical Leadership: the nineteenth century and beyond*, edited by Laura Hamer and Helen Julia Minors (London and New York: Routledge, 2024), pp. 624–633

Minors, Helen Julia, 'Soundpainting: A Tool for Collaborating during Performance', in *Artistic Research in Performance through Collaboration*, ed. by M. Blain and H. J. Minors (Basingstoke: Macmillan, 2020), pp. 113–38

Minors, H. J., P. Burnard, C. Wiffen, Z. Shihabi, and J. S, van der Walt, 'Mapping Trends and Framing Issues in Higher Music Education: Changing Minds/Changing Practices', *London Review of Education*, 15/3 (2017), November, 457–73

Morgan, Winston, 'Why is My Professor Still Not Black?', *Times Higher Education*, 14 March 2016, http://www.timeshighereducation.com/blog/why-my-professor-still-not-black

Nelson, Robin, *Practice as Research in the Arts: Principles, Protocols, Pedagogies, Resistances* (Basingstoke: Palgrave, 2013)

Östersjö, Stefan, 'Art Worlds, Voice and Knowledge: Thoughts on Quality Assessment of Artistic Research Outcomes', *ÍMPAR, Online Journal for Artistic Research*, 3/2 (2019), 60–89

Östersjö, Stefan, 'Thinking-through-Music: On Knowledge Production, Materiality, Embodiment, and Subjectivity in Artistic Research', in *Artistic Research in Music: Discipline and Resistance: Artists and Researchers at the Orpheus Institute*, ed. by Jonathan Impett (Leuven: Leuven University Press, 2017), pp. 86–107

Purves, R., N. A. Marshall, D. J. Hargreaves, and G. Welch, 'Teaching as a Career? Perspectives From Undergraduate Musicians in England', *Bulletin of the Council for Research in Music Education*, 161/162 (2004), 1–8

QAA (Quality Assurance Agency for UK Higher Education), 'Subject Benchmark Statement: Music', December 2019, https://www.qaa.ac.uk/docs/qaa/subject-benchmark-statements/subject-benchmark-statement-music.pdf?sfvrsn=61e2cb81_4

——, *UK Quality Code for Higher Education: The Frameworks for Higher Education Qualifications of UK Degree-Awarding Bodies*, 2014, https://www.qaa.ac.uk/docs/qaa/quality-code/qualifications-frameworks.pdf

Ritterman, Janet, 'On Teaching Performance', in *Musical Performance: A Guide to Understanding*, ed. by John Rink (Cambridge: Cambridge University Press, 2002), pp. 75–88

Sharma, S., E. Catalano, H. Seetzen, H. J. Minors, and S. Collins-Mayo, 'Taking Race Live: Exploring Experiences of Race through Interdisciplinary Collaboration in Higher Education', *London Review of Education*, 17/2 (2019), 93–205, https://doi.org/10.18546/lre.17.2.07

Small, Christopher, *Musicking: The Meanings of Performing and Listening* (Middletown, CT: Wesleyan University Press, 1998)

York St John University, 'Graduate Attributes', 2022, https://www.yorksj.ac.uk/careers-and-placements/graduate-attributes/

Williamon, Aaron (ed), *Musical Excellence: Strategies and techniques to enhance performance* (Oxford: Oxford University Press, 2004)

13. Conclusion: Probing, Positioning, (Re)Acting

Helen Julia Minors and Stefan Östersjö

Probing

How do we teach performance in higher music education? Or, should the question be how might we be teaching music performance in higher education if we were to base learning on artistic research rather than on skill acquisition in the traditional hierarchical European model of master-apprentice? Or, to rephrase, how might we teach performance according to a student-centred pedagogy—one which embeds employability skills, to ensure students have agency within and through their own learning, directed toward an authentic experience which is relevant to the student, to peers, and, also, for the global music industries now? The rephrasing of the question is necessary for our practices as artistic researchers and pedagoges because this book is about challenging how we teach performance to ensure we improve the student experience and that we share our own artistic practices with students and vice versa. An experiential basis to learning is vital. It situates the self and positions teaching as a sharing of practices. The balance of barriers and opportunities in HME is asserted by Heidi Westerlund and Helena Gaunt: 'Contemporary societal changes can thus be experienced both in terms of intense challenges and limitless potential for music'.[1] Moreover, we give a proposition: music educators must reflect on their teaching and change their practices to ensure they are inclusive. These must truly engage students as co-producers of knowledge, enabling them to understand the contemporary music industries with a global outlook.

Throughout the book, we have encountered a number of musicians who have developed artistic research practices. They are grounded in different art worlds and different cultures: the country music harmonica playing of Mikael Bäckman, and his explorations of the licks of Charlie McCoy; the electric bass of Fausto Pizzol, and his explorations of its potential for harmonic playing; Mariam Kharatyan's explorations

---

1 Heidi Westerlund and Helena Gaunt, *Expanding Professionalism in Music and Higher Music Education: A Changing Game* (New York: Routledge, 2022), p. xvii.

of improvisation as a tool to enhance the performance of classical piano repertoire; Robert Sholl's demonstrations of how improvisation may be a path to learning music theory. Their writing is sometimes analytical, sometimes descriptive, but they share the commonality that the practices they have developed only obtain their full meaning when manifested in context and shared with listeners, other musicians, or with students. The varying methodologies are necessary to articulate both artistic embodied experience and reflective practice through the creative process, then, not least, to embed artistic research effectively into pedagogic practice.

These artistic research practices are not merely means for individual development but also methods for sharing with students. The artistic researcher brings authentic practices and recent artworks into the teaching situation in order to nurture students' own creative practice and to develop their own personal artistic voices, with a critical understanding of the context. Much as the REACT model shows (see the Introduction to this volume), the intersectional overlap of how we contextualise our artistic practice, while exploring that practice and then sharing the practice in some way, ensures we are considering learning which is grounded on artistic research. This enables us as pedagogues to bring an authentic and inclusive experience to students in our global classrooms while also challenging them, and ourselves, to develop new practices. On our own and with others, we negotiate tradition and innovation in such a way that we are aware of what novel aspects we are bringing in our own work and continually reflect on our work in order to reconfigure our practice in ways that are relevant and sustainable. As such, we align ourselves with the position advanced by Paul G. Woodford:

> In [our] own field of music education, for example, curricula emphasise skills development, pedagogical methods, the acquisition of knowledge, national standards, and degree outcomes instead of teaching students how to research and develop arguments so they can think more critically about what they read, are told, see, hear, or do.[2]

In other words, education has become inherently political and, by readdressing the pedagogical ways in which we encourage students to develop their own critical voices in and through practice, we react to limiting factors in the pedagogical system to suggest ways in which we can revolutionise approaches to teaching music performance. The aim is to make our curricula and teaching more inclusive, more globally aware, more authentic in their practical creation to reflect the music industries, and, ultimately, to ensure we are encouraging students to work as artistic researcher right from the start of their creative journey.

Such close inquiries into specific artistic research practices embedded into a teaching and learning experience of performance are central to the book. In offering these varied case studies, the book shares some ways in which artistic research is becoming

---

2   Paul G. Woodford, *Music Education in an Age of Virtuality and Post-Truth* (New York: Routledge, 2019), p. 2.

central to performance learning in HME. It is, however, Euro-centric: the book builds on shared agreements from the Bologna process (detailed in the Introduction of this book), and authors were brought together through a European funded project. This is not to say that the examples cannot be applied globally, but we share this observation to draw attention to both the limitations of the book and the model and to clearly state our positionality (more on this below).

As can be seen in many chapters across this book, starting in Chapter 1, a defining factor of much artistic research in music is the use of recording technologies in the development of research methods. Such approaches also play a prominent role in the application of artistic research methods and practices in first- and second-cycle teaching. The use of audio and video recording enables both reflective practices as well as intersubjective learning, as is evident in Chapters 1 and 8. In artistic research, such practices have been employed to integrate artistic development with methods for documentation and analysis.

> If scholarly institutions of knowledge are founded on particular relations with archives, rather than specifically on the medium of writing — by which I mean all forms of numerical, textual, and musical notation — then the advent of audiovisual research stands to radically transform the university and perhaps knowledge itself. At issue here is not only the forms that research can be understood to take, but also who can be recognized as conducting research and what can be counted as knowledge.[3]

Recording technology has been proven to change our conception of musical listening and performance in ways that have led to the creation of entirely new institutional structures for music creation and novel ways of engaging with music in absolute solitude. But, recording technology also offers new opportunities for the teaching and learning of music performance. Further, it enables repeated listening, of listening reflectively, analytically, and, of course, 'musicianly'.[4] All of these modes of listening also constitute possibilities that are embraced by artistic research and brought to HME as practices that may both challenge and empower students.

We are proposing not only that teaching be student-centred but also that the learning situation be designed from an intersubjective perspective so as to widen the reflexive practice beyond the reflection of the individual (see Chapter 8). If we point back to John Dewey, who said that teaching should be 'one with the moral process'[5], our role involves helping students to develop critical approaches to how we make value judgments. The proposed approach, shown in the REACT model (see Introduction), places the student's voice at the heart of the pedagogic approach and collaborative artistic research.

---

3   Ben Spatz, *Making A Laboratory. Dynamic Configurations with Transversal Video* (Santa Barbara, CA: Punctum Books, 2020), pp. 35–36.
4   Pierre Schaeffer, *Treatise on Musical Objects: An Essay Across Disciplines*, trans. by Christine North and John Dack (Oakland: University of California Press, 2017 [1966]).
5   John Dewey, *Reconstruction in Philosophy* (New York: Mentor Books, 1950), p. 145.

Positioning

It is important to acknowledge how artistic research, when it was first introduced in Europe, was quite strongly characterised by a Eurocentric understanding of musical practice and, indeed, also, of artistic knowledge. The problem, therefore, has been that the positionality of reason has not previously identified its limited context, and now our context requires us to open our collective eyes to intersectionality, equality and diversity, and inclusive practices. As such, we need to address recent interventions which are challenging the Eurocentric, white-Western models which have dominated HME. It is imperative that we decolonise our curriculum, and work in many areas has begun with gusto to consider what this means in practice, how to do this work in a way which is co-created with students, and how it ensures genuine focus on intersectionality. The challenges are not merely individual, but also structural, as phrased by Darla Crispin:

> Can inequality and oppression be challenged by those who gain advantages from those same systems? And, in this age where so much of education is in danger of being instrumentalised, is artistic research and its training not also in danger of being entrained in a series of manifesto-based false promises, thus neutralising its potential for trenchant critique? How is artistic research to be accessed by those outside its privileged areas?[6]

We return below to how artistic research has come to address these challenges, through individual projects, but will first consider the implications of a decolonising approach in relation to teaching practices in HME. For example, it is no longer acceptable for academics to merely update a reading list for a course and to claim the work is done; rather they must each consider their role and how they address the subject matter with their students. Rowena Arshad articulated ways to get started, in her call for change, when she stated that:

> Decolonising is not about deleting knowledge or histories that have been developed in the West or colonial nations; rather it is to situate the histories and knowledges that do not originate from the West in the context of imperialism, colonialism and power and to consider why these have been marginalised and decentred.[7]

Within the UK in particular, work has begun to ensure that there is equality and equity in practices through two charter marks, which are assessed by Advance HE. This organisation gives Bronze, Silver, or Gold awards to reflect a university's work in relation to Athena Swan (gender equality) and Race Equality Charter (race, ethnicity). The decolonial work is one part of this effort.[8] For example, the EDI Music Studies Network (discussed in Chapter 12) has a working group looking to reimagine the curriculum to ensure it is both decolonised but also inclusive in all forms (considering

---

6   Darla Crispin, 'The Deterritorialization and Reterritorialization of Artistic Research', ÍMPAR, *Online Journal for Artistic Research*, 3(2019), 45–59 (p. 56).
7   Rowena Arshad, 'Decolonising the curriculum - how to get started?', *Times Higher Education*, 14 September 2021, https://www.timeshighereducation.com/campus/decolonising-curriculum-how-do-i-get-started
8   Race Equality Charter, https://www.advance-he.ac.uk/equality-charters/race-equality-charter

accessibility, learning needs, and so on).⁹ We must not, however, limit the work to one of a tick-box institutional exercise, as Paul Gilroy has warned. The work, when done effectively should we considered, careful, and thought-through:

> decolonising the curriculum does not mean forsaking the archives of knowledge built up here over centuries. It asks us to approach those treasured and error-strewn forms of knowledge in a new way. We are required to read them even more carefully, always mindful of the historical factors that formed them and eager to supplement them with other perspectives and commentaries.¹⁰

In order to reflect, and to make informed changes, the work needs broad discussion. At York St John University, referred to in Chapters 11 and 12, the discussion is presently active. Laura Key reiterates the purpose of the initiative as she lays out the university's next series of seminars on decolonising the curriculum: to 'critically engage with the vital work that staff and students across the sector are undertaking to develop anti-racist and decolonial praxis in Higher Education'.¹¹

More recently, an increasing number of critical artistic research practices have been developed. This can be seen in Luca Soudant's feminist and queer critique of sound art, which, quite importantly, looks also at human/non-human entanglements.¹² Similar perspectives are found in the work of violinist, composer, and sound artist Halla Steinunn Stefánsdóttir,¹³ who has also developed experiences from her artistic research in courses for the preparation of the degree project in the Malmö Academy of Music, highlighting their impact on the creation of a more diverse and inclusive curriculum.¹⁴ Combining research on diasporic identity with gender perspectives, Nguyễn Thanh Thủy, through an artistic PhD and continued postdoctoral research, has contributed to several perspectives in the pursuit of a decolonised approach to artistic research.¹⁵ As argued in Chapter 11, to develop intercultural competence, we need methods that enable critical thinking. Artistic research, such as in the examples above, points to how a practice-based understanding of intercultural dialogue demands methods that go even further. What a decolonising approach to artistic research enables is the development of practices that strive beyond

---

9   EDI Music Studies, https://edims.network/
10 Paul Gilroy, interviewed by Inho Park, 'Decolonising' Higher Education – An Interview With Professor Paul Gilroy', *RoarNews*, 27 November 2017, https://roarnews.co.uk/2017/decolonising-higher-education-interview-professor-paul-gilroy/
11 Laura Kay, 'Discussing Decolonisation: a mini-series at York St John University, 2023–24', https://blog.yorksj.ac.uk/tatlblog/2023/10/11/discussing-decolonisation-a-mini-series-at-york-st-john-university-2023-24/
12 Luca Soudant, 'Trans*formative thinking through sound: Artistic research in gender and sound beyond the human', *Open Philosophy*, 4 (2021), 335–46, https://doi.org/10.1515/opphil-2020-0189
13 Halla Steinunn Stefánsdóttir, 'HÉR! An Exploration of Artistic Agency' (Lund: Lund University, 2023).
14 Halla Steinunn Stefánsdóttir, 'The Degree Project – evaluation from within' (forthcoming).
15 Nguyễn Thanh Thủy, 'Vietnamese Diasporic Voices: Exploring Yellow Music in a Liminal Space', *VIS - Nordic Journal for Artistic Research*, 8 (2022), https://www.researchcatalogue.net/view/1513023/1513024/0/0

diversity, toward a fundamental reconsideration, and a widening of the foundations of knowledge within academia. This also implies that in music research, not only do theory and methods need to be decolonized but also the very foundations of our embodied practices, including our listening.[16]

The opportunity of a decolonised approach to artistic research and pedagogical practice in music therefore can afford us with a renewed self-awareness and a new critical understanding of the self within context. But, to achieve it, we need to rebuild our pedagogy afresh, recognising the need for institutional changes at every level.

(Re)Acting and EnActing

The REACT project has responded to the need to develop novel ways to deliver higher music performance education. This is the case even in institutional settings where increasing government regulation and administration, along with financial belt-tightening, have developed more barriers to the delivery of the courses and change the duties of academics. This book, therefore, shares the findings that proactive research and pedagogic interventions are necessary to advance a critical curriculum which has an embodied approach to practice.

In thinking about the REACT project and how it was conceptualised, in comparison to the practices it activated, focus on the prefix is illuminating. If 're' is suggestive of reproducing, it may be doubted that merely re-acting is enough to create change. In fact, with the prefix cut out, a more active or activist approach seems to emerge. But, given the nature of the practices discussed across the book, we feel that 'acting' needs further conceptual development, through an ecological understanding, which encompasses also the cultural and pedagogical. An EnActive approach, therefore, further emphasises how practices are always relational and situated. It demands that we advocate for an embodied pedagogic approach, which expects everyone to address his or her own positionality and habitus. We therefore advocate for such an approach, which we claim would be more inclusive of individuals' experiences and educational needs in relation to the current global music industries.

Paul Craenen summarises much of the examples given throughout the book of how artistic research has emerged as an integrating factor in the new curricula being developed in HME. Rather than merely integrating a research perspective in our teaching practices, artistic research offers approaches for how to integrate a more diverse curriculum into the individual path each student develops across his or her studies. Artistic skills and outcomes form part of an individual's portfolio, enabling a professional career in the increasingly diverse art worlds of music in contemporary society:

---

16   Stefan Östersjö, Nguyễn Thanh Thủy, David Hebert, and Henrik Frisk, *Shared Listenings: Methods for Transcultural Musicianship and Research* (Cambridge: Cambridge University Press, 2023), p. 5.

The concept of artistic research offers a platform where elements of practice, theory, experimentation, and reflection can meet in a tailored, personal learning trajectory. The relevance of such a trajectory in the master curriculum depends not so much on its production of knowledge and innovation, but in *the learning experience* of creating connections between those elements through independent research: as an experience that is assumed to set a motivational example for processes of learning and adapting to different contexts in a future professional life or further education. From this viewpoint, the integrative potential of artistic research does not only aim at specialisation, but also at learning *how* to learn.[17]

Craenen's argument is, in our understanding, in agreement with the fundamental idea of the REACT model: it is necessary to put artistic research practice at the centre of the rethinking of the teaching and learning of music performance in HME.

Fundamentally, we see novel possibilities offered by artistic research in developing new ways of 'learning how to learn', as teachers share their artistic research practices and methods with students. Examples of such teaching formats are presented throughout the book, perhaps most prominently in the first section. For instance, in Chapter 3, Mikael Bäckman shares with students his experience as an artistic researcher, developing his own voice, in order to facilitate their journeys in the creation of their own performative style. In Chapter 1, a more comprehensive demonstration of the outcomes of student projects based on artistic research approaches, through an analysis of finished degree projects, is illustrated. Further, the book provides several examples of how improvisation can be introduced in unexpected contexts, as an enactive approach to learning both musical interpretation as well as music theory (see Chapter 5).

Chapter 8 advocates the use of reflection in intercultural musicking and Chapter 11 proposes dialogic approaches to co-creation across genres. Chapter 6 discusses the need to enable group agency and engage student voices in co-creating the curriculum through a critical response method. This is similar to Chapter 12, which posits the need to integrate students' habitus into the creative approaches, which are assessed. These approaches all resonate with the more overarching perspective of deep learning, as outlined and discussed in Chapter 9.

The challenge of decolonising practices is a long-term project for teacher and student alike. In the context of music performance, this will always entail a critical, dialogical, and embedded engagement with the habitus of each individual. Hence, when artistic research is enacted in HME, learning how to learn, may at times even become a matter of re-learning how to learn.

---

17 Paul Craenen, 'Artistic Research as an Integrative Force. A Critical Look at the Role of Master's Research at Dutch Conservatoires', *FORUM+*, 27.1 (2020), unpaginated, emphasis in original, https://doi.org/10.5117/FORUM2020.1.CRAE

References

Arshad, Rowena, 'Decolonising the curriculum – how to get started?', *Times Higher Education*, 14 September 2021, https://www.timeshighereducation.com/campus/decolonising-curriculum-how-do-i-get-started

Craenen, Paul, 'Artistic research as an integrative force. A critical look at the role of master's research at Dutch conservatoires', *FORUM+*, 27.1 (2020), unpaginated, https://doi.org/10.5117/FORUM2020.1.CRAE

Crispin, Darla, 'The Deterritorialization and Reterritorialization of Artistic Research', *Online Journal for Artistic Research*, 3(2019), 45–59

Dewey, John, Reconstruction in Philosophy (New York: Mentor Books, 1950)

EDI Music Studies, https://edims.network/

Gilroy, Paul, interviewed by Inho Park, 'Decolonising' Higher Education – An Interview With Professor Paul Gilroy', *RoarNews*, 27 November 2017, https://roarnews.co.uk/2017/decolonising-higher-education-interview-professor-paul-gilroy/

Key, Laura , 'Discussing Decolonisation: a mini-series at York St John University, 2023-24', https://blog.yorksj.ac.uk/tatlblog/2023/10/11/discussing-decolonisation-a-mini-series-at-york-st-john-university-2023-24/

Östersjö, Stefan, Nguyễn Thanh Thủy, David Hebert, and Henrik Frisk. *Shared Listenings: Methods for Transcultural Musicianship and Research* (Cambridge: Cambridge University Press, 2023)

Race Equality Charter, https://www.advance-he.ac.uk/equality-charters/race-equality-charter

Schaeffer, Pierre, *Treatise on Musical Objects: An Essay Across Disciplines*, trans. by Christine North and John Dack (Oakland: University of California Press, 2017 [1966])

Spatz, Ben, *Making A Laboratory. Dynamic Configurations with Transversal Video* (Santa Barbara, CA: Punctum Books, 2020), p. 35–36

Soudant, Luca, 'Trans*formative thinking through sound: Artistic research in gender and sound beyond the human', *Open Philosophy*, 4 (2021), 335–46, https://doi.org/10.1515/opphil-2020-0189

Steinunn Stefánsdóttir, Halla, 'HÉR! An Exploration of Artistic Agency.' Lund University (2023)

——, 'The Degree Project: An Evaluation from Within', in Ylva Hofvander Trulsson and Hans Hellsten (eds), *Konstuniversitetet-högskolepedagogiska betraktelser* (Lund: Mediatryck. Lund University, 2024)

Thanh Thủy, Nguyễn, 'Vietnamese Diasporic Voices: Exploring Yellow Music in a Liminal Space', *VIS - Nordic Journal for Artistic Research*, 8 (2022), unpaginated, https://www.researchcatalogue.net/view/1513023/1513024/0/0

Westerlund, Heidi and Helena Gaunt (eds), *Expanding Professionalism in Music and Higher Music Education: A Changing Game* (New York: Routledge, 2022)

Woodford, Paul G., *Music Education in an Age of Virtuality and Post-Truth* (New York: Routledge, 2019)

About the Contributors

Mikael Bäckman started playing harmonica in the late 1980s. In 1995, he joined the blues-band Ramblin' Minds and has been with them ever since, releasing six albums and touring extensively. In 2008, Mikael formed John Henry, a Country-band that has released three albums and performed numerous concerts. Mikael took his Master of Education in 2006 and a Masters of Music Performance in 2017. Since 2019, Mikael is a PhD student in Music Performance. His PhD project is focused on the deliberate transformation of a performer's voice through the process of transcription and imitation. Mikael is a proud endorsee of Hohner Harmonicas since 2012. In 2017, Mikael was one of sixteen presenters at the World Harmonica Festival in Trossingen, Germany. In August 2022, Mikael was one of the featured performers at the annual SPAH (the Society for the Preservation and Advancement of the Harmonica) convention in Tulsa, Oklahoma.

Jorge Salgado Correia is Associate Professor of Musical Performance and Artistic Creation at the Department of Communication and Art of the University of Aveiro. He received his doctorate in 2003 for a dissertation on musical performance as embodied socio-emotional meaning construction. In 2007, he became an integrated researcher at the Institute of Ethnomusicology/Center of Studies in Music and Dance (Portugal) coordinating, from then until July 2022, the research group 'Creation, Performance and Artistic Research'. Jorge is a leading Flautist specialised in the performance of contemporary music but regularly playing other music genres like Portuguese popular music, Tango, or Brazilian Chôro. As a soloist and chamber music player, he has participated in more than 12 CDs and toured all over Europe, Latin America (Brazil, Colombia, Costa Rica), USA, Asia (Macau, Shanghai), and Africa (Mozambique). As one of the 3 artistic directors and founders of Performa Ensemble, a leading Portuguese ensemble for contemporary music, Jorge has collaborated extensively with the most prominent Portuguese composers from 2010 until today, playing and recording the première of dozens of new compositions. As conductor and artistic director, he founded in 2019 the project FLUTUA, a flute orchestra which has already commissioned about 12 new compositions for its specific formation and its transdisciplinary performance approach (music, dance, and staging). Jorge is currently Editor-in-Chief of *ÍMPAR-Online Journal for Artistic Research* and is the Coordinator of the project REACT–*Rethinking Music Performance in European Higher Education Music Institutions*—a strategic partnership involving five countries and financed by ERASMUS+.

Jorge is Director of the Doctoral Programme in Artistic Creation at the University of Aveiro, Portugal and President of the Portuguese Flute Association. ORCID: 0000-0002-2255-2063

Gilvano Dalagna is invited Assistant Professor at the University of Aveiro (Portugal), invited lecturer at the Alfonso X El Sabio University (Spain), and integrated researcher at the Institute of Ethnomusicology/Center of Studies in Music and Dance (Portugal). He concluded a European PhD (Music, with Honours and distinction) at the University of Aveiro, including an Erasmus-funded period at the University College London Institute of Education. His current research focuses on the links between performance (as creative practice) and music education. Between 2017 and 2019, he was postdoctoral fellow at the Instituto de Etnomusicologia/Centro de Estudos e Dança (SRFH/BPD/UI72/8071/2018) and invited lecturer at the Escola de Música e Artes do Espetáculo/Instituto Politécnico do Porto. Gilvano is currently a member of the coordinating team, quality manager, and phase leader for the project REACT–*Rethinking Music Performance in European Higher Education Music Institutions*. ORCID: 0000-0001-9123-1733

Randi Margrethe Eidsaa is a professor of music pedagogy at the University of Agder. She holds a PhD from the Danish University School of Education in Copenhagen. She teaches musicology, music history, concert production, and music didactics in the Department of Classical Music and Music Education. Eidsaa is affiliated with the research network Art in Context at the University of Agder and a leader of the research group Art and Conflict. In recent years, she has collaborated with partner institutions in Bosnia-Herzegovina, Israel, and Palestine. She has directed several artistic projects in different educational contexts and published articles on creative approaches to music-making. She is a member of the Norwegian team in the Erasmus+ projects BAIL: Business and Art Innovation (2022–2025) and REACT–*Rethinking Music Performance in European Higher Education Music Institutions* (2020–2023). ORCID: 0000-0002-0598-6062

Richard Fay has been based at The University of Manchester since the early 1990s. He is a Senior Lecturer in TESOL and Intercultural Education in the Manchester Institute of Education. He is also Academic Lead for Klezmer Ensemble Performance in the Music Department and a Research Fellow in the Centre for Jewish Studies. He coordinates the Lantern Doctoral Community where narrative and arts-based methods are now well-established. His PhD (Education) was narratively based and interculturally framed. He also has a narratively based Masters in Ethnomusicology. He is an active composer and performer with various klezmer ensembles. ORCID: 0000-0002-9171-5452

Clarissa Foletto is a junior researcher (CEECIND/03404/2017) at the Instituto de Etnomusicologia – Centro de Estudos em Música e Dança (INET-md/UA), in Portugal. She is the institutional coordinator of the project DigiMusi (Digital transformation in elementary music education) and a member of the coordinating team of the project REACT: Rethinking Music Performance in European Higher Education Music Institutions, both financially supported by the European Commission–Programme

Erasmus+. She holds a European PhD in Instrumental Teaching from the University of Aveiro and completed a traineeship at the Institute of Education, University College of London. Her research focus is on innovative approaches to instrumental teaching and learning, teacher and student communication, strings pedagogy, digital transition in music education, and early childhood in music education.

Sarah-Jane Gibson is a music lecturer at York St John University, United Kingdom. She completed a four-year post-doctoral research project into the Ethno-World organisation at the International Centre for Community music in December 2022. Her PhD research, completed in 2018, focused on community and identity formation through amateur choral singing in Northern Ireland. Her research interest is how to build intercultural understanding through music-making. Sarah-Jane has a background in music education, having worked as a classroom music teacher in Primary and Secondary schools in South Africa, the United Kingdom, and the United States. She is a singer, pianist, and choral conductor. Publications include the ethnographic monograph 'Building Community choirs in the Twenty-first century' (Intellect, 2023). ORCID: 0000-0003-3098-3231

Carl Holmgren is an Associate professor in Music Education at the Department of Creative Studies, Umeå University, Sweden. He holds a PhD in Music Education, and a master's in Music and Education in Music from the Luleå University of Technology, Sweden. Besides being a skilled piano teacher, Holmgren has extensive experience of playing for ballet classes. He has published in international and Swedish journals and presented at Swedish, Nordic, and international conferences. Holmgren's research, using hermeneutics, poetry, and translation, focuses on the teaching and learning elements of musical interpretation of Western classical music in higher education. ORCID: 0000-0002-8514-5422

The Armenian-Norwegian pianist **Mariam Kharatyan** performs internationally as a soloist and chamber musician and has appeared at festivals and concerts with orchestras in Sweden, Germany, Italy, Hungary, Poland, Romania, Bosnia-Herzegovina, Lithuania, the USA, and Armenia. She has two master's degrees in piano performance—from the Komitas State Conservatory in Yerevan, Armenia, and the University of Agder in Kristiansand, Norway. From 2015–2019 Kharatyan worked on her artistic research PhD project 'Armenian Fingerprints', interpreting the piano music of Komitas and Khachaturian in light of Armenian folk music. In 2019, she released two albums: 'Khachaturian, Chamber Music' and 'Komitas, Shoror' published with Simax Classics and Grappa Musikkforlag. Kharatyan is a member of the project REACT–*Rethinking Music Performance in European Higher Education Music Institutions*, 2020–2023, funded by ERASMUS+ and the European Commission. She is an Associate Professor in the Department of Classical Music and Music Education at the University of Agder, Norway.

Daniel J. Mawson is an Honorary Research Fellow and performance practitioner in the Music Department at The University of Manchester. He is the Performance Lead for the university klezmer ensemble, The Michael Kahan Kapelye, of which he is an alumnus and for which he is now Co-Director. He is a sound designer and performing arts producer, in addition to being a freelance reed player and band-leader.

Helen Julia Minors is Professor and Head of School of the Arts at York St John University, United Kingdom. She is also a Visiting Professor at Lulea Technical University, Sweden. She was founder and original co-chair of EDI Music Studies Network. Her publications include *Routledge Companion to Women's Musical Leadership*, co-edited with Laura Hamer (Routledge, 2024); *Music, Dance and Translation* (Bloomsbury, 2023); *Artistic Research in Performance through Collaboration*, co-edited with Martin Blain (Palgrave, 2020); *Paul Dukas: Legacies of a French Musician*, co-edited with Laura Watson (Routledge, 2019); *Building Intercultural and Interdisciplinary Bridges: Where Theory Meets Research and Practice*, co-edited with Pamela Burnard et al. (BIBACC, 2017); and *Music, Text and Translation* (Bloomsbury, 2013). Recent articles and chapters have also appeared in the *London Review of Education* (2017/2019), *Translation and Multimodality* (Routledge, 2019), *Opera and Translation* (John Benjamins, 2020), *Tibon* (2022), *Intersemiotic Perspectives on Emotions* (2023), and *Routledge Companion to Applied Musicology* (2023). ORCID: 0000-0002-0212-9030

Stefan Östersjö is Chaired Professor of Musical Performance at Piteå School of Music, Luleå University of Technology, Sweden. He received his doctorate in 2008 for a dissertation on musical interpretation and contemporary performance practice. In 2009, he became a research fellow at the Orpheus Institute. He is currently also a guest professor at Ingesund School of Music, Karlstad University of Technology; Professor II at Western Norway University of Applied Sciences; and associate professor at DXARTS, University of Washington. Östersjö is a leading classical guitarist specialising in the performance of contemporary music. As a soloist, chamber musician, sound artist, and improviser, he has released more than twenty CDs and toured Europe, the USA, and Asia. He has collaborated extensively with composers and in the creation of works involving choreography, film, video, performance art, and music theatre. Between 1995 and 2012 he was the artistic director of 'Ensemble Ars Nova', a leading Swedish ensemble for contemporary music. As a soloist he has worked with conductors such as Lothar Zagrosek, Péter Eötvös, Pierre-André Valade, Mario Venzago, and Andrew Manze. ORCID: 0000-0002-4704-5420

Nahielly Palacios is a Lecturer in Education at the Manchester Institute of Education, University of Manchester. She teaches in the areas of academic and research reflective practice, researcher reflexivity, teaching and learning online, language learning, and technology and methods in TESOL. Her research interests involve teacher professional development, reflection, narration, and intercultural sojourns. ORCID: 0000-0001-9527-751X

Ioulia Papageorgi is a Professor and the Associate Dean of the School of Humanities and Social Sciences at the University of Nicosia. Ioulia is the Convenor of the Board of Educational Affairs of EFPA and an elected Committee member of SEMPRE. She currently serves on the Cyprus National Bioethics Committee (President of the Review Bioethics Committee for Biomedical Research). Ioulia has served on the Board of Cyprus

Psychologists' Association (Vice-President, Treasurer). Her research interests include music performance anxiety, the development of expertise, the association between music training and cognitive development, psychometric testing, and teaching and learning in psychology. She has published multiple articles in peer-reviewed journals, book chapters, and has co-edited three books. ORCID: 0000-0001-8566-2457

Fausto Lessa F. Pizzol is a Ph.D. candidate in the Doctoral Programme in Music at the University of Aveiro, Portugal. He holds a master's degree in music performance from the University of Aveiro, a degree in Music Education from Universidade Federal do Espírito Santo – UFES (Brazil), and a sandwich degree in Jazz Performance from East Carolina University – ECU (USA). He is a former professor at Faculdade de Música do Espírito Santo – FAMES (Brazil). His current research, in the field of artistic research, investigates the potentialities of the harmonic use of the electric bass through the development of a proposal for its performance and musical creation. His interests include Artistic Research, Music Performance, and Music Education.

Robert Sholl teaches at The Royal Academy of Music and the University of West London and is an Assistant Organist at Arundel Cathedral. His has written extensively on twentieth-century music, including *Messiaen Studies* and *James MacMillan Studies*, coedited with George Parsons (both Cambridge University Press, 2007 and 2021); *Contemporary Music and Spirituality*, coedited with Sander van Maas (Routledge, 2017); *The Feldenkrais Method in Creative Practice* (Bloomsbury, 2021); and on musical improvisation to film (published in Princeton's journal *Perspectives of New Music*). He is the editor of *Olivier Messiaen in Context* (Cambridge University Press, 2024) and the author of *Olivier Messiaen: A Critical Biography* (Reaktion, 2024). He has released a CD (with Justin Paterson, Anna McCready, and Andy Visser) of organ improvisations entitled *Les ombres du Fantôme* (Métier, 2024), and he has also recorded around two-and-a-half-hours of improvisation to film on Youtube. Robert studied in Melbourne, then in Paris (with Olivier Latry, and at the Sorbonne, Paris IV), and in London (at King's College). In 2016–17, he played all of Olivier Messiaen's organ works, and in 2021–23 all of Louis Vierne's organ symphonies, the complete Duruflé organ works, and major works of Charles Tournemire at Arundel Cathedral. He has given recitals at the St John's Smith Square, St Paul's Cathedral, Westminster Abbey, and twice at the Madeleine and at Notre-Dame de Paris.

Jacob Thompson-Bell is a composer, curator, and researcher based in the United Kingdom. He creates music and multimedia work across live performance, release, and installation formats. Jacob's work is often inspired by issues and ideas from areas beyond music, such as food, science, and other art forms. He works in close collaboration with other artists and practitioners to play on these connections. Jacob's music has been programmed in venues including Le Delta (Namur), Tramway (Glasgow), Kings Place (London), Purcell Room (London), LSO St Luke's (London), Iklektik (London), Howard Assembly Rooms (Leeds), and BFI Southbank (London). Jacob's research work engages with themes around artistic practice and higher music education, and has been published by leading journals, including *Leonardo, International Journal of Food Design*, and the *British Journal of Music Education*. He is a founder member of multi-sensory collective 'Unusual Ingredients' and is a Principal Lecturer at Leeds Conservatoire, UK.

Odd Torleiv Furnes has a bachelor's degree in music composition and a master's and PhD in musicology. He has composed music for art installations and art films and practised as an electric guitarist and a guitar teacher. He has over 20 years of experience from teaching music in the teacher education programme in Norway. In his research, he has been investigating approaches to musical analysis of popular music as well as exploring the relationship between musical structure and the experience of musical hits from a psychological perspective. He has also done research on musical understanding and the concept of deep learning (in-depth) in music. He has recently published a book about this subject called *Deep Learning in Music – Musical Understanding through Sensations, Emotions, and Concepts* (translated from Norwegian). In his chapter in this anthology, he goes deeper into the reasoning behind his approach to deep learning in music, and how perceiving music as an object may aid our perceptual understanding and aesthetic experience.

Åsa Unander-Scharin is an artist-researcher in the intersection of opera, dance, music, interactive technology, and robotics. In 2008, her PhD thesis entitled *Human Mechanics and Soulful Machines*, was published. She holds a position as professor of music performance at Luleå University of Technology, Sweden. From 2013–15, she was member of The Committee for Artistic Research at The Swedish Research Council. Her internationally acclaimed artistic work started in 1998 when she created the first choreography for an industrial robot, *The Lamentations of Orpheus*, that was awarded an honorary mention from VIDA 2.0. In 2010, her emotionally captivating robotic swan *Robocygne* created a newsworthy item that reached as far as the USA, India, Canada, and Singapore. She has choreographed and directed two dance films for Swedish television, interactive and robotic installations, and about 40 dance and opera performances at Swedish Radio/Berwald Hall, Stockholm Royal Opera, The Dance Museum, Vadstena Academy, Operadagen Rotterdam, Deutche Oper am Rhein in Düsseldorf, Cape Town Opera, The Liszt Academy in Budapest, and Computer-Human-Interaction conferences in Toronto, Paris, and San José. Recent works include two experimental operas *Callas: Medea* for the Croatian National Opera and *The Tale of the Great Computing Machine* commissioned by the KTH Royal Institute of Technology. *Suite Procession* is a new creation for double choir, dancer, and hyperorgan for debut in September 2023.

List of Figures

Fig. I.1	A student-centred perspective on the teaching and learning of music performance grounded in artistic research practices.	p. 4
Fig. 1.1	A proportional representation of occurrences of the most prevalent categories in the qualitative content analysis.	p. 23
Fig. 1.2	A flowchart of the interaction between Mellberg and Andersson through the use of stimulated recall analysis.	p. 28
Fig. 2.1	Research design summarising the method adopted for the empirical experiments.	p. 56
Fig. 2.2	Diagrams for four and five-string electric bass.	p. 57
Fig. 2.3	Lydian Mode +IV Minor Seventh b5/Major(+IVb)—Principal Chord Family. From Russell, p. 27.	p. 58
Fig. 2.4(a–p)	Diagrams representing execution forms for the F#Min(b5) chord.	p. 61
Fig. 2.5	Harmonising the notes of the Lydian Diminished Scale that belong to the first-degree triad—closed position.	p. 63
Fig. 2.6	Harmonising all notes of the Lydian Diminished Scale with the first-degree triad—closed position.	p. 65
Fig. 2.7	Harmonising all the notes of the Lydian Diminished Scale with the first-degree triad—drop 2 position.	p. 67
Fig. 2.8	Execution of the Lydian Diminished Scale, on more than one string, accompanied by harmonisation with the first-degree triad—open position.	p. 69
Fig. 2.9	Delimitation scheme for the experiments of the second group.	p. 70
Fig. 2.10	Scheme of systematisation of the experiments of the second group.	p. 71
Fig. 2.11	Creative application: results articulation between the Lydian Flat Seventh Scale and the dominant chord of the first degree.	p. 77
Fig. 2.12	Articulation between LCCTO's principal scales and chords from the first degree—closed position.	p. 79
Fig. 2.13	Articulation between LCCTO's principal scales and chords from the second degree.	p. 81
Fig. 2.14	Creative Application: results from the articulation between LCCTO's principal scales and chords from the first degree.	p. 84

Fig. 3.1	Overview of the McCoy licks I chose with the intent of creating original licks inspired by his original recordings.	p. 92
Fig. 4.1	Number of students by course and year of study.	p. 116
Fig. 4.2	Students by instrument.	p. 116
Fig. 4.3	Correlation between instruments and students.	p. 117
Fig. 4.4	Themes and their respective sub-themes identified in the data analysis of the interviews.	p. 120
Fig. 5.1	J. S. Bach, *Goldberg Variations* (theme in facsimile).	p. 144
Fig. 5.2	*Goldberg* exercise.	p. 148
Fig. 5.3	Bach, *Goldberg Variations*, beginning of Variation 4 (facsimile).	p. 150
Fig. 5.4a	Based on *Goldberg* Variation 4.	p. 150
Fig. 5.4b	Based on *Goldberg* Variation 4.	p. 151
Fig. 5.4c	Based on *Goldberg* Variation 4.	p. 151
Fig. 5.4d	Based on *Goldberg* Variation 4.	p. 151
Fig. 5.5	*Goldberg* Variation 1 (facsimile).	p. 152
Fig. 5.6	Starter 'inventions' for *Goldberg* variations.	p. 154
Fig. 5.7	*Goldberg* variation based on the opening of BWV 781.	p. 157
Fig. 10.1	Jewel Longhorn Beetle and double bass (used with permission from the photographer Kristin Joyce Knox, McKnox.no).	p. 263
Fig. 10.2	Pleasing Fungis Beetle and guitarist (used with permission from the photographer Kristin Joyce Knox, McKnox.no).	p. 265

List of Tables

Table 1.1	The basic design of introductory courses and degree projects in the bachelor's and master's programmes in Music Performance at Piteå School of Music, Luleå University of Technology (LTU).	p. 18
Table 1.2	*Der Freischütz*; stable (S) and unstable (U) bar groups, drawn from Perčič, 2020, p. 26.	p. 29
Table 4.1	Professional competencies identified in the synthetic analysis.	p. 110
Table 4.2	Artistic career demands in music performance.	p. 112
Table 4.3	React training school structure.	p. 118
Table 8.1	Performance opportunities for the 2020–21 cohort of the KEP module.	p. 201
Table 8.2	Performances emphasised in the KEP module.	p. 211
Table 9.1	Deep learning vs traditional learning.	p. 227
Table 12.1	Aural, Analysis, and Improvisation, second-year module.	p. 298
Table 12.2	The Critical Presentation of Performance, master's module.	p. 300

List of Audio and Video Musical Examples

Video 2.1 Video of author presenting CMaj triad and inversions, uploaded by Fausto Lessa, 14 February 2022. https://hdl.handle.net/20.500.12434/c7435c81   p. 61

Video 2.2 Video of author presenting the harmonisation of Lydian Diminished Scale notes belonging to the first degree triad—closed position, uploaded by Fausto Lessa, 5 February 2022. https://hdl.handle.net/20.500.12434/df0f8785   p. 62

Video 2.3 Video of author demonstrating the harmonisation of all notes of the Lydian Diminished Scale with the first-degree triad—closed position, uploaded by Fausto Lessa, 5 February 2022. https://hdl.handle.net/20.500.12434/e6c0b76e   p. 63

Video 2.4 Video of author demonstrating the harmonisation of all notes of the Lydian Diminished Scale with the first degree triad—drop 2 position, uploaded by Fausto Lessa, 5 February 2022. https://hdl.handle.net/20.500.12434/0cb2636e   p. 66

Video 2.5 Video of author executing the Lydian Diminished Scale, on more than one string, accompanied by harmonisation with the first degree triad—open position, uploaded by Fausto Lessa, 5 February 2022. https://hdl.handle.net/20.500.12434/0874b874   p. 68

Video 2.6 Video of author demonstrating the creative application: articulation between the Lydian Flat Seventh Scale and the dominant chord of the first degree, uploaded by Fausto Lessa, 5 February 2022. https://hdl.handle.net/20.500.12434/56e02acf   p. 72

Video 2.7 Video of author demonstrating the articulation between LCCTO's principal scales and chords from the first degree—closed position, uploaded by Fausto Lessa, 16 May 2022. https://hdl.handle.net/20.500.12434/3636d83c   p. 78

Video 2.8	Video of author demonstrating the articulation between LCCTO's principal scales and chords from the second degree, uploaded by Fausto Lessa, 28 November 2022. https://hdl.handle.net/20.500.12434/35b6eccf	p. 79
Video 2.9	Video of author demonstrating the creative application: results from the articulation between LCCTO's principal scales and chords from the first degree, uploaded by Fausto Lessa, 28 November 2022. https://hdl.handle.net/20.500.12434/0dd3a1d7	p. 82
Video 3.1	Video of author documenting lick-generation session eight, https://hdl.handle.net/20.500.12434/f09a5320	p. 94
Video 3.2	Video of author documenting lick-generation session six, https://hdl.handle.net/20.500.12434/8ef03205	p. 95

Index

affordance 10, 47–56, 67–69, 84, 89, 93–94, 96, 201, 215–216, 238–239, 243
artistic experiment(ation) 3, 10, 15, 24–25, 31–32, 41–43, 56–57, 84–85
artistic research 1–3, 5–7, 9–11, 13–15, 17–18, 26, 31, 35, 37–38, 41–43, 47, 87–91, 94, 97, 104, 107, 113–115, 121, 127–129, 133–134, 136–138, 140, 158–159, 161, 182–184, 189, 221–222, 244–245, 287, 289, 296, 298, 307–309, 311–313
   methods 1, 6, 13, 15, 17–19, 26, 29, 35–38, 41–43, 47, 96, 121, 133, 309
   practices 1–4, 6–7, 10–11, 14, 17–19, 21, 30, 35–36, 38, 42–43, 87–89, 104, 107, 112–114, 128–129, 141–142, 159–160, 184, 193, 221–222, 287, 290, 296, 307–309, 311–313, 320–321
art worlds 1, 3, 14, 38, 114–115, 128, 133, 221, 253, 289–294, 298, 301–302, 307, 312

Bologna Declaration 1, 5, 13, 16, 36, 87, 108, 113, 309

careers 8, 90–91, 107, 109–112, 115, 121, 128, 160, 251–255, 257–258, 271, 287, 290, 292–294, 299–300, 312, 323
collaboration 3, 26–27, 35–36, 40, 43, 51, 110, 122, 134, 176, 184, 221, 254, 256–257, 261–262, 267, 282, 291, 294–295, 319
conservatoire model 2, 107–110, 113, 120–121, 128, 137, 142, 160, 216, 252–253, 259. *See also* master-apprentice model
content analysis 17, 19–20, 23, 36–37, 42, 321
counterpoint 6, 134–135, 140, 142–143, 146, 149, 151, 235
Craenen, Paul 134, 312–313
Crispin, Darla 15, 17, 310
Critical Response Process (CRP) 6–7, 134, 166, 171–172, 174–178
critical-response theory 6, 115, 313
critical thinking 2–4, 6, 17–18, 42, 109–112, 115, 128, 133–134, 191, 257, 259, 278, 280, 294, 302, 311

curriculum
   development of the 11, 16, 192, 255, 257, 266, 288
   inclusive 287–289, 291, 295, 297–298, 311
   new, innovative 6, 225–226, 241, 257, 291

Deardorff, Darla 272, 274, 278, 282

embodied music cognition 10, 27, 89, 175, 243–245
equality 274, 292, 310
equity 134, 166–167, 176–177, 294, 296, 310
exercises 6, 33–34, 85, 95, 100, 140, 143, 146, 149–150, 155, 158, 160, 216, 311
experimentation, experimental approaches 1, 3, 6, 10, 15, 17, 24–25, 30–32, 36, 38, 40–43, 47, 50–51, 55–58, 60–62, 69–71, 79, 81, 84–85, 88, 102, 114, 121, 139, 141–142, 160, 171, 184–185, 189, 193, 211, 215, 262, 295, 302, 313, 321. *See also* artistic experiment(ation)

Gaunt, Helena 259, 264, 266, 302, 307
Georgii-Hemming, Eva 15–17, 36, 38, 103, 246
Gibson, Eleanor Jack 48, 50, 53–54
Gibson, James Jerome 48–50, 52–53, 55, 89

improvisation 6–7, 20, 27, 32, 51, 92, 111–112, 134, 136, 139, 141, 153, 157–159, 161, 181–189, 191–193, 205, 230, 252, 254, 262, 264, 294–298, 308, 313, 319
inclusive practices 3, 113, 134, 264, 310. *See also* curriculum: inclusive
industry 7, 11, 110, 112, 115, 187, 216, 253, 257–258, 260, 271, 290–291, 301
innovation 1, 7, 134, 171, 190–191, 256, 303, 308, 313
interculturality
   intercultural competence 271–272, 274–275, 278, 280–283, 311
   intercultural dialogue 222, 271, 274–275, 279, 281, 283, 288, 311
   intercultural learning 7, 206, 273
   intercultural understanding 199, 246,

271–272, 274–275, 277, 280, 282–283, 317
intersectionality 221–223, 293, 296, 308, 310
intersubjectivity 3, 15, 21, 36–37, 309
intervention 4, 7, 39, 52, 107–108, 115, 123–124, 126, 128, 310, 312. *See also* pedagogical intervention

Johansson, Karin 15–17, 38, 99

Laboratory 10, 43
lifelong learning 2, 6, 16, 25–26, 35–37, 40–41, 43, 87–88, 101, 246–247, 273
listening 25, 32–33, 37, 51, 95, 99, 136, 138–139, 141–143, 145, 149, 155, 157, 172, 184–186, 191–193, 199, 214, 230–231, 238–240, 243, 277, 294, 296–298, 300, 308–309, 312
   music listening 230, 232

master-apprentice model 2, 30, 35, 40, 107–108, 133–134, 181, 257, 307. *See also* conservatoire model
Moberg, Nadia 16–18, 20, 22, 37–38, 42, 103
musicking 7, 51, 184, 195, 198–199, 201, 230, 247, 253, 258–259, 266, 301, 303, 313
music performance education 7, 107, 187, 252–254, 256, 258, 263, 312
music theory 6, 27, 134–138, 198, 281, 308, 313

ontonomy 18, 168, 170, 175, 177–178

pedagogical intervention 6, 11, 107, 128
performance practice 3, 6, 29–30, 109, 176, 181, 183–184, 186–187, 189–193, 205, 216, 259, 298, 318

REACT
   model 114, 129, 133, 221–222, 287, 289–290, 293, 296, 302, 308, 313
   project 2, 4–7, 11, 42, 107, 110, 114, 117, 119, 121, 124, 126, 134, 166, 181, 222, 251–252, 255–256, 273, 287, 312, 315
   training schools 4, 96, 107–108, 114–115, 118–129, 255–256, 323
reflection
   critical reflection 35, 39, 114, 216, 246, 271–272, 275, 280–283, 287, 289, 296
   reflection-for-performance 208–209, 213
   reflection-in-action 206–208
   reflection-in-performance 208–209, 211, 216
   reflection-on-action 208
   reflection-on-performance 208–209
   self-reflection 7, 15, 37, 110, 275, 288–289, 296

reflective practice 2, 7, 128, 205, 308–309, 318
reflexive methods 1, 6, 9, 15, 17–18, 36–38, 42–43, 115
research method(ologie)s 13, 19, 38, 41–42, 115, 121–122, 287, 309
research question 14, 18–19, 21–22, 38, 251, 266, 272–273

Schön, Donald A. 204–209
skills
   digital skills 256, 260, 267, 301
   employability skills 1, 3, 7, 221–222, 256, 258, 287–288, 290–291, 299, 301–303, 307
   instrumental skills 257, 259
   performance skills 16, 27, 51, 252, 257, 260, 264, 293–295, 297, 303, 312
   reflective skills 98, 110, 216, 278, 298
   technical skills 2, 33, 62, 111, 257–258
Small, Christopher 198–199, 230, 236, 253, 258, 301
stimulated recall analysis 21, 27–28, 35–37, 321
student autonomy 1, 6, 18, 35, 87–88, 97, 129, 191, 273. *See also* ontonomy
student-centred teaching and learning 1–2, 4–7, 13, 16, 18, 36, 39–40, 43, 108–109, 112–114, 124, 128, 134, 165, 171, 222, 307, 309, 321
student theses 11, 13–14, 17, 19, 21, 24, 26–28, 30–39, 41–43, 320
subjectivity 15, 30, 41, 114–115, 134, 137–138, 166, 170, 175, 177, 179, 221, 302

theory and practice 160, 198, 287, 289
transformation 1, 10, 88–89, 91, 93, 96–97, 100, 183–186, 273, 276–278, 283, 315–316

voice
   artistic voice 91, 97, 101, 117, 133–134, 188, 191, 221, 287, 302, 308, 313
   creative voice 6–7, 112
   musical voice 17, 32, 36, 88–89, 98, 190
   performer's voice 6, 27, 88, 315
   personal voice 3, 6, 10, 36, 88, 91, 96, 99, 101–104, 117, 175, 298, 313
   shared voice 3, 26–27
   student voice 4–7, 11, 14, 24, 108–110, 112, 126, 133, 175, 222, 259, 309, 313

Werktreue 181–185, 189, 191–192

About the Team

Alessandra Tosi was the managing editor for this book.

Jennifer Moriarty proof-read and indexed the manuscript.

Jeevanjot Kaur Nagpal designed the cover. The cover was produced in InDesign using the Fontin font.

Jeremy Bowman typeset the book in InDesign and produced the EPUB edition. The text font is Tex Gyre Pagella and the heading font is Californian FB.

Cameron Craig produced the PDF and HTML editions. The conversion is performed with open source software freely available on our GitHub page at https://github.com/OpenBookPublishers.

We thank Dr Christina Guillaumier and an anonymous referee. Experts in their field, these readers give their time freely to help ensure the academic rigour of our books. We are grateful for their generous and invaluable contributions.

This book need not end here...

Share

All our books — including the one you have just read — are free to access online so that students, researchers and members of the public who can't afford a printed edition will have access to the same ideas. This title will be accessed online by hundreds of readers each month across the globe: why not share the link so that someone you know is one of them?

This book and additional content is available at:
https://doi.org/10.11647/OBP.0398

Donate

Open Book Publishers is an award-winning, scholar-led, not-for-profit press making knowledge freely available one book at a time. We don't charge authors to publish with us: instead, our work is supported by our library members and by donations from people who believe that research shouldn't be locked behind paywalls.

Why not join them in freeing knowledge by supporting us:
https://www.openbookpublishers.com/support-us

Follow @OpenBookPublish

Read more at the Open Book Publishers **BLOG**

You may also be interested in:

Classical Music
Contemporary Perspectives and Challenges
Michael Beckerman, Paul Boghossian (eds.)

https://doi.org/10.11647/OBP.0242

The Power of Music
An Exploration of the Evidence
Susan Hallam and Evangelos Himonides

https://doi.org/10.11647/OBP.0292

Classical Music Futures
Practices of Innovation
Neil Thomas Smith, Peter Peters and Karoly Molina (eds.)

https://doi.org/10.11647/OBP.0353

www.ingramcontent.com/pod-product-compliance
Lightning Source LLC
Chambersburg PA
CBHW040741300426
44111CB00027B/2996